D0655973

PIRATES OF BARBARY

By the same author

Historic Houses of the National Trust
Country Houses from the Air
Life in the English Country Cottage
Visions of Power: Ambition and Architecture
The Polite Tourist: A History of Country House Visiting
The Arts & Crafts House
The Art Deco House
His Invention So Fertile: A Life of Christopher Wren
By Permission of Heaven: The Story of the Great Fire of London
The Verneys: A True Story of Love, War and
Madness in Seventeenth-Century England

PIRATES OF
BARBARY

Corsairs, Conquests and Captivity in the
Seventeenth-Century Mediterranean

Adrian Tinniswood

Jonathan Cape
London

Published by Jonathan Cape

2 4 6 8 10 9 7 5 3 1

Copyright © Adrian Tinniswood 2010

Adrian Tinniswood has asserted his right under the Copyright, Designs
and Patents Act 1988 to be identified as the author of this work

First published in Great Britain in 2010 by
Jonathan Cape
Random House, 20 Vauxhall Bridge Road,
London SW1V 2SA

www.rbooks.co.uk

Addresses for companies within the Random House Group Limited can be found at:
www.randomhouse.co.uk/offices.htm

The Random House Group Limited Reg. No. 954009

A CIP catalogue record for this book
is available from the British Library

ISBN 9780224085267 (HARDBACK)

The Random House Group Limited supports The Forest Stewardship Council (FSC),
the leading international forest certification organisation. All our titles that are
printed on Greenpeace approved FSC certified paper carry the FSC logo.
Our paper procurement policy can be found at
www.rbooks.co.uk/environment

Typeset in Bembo by Palimpsest Book Production Limited,
Grangemouth, Stirlingshire
Printed and bound in Great Britain by
Clays Ltd, St Ives plc

For
Carol, Clive and David:
absent friends

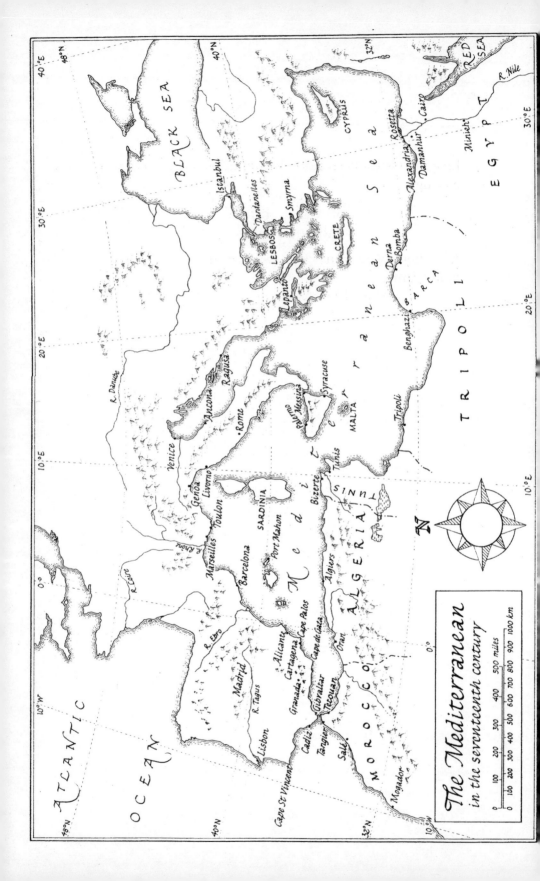

The Mediterranean
in the seventeenth century

Imagine (as thou readest) that thou hearest the cannon playing.

John Button, *Algiers Voyage* (1621)

And there were some who went on the sea *jihad* and found fame.

Ahmad bin Mohammad al-Maqqari (*c.* 1621)

Contents

List of Illustrations

Foreword

*P*irates are history.

The history of my own obsession with them goes back nearly ten years to a time when I was researching a seventeenth-century English family, the Verneys. In 1608 a country squire called Sir Francis Verney fell out with his step-mother, walked out on his teenage wife and went to North Africa, where he became a Moslem and embarked on a brief but spec-tacular career as a Barbary Coast pirate. How did *that* happen, I wanted to know. Did other Englishmen turn Turk like Sir Francis? I discovered that they did. And then I wanted to know what life was like for this community of renegades that operated at the interface of Christendom and Islam, a community that seemed to move effortlessly between those two worlds.

As I looked for answers to those questions I discovered the stories which make up this book – tales of bravery, brutality and betrayal, tales in which heroes and villains changed roles at the blink of an eye like the characters in some Cold War spy novel. I found that robbery on the high seas was far from being the private enterprise I'd imagined it to be: behind it lay a sophisticated system of socialised

crime, state-sanctioned and state-regulated, an early and efficient
example of public-private partnership. And I came to understand
the enormous economic importance of the Mediterranean trade
in slaves, a trade which took the liberty of around one million
Europeans and at least as many North Africans in the course of the
seventeenth century.

While I was working on the cluster of interlocking narratives
which make up *Pirates of Barbary*, stories of modern-day piracy
started to appear in the news. First it was Indonesia. Then there
were reports of Nigerian pirates using small speedboats to hijack
fishing vessels off the West African coast. There were an average
of two attacks a week in 2007, increasing to two a day in the first
month of 2008.

But it was the Somalis who really captured my attention.
Adopting the same tactics as the Nigerians – the same tactics, in
fact, as the Barbary pirates I was writing about – groups of Somali
militiamen began to prey on merchant ships as they passed along
the coast of Somalia, which at 1880 miles is the longest in Africa.
Some of their weapons were different – rusty Kalashnikovs and
dodgy looking grenade launchers rather than culverins and cutlasses
– but others hadn't changed in 400 years. They still relied, for
example, on shock and awe, intimidation and physical courage.
There were 130 robberies and attempted robberies on the high
seas involving Somali pirates in 2008. A Ukrainian cargo ship
packed with anti-aircraft guns, rocket-propelled grenades and
Russian tanks was hijacked that September, and two months later
pirates captured the $150-million *Sirius Star*, a colossal supertanker
three times the size of an aircraft carrier.

Pirates are history? History was repeating itself. As I wrote of how
a handful of men using small boats, scaling ladders and sheer nerve
had managed to hold the world to ransom in the seventeenth
century, I watched on TV as a handful of men using small boats,
scaling ladders and sheer nerve were managing to hold the world
to ransom in the twenty-first. And the sums involved were enormous. It cost the owners of the Ukrainian cargo ship the MV *Faina*
$3.2 million to get their vessel back. The *Sirius Star* with its crew
and its cargo of two million barrels of crude oil was handed over
in exchange for $3 million.

That winter, the winter of 2008–9, marine insurers from all over the world gathered in London to discuss the problem of African piracy. Senior figures condemned the Somali pirates as the scourge of modern shipping, calling them 'vermin' and demanding a concerted response from the international community – just as they had in seventeenth-century London. Meanwhile, shipowners began to avoid the Gulf of Aden – just as they had avoided the coast of Barbary four centuries earlier. The owners of very large crude carriers (VLCCs) refused to use the Suez Canal. Vessels were sent around the Cape of Good Hope, or through the Russian Northeast Passage, navigable without the aid of ice-breakers for the first time in history as a consequence of global warming. The Philippines barred its nationals from working on any vessel that was due to travel through the waters off Somalia, and other seafarers were given double pay as danger money. Iranian and Pakistani nationals were reported to be joining the Somalis, raising the spectre of *jihad* and links with Al-Qaeda. In the summer of 2009 a Republican Congressman introduced a Bill into the US House of Representatives giving immunity to any American merchant sailor who wounded or killed a pirate in response to an attack.

While the pirates' own communities hailed them as heroes, the international community sent in their navies. In 2009 the US Navy established a multi-national task force to carry out counter-piracy operations in and around the Gulf of Aden. Warships in the US Fifth Fleet's Combined Task Force 151 (CTF-151) were joined by ships from Operation Atalanta, the European Union's first ever naval operation, which mandated vessels to 'bring to an end acts of piracy and armed robbery which may be committed in the areas where they are present'. Norway, China, Russia and South Korea sent warships to the region; so did India and Pakistan and Turkey. Croatia, eager to take part in Operation Atalanta as a way of furthering its application to join the EU, was allowed to send a vessel only after promising to respect the human rights of any pirates its forces might capture. Japan relaxed its pacifist constitution to allow the deployment of two destroyers.

By the summer of 2009 warships, aircraft and military personnel from twenty-two nations were patrolling two million square miles of ocean in the biggest anti-piracy operation the world has ever seen. It failed. And it continues to fail, for exactly the same reasons that it failed in the past: as the story of the Barbary pirates shows, the long-term solution to the problem lies onshore, and it can only be achieved by making fundamental changes within a culture which regards piracy as a legitimate activity.

There is another parallel between the Barbary Coast corsairs of the seventeenth century and their twenty-first-century comrades in Somalia. In the West (although not in their own homelands) neither group has been able to boast the glamour of the buccaneers of America – the Henry Morgans and the Captain Kidds, the swashbuckling Errol Flynns of old romance. *Those* pirates have been held up by historians as heroic rebels without a cause, cheerful anarchists or ardent democrats, proto-marxists or proto-capitalists, promoters of gay rights and racial equality, praiseworthy dissidents rather than villains.

The pirates of Africa, past and present, have not. The white West regards them as the irreconcilable Other – not rebels against authority but plain criminals, not brave Robin Hoods (that would make us the Sheriff of Nottingham) but cowardly thieves. When the old pirates of Barbary described themselves as *mujahidin* on a sea *jihad* against encroaching Christendom, Christendom portrayed them as demons bent on world domination; when modern-day Somali pirate chiefs say that the real sea bandits are those who steal their fish stocks and pollute their coastal waters, we patronise them and then send a gunboat. An underlying racism and a more overt anti-Islamism make it hard to imagine Captain Blood or Jack Sparrow as North African Moslems. And which modern-day pirate movie is most likely to be in development in Hollywood as I write – a thrilling tale about a plucky little band of Somalis or a *Black Hawk Down* about the US military battling against underwhelming odds in the Gulf of Aden? You decide.

Pirates are history. The history of piracy, whether on the Barbary Coast or in the Horn of Africa, shows us – what? That we never learn? That we invent our heroes? That those we cast as demons play their parts too well?

All of those things. Above all, it shows us that the demons are human, too.

1

Prosperity at Sea: The Mediterranean World

On a wintry day in December 1609, a solemn group weaved its slow and stately way by barge down the Thames from the Marshalsea Prison in Southwark to Wapping. The tide was out, and as the first barge came to rest the sound of the water lapping at the foot of the steps and splashing over the thick, stinking mud was drowned by the shouts and laughter of a crowd which had gathered in front of the wooden cranes and warehouses.

The figures made their way through the jostling mass of people towards a gallows, which cast its long, sinister shadow over the river bank. At the head of the procession was a marshal from the High Court of Admiralty who carried a little silver oar as his baton of office. He was followed by the hangman, by a chaplain from the Marshalsea, by constables – and by seventeen men who walked with their heads down and their hands clasped tightly in front of them. All seventeen were Barbary pirates. None of them would see the sun go down that night.

Piracy is a hard business. To be a good pirate captain you need excellent seamanship, good leadership skills, a streak of brutality and a disregard for conventional morality. And, because you face death for a living on a regular basis, you need to be brave.

These men were brave. As they faced death together and alone on that cold winter's day, every one of them must have shivered to think about what they might have done differently – a path not taken, a stone left unturned. None of them realised – how could they? – that they were key players in a tradition that shaped relations between Christendom and Islam in the seventeenth century, a tradition that continues to inform those relations to this day. These Barbary pirates couldn't see beyond the sunset.

The first to entertain the noisy crowd was Captain John Jennings, whose bloody career in the western Mediterranean and the Atlantic had lasted a decade before his own crew betrayed him to the authorities. Two of his men had remained loyal: their reward was to hang with him, and it was to them rather than the jeering spectators that Captain Jennings addressed his final speech. The pair had followed him 'through the footsteps of transgression on earth', he reminded them, where 'bullets like hail have fallen about our ears'; and they must follow him still. 'I go before you on the highway to my salvation in heaven, where we shall meet amongst the fellowship of angels'.[1] With that rather optimistic prediction he turned and climbed the gallows to his death.

One by one, the other sixteen pirates followed him – some sullen, some penitent, all frightened and all determined to die well. William Longcastle, William Taverner and John Moore, who had always denied that they stole a merchant ship as it lay in a Moroccan harbour, now made a full and public confession; Taverner kept his eyes on the sky the whole time, declaring as he mounted the scaffold that 'this is Jacob's ladder, on whose steps I assure I shall be reared up to heaven'.[2]

Bristol-born Captain James Harris, leader of a gang which preyed on merchant shipping all the way along the Barbary Coast from Morocco to Tunis, went boldly to meet his maker, nonchalantly tossing away his hat as he climbed the ladder. He sang psalms in a loud voice and, when someone in the crowd asked if he had not had news from the King about a reprieve, replying 'None, sir, but from the King of Kings'.[3]

Two of the last to hang were the brothers John and Thomas Spencer, both members of Captain Harris's crew. John died cleanly, but the awful slowness of Thomas's death silenced the jeers of the crowd as he swung wildly on the short rope, beating his fists on the chest of his dead brother while he choked.

Pirates executed at Wapping were left to hang until three tides had washed over them

The seventeen executions were over in an hour. Harris, whose corpse had been bought by a relative, was cut down and taken away to be given a Christian burial. The others were left to hang, a traditional warning to others, until three high tides had washed over them. Then they were either sold for dissection, or tarred and caged in gibbets along the Thames, where their bodies twisted gently in the breeze, a reminder to passing sailors of the dreadful penalty for piracy.

Captain Harris had made a full confession, and copies of this were on sale all over London within hours of his death. He spoke of how he had turned to piracy after being captured and imprisoned in Tunis. How he had preyed on the small trading ships which

plied their trade in the Narrow Seas – the English Channel, the
Irish Sea and the stretch of the North Sea separating England from
the Netherlands. How he had cruised from the Atlantic coast of
Spain down to the Straits of Gibraltar in the hope of coming across
homeward-bound East India ships, merchants on their way back
from the Near East, perhaps even a straggler from the *Flota de
Indias*, the annual treasure convoy which brought silver, gold and
gems from the Americas back to Spain. 'Making my felicity out
of other men's miseries,' he recalled, 'I thought prosperity at sea as
sure in my grip as the power to speak was free to my tongue.'[4]

Harris's career came to an end early in 1609, when he was
ambushed by one of the King's ships as he put into Baltimore on
the Irish coast for supplies. Pirates often sought shelter in the
remote creeks and harbours of south-west Ireland, where the natives
were friendly and eager to offer all kinds of hospitality, much to
the exasperation of the English crown's representatives. Prostitution
was rife, and pieces of eight and Barbary ducats were accepted
in alehouses and stores along with the English shilling. 'Until
the sea coasts shall be planted with more honest subjects, and the
harbours better secured', said the Lord Deputy of Ireland, Sir
Arthur Chichester, in 1608, there was no hope of controlling the
problem.[5] Ireland 'may be well called the nursery and storehouse
of pirates', said the ex-pirate Henry Mainwaring.[6]

Only one of the King's ships was permanently stationed in the
area – the 22-year-old *Tremontane*, which was leaky, decrepit and
easily outrun by every pirate ship she met. And the provincial
governor of south-west Ireland, Sir Henry Danvers, adopted a
distinctly relaxed approach to piracy. On one occasion, after a group
of pirates appeared on the coast of Co. Cork and left again un-
challenged, word reached London that Danvers had somehow
acquired twenty chests of sugar and four chests of coral. His
superiors complained that this was 'a token of too much
familiarity', and recalled him.[7]

For the pirates, the problem with Ireland was that such familiarity couldn't be relied on, as Captain Harris found out to his cost.
One of the captain's gallows mates at Wapping, John Jennings, also
had his career terminated during a visit to Ireland. He was captured
in Limerick after he got so drunk that he was unable to stagger
back to his ship; in the meantime his comrades had made a deal

with the authorities, and they sailed away, leaving him to his fate.

The real hunting ground of pirates like Harris and Jennings was the Mediterranean, the 'sea in the middle of the earth'. Stretching from the Straits of Gibraltar in the west to the Holy Land in the east, and with a total area of nearly one million square miles, the Mediterranean was not only 'the meeting place of many peoples, and the melting-pot of many histories', as the great French historian Ferdinand Braudel describes it;[8] it was also the biggest marketplace in the world. Its tides ebbed and flowed over the shores of more than thirty kingdoms and republics, sultanates and beylicates, principalities and duchies. Those waters carried ships of all shapes and sizes: lumbering three-masted argosies from Venice and Ragusa (modern-day Dubrovnik); small lateen-rigged carvels hugging the coastline; fast, streamlined galleys with banks of oars and ranks of sweating, shaven-headed slaves to pull them; island-hopping polacres and settees and bertons and barks. And their cargos consisted of anything and everything that might conceivably be bought, sold or exchanged, from a salted cod caught off the Newfoundland Banks to a Nubian slave caught on the banks of the Nile.

The dominant power in the Mediterranean, and the largest market, was the Ottoman Empire, a vast conglomeration of conquered territories and vassal states which stretched for thousands of miles from the shores of the Caspian Sea in the east almost to the Atlantic, and south as far as the Red Sea and the Persian Gulf. Its centre was Istanbul, and citizens of Algeria, Athens and Armenia paid tribute to the Ottoman Sultan at the Topkapi Palace; so did Bulgaria and Baghdad, Cairo and the Crimea, Hungary and the Yemen.

Christian Europe was frightened of the Empire. Ever since Sultan Mehmed II's armies conquered Constantinople in 1453, Spain and Venice, the major Catholic powers in the Mediterranean, had felt challenged by the threat that the Turks posed to Catholic Europe's cultural identity. Some of that same anxiety was also permeating the nations of northern Europe. In Germany, Protestant congregations beseeched God 'graciously to preserve us from the monstrous designs of the Turk', while their ministers preached fear and loathing from the pulpit and warned that the Turk 'is an enemy who not only robs us of money and possessions, wife and child, and maltreats people in the most horrible manner, but whose whole purpose and

intention is to root out the name of Christ and put his own devil,
Mahomet, in His place'.[9] In 1575 the English clergyman Thomas
Newton wrote that Turks and Saracens were once 'very far from
our clime and region, and therefore the less to be feared, but now
they are even at our doors and ready to come into our houses'.[10]
By the beginning of the seventeenth century Islam was being called
'the present terror of the world'.[11]

Christian culture demonised Moslems as cruel, aggressive and
debauched, and it legitimised those who wished them harm. Ideo-
logically motivated attacks on Moslem shipping in the eastern
Mediterranean by the religious and military order of the Knights
of St John were just one expression of a crusader mentality which
taught that it was a Christian's duty to fight, as the Bishop of
Carlisle says in Shakespeare's *Richard II*, 'for Jesu Christ in glorious
Christian field, streaming the ensign of the Christian cross against
black pagans, Turks, and Saracens'.[12]

And the Empire fought back. Ottoman janissaries marched
down the valley of the Danube, threatened Vienna, fought with
Spain, took Cyprus and Crete from the Venetians. And in the
Mediterranean Istanbul allowed – sometimes actively encouraged
– its satellites to wage proxy wars against encroaching Christen-
dom from bases along the 2000-mile-long Barbary Coast of
North Africa, which stretches from Morocco, where the western
Sahara meets the Atlantic, north through the foothills of the Atlas
Mountains to the Straits of Gibraltar and eastward along the
southern edge of the Mediterranean until it reaches the Gulf of
Sidra and the Libyan Desert.

In the early years of the sixteenth century two brothers had
emerged as dominant figures in the Moslem fight against Christian
ambitions in North Africa. Known in Europe as the Barbarossas
on account of their red beards, Oruç and Hızır were the sons of
a retired Turkish cavalryman who ran a successful pottery business
on the Greek island of Lesbos. According to one source, Oruç
was attacked by the Knights of St John while returning on his
father's ship with a third brother, Ilyas, from a trading mission to
the Levant. Ilyas died in the fight and Oruç was captured and set
to work as a galley slave.

When he was ransomed three years later, he took to privateering, basing himself first at Antalya on the Turkish coast and then

with his younger brother Hızır at Tunis, from where the two corsairs preyed on Italian merchant shipping and waged a sea *jihad* against the Knights of St John. Their change of career coincided with the last stages of the *reconquista* of Ferdinand of Aragon and Isabella of Castile which, after the Spanish conquest of Moslem-held Granada in 1492, had evolved into a policy of establishing garrisons at strategic points along the Barbary Coast. In 1510 Oruç and Hızır were operating from the island of Djerba, fifty miles off the Tunisian coast, combining lucrative privateering with war against Spain, and often working in partnership with local leaders to repulse Spanish attacks. In 1513 and again in 1515 Oruç led unsuccessful attempts to retake the Algerian port of Béjaïa, which had been occupied by Spanish forces; he lost an arm in the first assault and wore a silver prosthesis for the rest of his life.

In 1516 the brothers moved their base of operations to Algiers, and Oruç extended his authority and his political ambitions west-ward, taking control of Algiers itself, repulsing Spanish attacks and leading assaults on territories where local warlords had accepted Spanish rule. Europe regarded him as the man 'who first brought the Turks into Barbary, and taught them to taste the sweets of the western riches',[13] the warrior who 'launched the powerful great-ness of Algiers and of Barbary'.[14] In 1517 he invaded Tlemcen, an important religious centre 280 miles to the west of Algiers whose rulers had submitted to Spain. He took the town easily and immediately began negotiations with Moroccan leaders, with a view to bringing them into the *jihad*. But he had overreached himself: a Spanish force from the garrison seventy miles away at Oran combined with Bedouin tribes to attack Oruç in Tlemcen. After a six-month siege he escaped from the town only to be overtaken by the Spanish and, after a battle in which he fought like a lion, he was overwhelmed and killed.

Hızır was left in charge of Algiers, and he responded to the news of his brother's death by asking Istanbul for military aid against Spain. In return he offered to bring the Sultan, Selim I, 'all, or the greatest part of Barbary'.[15] At this stage the Ottoman Empire's African possessions extended no further than Egypt, which had been conquered by Selim in 1517; and, presented with the opportunity to expand further westward into the Mediterranean, Selim accepted Algiers as a *sanjak*, or province of the Empire and

appointed Hızır as its governor. He also sent 6000 troops to reinforce Hızır's garrisons along the coast.

   With imperial backing, Hızır recaptured Tlemcen, consolidated
his influence along the Barbary Coast and turned Algiers into a
formidable naval base. By 1529 he commanded a fleet of eighteen
galleys 'and was become nothing less dreaded and renowned than
had been his brother'.[16] In that year he captured the vitally important fortress of El Peñón in the mouth of Algiers harbour, which
had been occupied by the Spanish for nearly twenty years; and
constructed an earthwork platform connecting the rocky island
on which it stood to the mainland. This 300-yard-long causeway,
the great mole, vastly improved Algiers as a harbour, creating an
anchorage that protected Hızır's fleet both from the elements and,
because defensive batteries were placed at strategic intervals along
it, from any unfriendly intruders.

A European impression of the Ottoman emperor Sulaimān

   From Algiers, Hızır and his captains took the sea *jihad* to southern
Europe, raiding the Balearics, Sardinia, Sicily and Calabria. He was
so successful that in 1533 he was summoned to Istanbul by Sultan
Sulaimān the Lawgiver, who was concerned at Spanish and Genoese

activity in the Mediterranean. Sulaimān appointed Hızır admiral of the Ottoman fleet and chief governor of North Africa, giving him the honorary name by which he is best known today, Khair ad-Din, 'Goodness of the Faith',[17] and charging him with the task of building up the Ottoman fleet.

Eight months later Khair ad-Din launched a successful assault on Spanish-held Tunis. His victory was short-lived − the Holy Roman Emperor and King of Spain, Charles V, counter-attacked the following year, and the Turks had to evacuate Tunis in a hurry − but within months Khair ad-Din was back in Algiers and raiding the coast of Spain itself. By the early 1540s he was at the head of the most powerful naval fleet in the Mediterranean, commanding 110 war galleys, 40 lighter galleys known as 'foists' and three great sailing ships filled with munitions. He also commanded a force of 30,000 men. After François I of France entered into a secret treaty with Sulaimān against Spain, the admiral fought alongside the French to capture Nice, then ruled by Charles V's ally the Duke of Savoy. To the horror of other Christian nations, Khair ad-Din and his fleet then put in at Toulon on the French Mediterranean coast. They spent the winter of 1543–4 there, François I having instructed the inhabitants to move out to make room for the Moslem troops. Even so, Toulon was crowded that year: there were fewer than 640 houses within its walls, and the surrounding fields were covered with a sea of tents. It was as if a second Istanbul had been built in Europe, muttered France's enemies.

Khair ad-Din retired to Istanbul in 1545, giving up command of the fleet and handing over the governorship of Algiers to his son Hasan. Described as a man whose 'stature was advantageous, his mien portly and majestic, well-proportioned and robust,' he died on 4 July 1546 at his palace on the shores of the Bosporus. He was in his late sixties. Two centuries later he was still held in such high regard by Ottoman mariners 'that no voyage is undertaken from Constantinople by either public or private persons, without their first visiting his tomb'.[18]

His legacy in the Mediterranean was threefold. He confirmed the strategic importance of North Africa, and of Algiers in particular, as the Ottoman Empire's front line in its struggle for regional dominance with the Holy Roman Empire. He showed the economic benefits which could accrue to a relatively poor state like Algiers from the proceeds of well-organised privateering expeditions. And he left behind him a group of effective and battle-hardened corsair captains.

In August 1551 Khair ad-Din's chief lieutenant, Torghūd, took Tripoli from the Knights of St John, who had been using the city for the past twenty-one years as a base from which to harass Islamic shipping in the eastern Mediterranean. Sulaimān subsequently made him governor, and he used the money obtained from privateering expeditions to build Tripoli into an important naval base and the capital of an Ottoman province. Torghūd was killed in an assault on Malta in 1565; but nine years later *his* chief lieutenant Uluj Ali, the man who had carried his body back to Tripoli, took Tunis from the Spanish. And this time the Ottoman Empire held on to it.

With the conquest of Tunis, the question of who would control North Africa was effectively settled, and in 1580 Sulaimān the Lawgiver's grandson Murad III made peace with Spain. Both sides agreed to respect each other's frontiers and not to molest each other's subjects.

But Tunis, Tripoli and Algiers relied on their attacks against Christian shipping to maintain their economies. Prize ships and their cargos paid the wages of government officials and furnished the governor's palace; they financed the building of mosques and mausoleums, harbour defences and residential housing, while Christian slaves, taken in coastal raids and attacks on merchant ships, provided the labour. England could sell its woollen goods in the *suks* of the Levant; Barbary had nothing to sell but its prowess at piracy.

The situation at the beginning of the seventeenth century was that three Barbary states – Tripoli, Tunis and Algiers – owed allegiance to Istanbul. The Ottoman Emperor sent governors to each of these cities to collect taxes and rule their citizens on his behalf, even though in reality all three possessed a considerable degree of autonomy. The fourth major presence in Barbary, Morocco, was an Islamic society like the others, but it was an independent state outside the Empire – or, rather, several independent states, since it had descended into a state of anarchy after the death in 1603 of Sultan Ahmad Al-Mansur, 'the Golden One', when several of his sons laid claim to the sultanate. The result was civil war and the partition of the country into two kingdoms centred on Fez in the north and Marrakesh in the south.

There was also a European presence in Barbary. Spain and Portugal were clinging on to a number of bases in North Africa: at Ma'amura and Mazagan on the Atlantic coast of Morocco; at Ceuta and Tangier on the North African side of the Straits; at Melilla, near the present-day Moroccan border with Algeria; at Oran, on the Algerian side of that border. Where they had been ejected, the remnants of colonisation often still dominated the architectural landscape. At Safi on the Atlantic coast, a favourite haunt of English pirates, the great Dar el Bahar, or 'castle of the sea', had been built in the 1520s by the Portuguese as the governor's residence. On higher ground, 500 yards inland, stood a larger Portuguese fortress, the Kechla citadel; and behind the walls of the *medina* was an incongruous Gothic church, the choir of a cathedral which was still unfinished when the Christian Portuguese pulled out of Safi in 1541.

Although they were unified by religion and, in the case of Algiers, Tunis and Tripoli, by their inclusion in the Ottoman Empire, the Barbary states never formed a coherent bloc; they frequently went to war with each other and with their own people, as well as with Christendom. But to Europe, Barbary was as much an idea as a defined geographical entity. The 'Barbarians', as the English called them – the origins of the word lie with the Berbers who inhabited the coastal regions of North Africa, but by the sixteenth century the pejorative meaning was in common use – were dismissively divided in the English popular imagination into 'Turks', who were part of the Empire; and 'Moors', who lived in or came from Morocco. The distinction was not hard and fast: both terms were loose, generic and often interchangeable. Barbarians manned the enemy's front line; they occupied the westernmost parts of the *dar al-Islam*, the territories where Moslems could practise their religion freely; and they fought against Christendom on behalf of the Empire, preying on Christian shipping in the Mediterranean, enslaving Christian mariners, and offering sanctuary to outlaws on the run from Christian justice.

Istanbul turned a blind eye: it suited Ottoman foreign policy to allow the Barbary states to chip away at the economic might of Christian powers, disrupting their trade, frightening their merchants and intimidating their coastal settlements. The Christian

Mediterranean responded in kind, and when Protestant and fiercely anti-Catholic northern Europe moved into the Mediterranean at the beginning of the seventeenth century, in the shape of England and the Netherlands, the potential for conflict and collaboration extended still further.

Yet they had to move into it. The Empire represented a colossal market for European goods. Besides Istanbul itself, 'the common mart of all commodities',[19] there was Smyrna on the Aegean coast of Anatolia, famed for its local cottons and carpets 'and all other commodities found in Turkey';[20] and the ancient city of Aleppo in Syria, whose lofty towers and massive walls were said by the Arabs to laugh in the face of Time. Aleppo was a natural trading centre for goods coming from Persia and Arabia, and every year huge caravans from Basra and Mecca snaked in and out of the desert bringing silks, gems and spices.

Such a vast storehouse of luxury goods, such a vast centre of consumption, was impossible to ignore. François I of France agreed to a trade treaty with Sulaimān the Lawgiver in 1536. Five years later Venice signed a similar treaty, followed by England in 1583 and Holland in 1613. Periodically renewed, amended and added to – under Ottoman law they were only valid for the life of the Sultan who had subscribed to them – these articles of capitulation, as they were known, guaranteed the rights and liberties of English, French, Venetian and Dutch citizens residing anywhere in the *dar al-Islam*. They guaranteed to Christians freedom of religion, access to their consul and free passage throughout the Empire either by land or sea. They capped the duty that merchants had to pay in all the Empire's ports:

> The English merchants, and all under their banner shall and may safely and freely trade, and negotiate in Aleppo, Cairo, Scio [the Aegean island of Chios], Smyrna and in all parts of our dominions, and according to our ancient customs of all their merchandise, they shall pay three in the hundred for custom and nothing more.[21]

And they explicitly provided for protection from pirates:

> If the pirates or Levents [*sic*], who infest the seas with their frigates, shall be found to have taken any English vessel, or to

have robbed or spoiled their goods and faculties; also if it shall be found, that in any of our dominions, any shall have violently taken goods of any English man, our ministers shall with all diligence seek out such offenders, and severely punish them, and cause that all such goods, ships, moneys, and whatsoever hath been taken away from the English nation, shall be presently, justly, and absolutely restored to them.[22]

England, France, the Netherlands and Venice all maintained ambassadors in Istanbul who combined their role as diplomats with that of commercial agent. Although he was appointed by the King, the English ambassador's post was actually financed by the London-based Levant Company, which held the monopoly on English trade with the Empire. The Company also retained consuls at Smyrna and Aleppo, and employed representatives at dozens of smaller ports from Alexandria to Zante. By the 1620s its merchants were sending goods worth £250,000 a year to Turkey; and as the century wore on, Mediterranean markets as a whole came to account for half of all English exports.

This was the world which attracted English pirates like Harris and Jennings. Those pirates who were prepared to concentrate their activity against Moslems found sanctuary among the Ottoman Empire's natural enemies such as the Spanish islands of Majorca and Sardinia, or the fiercely anti-Islamic sovereign states of Malta and Genoa.

But for those who weren't imbued with the crusader spirit, the Barbary Coast and its state-sanctioned piracy had a lot to offer: a friendly harbour where a ship could take on willing crewmen and supplies of food, fresh water, powder and shot; a safe place where a sea captain could carry out repairs without fear of being ambushed; a ready market for goods which might have a compli-cated past and no provenance.

More than this, the Barbary Coast offered the Protestant zealot a chance to continue the fight against Spain and popery. It offered the disenchanted outcast a chance to join a new and different social milieu, to renege on his own culture and religion and find a welcome in the *dar al-Islam*. It offered the brave, the unscrupulous and the adventurous the thing they wanted most of all – prosperity at sea.

2

Where Are the Days?
The Making of a Pirate

*I*n the summer of 1608 an Englishman arrived at the small *palazzo* near the Grand Canal that served as the official residence of Sir Henry Wotton, James I's ambassador at Venice. The sailor's name was Henry Pepwell, and he was just come from Tunis, where he had been gathering intelligence about an English pirate called Ward.

'Captain Ward' had been wreaking havoc in the Mediterranean for the past two or three years, and the English and Venetian authorities were desperate for any intelligence that might help them put an end to his activities. Pepwell told the ambassador how Ward's criminal career began when he stole a small ship on the south coast of England; how he had settled in Tunis and formed a lucrative partnership with the Moslem ruler there; how his pirate fleet was now heading for the Straits of Gibraltar and the North Atlantic, and how he had vowed 'to spare no one whom he can defeat'.

And in the course of his story, which Wotton took straight round to the Ducal Palace and presented to the Doge, the informant gave a description of the man who was fast becoming the most notorious pirate in Europe:

John Ward, commonly called Captain Ward, is about 55 years of age. Very short, with little hair, and that quite white; bald in front; swarthy face and beard. Speaks little, and almost always swearing. Drunk from morn till night. Most prodigal and plucky. Sleeps a great deal . . .[1]

This unprepossessing word picture is the only information we have about the physical appearance of the greatest pirate of his age. Half-man, half-legend, John Ward was the arch-pirate, the corsair king of popular folk culture. London street balladeers sang of how the 'most famous pirate of the world' terrorised the merchants of France and Spain, Portugal and Venice, and routed the mighty Knights of Malta with his bravery and cunning. Parents scared their children with tales of the demon who 'feareth neither God nor the Devil,/[Whose] deeds are bad, his thoughts are evil', and scared each other with reports that those who fell into his clutches would be tied back-to-back and thrown overboard, or cut in pieces, or shot to death without mercy.[2] Clergymen in their pulpits thundered that Ward and his renegades would end their days in drunkenness, lechery and sodomy within the sybaritic confines of their Tunisian palace, while congregations wondered idly if drunkenness, lechery and sodomy were really such a bad way to go.

The 'most famous pirate of the world' was one among thousands of disenchanted, disempowered sailors who turned to piracy in the early 1600s. Most had once been privateers, sailing with commissions which authorised them to capture for profit merchant shipping belonging to an enemy: the pirate leaders who were hanged at Wapping in December 1609 had begun their careers during the English wars with Spain which started in 1585 and dragged on intermittently for the next two decades. They attacked Spanish merchant shipping, but remained on the right side of the English law by obtaining letters of marque or reprisal, government licences which authorised them to attack ships belonging to Spain and her allies.[3]

This was an international tradition of state-sanctioned piracy which stretched back for centuries. When a group of London merchants had a huge cargo of wool and other merchandise confiscated in Genoa in 1413, the English king Henry IV issued letters of marque and reprisal allowing the merchants to detain Genoese

men, ships and goods until full restitution had been made. One
hundred and thirty years later, when Henry VIII was at war with
France and Scotland, he declared that any English citizen 'shall
enjoy to his and their own proper use, profit, and commodity, all
and singular such ships, vessels, munition, merchandise, wares,
victuals, and goods of what nature and quality soever it be, which
they shall take of any of his Majesty's said enemies'.[4] Elizabeth I's
government regularly issued letters of marque, and most of the
sixteenth century's greatest English sailors carried them or financed
expeditions that depended on them. The explorer Sir John
Hawkins promoted privateering ventures, as did the entrepre-
neurial Sir Walter Raleigh; Christopher Newport, one of the
founders of the Jamestown settlement in Virginia, brought prize
cargos of hides, sugar and spices taken from Spanish shipping in
the West Indies to the port of London in the 1590s; Martin
Frobisher and Sir Humphrey Gilbert were both involved in privateering. Sir Francis Drake was careful to take letters of marque
with him on his voyage round the world, authorising him to
harass Spanish and Portuguese shipping. (At least, he said he did:
he refused to show them to anyone who might have been able
to understand them.)

The legal rights and wrongs with regard to such letters of
commission could be hard to disentangle. If an English privateer
attacked and captured a Spanish merchantman while England was
at war with Spain, the status of the prize was fairly straightforward:
it belonged to the privateer and his backers. But what if an
Englishman operating with Dutch letters of marque took a
Venetian ship, claiming that it was carrying goods to one of
Spain's allies? Where did the Venetian merchant go for redress?
The English Admiralty might make sympathetic noises, but that
merchant would be fortunate indeed if he ever saw his goods
again. Elizabeth's government was notoriously flexible when it
came to interpreting the legitimacy of letters of marque. Senior
courtiers, and even the Queen herself, invested in privateering
ventures, and if this led to conflicts of interest, they frequently
resolved those conflicts in their own favour. And in 1585 the
government, concerned that prizes taken by English vessels were
being sold unsupervised in foreign ports, ordered that all prizes
must pass through the Admiralty Court in London for sentence

of forfeiture. Since the Lord Admiral thus came in for 10 per cent of their value, there was even more reason for Elizabeth's senior officials to turn a blind eye to the activities of mariners who blurred the distinction between privateer and pirate.

Privateering was big business. In the aftermath of the defeat of the Spanish Armada in 1588, 100 prizes were brought into English ports every year: together with their cargos of wines and calicos and sugar and spices, their value amounted to some £200,000, the equivalent of 15 per cent of all annual imports. Years later, the Venetian ambassador reckoned that 'nothing is thought to have enriched the English or done so much to allow many individuals to amass the wealth they are known to possess as the wars with the Spaniards in the time of Queen Elizabeth. All were permitted to go privateering and they plundered not only Spaniards but all others indifferently, so that they enriched themselves by a constant stream of booty.'[5]

This particular route to prosperity at sea came to an abrupt end when James I came to the throne in 1603. The pragmatic and peace-loving James was determined to make peace with Spain, and he immediately issued a proclamation declaring that recent prizes collected by English ships had to be returned, and that anyone who persisted in attacking Spanish shipping after the date of the proclamation would be treated as a pirate. In September 1603 another royal proclamation, this time 'to repress all piracies and depredations upon the sea', set out in no uncertain terms the consequences of ignoring the first:

> No man of war be furnished or set out to sea by any of his Majesty's subjects, under pain of death and confiscation of lands and goods, not only to the captains and mariners, but also to the owners and victuallers, if the company of the said ship shall commit any piracy, depredation or murder at the sea, upon any of his Majesty's friends.[6]

Over the summer of 1604 the Somerset House peace conference brought the Anglo-Spanish wars to an end; a treaty to that effect was signed on 16 August. In response, some English privateers offered their services to the Dutch Republic, which remained at war with Spain until the signing of the Twelve Years' Truce five years later – but in 1605, James I did his best to stop the looting of foreign ships by English privateers by calling home all English seamen serving with foreign powers and prohibiting vessels that carried letters of marque from victualling, or resupplying themselves, at British ports. Anyone who failed to comply would be regarded as a pirate and, warned the King, would face the 'peril of his heavy indignation, and the grievous pains belonging to the same'.[7]

At the same time as he was outlawing English privateering, James I was also running down his navy, and thus making it much harder for Englishmen who wanted a legitimate naval career to find work. By 1607 the English navy, which was once the envy of Europe, numbered only thirty-seven ships, 'many of them old and rotten, and barely fit for service', according to the Venetian ambassador.[8] The privateer Richard Bishop articulated the resentment felt by many seafarers when he complained that the King 'hath lessened by this general peace the flourishing employment that we seafaring men do bleed for at sea'. Having enjoyed prosperity at sea, many sailors found it hard to give up the life: 'We have spent our hours in a high flood, and it will be unsavory for us now, to pick up our crumbs in a low ebb.'[9]

John Ward began his maritime career as a fisherman

Those sentiments were echoed by John Ward. Born in the Kentish port of Faversham in about 1563 he first went to sea as a fisherman; then he became a privateer; and, after James I banned privateering, he joined the King's navy, serving aboard the *Lion's Whelp*, a fast, lightly armed vessel that patrolled the English Channel on the lookout for pirates operating out of Dunkirk. By all accounts he was a morose character, given to heavy drinking and self-pity. He spent his time ashore in taverns, where he would 'sit melancholy, speak doggedly, curse the time, repine at other men's good fortunes, and complain of the hard crosses [that] attended his own'.[10]

Andrew Barker, an English sailor who was held for ransom in Tunis after his vessel was captured by Ward's pirates in 1608, wrote a vivid account of his career. *A True and Certaine Report of the Beginning, Proceedings, Overthrowes, and now present Estate of Captaine Ward*, which appeared in October 1609, is imaginative, self-conscious and packed with rhetorical flourishes, but it nevertheless stays very close to the spirit, if not the letter, of the truth.

For instance, one night when the *Lion's Whelp* was in Portsmouth harbour and the crew had been given shore leave, Barker has his anti-hero launch into a tirade about how life has changed for the worse for English seamen since James I came to the throne:

> Here's a scurvy world, and as scurvily we live in it . . . Where are the days that have been, and the season that we have seen, when we might sing, swear, drink, drab [i.e., whore], and kill men as freely, as your cake-makers do flies? When we might do what we list, and the law would bear us out in it? Nay, when we might lawfully do that, we shall be hanged for and we do [it] now? When the whole sea was our empire, where we rob at will?[11]

The words which Barker put into Ward's mouth – for he must have, as he couldn't have heard him speak them – could have come from any one of a thousand disgruntled Jacobean sailors who longed, as Ward did, for the days that had been. Life in the English navy was hard for sailors like John Ward – so hard that, as Sir Walter Raleigh remarked, men went 'with as great a grudging to serve in his majesty's ships as if it were to be slaves in the galleys'.[12]

Conditions aboard even the best of the King's ships were insanitary and overcrowded. The 400-ton *Speedwell*, for example, a 30-gun man-of-war which was rebuilt at the beginning of the century, was about 90 feet long with a beam of less than 30 feet and a depth of about 12 feet. It carried a crew of 191, including 18 gunners, 50 small-arms men, 4 carpenters and 3 trumpeters. (The *Lion's Whelp* in which Ward was serving had a smaller crew, but then it was a smaller ship, probably only two-thirds the size of the *Speedwell*.) Hammocks were still something of a rarity, having only been introduced into the English navy in 1597 as hanging 'cabins or beds . . . for the better preservation of [sailors'] health'.[13] Most sailors shared a straw pallet with another man, although they did not usually occupy it at the same time: a two-watch system meant than one worked while the other was resting. They encountered other bedfellows, though: a Jacobean seaman rarely owned more than one set of clothes – typically a woollen Monmouth cap, a linen shirt and a pair of knee-length canvas slops – which he kept on waking and sleeping, until they were worn to rags. Clothes and bedding were riddled with lice and fleas.

The food at the beginning of a voyage wasn't too bad; it might consist of biscuit, salt beef, meal, cheese and beer. But the beef went bad, the beer turned sour and the biscuit and meal attracted weevils. Dysentery and scurvy were both common.

These horrors lay in store for every mariner, whether he sailed as a pirate, a merchantman or a member of His Majesty's navy. But aboard a private vessel, discipline was relatively relaxed. When the pirate captain John Jennings fell for an Irish whore and installed her in his cabin, for example, his crew burst in on the couple and lectured him on his lax morals, which they blamed for a recent run of bad luck. He lashed out at them with a truncheon, at which they chased him round the deck with a musket. He only managed to save his life by barricading himself in the ship's gun room. Eventually tempers cooled and he resumed command. But history doesn't record what became of his female companion.

That kind of behaviour from the crew was inconceivable aboard a naval vessel, where discipline was rigid and the consequences of any kind of insubordination or disobedience were brutal. A minor transgression could earn the hapless sailor a spell 'in the bilboes', shackled by his legs as though in the stocks; or bound to the mainmast or capstan for hours on end with a heavy basket of shot tied round his neck. He might be ducked at the yardarm: 'a malefactor, by having a rope fastened under his arms, and about his middle, and under his breech, is thus hoisted up to the end of the yard, from whence he is violently let fall into the sea, some-times twice, sometimes three several times one after another'.[14]

A refinement on ducking, reserved for more serious offences, was keel-hauling. A rope was rigged up from one yardarm to the other, passing under the keel, and the unfortunate offender was hauled up to one yardarm, dropped into the sea and dragged slowly under the ship and up to the other. The experience of being half-drowned was terrible enough, but much more serious damage was caused by being rasped over the razor-sharp barnacles that encrusted the ship's bottom. Keel-hauling was often a death sentence.

Keel-hauling and ducking were cruel, but relatively unusual punishments. By far the commonest penalty aboard ship was a thrashing. Minor offenders had to 'pay the cobty' by being spanked on the behind with a flat piece of wood called a cobbing-board. More serious crimes were dealt with by the marshal or the boatswain with a painful whip known as the cat-of-nine-tails.

Corporal punishment was an integral part of seventeenth-century life. Husbands beat their wives; parents beat their children; masters and mistresses beat their servants, and employers beat their employees. But the unrelenting harshness of naval discipline was of a different order altogether. Remarking that sailors preferred to take their chances 'in small ships of reprisal' – that is, in privateers or pirate ships – rather than serve the crown, the naval commander Sir William Monson (himself an ex-privateer) commented that this was because of 'the liberty they find in the one, and the punishment they fear in the other'.[15]

Monson had a point. But he glossed over another reason sailors preferred privateering. In the Royal Navy a Jacobean seaman's pay was ten shillings a lunar month before deductions (the navy calculated sailors' pay on the basis of a twenty-eight-day month right up until the beginning of the nineteenth century). That wasn't bad; but the crew of a privateer out on a cruise against the Spanish shared one-third of the prize money among them, and that could easily amount to ten or fifteen pounds for a voyage lasting only a couple of months. Little wonder that professional sailors, especially those who had prospered as privateers before England's peace with Spain, were less than happy to swap good money and relative freedom as a privateer for punishment and privation in the navy. Or that they wished, as John Ward wished, for the days that had been 'when the whole sea was our empire'.

According to Andrew Barker's *True and Certaine Report*, it was a wealthy Catholic who unwittingly offered Ward an escape route back to the days that had been. The man sold up his Hampshire estate with the intention of moving himself, his wife and children and all his worldly goods (including £2000 in ready money) to the more congenial religious climate of France. There was talk of this in the taverns and alleys of Portsmouth, and John Ward heard that the man had bought passage on a bark, a small merchant ship, which was currently at anchor in Portsmouth harbour. His valuables were already stowed aboard, while the passengers and most of the crew were lodging in the town, waiting for a fair wind for France.

One night, Ward persuaded about thirty of his comrades to desert from the *Lion's Whelp* and join him in storming the bark, arguing that they would have no problem in neutralising the two hands on watch and slipping out of harbour with the Catholic's fortune before anyone realised what was happening. Ward and his men duly crept aboard, overpowered the watch and 'straight shut [them] under deck, and commanded them not to squeak like rats'.[16] In the still darkness they piloted the little vessel out of Portsmouth harbour.

So far, so good. By dawn they were away from the guns of Portsmouth's fort and out in the English Channel, and the time had come for Ward to take a look at his ill-gotten Catholic gold. He had the captives brought up on deck — and received an unpleasant surprise: 'These poor wretches shaking for fear before this terrible thief, they replied, that his expectation was herein frustrate. Store of riches they must confess there was indeed, but upon what reason they knew not, it was the day before landed again.'[17] Ward's intended victim somehow had gotten wind of the plot to rob him, and his goods and money were sitting safe and secure back in his lodgings at the Red Lion Inn at Portsmouth.

Not quite knowing what to do or where to go, only that 'we

have proceeded so far into the thieves' path, that to return back we shall be stopped with a halter', the men got drunk on some wine they found in the hold and set off westward towards Land's End in Cornwall.[18]

Off the Isles of Scilly, about thirty miles from the south-west tip of Cornwall, they sighted a French merchant ship of 70 tons, fully laden and bound for Ireland. She was armed with six guns, which made her more than a match for the bark if it came to a fight. But Ward had no intention of engineering a head-on confrontation. He hailed the Frenchman – a perfectly normal procedure when two ships met on the high seas – and pulled alongside her, patiently 'passing many hours in courteous discourse . . . seeming glad of the other's acquaintance' while most of his men stayed hidden below deck.[19] When he judged that any suspicions the French crew might have had, had been lulled, he gave a signal; his men burst out on deck; and the novice pirates boarded their victim, seized her cargo and imprisoned all hands before 'any had time to think how they could be hurt'.[20]

The French prize gave Ward a more substantial ship and more firepower. Now he needed more men. So he anchored off Cawsand, a little fishing village overlooking Plymouth Sound known as a centre for smuggling, and went ashore in a longboat.

Throughout Ward's career as a pirate, one of his most effective qualities was his power of persuasion. He had convinced thirty of the *Lion's Whelp*'s crew to jump ship and steal the bark with its presumed cargo of Catholic gold; when that failed, he convinced them to take part in a daring act of piracy. In the years to come he would convince Ottoman officials to provide him with men and munitions; he would convince English agents who came to hunt him down that they should change sides. And now, on the beach and on the quay and in the alehouse, 'with the news of his success, and expectation to come',[21] he convinced the smugglers and fishermen of Cawsand Bay to follow him to the Barbary Coast.

Leaving ashore the two watchmen taken prisoner when he stole the bark in Portsmouth, Ward and his band of pirates sailed south, across the Bay of Biscay and down the coast of Spain and Portugal. Off Cape St Vincent they took a small flyboat, a flat-bottomed coastal trader used by the Dutch. She was laden with valuable merchandise, and as they turned east through the Straits of Gibraltar Ward put her crew into the bark and left them to steer their own course for home, while he and his little convoy doubled back and headed for the shelter of Larache on the Atlantic coast of Morocco. We don't know how long they stayed there, only that their next prize was a settee, a two-masted, single-decked transport ship used to carry spare galley slaves and more commonly found in the Levant than in the western half of the Mediterranean. Then Ward decided to take his squadron, which now consisted of the settee, the French merchantman and the flyboat, straight to the pirate haven of Algiers.

His timing couldn't have been worse. A few months before, an English privateer named Richard Giffard, a one-time friend of the Algerians who had subsequently changed sides and was now fighting against the Turks for the Duke of Tuscany, sailed into Algiers and tried to set fire to the Algerian corsair fleet. He failed, but the governor of Algiers, Mohammad the Eunuch, was angry. He rounded up a dozen of Giffard's crew who had somehow been left behind when their captain fled, and tortured them to death. English merchants in the city were imprisoned and ordered to pay heavy fines; English ships were banned from entering the port; and it was generally understood that Giffard's fellow countrymen were no longer welcome in Algiers.

So when John Ward arrived, hoping to dispose of his prize cargos and victual his ships in a city known throughout the western world as a safe haven for European renegades, he was surprised to meet with a frosty reception. In fact, several members of his crew were arrested the moment they went ashore, and it was only after some careful negotiation and a hefty bribe that Ward was able to procure 'the peace and enlargement of his followers'.[22]

According to another Englishman named Richard Parker who was in Morocco at the time to trade woollen goods for sugar, Ward made a hasty retreat and tried his luck next at Salé on the Atlantic coast. Arriving there late in 1604 he sold his booty, victualled and trimmed his vessels and recruited more men – mostly, it seems, from Parker's own ship, the *Blessing*, which was left so undermanned that the merchant thought he would never get back to England. He was left with little choice but to hitch a ride with the pirates. (Or so he told the Admiralty Court when he was brought before it and accused of piracy some years later . . .)

Early in 1605 Ward set sail from Salé on a course that took him through the Straits and back towards Algiers. This time, however, he kept going eastward along the Barbary Coast, past the ancient ruins of Hippo Regius, where St Augustine died as Vandals stormed the city walls in AD 430; past the Khroumirie Mountains with their forests of cork oak reaching almost to the sea; past the corsair bases of Tabarquea and Bizerte, which began life as Phoenician settlements more than 700 years before the birth of Christ. Eventually Ward and his little convoy rounded Cap Farina and entered the Gulf of Tunis.

Tunis had long been known in Europe as a refuge for outcasts and outlaws. In the early sixteenth century, when Oruç Barbarossa made the city his base for raids on Venetian shipping and an entire community of Christian merchants settled there to trade in stolen goods, the Hafsid ruler of Tunisia, Mohammad IV, was guarded by 'fifteen hundred most choice soldiers, the greatest part of whom are renegadoes or backsliders from the Christian faith'.[23] The subject of a drawn-out struggle between the Ottoman Empire and Spain during the 1500s, Tunis was occupied in 1534 by Turks under the command of Khair ad-Din; then by the Spanish; again by Turks in 1569; again by the Spanish; and by the Turks for a third and final time in 1574, when the Hafsids, who had become little more than puppet kings of the Spanish, were ousted, and the Ottoman Emperor installed a *beylerbey*, or provincial governor, whose authority was enforced by a garrison of 4000 janissaries.

The janissary corps was the nucleus of the Ottoman army. All of its members were converts to Islam who had been recruited from the children of the *devshirme*, the child-tribute that the Empire exacted from Christian subject states in the Balkans. Highly disciplined and rigorously trained in the use of arms, they were a hierarchical warrior class that was accountable to its officers and to Istanbul, and not to the civil authorities in the various provinces where the corps was stationed. Janissaries played a vital social and political role in all of the Ottoman outposts on the Barbary Coast, and for a governor to ignore their interests was to court disaster.

The Ottoman Empire's objective in taking and holding Tunis

Tunis, with the harbour of La Goulette in the foreground

was primarily strategic: because the city was regarded as a bulwark against expansionist Christian powers in the Mediterranean, a base from which to launch military operations against the West, no real attempt was made to colonise the country, and the fact that Istanbul appointed a *pasha* to govern for only one year at a time did little to encourage stability.

In 1591 the rank and file janissaries garrisoned in Tunis rebelled against their senior officers, whom they accused of treating them badly. The mutineers chose leaders of their own, whom they called *deys* (from the Turkish *dāī*, 'maternal uncle'), and forced the *pasha* to accept a nominal role as the Sultan's representative and to cede real power to the *dey*.

For seven years ruling *deys* came and went with alarming frequency, none of them strong enough to keep the different factions within the janissary corps in check. Then in 1598 a junior officer named 'Uthmân emerged as the leader Tunis needed and, with a little help from 2000 local Arab troops, he took control of the corps and the capital.

Known in England as Kara Osman, Osman Bey, Crosomond and the Crossymon, described at different times as Vice Roy, Captain of Janissaries and Lord Admiral of the Sea, and regarded as the archetypal sinister Turk, 'Uthmân Dey was an able administrator and a clever manager of men. His rule, according to a seventeenth-century history of Barbary, was characterised by gentleness, justice and a profound tranquillity.[24] Among the many achievements of his reign were an important trade treaty he concluded with France, which included a reciprocal renunciation of the right of search; success in maintaining harmonious relationships both within Tunisia and between Tunisia and the rest of the Ottoman Empire; and the welcome he gave to tens of thousands of Moriscos, Spanish Moslems expelled from Andalusia in 1609. According to the seventeenth-century historian Ibn Abi Dinar, 'Uthmân Dey 'made room for them in the town, and distributed the neediest of them among the people of Tunis'[25], bringing an army of skilled artisans and labourers into his country, and revitalising Tunisian arts and crafts.

In the West, 'Uthmân Dey is remembered for one thing and one thing only – piracy. As part of his efforts to build a prosperous new Tunis, he worked closely with the head of the navy,

the *qaptān*, and the powerful guild of corsairs, the *tā'ifat al-ra'īs*,
to establish the city as one of the most important corsair bases
on the Barbary Coast. European renegades and 'Turks' – that
catch-all English euphemism both for citizens of the Ottoman
Empire and for all Moslems, no matter where they came from –
had operated out of Tunis for generations, paying tribute to officials
and duty on the prizes and slaves they brought in for sale. But
'Uthmân invested in corsairing expeditions and provided each
corsair captain, or *raïs*, with troops, guns and money. He ensured
that janissaries received a share of the profits. (Janissaries served as
the fighting force aboard all corsair vessels and the janissary officer
in command was theoretically in charge of the ship, since he
outranked its *raïs*.) By the time of his death he had managed to
weave piracy so deeply into the fabric of Tunisian society that it
was a major state industry.

The state industry, as it was turning out to be for smaller maritime
nations all over the Mediterranean. Unable or unwilling to compete
with the big trading powers like Spain, France, the Venetian
Republic, or their up-and-coming rivals, England and the Dutch
Republic, such states turned privateering into a mainstream
commercial activity. This meant that strictly speaking the corsairs
of the Mediterranean weren't pirates, just as the privateers of
western Europe weren't pirates. Much has been made of the distinction by twentieth-century apologists, who stress the institutional
and legalistic aspects of corsairing: the issuing of commissions, the
way that prizes were taxed by the state, the restrictions on who
could and who could not be attacked. In most Mediterranean
languages the word 'corsair' – the French *corsaire*, the Provençal
corsari, the Spanish *corsario*, the Italian *corsaro* – means 'privateer' as
distinct from 'pirate'. It was only the lazy English who persisted
in treating the two words as synonymous: in the 1599 edition of
his *Voyages*, for example, Richard Hakluyt spoke of 'the Turkish
cursaros, or as we call them pirates or rovers'.[26] Over 100 years
later an English historian could still talk of 'the corsories or pirates
of Tripoli'.[27]

These are muddy semantic waters. Christian and Moslem states
adopted increasingly legalistic positions in the course of the seventeenth century, as jointly ratified and (in theory) binding articles
of peace came to occupy a position of importance in Europe's

stance towards Barbary. From the 1670s onwards, English government sources tended to reserve the charge of piracy for the buccaneers of the Caribbean, who were becoming an increasing menace.
(In 1684 Henry Morgan wrote from Jamaica to instruct his London
lawyers to sue a publisher for describing him as a 'pirate' rather
than a 'privateer'; he won £200 in damages, plus costs.) English
consuls in Barbary were careful never to refer to corsairs as pirates,
even though the absence of a treaty rather than the presence of a
state of war was enough for those corsairs to justify taking a vessel
from a militarily weak nation such as Naples or Ragusa or Genoa.

Most seventeenth-century Englishmen were less particular. The
word 'corsair' wasn't common in English anyway, and the charge
of piracy was routinely and casually levelled at the warships of
any nation the English didn't like, including all the Barbary Coast
states. In any case, what *was* the legal status of Tripoli or Tunis or
Algiers – all part of the Ottoman Empire – when they declared
war on a European state to legitimise the plundering of its merchant
ships, while their political masters in Istanbul simultaneously assured
the state in question that the Ottoman Empire was friendly and
that no such hostilities were intended? What if a state's *tā'ifat
al-ra'īs* was so bound up with government, as it frequently was,
that it could engineer a declaration of war in order to legitimise
the search for lucrative victims, thus turning diplomacy itself into
an instrument of piracy? After pointing out the confusion and
stressing the difference between a privateer and a pirate, the *Oxford
English Dictionary* deftly sidesteps the problem by defining a corsair
as 'a pirate-ship sanctioned by the country to which it belongs'.

A further complication was the wars of religion that were being
fought out in the Mediterranean – sometimes by proxy, sometimes not – all through the seventeenth century. The fiercely anti-
Islamic tendency in Catholic southern Europe had its counterpart
in the devout Moslems who still saw the Barbary Coast corsairs
as front-line troops against encroaching Christendom. 'And there
were some who went on the sea *jihad* and found fame,' wrote
the Algerian historian Ahmad bin Mohammad al-Maqqari in the
1620s.[28] Forty years later a Moroccan pilgrim who paused in
Tripoli on his way to Mecca referred to corsairs as *mujahidin* and
again described their activities as *jihad*. They were warriors for
Allah, *ghuzat mu'mineen*, and by attacking European shipping they

were resisting the colonising forces of Christendom, who had not
given up their intention to gain a foothold in North Africa and
erode the *dar al-Islam*.

Like the truth, the motives of individuals are rarely pure and
never simple. Circumstance, history, ideology, the opportunity to
strike back, the thrill that can accompany an act of violence – all
played their part in the creation of a corsair culture along the
Barbary Coast. So did profit. Ibrāhīm bin Ahmad, an Andalusian
sailor and master gunner who came to Tunis with other Morisco
refugees in 1609, was delighted at the warm welcome he was
given when he arrived. 'The ruler, ʿU<u>th</u>mân Dey – God have
mercy upon him – took an interest in me and appointed me to
the command of two hundred Andalusians, giving me the sum of
five hundred *sultanis* [gold coins] and two hundred hand-guns and
daggers plus whatever was necessary for a sea voyage.' Suitably fitted
out, Ibrāhīm set off 'in search of the infidel and his wealth'.[29]

When John Ward and his men arrived in Tunis in 1605, ʿU<u>th</u>mân
Dey's enthusiasm for piracy, and the eagerness of English outlaws
to play their part in the war against Christendom, were already
causing anxiety in Europe. In February 1603 the French vice
consul at Zante counted eleven English pirates who had taken
French shipping and brought their prizes into Tunis over the
previous nine months (the list was headed by Richard Giffard);
and the Venetians, who were forced to ask the Sultan himself to
intervene when an English corsair robbed 'the Consul of the
Republic and many other rich merchants' and sold their goods
at Tunis,[30] reckoned the current *pasha* had amassed so much wealth
from English privateering that he could afford to send the Sultan
a present of 4000 gold coins to secure his early return to the court
at Istanbul.

Unusually for a pirate base, the city of Tunis lies a good five miles
from the coast, at the western end of a shallow saltwater lagoon
called el-Bahira ('the little sea') which is known to Europeans as
the Lake of Tunis. At the narrow eastern mouth of the lagoon is the
harbour of La Goulette, 'the throat', which controlled access from
the Mediterranean into el-Bahira, and which was a natural focus

for the city's naval defences. The Spanish king Charles V built a fortress across the entrance to el-Bahira when his forces took Tunis in 1535, but it was destroyed forty years later by the Turks, who constructed a massive citadel, the Borj el-Karrak, in its ruins. By the early seventeenth century a small town had grown up around the citadel, and La Goulette boasted two mosques, warehouses, a customs house, holding cells for slaves and a small community of a hundred or so Jewish and Italian merchants.

El-Bahira was only a few feet deep, and although a channel had been cut through the lagoon to allow shallow-drafted Mediterranean galleys access to Tunis itself, strangers were required to come ashore at La Goulette to make themselves known to 'Uthmân Dey's customs officials and the merchants who gathered at the quay to appraise the new arrivals.

What did they make of John Ward and his motley crew of disaffected naval men and Cornish smugglers? Heavily bearded, with long lank hair beneath their knitted Monmouth caps, and wearing short canvas breeches and a bizarre assortment of brightly coloured velvet jackets and leather jerkins, stolen doublets and clanking body armour, the pirates must have attracted stares as they moved through the sunlit streets and dark little alleys of La Goulette – stares from the janissaries in their vivid woollen coats and elaborate gold-banded hats, stares from turbanned artisans and fishermen, stares from the veiled women whose 'multifarious coverings at a distance make them appear of a much larger size than ordinary'.[31]

La Goulette seemed just as strange and exotic to Ward and his men, and Tunis itself was another world. Before the sieges and counter-attacks of the sixteenth century reduced it to ruins, it had been a thriving, cosmopolitan city. Writing in the 1520s, the Andalusian chronicler Al Hassan ibn Mohammad al-Wazzan al-Fassi (known in the West as Leo Africanus) recalled Tunisia as 'the richest kingdom in all Africa',[32] praising its capital as a 'stately and populous city' set amid olive groves, with a fine mosque, 'colleges and monasteries . . . maintained upon the common benevolence of the city',[33] and a great diversity of commerce and industry: linen weavers, drapers and artificers of all kinds, butchers, grocers, apothecaries, tailors, 'and all other trades and occupations'.[34] Houses were built of stone and decorated with carved and painted work:

They have very artificial pargettings or plaster-works, which they beautify with orient colours: for wood to carve upon is very scarce at Tunis. The floors of their chambers are paved with certain shining and fair stones: and most of their houses are but of one storey high: and almost every house hath two gates or entrances; one towards the street, and another towards the kitchen and other back-rooms: between which gates they have a fair court, where they may walk and confer with their friends.[35]

Suburbs had grown up beyond the walls to the north and south, and another between bāb al-Bahr, the eastern entrance to the city, and the shore of el-Bahira: this was where Genoese, Venetian and other European merchants lived, 'out of the tumult and concourse of the Moors' in their separate factories, or *wakāla*.

'Before the last assault made upon it by the Turks', wrote a seventeenth-century English traveller, referring to the Ottoman conquest of Tunis in 1574, 'there were many bulwarks and forts, but most of them are since slighted'.[36] But plenty of monumental architecture survived, most notably the Great Mosque that had stood at the heart of Tunis since the eighth century. At the time of John Ward's arrival 'Uthmân Dey was busy adding a monument of his own. His house, Dâr 'Uthmân, was the most impressive seventeenth-century palace in the whole of Tunis.

'Uthmân's enthusiasm for piracy was attracting merchants back after the upheavals of the previous century; and the ready market for stolen goods, coupled with the promise of a safe haven and the prospect of official backing in the form of men, supplies and money for any ventures against European shipping, were enough to persuade John Ward that Tunis was a suitable base of operations. 'Thus as the sea might by experience relate his spoils and cruelty', reported a scandalised Englishman, 'so the land was an eye-witness of his drunkenness and idle prodigality.'[37]

For the next year, nothing was heard in Europe of John Ward. He was working hard to establish a relationship with 'Uthmân Dey, who 'held share with Ward in all his voyages, prizes, and shippings and [was] his only supporter in all his designs'.[38] Driven by mutual respect and mutual self-interest, the two men seemed to hit it off almost immediately. Ward was given lodgings in the house of the *dey*'s treasurer, Hasan the Genoese, and was trusted to look after 'U<u>th</u>mân's money when Hasan was away.

Tunis at the beginning of the seventeenth century was a cosmopolitan society. Along with the native Tunisians and the Turks, there were Greek and Armenian merchants and brokers, tribesmen from the interior, and outcasts from just about every seafaring nation in Europe. John Ward and his English crew brushed shoulders in the *suks* and alleys with Dutchmen, Spaniards, Frenchman, Irish, Portuguese. Algiers was the same: a list of thirty-five corsair captains who owned war galleys in Algiers in the 1580s included just ten Turks, along with six Genoese, three Greeks, two Venetians, two Spaniards, two Albanians; one apiece from Naples, Sicily, Calabria, France, Hungary and Corsica; one Jew; and three sons of renegades. Even the admiral of the Algerian fleet was an Italian renegade.

And the Franks, as the Levant contemptuously called all European nationals, not only used the Barbary States as bases for piracy; they occupied positions of power in governments all the way along the coast of North Africa. Before his capture and conversion to Islam, the treasurer to the *pasha* of Algiers in the 1580s, now a eunuch named Hasan Aga, had been a Bristol merchant's son named Rowley. From 1649 to 1672 the roles of both *pasha* and *dey* of Tripoli were occupied by a Greek renegade. Later on in the seventeenth century, after the dual role was divided into separate posts again, the *dey* was a Venetian and the *pasha* an Albanian.

Although Ward quickly became a minor member of the Tunisian court, his real value to 'U<u>th</u>mân didn't have much to do with his abilities as an administrator. Towards the end of 1606 he was out on the cruise again, prowling around the islands of the Aegean and the Ionian seas in his Dutch flyboat, which he had rather wittily renamed the *Gift*. She was armed with thirty guns and carried a crew of sixty-seven Englishmen, Dutchmen and Spaniards. There were also twenty-eight 'Turks' aboard, either North African sailors recruited at Tunis or La Goulette or, more likely, a contingent of janissaries provided by the *dey* to act as marines and to keep an eye on his investment. A further nineteen English seamen sailed in a pinnace, a small, light sailing vessel, that accompanied the *Gift*.

Late one evening at the beginning of November 1606 the watch on the *Gift* caught sight of an English ship, the *John Baptist*, which was on its way from Messina in Sicily to the island of Chios in the Aegean Sea with a consignment of silks. The pirates caught up with the merchantman after midnight just outside the Ottoman-held port of Koroni on the south-west coast of the Peloponnese. Her master surrendered and Ward's men duly came aboard and loaded the cloth into the pinnace, which set off back to Tunis, while the pirates commandeered the *John* and forced its officers to join their company.[39] (Or so the master of the vessel later claimed when he was hauled before an Admiralty Court in London.)

Two weeks later, on 16 November 1606, a Venetian merchant galley named the *Rubi* disappeared in the eastern Mediterranean on its way home from Alexandria. Its cargo was valuable – spices, indigo, flax and luxury goods – and the rumour was that it had been taken by an English privateer. It had, and the culprit was John Ward.

At the turn of the year another Venetian ship, the *Carminati*, left Návplion in the Peloponnese for Venice, carrying a mixed cargo of acorns, gall–nuts, blankets, silk and grain. Driven off course by strong winds, she was intercepted near the Greek island of Milos by pirates in a Savoyard ship flying the Maltese flag, who stole her cargo but let her go on her way. Good fortune didn't sail with her. On 28 January 1607 the *Carminati* was intercepted again, this time by an English vessel flying Flemish colours. (Who needed a Jolly Roger? One can see why the Admiralty Court in London used to complain that 'so many banners and colours are promiscuously used at sea to disguise themselves and entrap others [that it is not possible] to know which ships are piratical or not').[40] The 'Fleming' was John Ward, with a crew of 110, mainly English but with a contingent of Turks. He boarded the *Carminati* and her master, crew and passengers were put in a small boat with a supply of ship's biscuit and left to find their own way home, while the pirates sailed off with her in the direction of the Barbary Coast.

There were plenty of renegades operating in the eastern Mediter-ranean at this time, and so far there was little to mark Ward out as any different from the rest. That was about to change dramat-ically. Ward took the *John Baptist*, the *Rubi* and the *Carminati* back to La Goulette and spent late February and March rigging out his prizes for battle with backing from partner-in-piracy 'Uthmân Dey. In April 1607 he put to sea again, this time in the converted *Rubi*, and now in command of a small war fleet, which seems to have consisted of the *John Baptist* (renamed the *Little John*), the *Gift* and the *Carminati*. A storm scattered the four vessels before they reached the northern Adriatic, where they planned to prey on returning Venetian merchantmen; Ward lost contact with the *Little John* and the *Carminati* and, blown far off course, he changed his mind and took the *Rubi* and the *Gift* into the eastern Mediterranean.

On 26 April, while cruising between Cyprus and the coast of Turkey, he came in sight of the biggest ship he – or any of the other pirates – had ever seen.

There were some gigantic merchant vessels afloat at the turn of the seventeenth century. The *Madre de Dios*, a Portuguese carrack captured by the English off the Azores in 1592, was an 1800-ton monster, so huge that her captors had to bring her into Dartmouth instead of London because the Thames wasn't deep enough to take her.[41] Five years later a visitor to Marseilles was astonished at the sight of a captured Genoese vessel coming into harbour 'like a great house of five storeys rising from the middle of the sea'.[42] The Dutch built a series of massive ships in the early 1600s to ply the East Indies trade; the Venetian ambassador to England remarked in the summer of 1609 on a sighting of four great Dutch ships passing the English coast on their way home from the Indies. 'They are reported to vary from 1400 to 2000 tons', he said.[43] And the Venetians had leviathans of their own, the seventeenth-century equivalents of the very large crude carriers and ultra large crude carriers (VLCCs and ULCCs) that ply their trade between east and west today. They were useful for transporting bulky cargos like cotton from Cyprus and the Levant and, although they were slow in the water, they were much less vulnerable to attack by corsairs. They were manned by hundreds of sailors and marines, and they towered over the galleys, flyboats and bertons favoured by most Mediterranean pirates.

It was one of these massive Venetian merchantmen that John

Ward encountered as the *Rubi* and the *Gift* cruised off the Turkish coast in April 1607. The *Reniera e Soderina*, 'a great argosy of fourteen or fifteen hundred tons', was on her way back from Aleppo with a mixed cargo of cotton, silks, indigo, salt and other merchandise 'esteemed to be worth *two millions* at the least'.[44]

Too heavy to manoeuvre in the light winds, the *Soderina* was a sitting target, and Ward's much smaller vessels, which *were* able to make use of the wind, opened fire as soon as their guns were within range. For three hours they blasted away at the Venetian, smashing holes through her hull in five places and starting fires among the cotton bales which the ship's company had dragged up from the hold to use as cover. Eventually Ward ordered his men to prepare to board her.

As the pirates approached, the *Soderina*'s captain mustered his crew and passengers on deck and asked them whether or not he should surrender; finding that they still had stomach for a fight, he handed out small arms and deployed the defenders on the quarterdeck (the area of deck aft of the mainmast) and the poop, the raised deck at the stern of the vessel. The *Soderina*'s gunners got off another two or three shots at the corsairs as they closed; everyone else held steady and waited for the iron grapnels to come flying into the rigging and over the gunwales, the inevitable prelude to being boarded.

Not yet. Not quite yet. When they were within a hundred yards of the *Soderina*, the *Rubi* and the *Gift* each fired six rounds of chain shot. Some of it tore into the rigging and sails, some smashed into the gunwales and the bales, sending up clouds of shredded cotton and splinters. And one round scored a direct hit on a group of defenders. It blew two of them into pieces. Terrified, the rest dropped their weapons and ran, locking themselves in the fore-castle or below decks. When the unfortunate captain ordered his crew back to their stations, the ship's carpenter and a couple of others confronted him with weapons in their hands and told him he was no longer in command.

In the midst of all this panic, first the grapnels and then the pirates made their fearsome appearance on deck, with Ward in the thick of the fight. 'He did in the deadly conflict so undauntedly bear himself', said one of his men later, 'as if he had courage to out-brave death, and spirit to out-face danger, bastinadoing the

Turks out of his ship into theirs, and pricking others on even with the point of his poignard'.[45] Another henchmen, William Graves, was even more eloquent. The battle 'was long, and it was cruel, it was forcible, and therefore fearful', he said. 'But in the end our Captain had the sunshine, he boarded her, subdued her, chained her men like slaves, and seized on her goods, as his lawful prize, whom the whistling calm made music unto, ushering her and our general into Tunis.'[46]

3

Hellfire Is Prepared: Turning Turk on the Barbary Coast

The capture of the *Soderina*, magnificent though it was, almost proved to be Ward's undoing. After a triumphal entry into Tunis, he spent the summer and autumn of 1607 refitting her and arming her as an awe-inspiring man-of-war. 'So inflated with pride, and puffed up with vain glory, that he now thought, nay did not spare to speak, he was sole and only commander of the seas',[1] he sailed out again that December at the head of a small fleet of pirate ships on an expedition financed in part by himself and his commanders, in part by 'Uthmân Dey and other wealthy Algerians. The *Soderina* now carried sixty bronze cannon, a vast quantity of ammunition and a fighting force that consisted of 350 of 'Uthmân Dey's janissaries. The crew, a mixture of English, French and Flemish renegades, was captained by an Englishman, Abraham Crosten or Grafton, and Ward himself sailed as admiral of the fleet.

The news that Ward was out on the cruise again with such a strong force caused panic in Christendom. James I offered to send three or four naval vessels to help the Venetian Republic track him down. The Doge and Senate forbade any of their merchants from sailing east of Corfu unaccompanied, and ordered three great war galleys down to escort ships in convoy to and from Alexandria and Aleppo.

Then, in March 1608, reports started to circulate that a ship bound for Marseilles had sighted wreckage 100 miles off the Greek island of Kythira, which was a favourite haunt of corsairs because of its strategic position between the Aegean and Ionian seas. Four men and a boy, all Turks, had been found clinging to a makeshift raft, and they claimed they were the only survivors of the wreck of the *Soderina*. The vessel had got into difficulties during a storm and Ward had taken to one of the boats. He was presumed to have drowned. 'Would to God the news were true!' exclaimed Sir Henry Wotton.[2]

It wasn't. At least, the part about Ward's death wasn't. The *Soderina* had indeed gone down off Kythira, 'being much disabled with cutting so many holes out of her sides for the planting of ordinance', according to Andrew Barker.[3] Ward's attempt to convert her into a fully-armed man-of-war had fatally weakened her hull and left her unable to withstand one of the sudden powerful storms that plague the eastern Mediterranean. Her entire crew went down with her, as did all the janissaries except for the five who were picked up clinging to the wreckage.

But John Ward hadn't been aboard the *Soderina* when she sank. When intelligence came from Tunis that he was still alive, it suited the Venetians to announce that he had deserted his men. Henry Pepwell, the informant who had provided the English ambassador with such a vivid picture of the balding, drunken prodigal in Venice that summer, reported that the arch-pirate had transferred to a 22-gun French prize because the *Soderina* was leaky and rotten. Another story was that Ward hadn't been sailing on the *Soderina* at all, but had gone aboard temporarily to put down a quarrel between the English and the Turks – it was sheer good fortune that he was already back aboard his own vessel when the storm hit.

Whatever the truth of the matter, Ward faced a bitterly hostile reception when he sailed into Tunis without the *Soderina*, and without her crew. The friends of the lost men wanted to know how it was that the English admiral had survived when their loved ones hadn't. For a time he didn't dare walk the streets for fear of 'the outcries and cursings blown in his ears, of wives, fathers, and kindred, for the loss of so many of their friends at one blow'; and it was only the continued support of 'U<u>th</u>mân Dey that enabled him to recruit a new crew. Even then, no Turk would sail with him for some time to come.

Yet for all his woes, the taking of the *Soderina* transformed Ward from just another Barbary Coast renegade into an arch-pirate. *The* arch-pirate, in fact. Its cargo had made him so much money that he tried to buy himself a pardon from James I so that he could return to England. In mentioning the subject to the Doge of Venice, Sir Henry Wotton described him as 'beyond a doubt the greatest scoundrel that ever sailed from England'.[4] For their part, the Venetians were so outraged at the damage done to their reputation by the *Soderina*'s capture that *their* ambassador told the Earl of Salisbury that 'the Republic will never consent to Ward's pardon'.[5] Their outrage was increased by the swift arrival in Bristol of no fewer than three English vessels carrying goods bearing the *Soderina*'s stamp. When challenged, the merchants admitted that their cargo was bought in Tunis. They said that Turks sold it to them, not Ward. And they claimed that although that cargo might well include stolen goods, the goods weren't stolen from the Venetians. The case was still going through the English courts three years later.

Now every corsair who ever cruised the Barbary Coast was described as a follower of Ward the arch-pirate. Henry Pepwell, who had returned to England, wrote to Sir Henry Wotton at Venice to say 'that on the strength of his knowledge of Ward and even of a certain friendship for him, he was prepared to kill him and burn his ships'.[6] All he needed was a ship of his own to get him to Tunis, and he hoped that might be provided by the Venetians. Wotton duly broached the subject during an audience at the Ducal Palace, but received a frosty response from the Doge, who thanked him for the idea, but said 'he believed Ward was not at Tunis but outside the Straits'.[7]

The mere fact that an English ambassador could discuss a pirate's assassination with a Venetian head of state, and that the head of state was already well briefed on that pirate's current whereabouts, says a lot for Ward's reputation. One of James I's proclamations against pirates singled out Ward by name, commanding English naval officers, justices, vice admirals, mayors and bailiffs to do everything in their power to apprehend 'Captain John Ward and his adherents, and other English pirates'. The same proclamation threatened death to any of the King's subjects who supplied 'this pirate Ward and others' with munitions.[8]

Despite his growing reputation, Ward suffered his share of setbacks. The Venetians built a huge warship, the 1500-ton, 80-gun *San Marco*, which they sent against him with twenty or thirty galleys 'to beat him out of the Gulf [of Venice]'.[9] Andrew Barker was told that this fleet came on Ward's flyboat and forced her ashore, sending the crew running for their lives. The arch-pirate himself doesn't seem to have been aboard at the time, which was as well for him – Venetian marines killed several of the pirates and captured thirty-two more, whom 'they hung up for carrion in the island of Corfu'.[10] Ward's lieutenant William Graves was captured by a French vessel and hanged at Marseilles; his crew, 'which were about an hundred infidels, are all made slaves'.[11] And in the summer of 1609 a French force entered the harbour at La Goulette and burned twenty-three privateers, all said to belong to Ward.

None of this made any difference to Ward's reputation. Although he rarely went to sea now, Europe still regarded him as a sinister puppet master, directing a vast pirate fleet from his stronghold in Tunis. 'Uthmân Dey gave him a ruined castle in the city, and on the site he built a mansion, 'a very stately house, far more fit for a prince, than a pirate', according to one account.[12] Stories of his extravagant and amoral lifestyle spread, growing more outrageous with every telling. It was said that whenever he went to sea, his cabin was watched by his personal guard of twelve janissaries. On land he held court like a nobleman, 'his apparel both curious and costly, his diet sumptuous'. He had two cooks to dress his meat, a man to taste it for him, and an entourage of renegades who had to be bribed before any petitioner was admitted to his presence. 'Swearing, drinking, dicing, and the utmost enormities that are attended on by consuming riot, are the least of their vices.'[13] It was even said that Jews queued up to offer him their sons to satisfy his unnatural lust.

As stories of Ward's exotic lifestyle spread, he found his own peculiar niche in popular culture. The prolific bookseller Nathaniel Butter, publisher of the first quarto edition of *King Lear*, commissioned a hack writer named Anthony Nixon to produce *Newes from Sea, Of Two Notorious Pirates, Ward the Englishman and Danseker the Dutchman, With a true relation of all or the most piracies by them committed*

unto the 6th of April 1609. (Ward's name was often coupled with that
of Simon Danseker, another Barbary Coast pirate with a reputation.) The pamphlet sold well – rather better than *Lear*, in fact –
and it was quickly reprinted with a slightly different title, *Ward and
Danseker, Two Notorious Pirates.* 'The Seaman's Song of Captain Ward',
which draws heavily on Nixon's account, was registered at Stationers'
Hall on 3 July 1609; and at the end of October Andrew Barker's
True and Certaine Report appeared, claiming to set the record straight
since 'so many flying fables, and rumoring tales have been spread,
of the fame, or rather indeed infamy, over the whole face of Christendom, of this notorious and arch pirate Ward'.[14]

All these works hover ambiguously between condemnation of
Ward's crimes, a grudging admiration of his courage and a ghoulish
relish at his more exotic atrocities. But in December 1610 a new
rumour reached the Venetian ambassador in England, a rumour
so awful that it eclipsed all his other misdeeds.

Ward had become a Moslem.

Whenever a Christian converted to Islam before the Sultan in
Istanbul, the imperial scribe who recorded the fact sprinkled
gold dust over the black ink in celebration.[15] After reciting the
shahada, 'There is no other God than God, and Mohammad is his
messenger', the new Moslem was presented with a ceremonial
purse of coins, a length of white muslin with which to make a
turban, and a cloak that, in the case of the more distinguished
converts, might be lined with sable and brocaded in silver and
gold. (Female converts were given slippers instead of turbans.)
Men were then whisked away to a convenient corner by the
waiting imperial surgeon, who circumcised them on the spot. It
was common, particularly among Europeans, to confirm and celebrate conversion to Islam by adopting a new Islamic name.

The moment when John Ward was honoured by the glory of
Islam in the Tunisian *qasba* might have been less formal than the
ceremonies at the Ottoman court, but even shorn of gold dust,
sable and silver brocade, the basic elements remained the same:
the devastatingly simple profession of faith; the symbolic reclothing
of the convert to signify his new identity and a new life in the

community of Islam; the ritual mutilation. Ward took the name Yûsuf, the Arabic form of Joseph – and also the name of 'U<u>th</u>mân's son-in-law and heir, who succeeded as *dey* of Tunis around the time of the pirate's conversion.

News that the arch-pirate had apostatised reached England towards the end of 1610. In his regular newsletter to the Doge, the Venetian ambassador, Marc' Antonio Correr, wrote on 23 December that 'there is confirmation of the news that the pirate Ward and Sir Francis Verney, also an Englishman of the noblest blood, have become Turks, to the great indignation of the whole nation'.[16]

Istanbul, the heart of a vast Islamic empire

This was the ultimate betrayal, as far as the English were concerned – worse, even, than robbery or murder. Turning to crime was bad, but for Ward to compound his crimes by voluntarily handing over his immortal soul to the enemy was horrible. We can get a hint of the righteous fury that his conversion provoked in the opening lines of 'To a Reprobate Pirate that hath renounced Christ and is turn'd Turk', a 1612 poem by the satirist Samuel Rowlands:

Thou wicked lump of only sin, and shame,
(Renouncing Christian faith and Christian name),
A villain, worse than he that Christ betray'd . . .

At least Judas eventually acknowledged Christ, says Rowlands, before going on to condemn his reprobate pirate as a 'cursed thief' and a 'devouring monster' who was 'worse than devils'. The poem ends with a prediction:

Receive this warning from thy native land;
God's fearful judgements (villain) are at hand.
Devils attend, hellfire is prepared:
Perpetual flames is reprobate's re-ward [*sic*].[17]

Ward earned himself another damnation in Thomas Dekker's comedy about Hell, *If it be not good, the Divel is in it*, which also appeared in 1612. 'Where's Ward?' asks Pluto, god of the underworld, to be told the pirate is still alive and doing his bidding by flaying merchants; when he's done he will bring down with him 'fat booties of rich thieves'.[18]

The year 1612 was a good one for consigning Ward to Hell. His most spectacular appearance in Jacobean literature was the work of a rather minor playwright who wrote for the Whitefriars Playhouse off Fleet Street. As its title suggests, Robert Daborn's *A Christian Turn'd Turk* took as its centrepiece Ward's conversion, to which he was driven – according to Daborn at least – by his lust for 'Uthmân's beautiful but duplicitous sister Voada. Too dreadful to depict in words, the pirate's apostasy was presented to London audiences as a lurid and prop-laden mime:

Enter two bearing half-moons, one with a Mahomet's head following. After them, the Mufti, or chief priest, two meaner priests bearing his train. The Mufti seated, a confused noise of music, with a show. Enter two Turks, one bearing a turban with a half-moon in it, the other a robe, a sword: a third with a globe in one hand, an arrow in the other. Two knights follow. After them, Ward on an ass, in his Christian habit, bare-headed. The two knights, with low reverence, ascend, whisper the Mufti in the ear, draw their swords, and pull him off the ass. He is laid on his belly, the tables (by two inferior priests) offered him, he lifts his hand up, subscribes, is brought to his seat by the Mufti, who puts on his turban and robe, girds his sword, then swears him on the Mahomet's head, ungirts his sword, offers him a cup of wine by the hands of a Christian. He spurns at him and throws away the cup, is mounted on the ass, who is richly clad, and with a shout, they exit.[19]

The next step should have been the convert's circumcision. Since Jacobean audiences were incapable of distinguishing between circumcision and castration, that left Daborn's all-for-lust plotline with something of a problem, which he solved by having Ward substitute the end of a monkey's tail for his foreskin during the ritual, which took place discreetly offstage.

An apostate pirate could hardly be allowed to live happily ever after. At the end of the final scene (a Jacobean bloodbath, which leaves a total of seven corpses strewn about the stage) Ward is betrayed by Voada. He kills her and then stabs himself before 'Uthmân can carry out a promise to torture him to death. With his dying breath he recants, curses the 'slaves of Mahomet' for their ingratitude to one 'that hath brought more treasure to your shore/Than all Arabia yields', and delivers a dire warning to his fellow pirates:

> All you that live by theft and piracies,
> That sell your lives and souls to purchase graves,
> That die to hell, and live far worse than slaves,
> Let dying Ward tell you that heaven is just,
> And that despair attends on blood and lust.[20]

Daborn's account of Ward's Faustian fall, like the pirate's repudiation of Islam, was greatly exaggerated. While *A Christian Turn'd Turk* was playing off Fleet Street, its subject was living happily in Tunis. But anger and horror in Europe at the idea that a Christian was capable of such a terrible piece of treachery was the normal response to news of an Englishman turning Turk; and when one was in control of one's world, as Daborn was, death and damnation were bound to follow.

Not in the real world, though. Direct contacts with Moslems,

A
Christian turn'd Turke:
OR,
The Tragicall Liues and Deaths of
the two Famous Pyrates,
WARD and DANSIKER.
As it hath beene publickly Acted.

WRITTEN
By ROBERT DABORN, Gentleman.

Nemo sapiens, Miser est.

LONDON,
Printed by for *william Barrenger*, and are to be sold
at the great North-doore of *Pauls*. 1612.

The title page of Robert Daborn's A Christian Turn'd Turk

as opposed to the stage Turks who fascinated and appalled, were few and far between. Apart from the occasional renegade or native-born Barbary corsair whose rotting corpse dangled in the breeze at Execution Dock, the only real-life Moslems that Londoners would have seen were the sixteen members of the Moroccan embassy that visited the city in the summer of 1600 in search of an Anglo-Moroccan alliance against Spain. Throughout its six-month stay in London, the embassy, which was led by the Sultan's secretary, 'Abd al-Wāhid 'Annūn, was regarded with suspicion and hostility. The Moors were 'very strangely attired and behavioured'.[21] They were mean, because they didn't bring rich presents for the Queen or give alms to the English poor. They were sinister because 'they killed all their own meat within their house . . . and they turned their face eastward when they killed anything'.[22] It was generally reckoned that their real purpose was to gather intelligence about the market for sugar, which was one of Morocco's main exports to England, so that their merchants could raise their prices; and when the time came for them to continue on their way to Aleppo in the Levant, which was their next destination, no ship could be found to take them, because English merchants and mariners 'think it a matter odious and scandalous to the world to be friendly or familiar with infidels'.[23] They had to go home to Morocco instead.

The vast majority of English men and women had no knowledge of Islam. There were no mosques in England. There was no English-language version of the Qur'an – nor would there be until the 1649 publication of Alexander Ross's poor English translation of a poor French translation from the Arabic, *The Alcoran of Mahomet*. The word 'Moslem' was virtually unknown, English-speakers preferring the generic 'Turk'. A different faith, different cultures, different nations, were all lumped together in a single indiscriminate Other, a non-Christian, anti-Christian empire that stretched from the Persian Gulf to the borders of the Holy Roman Empire and threatened the very fabric of Christendom. Islam was the enemy, and turning Turk was treachery.

Words betray their secrets. To seventeenth-century England, every follower of Islam was a Turk, every Turk a follower of Islam. Moors were 'barbarians', both in the sense that they were Berbers, and hence came from Barbary, and more contemptuously because they were beyond the boundaries of Christian civilisation. The word 'renegade' or 'renegado' or 'runnagate' originally meant 'apostate', one who deserts his or her religion – except that the West never referred to the rare Moslem convert to Christianity as a 'renegade'.

Sir Francis Verney, the 'Englishman of the noblest blood' whose conversion to Islam was reported along with John Ward's, aroused particular consternation in England. Sir Francis was unusual for a Jacobean pirate in that not only did he come from further up the social scale than most – his family had a long and respected pedigree as Buckinghamshire gentry – but he had absolutely no previous experience of seafaring. In 1606, when he was twenty, he got into a fearsome row with his stepmother over the rights to a small field. (He was married to her teenage daughter, so the stepmother was also his mother-in-law.) The dispute over this field went all the way to Parliament, and when Sir Francis lost the case he sold his estates in a fit of pique and, in 1608, walked out on his wife and his stepmother/mother-in-law.

According to family tradition, Sir Francis went to Morocco and joined up with a band of English mercenaries who were fighting for Mawlay Zidan, one of the claimants to the Sultanate of Morocco. The legend gains credibility from the fact that he was related to the commander of the mercenaries, Captain John Giffard, and also to his second-in-command, Philip Giffard. Both men were later killed in a desert skirmish, and the same family tradition suggests that Sir Francis then made contact with another Giffard kinsman – Richard, whose attempts to set fire to the Algerian fleet as it lay at anchor in its home port had caused so many problems for John Ward. According to this version of events, it was Richard who was responsible for launching Sir Francis Verney's career as a pirate.

Unfortunately for the accuracy of the story, Richard Giffard was stuck in a Florentine jail from 1607 to the spring or summer of 1610, which rules him out as Sir Francis's piratical mentor, since in 1609 the English embassy in Madrid reported that Sir Francis was operating as a pirate and that he had captured three or four ships from Poole in Dorset and one from Plymouth. In October the same year London was gossiping about the rumour that 'Sir Francis Verney, who is become a strong pirate on the Barbary Coast, hath seized the provision of wine coming for the King from Bordeaux';[24] and six weeks later the rumour was confirmed, and it was said that Sir Francis had also taken 'a much richer prize'.[25] King James I was so alarmed that he dispatched a man-of-war to escort an English merchant convoy en route for the Levant; and the Venetians reported that the corsairs had recently been joined by 'a certain Francis Verney, an Englishman of very noble blood' who had squandered his fortune.[26] Around the same time Sir Francis was said to be living in Tunis, as part of John Ward's entourage.

Verney's fall was as meteoric as his rise. Six months later he lost two or three ships in the space of a few days, and was reduced to living in great poverty and deeply in debt to the Turks. For his family and friends in England, the news of his conversion to Islam set the seal on a real-life Jacobean morality tale of a wild young man who made an effortless transition from gentleman to outlaw to outcast. He was dead to them.

The last account we have of both Sir Francis Verney and his captain, John Ward, comes from a Scottish traveller, William Lithgow, who arrived in Tunis in 1615 en route for Algiers, and was invited to supper by Ward. Sprawled on cushions in the cool interior of a palace that shone with marble and alabaster, he chatted to the old pirate as he sat surrounded by his entourage of English renegades, fifteen in all, 'whose lives and countenances were both alike, even as desperate as disdainful'.[27] Ward himself was mild and agreeable: during Lithgow's ten-day stay in Tunis, the old man entertained him to dinner or supper a number of times, and when he heard that the Scot wanted to travel overland to Algiers, he personally arranged for him to have a safe conduct signed by the *pasha*.

Lithgow described the man he met in the palace by the *qasba* as 'once a great pirate, and commander at seas'; and the truth was that by 1615 Ward's career was all but over. If his conversion to Islam had been a cynical attempt to curry favour with the new *dey*, Yûsuf, following the death of Ward's mentor 'Uthmân in 1610, it didn't work. Yûsuf surrounded himself with young and ambitious renegades – Genoese, Corsican, French, Venetian, Ferrarese. They held all the high state offices; they controlled the janissary corps; they commanded the harbour at La Goulette. But there was no place at Yûsuf's court for an Englishman in his sixties who belonged to yesterday.

Too tired to go out on the cruise any more and too notorious to sue for peace with James I and go home, Ward made a life for himself in Tunis, marrying a renegade woman from Palermo called Jessimina. Perhaps he used the profits from piracy to finance new ventures; perhaps, as one rumour had it, he taught gunnery and navigation to a new generation of corsairs. Most likely he lived in quiet retirement with his desperate and disdainful entourage, swapping old men's stories of death and fire on the high seas. William Lithgow, who stopped off again in Tunis on the way back from his trip along the Barbary Coast, left a final vignette of Ward. Twice while he was in Tunis this second time, says Lithgow, Captain Ward dispatched one of his servants to show him 300 or 400 chickens' eggs as they hatched after being kept in ovens. The heat from each oven, said Lithgow, was 'answerable to the natural warmness of the hen's belly; upon which moderation, within twenty days they come to natural perfection'.[28] There is something oddly moving about the idea that a brutish, violent man like Ward, who had been the death of so many, many people, was so fascinated at the end of his life by chicks in an incubator. Still settled in Tunis, he died of the plague in the summer of 1622.

There are worse fates. On his way home from Tunis William Lithgow called in at Sicily, where he found Sir Francis Verney close to death in the great hospital of St Mary of Pity at Messina. Sir Francis's career as a pirate had ended soon after he converted to Islam in Tunis. Taken at sea by Sicilians, he spent two years as a slave on their galleys before being redeemed by an English Jesuit who made him promise to return to Christianity. After another year or so as a common soldier, he fell sick and applied for admission to St Mary of Pity where, on 6 September 1615, he died.

Lithgow arranged for his burial in the grounds of the hospital, and his turban and slippers were sent home to his family in England. Whatever they thought of him, the Verneys kept the things. They're still in the family home today, treasured heirlooms in a glass case, souvenirs of a wrong but romantic ancestor.

4

The Land Hath Far Too Little Ground: Danseker the Dutchman

*E*ven more than poor Sir Francis Verney, one corsair was inextricably linked with John Ward in seventeenth-century imagination – Simon Danseker, the 'Devil Captain of Algiers'. Andrew Barker promised that his *True and Certaine Report* would tell all about the 'beginning, proceedings, over-throws, and now present estate of Captain Ward and Danseker, the two late famous pirates'. 'The Seaman's Song of Captain Ward' that appeared in the summer of 1609 had as its companion piece 'The Song of Dansekar the Dutchman'; and the full title of Robert Daborn's 1612 play is *A Christian turn'd Turk: or, The tragical lives and deaths of the two famous pyrates, Ward and Dansiker.*

Danseker plays second fiddle to John Ward in all of these works, with English publishers preferring to thrill their English readers with the villainy of an English pirate. He scarcely gets a mention in Barker's pamphlet, and even 'The Song of Dansekar' can't resist bringing in the Dutchman's rival, focusing throughout on the exploits of the two men together: 'All the world about have heard/ Of Dansekar and English Ward,/And of their proud adventures every day.'[1] But Danseker's career is the stuff of legend. He deserves a song of his own.

Simon the Dancer came from Vlissingen and served in the Spanish wars before moving to Marseilles in the early years of the seventeenth century. According to Thomas Butler, an English merchant who picked up stories about him as he travelled towards the Levant in the summer and autumn of 1608, Danseker had married the Governor of Marseilles's daughter and then quarrelled with the authorities, who presumably included his father-in-law. In 1607 he stole a ship in Marseilles harbour, used her to take another and set out to sell his prizes – in Algiers. Within a matter of months he had established himself as a piratical power to be reckoned with in the Mediterranean, capturing twenty-nine English, French and Flemish vessels.

Danseker had a short but spectacular career as a corsair. In 1608 Henry Pepwell, the spy who had offered to kill John Ward, listed 'Captain Dansker [*sic*] of Flushing' as one of Ward's commanders at Tunis. Soon afterwards the Dutchman moved his base to Algiers, where he operated under the protection of the *pasha*, Redwan, and acquired the title by which he was known on the Barbary Coast – Dali Raïs, the 'Devil Captain'.

At the end of 1608 Danseker pulled off a major coup. He and his crew of Dutch, English and Turks ambushed a Spanish grain convoy off the coast of Valencia. The corn was useful, but the prizes' real value lay in their human cargo: among the 160 passengers found aboard the main vessel, the *Bellina*, were the son of Viceroy Sandoval of Majorca and the illegitimate son of Viceroy Viliena of Sicily, one of whom (the dispatches aren't clear which) was transporting 300,000 crowns to Spain for his father. Needless to say, neither the Spaniards nor the 300,000 crowns ever reached their destination.

A month later there was an unconfirmed report that Danseker was in the eastern Mediterranean and that he had taken a Venetian merchantman six miles off the southern coast of Cyprus. By April 1609 he was threatening to blockade the Spanish fortress on Ibiza with a fleet of five ships, including the *Bellina*.

Among his victims was one particularly unlucky English merchantman. On 15 March 1609 the *Charity* put out from Ancona on the Adriatic coast of Italy with a cargo of corn, bound for Malaga and home. As she rounded the heel of Italy she met with the *Pearl* of London; and, mindful of the corsairs who hunted in those waters, the *Charity*'s master, Daniel Banister, suggested the two vessels should stick together as they headed west to the Straits.

The charity of M. *Megs* of London, taken twice

The Charity *of London, which was taken by pirates twice in the same voyage*

With a steady wind from the north-east (known by sailors as a 'Levant') the pair made tremendous progress, covering the 1300 miles or so to Cartagena on the southern coast of Spain in only fifteen days. Then things began to go wrong. On 3 April, as they struggled in choppy seas with a wind now coming from the west, the watch on the *Charity* sighted three vessels closing fast. They reached the *Pearl*, which immediately lowered her topsail in a gesture of surrender, confirming Banister's fears that the three ships meant them no good. The *Charity*'s crew gave her all the sail they could and tried to run, but after a long chase the pirates over-took them and ordered the ship to stand to in the name of their master, the Great Turk.

What shocked the men aboard the *Charity* more than anything else was the realisation that their pursuers were a mixture of Englishmen and Turks, and that all three ships were commanded by Englishmen. They later discovered that the pirates were members of John Ward's Tunisian fleet.

What followed was a perfect example of typical pirate tactics.

The corsairs began by trying outright intimidation. One of their commanders, an old man named Foxley, 'most sternly looking up, as sternly told us, that if we would not presently strike our topsail, thereby to show our yielding was immediate, they would lay us directly aboard with their ships and as readily sink us'.[2]

That approach produced no results, even though the crew of the *Charity* numbered just twenty men and faced three heavily-armed opponents – one with thirty guns, the other two with twenty-eight apiece – and a small army of about 600 Turks brandishing small arms. With a splendid rhetorical flourish, Banister bid the pirates welcome and invited them to board, telling them that 'such a hot entertainment should they find, as all the water that bare them, should hardly bring them into a cool temper again'.[3] Every man made frantic preparations to fit the ship for action and to fit his soul for heaven. Cannon were unlashed and dragged into place; rope netting was suspended above the deck, so that boarders trying to jump down into the vessel would find themselves entangled; canvas drabblers were laced to the bottoms of the sails to give extra speed when the ship was manoeuvring. And the crew waited.

But the pirates didn't want a fight. They wanted prizes. Their next step was to parade a group of English captives on deck, clanking their chains. Foxley and the other commanders had recognised Banister – the *Charity* was well known on the Barbary Coast for transporting passengers between Tunis, Algiers, Alexandria and Istanbul. Unnervingly, their prisoners called on him by name and begged him to surrender. If his crew ever wanted to see their homeland again, they shouted across at him, 'if we had parents to mourn for their sons, wives to lament for their husbands, or children to cry out for their fathers' they should not fire so much as a single shot.[4] The corsairs had sworn to show them no mercy if they put up the least sign of resistance: the lucky ones among the *Charity*'s crew would die; the rest would be taken into slavery.

This display was enough for Banister. He struck his topsail and surrendered. As night fell he and his company were taken aboard the pirate ships and placed under guard.

The pirates hadn't finished with them. It was customary for sailors on merchant ships to do some trading on their own account

– a piece of silk or woollen cloth, perhaps, or a little oil – and the crew of the *Charity* was no exception. Every single man had 'some little particular venture for ourselves, or our friends', and when the *Charity* was boarded they all pleaded with Foxley and the other English pirates not to take their personal possessions. There was no need to worry, they were told: 'it was in no way their intents, neither was it their captain Captain Ward's pleasure that any private seafaring man's venture should be in any ways hindered'.[5] But the renegades said they couldn't vouch for their shifty Turkish comrades, who would steal the shirts off their backs if they had the chance. Perhaps the captives ought to hand their things to the English pirates so they could keep them safe overnight from the greedy, dishonourable janissaries?

They did. No one ever saw their possessions again.

A fight at sea: Barbary corsairs have hanged two European captives from the yardarm

But they did see their freedom. It so happened that on a recent voyage the *Charity* had carried the *pasha* of Tunis from Istanbul, and in consideration of this Foxley and his comrades decided to let the ship go, together with her entire crew and the crew of the *Pearl*. They took the *Pearl* herself back to Tunis as a prize; and while they ignored the *Charity*'s cargo of corn, they took her powder, muskets, match, pikes, ladles, sponges, swords and daggers; her cables; most of her beef, pork, butter, cheese and oil. And 'when they saw they could take no more, they heaved up their hands and bade us be gone'.[6]

If the sailors were feeling sorry for themselves, they were soon reminded of how much worse things might have been. At dawn the next day they saw the same pirates about a mile away, engaged in a confrontation with a French vessel whose crew was rash enough to put up a fight. The men of the *Charity* watched appalled as the corsairs boarded her, hanged the master from the yardarm and forced the eighty-four survivors to plead on their knees for their lives. They were all destined for the slave market in Tunis.

But it turned out that the *Charity* wasn't as fortunate as its name might suggest. The ship steered a course for the Spanish coast. The next morning they sighted a French vessel, which unfortunately for them also turned out to be a pirate, and one, moreover, 'of whose cruelty we had heard of so many [times] before, that we accounted ourselves compassed even in the arms and grip of death'.[7] For two days she chased them, getting closer and closer with each passing hour, until there was less than a mile between them. The *Charity*'s crew had all but given up hope when they saw on the horizon five ships under sail. Not caring who or what they were, they made straight for them, shouting, kneeling on the deck, holding up their hands and generally expressing 'the lively motions of distressed men'.[8]

The convoy, which consisted of four merchantmen from the east coast of England and one Fleming, realised what was happening and steered a course towards the *Charity*; and the Frenchman veered off, unhappy at the odds. It seemed the *Charity*'s luck had changed.

It hadn't. While the crews were exchanging greetings and news, another vessel came into view. It was Danseker – terrifying, irresistible Danseker the Devil Captain, in a huge man-of-war that bristled with cannon and Turkish janissaries:

Comes he amongst the thickest of our fleet, as if he had the power to sweep us away with his breath. But when he came near to us, he caused his followers to waft us amain with their glistering swords, threatening to sink us one after the other, if at his command we did not immediately strike.[9]

This was too much. The master of the *Prosperous*, the first vessel Danseker approached, was an Englishman named Startop. He was so overawed by the spectacle of 400 Turks brandishing small arms and scimitars that he struck his sails immediately. Even when his comrades rallied round and shouted out that 'they would never forsake him, they would fight for him, rescue him, or die with him', he steadfastly refused to put up any resistance. The three remaining Englishmen scattered, leaving the *Prosperous*, the *Charity* and the *Fleming* to the mercy of Captain Danseker and his Algerian janissaries.

There is something magisterial, almost theatrical, about accounts of Danseker in action. An English seaman who was on the *Swan*, which put into port along the coast from Algiers in 1609, told of how Danseker boarded the vessel and declared 'after his Dutch pronunciation, "Aha Swan, dow binst myne!"'[10] And now, as he drew alongside the *Charity*, the first words he spoke were 'I command you to strike sail and follow me!'

Banister did as he was told. What choice did he have, with no powder, no weapons, not even a dagger among twenty men? But he did point out to Danseker that they had been robbed by Ward's men less than six days before. The Devil Captain's response was as grandiloquent as his other gestures. 'Since the men of Tunis had had us in hand, he scorned to rob a hospital, to afflict where there was misery before, or to make prey of them who had nothing left.' He would let the *Charity* go free – all the crew had to do was to fire a three-gun salute by way of tribute, 'as a thanks to him or ransom for our liberty'.[11]

Banister pointed out that 'such was the cruelty of our enemies' that he didn't even have enough powder to do that, so Danseker simply sent them on their way, although he kept the *Prosperous* – and the Flemish vessel, which was carrying £20,000 in silks and other precious materials. In fact, when the crew of the *Pearl*, still aboard the *Charity* and rather tired of being captured by pirates, begged Danseker to put them ashore, he presented them with four shillings each 'to help to carry them up into the country of Spain'.[12]

Detaining sailors only to give them money was not the usual practice among pirates of the Barbary Coast, and Danseker's Robin Hood habit of robbing merchants and respecting mariners, coupled with his refusal to convert to Islam, earned him the admiration of the *Charity*'s crew, who contrasted his behaviour with that of Ward's men:

> This is the difference between these two pirates . . . Ward makes prey of all and Danseker hath compassion of some: the one contemning [i.e. disdaining] to be charitable to any, the other holding it hateful to take any thing from them, who labour in continual danger to maintain their lives.[13]

Back in London, the merchant community was less impressed. The news of the loss of both the *Pearl* and the *Prosperous* brought a temporary halt to the Levant trade, and merchants petitioned the government for protection.

Danseker may have been the most famous Dutch renegade, but he wasn't the only one. *Zeerovers* with Barbary Coast connections attracted attention and alarm throughout the early seventeenth century. They included Simon Maartsszoon Stuijt, who commanded a fleet of corsairs off Tangier in 1611; 'Big Pete' (*Grote Piet*) who terrorised shipping in the English Channel in the early 1610s; and – a rare example of a corsair dynasty – Simon Danseker the younger, who, after his father's death, became a renowned pirate in his own right, ending his days in Morocco, where he ran a successful business dealing in stolen goods. And unlike the 'Great Danseker', numbers of Dutch pirates converted to Islam. Hassan Raïs began life as Meinart Dircxssen; Murad Flamenco came from Antwerp; and Assam Raïs was better known in his home town of Sommelsdijk as Jan Marinus.

With all the different nationalities that frequented the Barbary Coast, communication was something of a problem. Arabic, the language of Islam, was universal throughout North Africa, although in a variety of different dialects. Turkish was the official language of the Ottoman Empire, and in the three Barbary states which owed a nominal allegiance to Istanbul – Algeria, Tunis and Tripoli – it was the language in which government business was conducted. The situation was slightly different in

Morocco, which wasn't part of the Empire. There, Arabic was also used in government and diplomatic circles, although the Sa'dī sultans didn't necessarily confine themselves to Arabic – the Spanish said of 'Abd al-Malik, Arab ruler of Morocco from 1576 to 1578, that he knew Turkish, Spanish, German, Italian and French.

Corsairs and other renegades who spent any length of time in the Barbary states obviously picked up a fair smattering of Arabic. But there was an alternative. When the Puritan William Okeley was captured by Algerian pirates on his way to the West Indies in 1639, he found himself chained below decks with some English galley slaves. 'From them', he wrote, 'we learnt a smattering of the common language, which would be of some use to us when we should come to Algiers.'[14]

The common language to which he referred was the language of the Franks, a curious pidgin tongue in which Italian predominated, but which included Greek, Provençal and Turkish words with a dash of Spanish and Portuguese thrown in. (When Daniel Banister's *Charity* was first boarded by pirates, the Turks among them addressed his crew in a language he thought was Italian.) Spoken by pirates and the merchants, brokers and slave masters they dealt with, this pidgin language originated in Palestine around the time of the Crusades, perhaps at Acre, where Venetian, Pisan and Genoese communities settled close to each other around the harbour. In Egypt it was *lisàn al ifràng*, in North Africa *sabir* and, later, *petit mauresque*. By the seventeenth century it was being referred to in the West by its most common name, *lingua franca* – so common, indeed, that the phrase has since come to mean any common medium of communication between people who speak different languages.

Lingua franca was primarily a spoken language. Its purpose was to facilitate face-to-face communication between traders and sailors around the Mediterranean basin, and documentary sources are few and far between, although almost every European who set foot on the Barbary Coast, from William Lithgow to Samuel Pepys, mentions it. The Spanish poet Juan del Encina used the language in a *villancico*, a song he wrote after returning from a pilgrimage to the Holy Land in 1520. Dryden parodied it in his 1678 comedy *Limberham, or The Kind Keeper.*

Limberham: Now I understand him; this is almost English.

Mistress Tricksy: English! away, you fop: 'tis a kind of *lingua Franca*, as I have heard the merchants call it; a certain compound language, made up of all tongues, that passes through the Levant.

Limberham: This *lingua*, what you call it, is the most rarest language! I understand it as well as if it were English; you shall see me answer him: *Seignioro, stay a littlo, and consider wello, ten guinnio is monyo, a very considerablo summo.*[15]

And Molière's *Le Bourgeois Gentilhomme* (1670) contains a 'Turkish ceremony', probably written by the Florentine composer Jean-Baptiste Lully, in which the Mufti speaks in *lingua franca*:

> Se ti sabir,
> Ti respondir;
> Se non sabir,
> Tazir, tazir.
> Mi star Mufti:
> Ti qui star ti?
> Non intendir:
> Tazir, tazir.

(If you know [*lingua franca*],/You will reply;/If you do not know it,/Be silent, be silent./I am the Mufti:/Who then are you?/If you do not understand:/Be silent, be silent.)[16]

Such literary sources are stylised, concerned more with dramatic impact than accuracy. And because of its amorphous and unstable nature, because of the paucity of written sources, because by the nineteenth century it had all but been replaced in North Africa by French and in the Levant by a more correct Italian – for all these reasons *lingua franca* remains strangely elusive. (Bizarrely enough, fragments are thought to survive in Polari, the secret language used by fairground people, street entertainers and the gay community in nineteenth- and twentieth-century London.) But it is still possible to catch a hint of its real and fluid nature here and there in Tunisian and Algerian letters of marque and other official and semi-official documents. For example, the Genoese renegade Agostin Bianco, known also as Murad Raïs, is referred to as 'agostin bianco alis morato raixi genovesz'; and 'Caytto Morato Genovese Turco'; and also as Juldàg bene Abedolo [ibn Abdullah] Turco Genovese'.[17] And a whole raft of Italian, Greek and Spanish nautical terms found their way into the Turkish language via *lingua franca*. So *galión*, the Venetian word for 'galleon', was absorbed into Turkish as *kalyon*; *disbarco*, disembarcation, became *dizbarko*; and *corsar*, corsair, became *korsar*. Lithgow claimed that the Turks 'borrow from the *Persian* their words of state, from the *Arabic*, their words of Religion, from the *Grecians* their terms of war, and from the *Italian* their words and titles of navigation'.[18]

'Since it is only recently that the Moslems have conquered the Land of the Rhommaioi [Romans] and begun to sail the seas', wrote the Ottoman encyclopaedist Hadji Khalifa in the mid-seventeenth century, 'most of the terms and names given to things pertaining to ships and to the sea are some Spanish, some Italian, and some Greek; they have taken them over at their pleasure'.[19] We can only guess how much the renegade corsairs of the Barbary Coast facilitated this process; but there is no doubt that Ward and Danseker conversed with their victims and their friends in this lost pidgin tongue.

In July and August 1609 rumours reached England that Simon Danseker wanted to negotiate a pardon with Europe and retire to Italy or France. Perhaps he had amassed enough wealth to retire from piracy; perhaps he was just tired. Certainly, the Mediterranean was becoming a more dangerous place for corsairs that summer. Amsterdam, Middelburg and Vlissingen launched a combined expedition to Barbary in an attempt to stamp out the threat to their shipping (although the Venetians, always suspicious of other European powers, were privately convinced their real motive was to establish trading links with the Turks); and a fleet of more than a dozen Spanish galleons under the command of Don Luis Fasciardo passed the Straits with express orders to hunt down corsairs, at one point forcing Danseker to take refuge in Algiers harbour. Anthony Sherley, an English ex-privateer employed by the King of Spain to suppress piracy in the Mediterranean, wrote a letter to Ward and the other corsairs urging them to bear arms against the Turks instead of siding with them. Ward's response was to say he felt safer with Turks than with Christians; Danseker, in a characteristically flamboyant gesture of defiance, released a captured Spanish carvel and its crew on condition that they seek out Sherley and tell him that if he cared for a fight, the pirate would wait for him at the mouth of the Straits. 'This was the pride of his mind, this was (as he thought) a revenge for the letter, and in manner of a challenge upon the same.'[20]

But in spite of the outward show of defiance, the rumours that Danseker wanted to give up the life of a sea raider were true. In October he suddenly turned on his Algerian comrades, killing some, taking others prisoner and liberating several hundred Christian slaves. Then he headed for the Straits. As he reached the Gulf of Cadiz he came on a Spanish treasure fleet entering the Guadalquivir estuary on the way to Seville, and captured a great galleon and two ships. According to the Venetian ambassador at Madrid, 'half a million of gold in booty was taken and that, one may say, in the very harbour of Seville'.[21] Reasoning that it would be hard for the French authorities to take a high moral tone towards him when presented with gifts such as these, he sailed into Marseilles harbour, where he was met by the governor of Provence, Charles, Duke of Guise, 'with every sign of joy'.[22] No wonder, since he presented the Duke with a hefty bribe, the freed Christian slaves, and his Moslem prisoners, who were to be held hostage against the release of some of Danseker's comrades in Algiers who had been arrested in the aftermath of his escape.

The Duke of Guise secured a safe conduct through France from Henry IV for the pirate and accompanied him on a public progress to the French court at Paris, where he arrived in the middle of December 1609. Conservative estimates put his personal wealth at 500,000 crowns – he laid out 60,000 on various things as soon as he landed in Marseilles – but attempts by the Spanish and English governments to obtain compensation were waved aside by Henry IV, who told them airily that Europe ought to be grateful to France 'for clearing the sea of such a famous pirate'.[23]

And that should have been that for Danseker and the Barbary Coast. Reunited in Marseilles with his wife and young son after an absence of two years, feted as 'a famous pirate' by the French court, rich enough to live in comfort for the rest of his life, he had no need to go to sea ever again.

The French had other plans.

Those plans had their origins in an idea mooted in March 1610 by Henry IV's loyal old Protestant general, the Duc de Lesdiguières, for a seaborne assault on Genoa, using a fleet led by Danseker. Henry IV was assassinated on 14 May and the scheme came to nothing, but by the end of that month Danseker was preparing to go back to sea on behalf of the merchants of Marseilles, who were up in arms at the losses they were suffering at the hands of corsairs. Still only in his thirties, and perhaps a little bored with life ashore, the 'most notable freebooter'[24] had been persuaded out of his early retirement to lead an expedition under French colours against his old allies, the Algerians. His knowledge of the Barbary Coast was too valuable to lose, and the Marseilles merchants clubbed together and spent 24,000 crowns on equipping and victualling three men-of-war to sail for Algiers under his command. Most of the crews were Marseilles men – Danseker was allowed to keep 'only two or three of his old lot with him'[25] – and he was asked to leave his fortune behind as a deposit against his return. The French crown authorised a tax on imports and exports to help pay for the expedition, which was to cruise between Tunis and Algiers, intercepting, intimidating and if possible destroying any pirate vessels that ventured out of port. Danseker promised that if the French came up with three more ships to reinforce his own, he would 'clear out those pirates' nests within a year'.[26]

The expedition sailed on 1 October 1610, and before the end of the year reports were filtering back to Europe that Danseker was dead. According to Antonio Foscarini, the Venetian ambassador in France, the Dutchman scored a few successes against the Algerians and then, with characteristic directness, he hoisted a flag of truce and sailed right into Algiers harbour, asking for a parley. Invited to come ashore and discuss the matter of corsair attacks on Marseilles shipping, he accepted, whereupon he was 'made prisoner and has paid by his death for his excessive credulity'.[27]

The reports, which Foscarini admitted were still unconfirmed, were premature. But they were eerily prophetic. Danseker survived the Algiers expedition, returning safe home to France in late 1610, although he wasn't successful in putting an end to Algerian raids on Marseilles's Mediterranean trade.

For the next four years he lived quietly with his family. Then history repeated itself. At the end of 1614, Louis XIII asked him to come out of retirement once again for a last mission to the Barbary Coast. In recent months pirates operating out of Tunis (including renegades working for the ageing John Ward) had captured a total of twenty-two French vessels. They and their crews were being held at La Goulette at the mouth of the Lake of Tunis, and the young king – or, more probably, the irate Levant merchants of Marseilles – pleaded with Danseker to go to Tunis and negotiate with Yûsuf Dey for their release.

Danseker agreed. He eventually anchored in the Gulf of Tunis with two French ships in February 1615, and immediately sent a party of men ashore to pay his respects to the *dey* and to open negotiations. They were welcomed, and the next day Yûsuf himself came aboard Danseker's ship with twelve followers. He was perfectly amenable to the request to free the French vessels – in fact he had them brought out into the bay as the two men talked – and Danseker, who was pleasantly surprised at his reception, put on a great feast in return, 'with good cheer, great quaffing, sounding trumpets, and roaring shots', according to William Lithgow, who was in Tunis at the time and visiting John Ward.[28]

The rituals of hospitality demanded that the following day Danseker should come ashore to be entertained to dinner in his turn by Yûsuf Dey at the Borj el-Karrak. As the Dutchman crossed the drawbridge at the head of his own entourage, a pair of janissaries came out to greet him and lead him into the fortress.

There was nothing unusual in that. But when Danseker stepped inside, things went quickly and terribly wrong. The janissaries slammed the gate in the faces of his twelve followers and, leaving them to wait in confusion, marched Danseker straight to the *dey*. Far from welcoming him to dinner, Yûsuf berated him at some length for his crimes against Islam. The ex-pirate was forced to his knees and made to listen to a tirade of accusations about 'the many ships, spoils, and great riches he had taken from the Moors, and the merciless murder of their lives'.[29] Then a janissary stepped forward and cut off his head.

Danseker's corpse was thrown over the fortress wall into a ditch, a signal for every cannon on the ramparts to open fire on the two French ships at anchor in the bay. The ships cut their cables and fled, leaving their dead captain and their twelve live comrades behind. The survivors were, in fact, treated decently by the Tunisians, who obviously felt that their point had now been made. They escorted the men aboard one of the redeemed merchantmen and allowed them to set sail for Marseilles with the news of their commander's death.

The rise and fall of Simon Danseker the Devil Captain was more theatrical, more tragic, than the careers of most Barbary Coast renegades, which tended to be squalid, fragmentary, or both. His adherence to a moral code of sorts, his refusal to renounce Christendom, his return to the European fold and the manner of his death at the hands of 'Turks' gave commentators a licence to admire him. The Scottish Protestant Lithgow, who loathed Islam almost as much as he hated Catholicism, was convinced that Yûsuf Dey had arranged the taking of so many French merchant ships purposely to lure Danseker to his doom: 'There was a Turkish policy more sublime and crafty', he wrote, 'than the best European alive could have performed.'[30] And even before the Dutchman's rejection of piracy, English ballad-writers were marvelling at the majestic scope of his ambition with a frank admiration which wasn't often accorded to corsairs:

> His heart is so aspiring,
> That now his chief desiring
>   Is for to win himself a worthy name;
> The land hath far too little ground,
> The sea is of a larger bound,
>   And of a greater dignity and fame.[31]

There was precious little dignity in Danseker's brutal death. In life, though, there was a certain fame. 'Mondo cosi, cosi', as his *lingua franca*-speaking friends might have said. The world is such.

5

Your Majesty's New Creature: Pardons and Pragmatism under James I

*T*he summer of 1611 was hot and dry. James I postponed his annual progress on account of the drought, and while he was stuck in Whitehall he mustered the Privy Council to advise him on a delicate problem of ethics. Word had come from Sir Arthur Chichester in Dublin that a pirate was offering to surrender himself to the authorities in return for a royal pardon. And James, punctilious and principled, was unhappy at the prospect. His conscience, he said, would not allow him to grant impunity so easily to one who had done so much harm to shipping in the Atlantic and the Mediterranean.

It might have been easier for the King to maintain the moral high ground – or, indeed, to grant a quiet pardon – if Peter Eston had been just any pirate. But he wasn't. *Il Corsaro Inglese*, as the Venetians called him, was known all over Europe as a fearsome general-at-sea who sailed at the head of a fleet that numbered up to twenty-five ships. Like most English pirates of the period, he divided his time between Barbary and the west of Ireland, 'the former of which is beyond all rule and justice, being wholly given up to barbarism', commented an exasperated English government official, 'while the latter is inhabited either by natives who, from motives of interest or of fear, are ready to supply their necessities, or by persons of our own nation who have taken places there with the express purpose of commercing with the pirates'.[1]

Nothing is known for certain of Eston's early life: he first attracted attention in 1608, when he was seen in command of a vessel anchored off Baltimore, Co. Cork, and then at Essaouira on the Moroccan coast. Both times he was in the company of Tibault Saxbridge, an associate of John Ward. Within a couple of years Eston had acquired such a formidable reputation inside and outside the Straits that his mere presence at the mouth of the Avon was enough to send Bristol merchants begging the Lord High Admiral for help to safeguard their ships. Unlike some English pirates, who still thought of themselves as privateers, Eston felt no compunction about attacking the ships of his own nation. He released the master of one English vessel he captured, for instance, and sent him to London with a warning. Tell the merchants on the Exchange, he said, that Eston 'would be a scourge to Englishmen' and that 'he esteemed English men no other than as Turks and Jews'.[2]

But in spite of his success and his fearsome reputation, Eston had grown tired of the pirate's life. He wanted to come home, which was why in the late spring of 1611 he turned up off the coast of Cork with a squadron of ships and a request to parley.

Lord Deputy Chichester's response was to offer Eston a forty-day promise of protection while he consulted Whitehall. The pirates must report to the vice president or deputy vice admiral of Munster if they wanted to come ashore, and could only buy enough fresh supplies to last them a day or two at a time. (They couldn't revictual for their next expedition, in other words.) In the meantime, King and Council wrangled over what was right and what was expedient.

The arguments in favour of pardoning a man like Eston were powerful. A pardon would take him out of circulation. It would act as an incentive to others to abandon piracy. It would reduce the numbers of pirates and make those who remained less capable of resistance. And if Eston and his men could be enlisted in the King's cause, their experience of seamanship – and piracy – could be turned to good use.

There were precedents. Gilbert Roupe had received a pardon

in 1609, although that had been in return for turning in his comrade, John Jennings. (It hadn't been an unqualified success, either. Roupe was currently out on the cruise again – with Eston, as it happened.) Richard Bishop, who had sailed with Jennings and with John Ward, had turned himself in a few months before Eston made his offer to retire. Bishop hadn't actually been pardoned, but he had been granted a protection and allowed to build himself a house and settle quietly in West Cork.

Against all this was the niggling feeling that pardoning pirates was wrong – the same moral qualms that were felt in the United Kingdom in the 1990s when the Blair administration agonised over the morality of releasing terrorists in return for peace in Northern Ireland. For James I to promise one moment that he would wield his 'royal sword of justice' against the common enemies of mankind, and to let them off scot free the next, was inconsistent with England's sense of honour, conscience and natural justice.

IACOBUS DEI GR: MAGNÆ BRITANNIÆ FRANCIÆ ET HY-
BERNIÆ etc: REX.

Magnus honor magni si (quod decet) Orbis habetur,
Major et heroïs gloria rebus inest.
Quis, REX MAGNE, tuas exæquet carmine laudes?
Quis Ti divinum munus inesse neget?

El: Kiger exc: Daniel Mÿtens Connoub. Bâ:

James I, who swore to wield his royal sword of justice against pirates, 'the common enemies of mankind'

Eventually James's advisers, always more pragmatic than their sovereign, prevailed. They agreed to pardon Eston, but there were conditions: he had to surrender the ships and goods in his possession, so that they might be restored to the poor men he had ruined. But he could come in. 'Out of consideration for the safety of the persons and goods of his subjects, which were imperilled by so formidable and so wicked a course of piracy,' recalled the Lords of the Council later, the King 'consented to forgo the strict course of justice'.[3] Messengers were dispatched to Ireland with the good news.

They soon discovered that pardoning pirates was more difficult than anyone had imagined. Eston had gone, even before the forty-day grace period was up. He wasn't a patient man, and he was used to being in control of his own destiny. So while the King and Council discussed his fate in London, he grew bored and took his squadron down to Cornwall. A few weeks later he was back in Ireland, putting in with nine men-of-war and four prize ships at the isolated harbour of Leamcon in West Cork.

Leamcon was a favourite haunt of pirates. Some of Eston's men kept families there, and there were rumours of treasure being brought ashore and buried. It was a wild place, more like a frontier town than an Irish village. Captain Henry Skipwith, the deputy vice admiral of Munster, made his way there as fast as he could and obtained an audience with Eston, acquainting him with the King's intention to grant his request for a pardon on the condition that he returned any stolen goods and ships in his possession.

The trouble was, there were rather more stolen goods and ships in Eston's possession than there had been a couple of weeks earlier. During his brief cruise he had captured a richly laden English merchant ship, the *Concorde*, killing one crew member and frightening three others so much that they leaped overboard (he claimed). Moreover, he had in the meantime received letters of protection from Cosimo II de' Medici, Grand Duke of Tuscany, who offered him sanctuary and citizenship in return for his expertise and his loot. Skipwith found him busily adapting the *Concorde* for fighting and arming her with ordnance. He didn't want the English king's pardon after all, he said. He had no intention of surrendering any goods: in fact, he was preparing to set sail for Barbary, where he would sell the *Concorde*'s cargo, spend one last season raiding around the Straits and then head for Florence and retirement. 'I told the merchants [in the *Concorde*] that if I might have any pardon, I would surrender up their ship and goods; but now in respect of the Duke of Florence's offer and the greatness of this wealth, I am otherwise resolved.'[4]

Skipwith was not pleased. He told Lord Deputy Chichester that if he'd had the men and the guns with him, it would have been more to the King's honour to have taken and killed every one of the pirates instead of offering them mercy.

But he persevered. The reformed pirate Richard Bishop was brought in to mediate and, after refusing an offer from Eston to sail away to Tuscany with his old comrades – 'I will die a poor labourer in mine own country, if I may, rather than be the richest pirate in the world'[5] – Bishop managed to persuade Eston at least to consider giving up the *Concorde*, and to wait for one of the King's agents to arrive from London with the pardon, rather than rejecting it out of hand.

The agent, Captain Roger Middleton, was dispatched from Plymouth at the beginning of August; when he reached Co. Cork on the 17th, he found he had missed his man by ten days. Eston had heard a rumour that the King's ships were preparing an assault, which they weren't; and another that a Dutch naval squadron was cruising off the coast of Munster with the intention of flushing pirates out of little harbours like Leamcon – which it was. Unsure about whether Eston and his men would accept their pardons, and still uncomfortable at having offered them, James had duplicitously salved his conscience by giving Dutch men-of-war permission to pursue pirates into the harbours and creeks of Ireland. Eston's men, 500 of them, had taken fright and taken flight. They bought victuals, powder and shot, split into three squadrons of three ships each and set sail on 7 August. With the first fair wind Middleton intended to follow them to Barbary, pardons in hand.

He didn't find them. Instead of retiring to Tuscany, 'that famous Arch-Pirate Peter Eston' went to Newfoundland, where his fleet, which now consisted of ten 'well-furnished and very rich' warships,[6] found easy prey among the fishing vessels out on the Newfoundland Banks, capturing their crews and taking their catches and supplies. He seems by now to have got into the habit of asking for pardons: although he announced to the world that 'he would not bow to the orders of one king when he himself was, in a way, a king as well','[7] at the same time he begged a captured English sea captain, Sir Richard Whitbourne, to go to England and find some friends of his, 'and solicit them to become humble petitioners to [King James] for his pardon'.[8] By the time Whitbourne reached London he was told that a pardon had already been dispatched to Newfoundland, where again it failed to reach its intended recipient, who was now either in Morocco or off the coast of Munster or heading for the East Indies to lie in wait for a Spanish treasure fleet, depending on which of the increasingly wild rumours one believed.

By this stage, the English government had decided to extend a general pardon to all subjects of James I who had taken to piracy, around 3000 men in all. The idea was supported by the King's eldest son, Prince Henry, who wanted to see 'the mariners of this kingdom augmented by those who are now buccaneering';[9] but it was also a tacit admission that Eston and his fellow pirates were so powerful that James I's ramshackle navy simply wasn't capable of overcoming them by force. The Privy Council secured the agreement of merchants, clearing the way for an amnesty that allowed pirates to hold on to goods they had stolen prior to entering into negotiations for pardon; and in February 1612 the general pardon was announced. 'What effect it will have is the subject of various opinions', reported the Venetian ambassador, diplomatically.[10]

It was the news of this general pardon that missed Eston in Newfoundland. King James issued another pardon in Eston's name in November 1612, still insisting rather fretfully that the *Concorde* be restored to its rightful owners. But by the time the reluctant penitent read it (if he ever did), he had moved on to sunnier climes. At the beginning of 1613, in an attempt to compete with the Grand Duke of Tuscany's free port of Livorno on the north-west coast of Italy, the Duke of Savoy declared Nice and Villefranche, both then part of the Duchy of Savoy, to be free ports also. Bonded warehouses were opened where goods could be stored and sold, no questions asked; and 'all mariners and merchants belonging to any nation, none excepted, shall have safe conduct'.[11] Weeks later Eston sailed into Villefranche with four ships, 900 men and, according to the rumours, a colossal fortune of 400,000 crowns and goods 'to an amount that seems incredible'.[12] Then aged about forty, he bought himself a palace and a title and married a wealthy woman from Nice.

And as far as I know, he lived happily ever after.

Eston wasn't the only pirate to reject James I's advances. Within weeks of the general pardon being announced in 1612, an English naval officer caught up with a fleet of thirty pirates who were terrorising the Straits and told them the good news. But they turned down his offer of a pardon out of hand, replying that 'in the present state of peace they could not maintain themselves in England'.[13] There was little legitimate employment at home for sailors, and what there was was so poorly paid that they preferred life on the cruise with all its dangers and uncertainties but greater prospects for profit.

As the years passed, however, James's pragmatic approach proved effective. As times changed and it became more difficult to make a living as a pirate, one captain after another came in and claimed amnesty. Various reasons have been proposed to explain this change of heart: Spanish attacks against traditional pirate bases on the coast of Morocco; the outbreak in 1618 of the Thirty Years War, which provided rich pickings for mercenaries; the development of new trade routes to English possessions in the Americas. Taken by themselves, none of these reasons is particularly compelling, but perhaps they each contributed something to the indisputable fact that by the end of James I's reign in 1625, the threat posed by the English pirates who drifted between Barbary, Ireland and the Newfoundland Banks was, if not exactly eradicated, at least eclipsed by the highly organised state-sanctioned Islamic corsairs of North Africa.

The giving and receiving of pardons took place in a dark and treacherous world, as the case of John Nutt demonstrates. Nutt was a bad man and a good representative of the less romantic side of seventeenth-century piracy. In the early 1620s he haunted the seas off the south-west coast of England in a small but heavily armed vessel of 120 tons, preying on the merchant ships that sailed between the western ports and Ireland and selling the goods he stole in Holland.

'A merciless villain [with] a crew of wicked villains', Nutt kept a wife and three children at Topsham, near Exeter, and in May of

1623 he decided the time had come for him to settle down with his family.[14] After a terrifying spree off the Irish coast, in which he and his crew kidnapped a man out of Youghal harbour, ransacked four ships, took rings, jewellery and ready money from sixty or seventy passengers and raped fourteen women – one of whom, a saddler's wife from Cork, he kept locked in his cabin for several weeks – he dispatched a man to England to enquire about a pardon. He had already obtained one from the Dutch; but he had heard that the English government had issued another in his name. What he did not know was that it was time-limited – it had, in fact, already lapsed.

A fortnight later Nutt sailed into Dartmouth harbour looking for news of his pardon. The young, eager, newly appointed vice admiral for Devon, Sir John Eliot, was determined not to lose such a prize. After negotiating with the pirate for days on end, and waiting for detailed guidance from London, he went aboard Nutt's ship at some personal risk, where he waved the expired pardon under the pirate's nose and induced him and his crew to come ashore. Then he had them all arrested. Nutt was sent to London for trial and his men were packed off to Exeter jail.

A victory for truth and justice? Not even close. Before the summer was out Nutt was free and complaining of his ill treatment to anyone who would listen, while Eliot was in the Marshalsea Prison awaiting trial at the Admiralty Court.

The explanation of how this happened depends on whose lies one believes. Nutt claimed that he offered £500 for a pardon that would allow him to keep his stolen goods; and that when he came in and told Eliot he didn't have it, the vice admiral told him to go and find it in money or goods, whereupon he took an English merchant ship with a cargo of sugar worth £4000. The master of that ship claimed that Eliot had come aboard and taken away fourteen chests of sugar while Nutt looked on.

Eliot admitted taking £500 for the pardon, saying it was for the Lord Admiral's use. He also admitted that his deputies had accepted on his behalf six packs of calfskins and four pieces of baize – clearly stolen goods – which were also laid aside for the Lord Admiral's use. He flatly denied encouraging Nutt to commit any further acts of piracy and taking the sugar from the merchant ship, and said he had urged the pirate to restore the vessel to her master, at which 'the said Nutt presently fell into a passion and vowed not to accept the pardon but upon condition to enjoy what he had'.[15]

Eliot made two mistakes in his dealings with Nutt. He spent several hours alone with the pirate in his cabin with no witnesses present, which was stupid, because it raised the suspicion that some underhand dealings were taking place. And he didn't realise until it was too late that Nutt had a powerful patron at court. A year or so earlier the pirate had helped to defend the young English colony in Newfoundland against an attack by the French. The chief promoter of the colony was Sir George Calvert, James I's Secretary of State, and it was Calvert who had procured Nutt a pardon in the first place, and Calvert who now secured Nutt's release from prison. 'The poor man is able to do the king service if he were employed', he told Sir Edward Conway, his fellow Secretary of State; 'and I do assure myself he doth so detest his former course of life as he will never enter into it again. I have been at charge already of one pardon, and am contented to be at as much more for this, if his majesty will be graciously pleased to grant it.'[16]

Without even knowing it, Eliot had managed to irritate Sir George Calvert, 'who may suppose himself therein crossed by me', as he plaintively wrote to Conway. To teach him a lesson, Calvert ensured Eliot was kept in prison over the summer, leaving the indignant vice admiral to rant against the unfairness of a system in which 'the words of a malicious assassin now standing for his life, shall have reputation equal to the credit of a gentleman'.[17] Nutt was released immediately, and went home to a quiet retirement in Devon.

The most distinguished product of James I's amnesty for English pirates was Sir Henry Mainwaring, whose route to redemption was accompanied by a seemingly effortless transition from outlaw to senior naval officer. After giving up a life of piracy himself, Mainwaring went on to become an MP and a master of Trinity House, the guild that looked after the interests of seamen and shipping of England. He became vice admiral of the royal fleet that guarded the Narrow Seas in the late 1630s, and as a staunch Royalist in the English Civil War he was one of the captains entrusted with taking the teenage Prince of Wales to safety as the King's cause unravelled in the autumn of 1645. When Mainwaring joined Charles I's court at Oxford in 1643, the University made him a doctor of physic – an honour not usually granted to ex-pirates, but a credit to Mainwaring's support of the Royalist cause.

But Mainwaring's background was not the usual one. Born into a gentry family in Shropshire in about 1587, he graduated from Brasenose College, Oxford, at the age of sixteen and entered the Inner Temple in London to study law two years later. Around the same time he became a student of the writing master John Davies of Hereford, 'the greatest master of the pen that England in her age beheld'.[18] In 1612, when Mainwaring was preparing to escort the Persian ambassador on his return journey to the shah's court, Davies addressed him in a farewell ode as 'heroic pupil, and most honoured friend'.[19]

This embassy was the unwitting cause of Mainwaring's decision to turn to piracy. The Persian ambassador was actually a flamboyant Englishman, Robert Shirley, who had converted to Catholicism (and married the daughter of a Circassian chieftain) during an eight-year stay at the shah's court. Shirley, who had been created a count twice – once by the Pope and once by the Holy Roman Emperor – habitually wore Persian dress with a large gold crucifix attached to his turban. He was sent to Europe by Shah 'Abbas I to enlist support for Persia's struggle against the Ottoman Empire; but while he was negotiating a military alliance with James I, a declaration of peace between the Persians and the Turks made his mission pointless and he decided to return to Persia.

Four English merchant ships were to accompany Shirley through the Straits and the entire length of the Mediterranean, and Henry Mainwaring, who paid over £700 for the 160-ton *Resistance* that summer in England, was meant to sail with this fleet, perhaps even as its commander. But Spain and Venice were both convinced that as soon as the English ships reached the eastern Mediterranean they would turn to piracy, and in 1613 pressure from the Spanish ambassador caused the English to abandon the plan and send Shirley back to Persia in a single vessel. Mainwaring was so angry at being deprived of the mission that he took off for Barbary in the *Resistance* and proceeded to work out his frustration on Spanish shipping.

Looking back in later years at his career as a pirate, Mainwaring portrayed himself as the scourge of the Mediterranean. He treated his listeners to incredible stories of his escapades on the Barbary Coast: how the Emperor of Morocco called him 'brother' and gave him a castle to protect his fleet of twenty-four galleys; how he amassed a vast fortune in gold and silver and used it to ransom English slaves in Tunis and Salé, and compelled all the pirates in Ma'amura – his base on the Atlantic coast of Morocco – to swear they wouldn't attack any subjects of James I. How he was so feared by European nations that he received offers of pardon from Spain, Savoy and Tuscany, while Yûsuf, the *dey* of Tunis, swore 'that if I would stay with him he would divide his estate equally with me, and never urge me to turn Turk'.[20] How, with all his ammunition gone, he fought off an attack by a superior force by loading his guns with pieces of eight.

There may be traces of truth in some of this, although there is little corroborative evidence for most of it. But Mainwaring was a famous pirate – famous enough for the naval officer Sir William Monson to impersonate him during an operation in the west of Ireland to root out sympathisers and suppliers of pirates. His base in 1613, Ma'amura, lay at the mouth of the Sebou river about 150 miles south of the Straits, and had enjoyed something of a vogue as a popular pirate stronghold in the early 1600s, a 'place of rendezvous' for a reported forty ships and 2000 men.[21] But a Spanish force under Don Pedro di Toledo had managed to close off the harbour in 1611 by sinking eight ships in the entrance; and although the Moors soon cleared away the wrecks, crews were starting to drift away to the safer havens of Algiers and Livorno.

Not Mainwaring. For more than a year he used Ma'amura as a base from which to raid Spanish, Portuguese, French and Dutch shipping. Unlike some of his contemporaries, he was particularly careful not to take vessels or goods belonging to his own countrymen, later telling King James that 'I have abstained from doing hurt to any of your Majesty's subjects, where by it I might have enriched myself more than £100,000'.[22] Then in the late spring of 1614 he headed north, intending to prey on the fishing fleets off the Newfoundland Banks. It was a timely decision: in August an armada of ninety-nine ships and several thousand men under the command of Don Luis Fajardo de Cordoba stormed Ma'amura's defences and occupied the town, declaring it to be Spanish territory.

Mainwaring arrived in Newfoundland 'with divers other captains' on 4 June 1614. His fleet of six ships was quickly augmented by two prizes, 'one whereof they took at the bank, another upon the main', according to a list of piratical depredations drawn up by the Newfoundland Company.[23] He spent three and a half months cruising off Carbonear on the south-east coast of Newfoundland, helping himself to victuals and munitions he found on French and Portuguese ships. He helped himself to men, too, by all accounts: when he left for warmer waters on 14 September he took with him about 400 sailors and ships' carpenters, 'many volunteers, many compelled'.[24]

The borderline between volunteers and 'perforced-men' was often blurred, and the records of the Admiralty Court are full of stories of men who claimed to have been abducted by pirates against their will, or captured at sea and forced to serve aboard pirate ships. A Richard Hayman swore he had only gone aboard Tibault Saxbridge's ship as it rode at anchor in Cawsand Bay in Devon to see a friend, 'but despite his entreaties Saxbridge would not then set him on land again'. Simon Ashdon's ship had sprung a leak; he had joined Richard Bishop's company in Tunis because it was the only way he could get back to England. John Baker explained to the court that he had had a dangerous fall from a cliff at Baltimore, and 'was forced to go aboard Saxbridge's ship to have the help of his surgeon'; then Saxbridge set sail, taking him to sea against his will. Mainwaring later explained to King James how such things worked:

> Having fetched up and commanded a ship, some of the merchants-men would come to me, or to some of my captains and officers, to tell me they were desirous to serve me, but they durst not seem willing, lest they should lose their wages, which they had contracted for with their merchants; as also that if by any occasion they should come home to their country, or be taken by any other princes, it would be a benefit to them, and no hurt to me, to have them esteemed perforced-men. In which

respect I being desirous to have men serve me willingly and cheerfully, would give them a note under my hand to that purpose, and send men aboard to seem to take them away perforce ... The inconvenience and mischief whereof is this: that such men knowing themselves to be privileged are more violent, head-strong, and mutinous, than any of the old crew, either to commit any outrage upon their own countrymen, or exercise cruelty upon other, as also the most unwilling men to be reduced home, till they have struck up a hand [i.e. obtained their share of the prizes], and then they apprehend the first occasion they can to get ashore in any your Majesty's dominions, where concealing their wealth they offer themselves to the next officers or justices, complaining of the injury they have received in being so long detained by force, and so they are commonly not molested but relieved.[25]

Unable to return to Ma'amura because of Don Luis Fajardo de Cordoba's occupation of the city, Mainwaring, like Peter Eston, moved his base of operations to Villefranche. Information about his movements over the next couple of years is sketchy. He spent five months at Tunis, recalling later that Yûsuf Dey was 'a very just man of his word', whose firm but fair rule had produced a notably stable and safe society.[26] And he was said to have engaged with a squadron of four Spanish men-of-war off the coast of Portugal on midsummer day 1615, and to have got the better of them; soon afterwards, by his own account, Spain offered him a pension of 20,000 ducats a year if he would serve in their navy.

By then, however, he seems to have resolved to take the King's pardon, and he arrived off the Donegal coast at the beginning of November to begin negotiations. They were uneventful but protracted, and it wasn't until 9 June 1616 that 'Captain Mainwaring, the sea captain, was pardoned under the great seal of England'.[27]

Mainwaring's importance for the history of piracy has less to do with his exploits, real or imagined, than with his writings. His *Discourse of the Beginnings, Practices, and Suppression of Pirates*, which was begun shortly after his pardon and presented to James I in 1618 'as some oblation for my offences', is an elegant forty-eight-page manuscript, strewn with learned Latin phrases and illuminated in gold. It earned a knighthood for the born-again Mainwaring, who described himself in the dedicatory preface as 'your Majesty's new creature'. Also known as the *Treatise of Piracy*, it was transcribed and circulated (at least nine copies still survive) and became a standard text for those in government trying to understand the threat posed to the economy by the pirates 'who now so much infest the seas'.[28]

The *Discourse*'s five chapters displayed an impressive combination of intelligent thought, inside knowledge and sound common sense. Mainwaring began by describing how so many of the King's subjects turned to piracy and how they managed to keep themselves supplied. Far too many shipowners neglected to mount a watch while they were in harbour, he said; and they left their sails aboard, making it easy for a dozen discontented sailors to steal a small bark. Once in possession of a vessel of their own, they could recruit more crewmen at almost any small fishing village, 'by reason that the common sort of seamen are so generally necessitous and discontented'.[29] With a strong crew they could overpower one of the coastal vessels which plied their trade off the French coast. With that they could run down and take any small lightly armed ship. 'And so by little and little [they] reinforce themselves, to be able to encounter with a good ship.'[30] (This was just the career path that John Ward had taken a decade earlier.) And once they had amassed a little capital in the form of stolen goods or hard cash, Ireland was a popular stopping-off point for supplies and munitions. Irish country people wouldn't openly sell to the captain of a pirate ship for fear of the consequences, but they would let him know where he might find anything he needed. He was expected to 'steal' the goods with a show of force, and then leave goods or money worth considerably more than the items' market value in a mutually agreed spot.

With a touching lack of irony, Mainwaring chided the King for his policy of offering pardons, which meant that now every English pirate was confident of being able to come in and negotiate terms as and when it suited him. And the ordinary sort of pirate didn't worry much about the consequences of being taken and brought to trial, since 'none but the captain, master, and it may be some few of the principal of the company shall be put to death'.[31] The rest might be condemned to 'a little lazy imprisonment'; but it wouldn't be any worse than conditions aboard ship. Rather than hanging entire crews, however, he proposed putting them to work as galley slaves, or dredging silted-up harbours or repairing the coastal forts which were, he pointed out disapprovingly, 'miserably ruined and decayed'.[32]

These reflections took up the first two chapters of the *Discourse*. In the third, the reformado offered a short account of how pirates typically went about catching their prey. A little before dawn, he wrote, a ship would take in all its sails so that it lay still in the water. As the sun came up, the watch could make out what else was in sight and the pirate ship would set sail to intercept its chosen victim. To anyone watching from the other vessel, she hadn't altered course to chase them; it would seem as though she was just another merchantman bound on the same course as themselves. She would allay suspicion by showing the appropriate colours: if she was a Flemish flyboat, for example, she flew a Flemish flag. 'In chase,' said Mainwaring, 'they seldom use any ordnance, but desire as soon as they can, to come a board and board [i.e. alongside], by which course he shall more dishearten the merchant and spare his own men'.[33]

Rather disappointingly, Mainwaring didn't have much more to say about tactics, apart from a couple of intriguing asides. If a pirate wanted to lull a pursuer into a false sense of security, she heaved out all the sail she could make and hung out drags to slow her down, so that the other ship would think she was running scared and make haste to overhaul her. (Sir Francis Drake used the same trick against the Spanish in the Pacific.) And when pirates sailed as a fleet, all vessels kept their tops manned constantly and used a system of 'signs' – flags? A pre-cursor of semaphore? – to communicate with each other.

Eighteen of the *Discourse*'s forty-eight pages are taken up with a remarkable piratical gazetteer. From Flores in the Azores, where pirates 'may water, wood, and ballast, and the inhabitants will not offer to molest them', to Tripoli, where they 'shall be entertained and refreshed, and ride in command [i.e. protected by a fort]; but these are dangerous people', Mainwaring gave terse but telling descriptions of harbours and havens where pirates could trade or shelter or resupply in safety. He confined himself to 'the most important and the most used', and he didn't include individual bays and coves in Ireland, since pirates could find 'all the commodities and conveniences that all other places do afford them' at virtually any coastal village or town beyond the pale. 'They have also good store of English, Scottish and Irish wenches', he added. 'And these are strong attractors'.[34]

Even so, he managed to produce a list of over forty places where pirates could expect to find sanctuary of sorts and where, therefore, the King's ships could expect to find pirates if they were minded to look. Some were remote islands out in the Atlantic, or quiet coves on the shores of Spain or Portugal, where it was possible to rest for a day or two, take in water and perform running repairs to a ship. On the Desertas Islands, south-east of Madeira, for example, pirates could 'water and perchance get some beeves [oxen]'; the tiny Lobos Island in the Canaries offered 'goats but nothing else'.[35]

But at somewhere like Santa Cruz on the Atlantic coast (modern-day Agadir in Morocco), pirates could resupply, and ride safe at anchor in the shadow of the fort, 'so that there they stay long and use much'.[36] Tetouan, just inside the Straits, was a good place to dispose of stolen goods and to buy powder and munitions, which were brought in for trade by English and Flemish merchants. 'The people are very just and trusty'[37].

Pirates based at Tunis tended to hunt off Sardinia or the southern coast of Sicily, or further east among the Greek islands. In the spring, those who operated out of Algiers or the Moroccan ports might lurk off the south-west coast of Spain, waiting just outside the Straits 'for Indies men outward bound'.[38] Others lay off Portugal on the lookout for Baltic merchantmen carrying copper, linen and victuals on their way to supply the Spanish fleet; they were also well placed to meet with the ships of the annual Spanish Brazil fleet, 'which commonly are going and coming all the year long'.[39] From May to August 'the Spanish and Flemish men of war do more diligently keep the seas than in winter weather', and to avoid their patrols pirates moved north to raid the fishing fleets on the Newfoundland Banks, before returning to patrol the Atlantic between the Azores and Portugal at a latitude of $37\frac{1}{2}°$ to $38\frac{1}{2}°$, 'at which height the Indies men come in'.[40]

Of the dozen or so havens within the Straits, Mainwaring singled out Algiers and Tunis for special mention. In both, he told the

King, pirates 'may be fitted with all manner of provisions and . . .
ride safely from the Christian forces'.[41] But he distinguished unwittingly between their brand of structured, state-sanctioned warfare
– which would have been called privateering if it had been
conducted by a Christian state – and the more haphazard, opportunistic way in which the coastal settlements of Morocco traded
with European fugitives. Pirates needed to obtain passes from the
Tunisian authorities, he said, before trading with Porto Farina,
Sousse, or any of the other harbours along that coast; and it wasn't
a good idea to call in at Rhodes or Cyprus without letters of safe
conduct from Tunis or Algiers. At Bona and Bougie (present-day
Annaba and Béjaïa respectively), they 'may be very well refreshed
with victual, water, and bread, and also sell goods well, and these
are good roads for pirates, but they dare not trade with any unless
they bring with them the letters of Algiers'.[42] He also misrepre-
sented – or perhaps misinterpreted – the symbiotic relationship
that existed at Algiers between janissaries and Christian or renegade pirates, characterising it as a kind of treachery on the part
of the perfidious Turk. At Algiers, English pirates were liable to
have their ships 'betrayed from them and manned out by the Turks,
after the proportion of 150 Turks to 20 English'.[43]

In the final section of the *Discourse* Mainwaring turned his
attention to the question of how to suppress piracy. Some of what
he had to suggest was sound common sense: instituting regular
coastal patrols in the west of Ireland; having unemployed sailors
bound over to keep the peace; training up naval officers and
commissioning armed merchantmen. But his big idea was less
happy. 'Your Highness must put on a constant immutable resolution never to grant any pardon, and for those that are or may be
taken, to put them all to death, or make slaves of them . . . for
questionless, as fear of punishment makes men doubtful to offend,
so the hope of being pardoned makes them the apter to err.'[44]

The spectacle of Mainwaring trying to pull up the ladder behind
him after making his own successful escape is not attractive. More
to the point, he was plain wrong. After a patchy start James I's
policy of pardoning pirates had yielded results, as crews followed

Mainwaring's example and came in. That didn't mean that piracy *per se* was on the decrease, though – far from it. By the end of James I's reign in 1625 the nomadic community of English pirates who had spent their lives drifting between the west of England, Ireland, Barbary and the Newfoundland Banks – the Bishops and the Estons and the Mainwarings – were being superseded by more professional sea rovers based in Algiers or Tunis, men who regularly sailed out beyond the Straits with large companies of janissaries in search of prizes, goods and slaves.

Contemporaries were convinced of the reason for this. It was because Europeans had betrayed Christendom by teaching the Turks and the Moors how to navigate the oceans in sailing ships. Captain John Smith of Pocahontas fame claimed that Ward and Danseker and Bishop and Eston 'were the first that taught the Moors to be men of war';[45] and Londoners who went to see *A Christian Turn'd Turk* gasped as Robert Daborn's stage-Ward told the stage-Turks that it was him 'that hath shown you the way to conquer Europe, [who] did first impart what your forefathers knew not, the seaman's art'.[46] The English sailor Sir William Monson even thought he knew exactly when it happened. Writing in 1617 in a report on how to combat the threat from Algerian pirates, he told the Privy Council, 'it is not above twelve years since the English taught them the art of navigation in ships'.[47]

The traditional Mediterranean galley was faster and more manoeuvrable than a sailing ship. With a clean bottom and a fresh crew, a heavy war galley, with twenty-four oars to a side and three men to each oar, could cover well over two nautical miles in twenty minutes.[48] Its speed and direction didn't depend on the prevailing wind, or lack thereof, and its shallow draught meant it could come close in to shore, allowing its crew to escape from pursuers or launch amphibious assaults as the occasion demanded.

The galley was well suited to the kind of shock tactics in which the Mediterranean corsair excelled. Ordnance was light and mounted on the bow. It might typically consist of a heavy, centrally mounted gun firing a 52-lb shot, flanked by a pair of 12-pounders and a pair of 6-pounders. Small wooden fighting platforms over the guns gave a degree of cover to the gunners, and were themselves mounted with breechloading swivel guns (that is, light guns fixed on swivels to allow them to be turned horizontally in any direction).

The slender prow was reinforced with a raised iron beak. In an attack, a pirate galley would close at alarming speed with its prey, presenting a minimal target to the victim's guns and ramming hard on impact into the planking of its hull. The prow stayed fast and acted as a boarding plank; after the janissaries had fired at point-blank range into the rigging and raked the decks with their swivel guns, they would storm the enemy vessel, which was powerless to free itself from the unrelenting iron spur.

The Mediterranean galley, a formidable fighting machine

But the features that made the galley so formidable were also the reasons for its decline as a fighting ship. A twelve-bank raiding galley – a galley with twelve oars on each side – required a rowing gang of seventy-two (twenty-four oars in total, with three men to each oar). It would also carry perhaps ten spare oarsmen. This was small compared with a typical heavy war galley, which was powered by twenty-four banks of oars and a standard rowing gang of 164 slaves (including twenty spares). The oarsmen needed food and water, not only as a matter of common humanity, but because a healthy rowing gang was an efficient rowing gang; and there was hardly any storage on a galley, around 95 per cent of the space being taken up by the oarsmen's benches. It has been calculated[49] that a voyage by a war galley with 144 oarsmen and 40 soldiers and officers would require 1800 gallons of water, limiting its cruising radius to ten days at the most before it was forced to take on more water. Even a lighter galley of the kind favoured by corsairs needed to take on water at fourteen-day intervals.

Within the Straits, an undefended beach wasn't too hard to find and it was easy to put a small foraging party ashore, even on a hostile coast. The wilder northern waters of the Atlantic were a different matter. While the clear, non-tidal waters of the Mediterranean allowed a corsair captain to moor relatively close to shore without much difficulty, the shifting tides, contrary winds and vicious currents of the seas around the coasts of northern Spain, France, England and the Low Countries required local knowledge and navigational skills beyond the reach of the Mediterranean galley captain.

The European renegades of the early 1600s may well have played their part in introducing 'the seaman's art' into Barbary, although the Moriscos of Spain who settled in North Africa after their expulsion also contributed their knowledge and experience as, no doubt, did the English and Dutch traders who made a living by supplying munitions and buying stolen goods all the way along the coast from Safi to Tunis. But while contemporaries might debate whether Ward or Danseker was responsible for empowering the Turk, no one was in doubt that the switch from galley to sailing ships had happened, or that it made the corsairs of Algiers and Tunis more formidable as a result.

Mariners' accounts of attacks reflect the change. The *Three Half Moons*, an English merchant ship captured near the Straits in the 1560s, fell victim to 'eight galleys of the Turks'.[50] In 1582 the *Mary Marten* was attacked and sunk by two galleys off Cabo de Gata on the Spanish coast. Forty years later the *George Bonaventure* and the *Nicholas* were both overtaken and boarded off Gibraltar by Algerian pirates in five sailing ships (two of which were recently captured merchantmen). From the 1620s onward it was rare indeed to find Barbary Coast pirates using galleys in the western Mediterranean or outside the Straits.

They had a cheap and unending source of ships, of course, in the prizes they took. 'You must understand', wrote Sir William Monson in 1636, 'that all the Turkish pirate ships are vessels of Christians, taken from them by violence, which when the Turks are possessed of [them] they use all art and industry to make better sailers [*sic*] than all other ships.'[51] They would convert a merchant ship by stripping away as much of the superstructure as possible, and removing many of the timber supports which strengthened the hull. 'They never regard the strength of their ships more than for one voyage', said Monson, 'for they want not continual prizes which they take of Christians and thus use.'[52] No weight was carried overhead or in the hold except for food, water and munitions, and even heavy armament was kept to a minimum. Speed was the object – speed in escaping unwelcome attention and speed in pursuit. And they were quick learners. Within a decade or so the English were forced to acknowledge that no European ship was equal to the Turks of Barbary with their modified vessels. That made the merchants and mariners of Europe very afraid indeed.

'The Turkish pirates domineer in the Mediterranean Sea', reported the English courtier George Carew in June 1617. 'Our merchants are daily taken by them, in so much as, if the Christian princes do not endeavour their extirpation, the trade into the Levant will be utterly destroyed.'[53]

Carew's sense of apprehension was shared in courts and council chambers all over Europe. In Madrid, Sir Francis Cottington complained to Philip III that Spain wasn't doing enough to control piracy in its waters, while the Spanish were thrown into panic by the exploits of two pirate fleets that were raiding along the coast all the way from Malaga to Seville. 'I have never known any thing to have wrought a greater sadness and distraction at court', Cottington reported.[54] The Dutch threatened the *pashas* of Algiers and Tunis that if they didn't curb their subjects' activities, the States General 'would try another way to free themselves from the constant losses which they suffer'.[55] James I's Secretary of State, Sir Ralph Winwood, echoed Carew's concerns over the impact of piracy on the economy, warning that Barbary pirates 'will shortly grow so insolent and presumptuous that they will adventure to possess our seas, and to assail us in our ports'.[56]

As he wrote, there were reports that a band of renegades operating out of Salé on the Atlantic coast of Morocco had been taken by poacher-turned-gamekeeper Henry Mainwaring in the Thames at Leigh-on-Sea, only thirty miles from central London. On the south coast, the citizens of Swanage demanded that their harbour be fortified, 'the Turks being grown exceedingly audacious'. In Cornwall, there were objections to setting up a light on the Lizard, the most southerly point in England, since it would act as a guide for pirates.[57]

James I hated piracy. There is a memorable description of him at Woodstock Palace in Oxfordshire back in 1603, listening to a personal complaint from the Venetian ambassador about the activities of English pirates. As the tale of woe unfolded, the king began twisting his body, striking his hands together and tapping his feet. Eventually he interrupted the ambassador, standing up and shouting, 'By God! I'll hang the pirates with my own hands!'[58]

So when members of the Levant Company, the hardest hit of the London trading companies, came to James for help against the pirates of Barbary in the spring of 1617, the knowledge that in spite of years of hanging, haranguing and pardoning pirates, in spite of cajoling every head of state on the Barbary Coast, in spite of sending stern messages to Istanbul, the self-styled *rex pacificus* had not been able to solve the problem struck hard at his sense of self-esteem. He decided it was time for direct action. Time, he declared, 'to draw our sword against the enemies of God and man. That is, the pirates.'[59]

6

Rich Caskets of Home-Spun Valour: Fighting Back Against the Pirates

*J*ust after dawn on 12 January 1617, the morning watch aboard the *Dolphin* caught sight of a sail making towards them from the Sardinian shore. She was still a mile or so away, but as she came closer the sailor could see that she was a two-masted settee, the kind of ship which was often used by the Turks to transport men and supplies. That meant there were likely to be other Turks in the area.

The watch woke the master, Captain Nichols, who sent a man up into the maintop with a prospect glass, a new and useful device for seeing faraway things as if they were nearby. Sure enough, a line of five men-of-war in full sail was coming up on them before the wind. And they were pirates.

We know this because an unnamed member of the *Dolphin* wrote a narrative of the day's events – one of a handful of extraordinary eyewitness accounts of encounters with pirates that appeared in the late 1610s and early 1620s, describing in vivid detail what it felt like to be attacked on the high seas.

The 280-ton *Dolphin* was on her way home to London and eleven days out from her last port of call, the Ionian island of Zante, an important centre of trade in honey, oil, wine and currants. She had left Zante on 1 January 1617, and in a little over a week 'a prosperous gale' had carried her westward past Sicily, until she was within sight of the watchtowers which lined the coast of Spanish-held Sardinia.[1] But contrary winds had held her there, south of Cagliari and three leagues to the east of Cape Pula on Sardinia's southern tip. These were dangerous waters, where corsairs from Tunis and Algiers cruised with impunity.

Sea battles were often fought at very close range

The five pirates were 'all well prepared for any desperate assault', wrote the anonymous author of *A Fight at Sea, Famously fought by the Dolphin of London*.[2] The leading ship was carrying thirty-five guns. The other four had between twenty-two and twenty-five apiece. All five had crews which were 200–250 strong. The *Dolphin* was outgunned and outnumbered.

But she was not defenceless. She was armed with nineteen heavy guns, nine anti-personnel 'murderers' and an assortment of muskets, pikes and swords; and her crew of thirty-six men and two boys included at least one master gunner, whose job it was in situations like this to turn ordinary seamen into soldiers. Since there was no chance of outrunning the pirates, and since they lay between the *Dolphin* and the safety of the shore, Captain Nichols immediately decided to fight. Small arms and swords were handed out and all the paraphernalia of violence was checked and distributed – the round shot and hail shot and chain shot, the powder measures and ladles and rammers and sponges, the baskets to carry the shot to each piece, the barrels to carry the powder, the wedge-shaped quoins used to adjust the elevation of each gun barrel and the fuses used to fire the cannon.

Then the crew assembled on deck and prayed together, before sitting down with remarkable sangfroid to an early dinner, which was followed by a rousing speech from Nichols.

A sea battle was a slow, complicated and chaotic business, especially for merchantmen who weren't used to fighting. In his 1626 manual on seafaring, *An accidence or The path-way to experience Necessary for all young sea-men*, Captain John Smith offered a dramatic description of an encounter with an enemy ship:

A broadside, and run ahead. Make ready to tack about. Give him your stern pieces, be yare [ready] at helm, hail him with a noise of trumpets.

We are shot through and through, and between wind and water. Try the pump. Master, let us breath and refresh a little; sling a man overboard to stop the leak.

Done, done, is all ready again? Yea, yea: bear up close with him, with all your great and small shot charge him. Board him on his weather quarter [the stern quarter on which the wind blows]; lash fast your graplins [grappling irons] and shear off, then run stemlings [ram her] the midships. Board and board, or thwart the hawse [pull alongside, or cross her bow]. We are foul [tangled] on each other.

The ship's on fire! Cut anything to get clear, and smother the fire with wet clothes.

We are clear, and the fire is out, God be thanked. The day is spent; let us consult. Surgeon, look to the wounded. Wind up the slain, with each a weight or bullet at his head and feet; give three pieces [fire a three-gun salute] for their funerals.

Swabber, make clean the ship. Purser, record their names. Watch, be vigilant to keep your berth [position] to windward, and that we lose him not in the night. Gunners, sponge your ordnances; soldiers, scour your pieces. Carpenters, about your leaks. Boatswain and the rest, repair the sails and shrouds. Cook, see you observe your directions against the morning watch.[3]

There can't have been a man aboard the *Dolphin* who didn't play out a scene like this in his head as he waited for the action to begin. By the time the meal was over it was nearly 11 a.m., and the leading pirate ships were closing. In a show of defiance Captain Nichols stood on the poop deck in plain view of his pursuers and waved his sword at them three times, 'shaking it with such dauntless courage as if he had already won the victory'.[4] His men followed suit; the ship's trumpeters blew their trumpets; and as the first of the pirates came within range, Nichols gave the order for his gunner to take aim and fire.

It was very hard to hit another ship. William Bourne, whose 1587 manual on *The Arte of shooting in great Ordnaunce* was a standard text for gunners, devoted an entire chapter to the problem. In a pitching sea, when your ship was rocking from bow to stern, it was best to place your gun on the lowest deck and as near as possible to the mainmast, the point at which she 'doth hang as though she were upon an axiltree'.[5] Similarly, if the vessel was rolling, then 'the best place of the ship for to make a shot is out of the head or stern'.[6] In either case, reckoned Bourne, 'the principallest thing is that he that is at the helm must be sure to steer steady, and be ruled by him that giveth the level [that is, adjusts the elevation of the gun], and he that giveth fire, must be nimble, and ready at a sudden'.[7]

In practice, it was usual to fire point-blank – that is, when you were so close to your adversary that your shot would travel in a straight line, and you didn't have to worry about trajectory. That meant closing to within a hundred yards or so of the target, and, since that involved your target's guns coming within point-blank range of you, it required an iron nerve, especially if you weren't particularly experienced in combat.

All of which is by way of excusing the fact that the *Dolphin*'s gunner missed.

The man in charge of the pirate fleet was a one-armed Londoner named Robert Walsingham, whose addiction to piracy had led to his being forced out of Ireland and then Morocco before settling on Algiers as his base of operations. He usually hunted with two other British pirates, Captains Kelly and Sampson, both of whom were with him now. Walsingham immediately returned fire, aiming to disable the *Dolphin* and demoralise her crew. At noon he drew alongside and his men clambered aboard, yelling and waving scimitars, hatchets and pikes. They hacked at the planking on the raised poop deck and tried to prise open the main hatch to get at the cargo below.

Fear and intimidation were the pirates' most potent weapons. But the *Dolphin's* crewmen held their nerve and bided their time. When they were sure of their targets they opened fire with one of the anti-personnel 'murderers', which their gunner had mounted in a cabin under the poop so as to be able to rake anyone who came into view on the open deck. In a hail of dice shot the boarders were forced back on to their own vessel, only to come under musket fire from more of the defenders who shot from the cover of the closed-in gallery which ran round the *Dolphin's* stern below the poop deck. At the same time the *Dolphin's* gunner directed his heavy ordnance at Walsingham's ship, now so close that it was hard to miss. The pirates returned fire; but whereas the *Dolphin* was intent on causing them major structural damage, the pirates had no wish to sink the *Dolphin*, and confined themselves to aiming rounds of chain shot at their adversary's masts and rigging. After several hours the pirate ship had sustained enough damage for Walsingham to break off the engagement, and as he pulled ahead of the *Dolphin*, she gave his vessel such a broadside that it played no further part in the battle.

The *Dolphin's* troubles weren't over yet. Captain Kelly moved up on one side, and another unnamed pirate commander came up on the other, so that they sandwiched the merchantman between them. Parties from both vessels boarded the *Dolphin*, 'entering our ship thick and threefold, with their scimitars, hatchets, half pikes and other weapons'.[8] One of the Turks climbed into the rigging and up the mainmast, determined to bring down the flag, 'which being spied by the steward of our ship, presently shot him with his musket that he fell headlong into the sea, leaving the flag behind him'.[9] Again the pirates were forced back to their own vessels; and again they drew off to mend their leaks, 'for we had grievously torn and battered them with our great ordnance'.[10]

The final assault came late in the afternoon. By now the *Dolphin* was badly damaged herself, shot through and through and leaking. Several of the crew were dead; others were hurt, including Captain Nichols, who had been shot twice in the groin while he stood at the helm trying to hold the ship steady for the guns. But there was still powder and shot, and the knowledge that by resisting they had forfeited any chance of mercy gave the survivors a desperate courage. They had no choice now but to fight.

As the last two pirate ships closed in, shot from the *Dolphin's* guns went straight through the hull of one of them, and its pirate commander aborted the attack. The other vessel came up on the starboard quarter, and yet again janissaries stormed aboard. They were blowing trumpets, running to and fro on the deck and 'crying still in the Turkish tongue, yield your selves, yield your selves', and throwing grenades filled with wildfire, an incendiary mixture of gunpowder, brimstone and oil of petrol, which 'being once set on fire can hardly be quenched'.[11] It must have been terrifying.

One ball of wildfire landed in the basin which the ship's surgeon was using to tend a wounded man, and with commendable presence of mind he hurled the basin into the sea; but others landed on the deck in the midst of some bloody hand-to-hand fighting, and almost before anyone realised what was happening the *Dolphin* was burning.

Ironically, this potentially catastrophic fire saved both the ship and the lives of its surviving crew. As the flames took hold, the pirate captain called his men back. 'Thinking that our ship would have therewith been suddenly burned to the water, they left us to our fortunes.'[12] The corsair fleet fell astern, and as night came on and the crew managed to bring the fire under control, the battered *Dolphin* limped towards the Sardinian coast and safety. She was badly damaged in four places: between decks, in the gun room, in Nichols's cabin and in the helmsman's cabin where the captain had been standing when he was shot. Of the ship's complement of thirty-eight, seven were killed in the battle and nine more injured. Four of these had died of their wounds by the time the ship put in at Cagliari for repairs. Captain Nichols was one of the survivors.

There were plenty of occasions when merchant ships outran pirates, but victory in pitched battle, especially against such over-whelming odds, was a rare event. One of the survivors 'that was then present and an eye witness to all the proceedings' published his narrative of the *Dolphin*'s encounter soon after he reached London in February 1617. He gave due thanks to God and praised 'the magnanimity and worthy resolution of this our English nation'. He might also have pointed out the advantages of providing merchant ships with heavy ordnance, a decisive factor in the *Dolphin*'s deliverance. But his real purpose was to celebrate the courage of ordinary seamen, who were often criticised at home – particularly by the merchants and shipowners who had to bear the loss – for yielding too quickly and giving up their cargo to save their own skins. The anonymous author of *A Fight at Sea* was at pains to emphasise that the *Dolphin*'s crew chose 'rather to die, than to yield, as it is still the nature and condition of all Englishmen'.[13]

Four years after the *Dolphin*'s clash with Walsingham's pirates, the affair of the *Jacob* offered England another opportunity to celebrate the bravery of English sailors.

Towards the end of October 1621 the 120-ton *Jacob* of Bristol was passing through the Straits of Gibraltar when she was attacked and captured by a squadron of Algerian corsairs. The pirates ransacked the ship, shackled most of the Englishmen below decks on their own vessel and installed a crew to sail their prize back to Algiers. Four youths – John Cooke, William Ling, David Jones and Robert Tuckey – were kept aboard the *Jacob* to help sail her back to Algiers.

For five days and nights the *Jacob* sailed east, along the coast of Morocco, past Cape Tres Forcas and the tiny Spanish-held Isle of Alboran, all the time coming closer to a future that looked distinctly bleak for the four English boys. All they had to look forward to was 'to eat the bread of affliction in the galleys all the remainder of their unfortunate lives, to have their heads shaven, to feed on coarse diet, to have hard boards for beds, and which was worst of all, never to be partakers of the heavenly word and sacraments'.[14]

The wind began to rise late on the fifth night. By the early hours of the following morning the *Jacob* was being tossed around the ocean at the mercy of one of the sudden and violent storms that afflict the Mediterranean between mid-October and mid-March. Robert Tuckey was at the helm. John Cooke, William Ling and David Jones were together on deck, wrestling with the rigging. They struck the topsails and then, realising they were going to have to strike the mainsail as well, called out for help. The pirate captain, 'a strong, able, stern and resolute fellow',[15] came to their aid; and as the four of them struggled to haul in the billowing canvas, Cooke and Jones seized their chance and toppled him over the side.

He came back. By a stroke of good fortune (for him, if not for the boys) the man fell into the belly of the sail, and he grabbed hold of a rope and began to haul himself back up to the deck.

But his good fortune was about to run out. Seeing what was happening, Cooke dashed to the mainmast, wrenched the wooden handle off the pump that stood there and threw it across to Ling, yelling at him over the roar of the wind to clout the pirate with it before he could climb over the gunwale. Ling smashed the pump handle down on the man's head and he fell back into the sea and vanished.

There were still twelve pirates to contend with. Five or six were forward, busy trimming the foresail, while the rest were gathered aft. It was pitch dark, and the noise of the wind 'whizzing and hizzing in the shrouds and cordage' had drowned out the captain's cries.[16] Cooke remembered there were weapons unsecured in the master's cabin and, pushing past some Turks in the darkness, he burst in, grabbed two cutlasses and handed one to Ling. The two youths laid into their captors, stabbing two of them to death and slashing so savagely at a third that he leapt overboard to escape them.

That left nine bewildered and surprised Turks, who were chased round the ship by these two cutlass-wielding boys all the time slashing and cutting at them, until they ran below deck and Cooke secured the hatch.

Robert Tuckey was at the helm all this time. There was no wheel. Until the beginning of the eighteenth century larger sailing ships were steered with a whipstaff, a vertical wooden rod that was attached to the tiller. Now, as Tuckey struggled to keep the *Jacob* steady, the whipstaff fell loose in his hand. In desperation the pirates below had broken the link with the tiller, and the ship 'lay tumbling and rolling unguided in the raging and boisterous billows of the sea'.[17]

The pirates must have hoped that their action would at least prompt the boys to negotiate. They reckoned without John Cooke and William Ling, whose reaction to Tuckey's announcement that he no longer had the helm was to load a pair of muskets, go below decks and threaten to shoot their erstwhile captors dead. Within minutes the Turks had reconnected the whipstaff and delivered control of the vessel back to Tuckey.

The *Jacob* survived the storm and the next day the boys set a course for Spain. By keeping the nine pirates below deck and calling up two or three at a time to undertake 'necessary and laborious employments' they eventually reached St Lucas, where they sold the pirates for galley slaves and, presumably, took on fresh crew before sailing the *Jacob* home to Bristol and fame.

On their return to England their exploits were celebrated in print; and, as with the *Dolphin*, the anonymous author took the opportunity to emphasise that the boys were from humble backgrounds:

> Had John Cooke been some colonel, captain, or commander, or Williame Ling, some navigating lord, or David Jones some gentleman of land and riches, or had Robert Tuckey been one of fortune's minions, to have had more money than wit, or more wealth than valour, oh what a triumphing had here been then.[18]

But these 'four rich caskets of home-spun valour and courage' were just ordinary people performing acts of extraordinary bravery. Their actions made Bristol famous and Britain glorious.

A year later, on 26 December 1622, the *Jacob* was again attacked by pirates near the Straits. This time she put up a fight and was sunk with the loss of all hands except two, who were rescued by the Turks and sold as slaves in Algiers. There is no record of what happened to the four boys.

In the middle of November 1621 two small English merchantmen, the *Nicholas* and the *George Bonaventure*, were in the Straits within sight of Gibraltar when they were intercepted and boarded by a squadron of three pirate ships. This was only a couple of weeks after the *Jacob* was first captured and the same pirates may have been responsible in both cases. They already had two prizes and a quantity of English prisoners, so they had been on the cruise in the Straits for some time; and their tactics were similar. They put a prize crew of thirteen into the *Nicholas* and left four English crewmen on board to help them while keeping the rest below deck on one of the pirate vessels.

The master of the *Nicholas* was John Rawlins, an experienced West Country mariner with a disabled hand who had been sailing out of Plymouth for twenty-three years without incident. Before he saw his home again he was to become involved in one of the most audacious acts of mutiny in the history of Barbary Coast piracy.

Along with the rest of the captives Rawlins was brought into Algiers, valued and put up for sale in the *qasba*. 'Although we had heavy hearts, and looked with sad countenances', he later recalled, 'yet many came to behold us, sometimes taking us by the hand, sometime turning us round about, sometimes feeling our brawns [i.e. muscles], and naked arms, and so beholding our prices written in our breasts, they bargained for us accordingly'.[19] Because of his disability Rawlins was the last to be sold. He was bought for 150 doubles (about £7.50) by the pirate who had taken him, a renegade named Villa Raïs.

The fact that a pirate had to buy his own prisoner is a reminder of how formalised the slave trade was on the Barbary Coast: just like the captain of any Levant Company merchantman, Villa Raïs worked in partnership with financial backers, who sponsored his expedition in return for a share of the profits.

What happened next to Rawlins also sheds light on the logistics of piracy and the economics of slavery. After being put to work to repair Villa Raïs's ship over the winter, he was sold on to an English renegade, John Goodale. Goodale's captain, Ramadan Raïs – a candlemaker's son from Southwark, who until his conversion to Islam had been Henry Chandler – had just bought a ship, the *Exchange* of Bristol, from some Turks who had captured her earlier that year. He and Goodale intended to take her out hunting as soon as possible, and since neither man was a particularly experienced mariner they were in need of a good pilot. Villa Raïs demanded 300 dollars for Rawlins – twice the price he had paid for him only a couple of months previously – and after some haggling, Goodale and two more Turks formed a consortium to buy him, putting up 100 dollars each.

The *Exchange* set sail from Algiers, streamers and banners flying, on 7 January 1622. She was armed with '12 good cast pieces, and all manner of munition and provision',[20] and a polyglot crew consisting of sixty-five Moslems, a number of whom were European renegades; one French slave; nine English slaves (including Rawlins and two of his men from the *Nicholas*); and four free Dutchmen.

From the start, Rawlins refused to accept his fate, ranting so violently against 'these cruel Mahometan dogs' and their treatment of him that the other slaves begged him to be quiet or it would be the worse for all of them:

> The worse [he said]? What can be worse? Death is the determiner of all misery, and torture can last but a while. But to be continually a dying, and suffer all indignity and reproach, and in the end to have no welcome but into the house of slaughter or bondage, is unsufferable, and more than flesh and bloud can endure. And therefore by that salvation which Christ hath brought, I will either attempt my deliverance at one time, or another, or perish in the enterprise.[21]

As the *Exchange* cruised towards the Spanish coast and the Straits, Rawlins devised a desperate plan to take over the ship and sail it back to England. If enough of the crew could be persuaded to help, he was convinced it would be possible to jam shut or bind up all the cabin doors, gratings and portholes when Chandler and his confederates were below deck. This would buy the mutineers enough time to storm the gun room. Once in control of the ordnance, they would be in a position either to blow the pirates into the air 'or kill them as they adventured to come down, one by one, if they should by any chance open their cabins'.[22] With some effort, he managed to convince his fellow slaves that his plan was their only hope of freedom. Then he took a couple of English renegades into his confidence, and the four Dutch Christians, who in turn persuaded two Dutch renegades to join with them. The signal for the mutiny to begin was a cry of 'For God and King James and St George for England!'

The rebels still faced odds of nearly four to one. But as the days went by and the *Exchange* headed towards the Atlantic in search of prey, the pirates unwittingly conspired to reduce them. In the middle of January they chased a little three-masted polacre aground on the Spanish coast; when the crew ran off, Captain Chandler refloated her and put a prize crew of nine Turks and one slave aboard to sail her back to Algiers.

Then, on 6 February, off Cape Finisterre, the pirates captured a bark on its way home to Torbay with a cargo of Portuguese salt; Chandler brought seven of the English crew aboard the *Exchange* and replaced them with ten Turks (three of whom, however, were renegades who were in on Rawlins's plan). The Torbay men agreed to join the mutiny, and that meant there were twenty-four rebels pitting themselves against a pirate force of forty-five.

When the sun rose the next day, there was no sign of the Torbay bark. (The renegades had decided to persevere with their plan: they secretly set a course for England during the night, and the first the other pirates knew of it was when they came within sight of the Cornish coast and puzzled 'that that land was not like Cape Vincent'.[23]) Chandler was so angry at the loss of his prize that he threatened to turn the *Exchange* for Algiers, and although he eventually calmed down, Rawlins decided he must act quickly if they weren't to lose their chance of freedom. On 8 February he took Chandler down into the hold and showed him a quantity of water that had gathered in the bow. There was nothing unusual in that, but Rawlins convinced the captain that it wasn't coming to the pump, which was placed amidships, because the *Exchange* was 'too far after the head' – that is, her bow was too low in the water. Chandler's only course of action, he said, was to drag four of the heavy pieces of ordnance aft – Rawlins's confederates lashed two of them down on the deck with their barrels pointing at the poop deck – and to order as many men as possible to gather on the poop. The weight of men and ordnance would bring the stern down, so that Rawlins and the other slaves could pump out the water from the hold.

Chandler followed Rawlins's advice, and all day the slaves manned the pumps, while twenty or so pirates lounged around on the poop deck. The routine was repeated the next day, 9 February, and again half the pirate crew was ordered to gather on the poop, in order to bring up the bow.

At two o'clock that afternoon one of the rebels fired off one of the guns. The shot, which splintered the binnacle housing and threw the pirates into confusion, was the signal for the rebels to storm the gun room and grab all the muskets they could find. Chandler, who had been writing in his cabin, dashed out on deck waving his cutlass, only to come face to face with Rawlins, at which he threw down his cutlass and begged for mercy.

The other pirates were made of sterner stuff. They set to work to tear up the planking of the deck with anything they could find – hammers, hatchets, knives, cutlasses, boathooks and oars, even the stones and bricks from the cookhouse chimney. Their object was not only to get at the slaves, who were most of them below deck, but also to break through to the helm and thus take control of the *Exchange*. But they were too late. The rebels subjected them to volley after volley of musket fire from cover, killing some and injuring more, until at last the Turks called for a truce and asked to negotiate with Rawlins. With an armed guard he went up to talk with them, 'and understood them by their kneeling, that they cried for mercy, and to have their lives saved, and they would come down, which he bade them do'.[24]

But he wasn't interested in mercy. He was too angry, too exhil-arated at the rising's success and – perhaps – too well aware that he and his men were still outnumbered and that thirty-odd prisoners would pose a threat to the ship's security. So he did something which to twenty-first-century sensibilities seems terrible. As the beaten pirates clambered down below deck, one by one, they were disarmed, bound – and then killed with their own cutlasses. The screams of the dying soon alerted the survivors above to the awful truth of what was happening, and a few jumped overboard in a futile attempt to escape. For the rest, Rawlins's men moved through the ship, cutting down anyone who resisted, and putting those who didn't in manacles before tipping them into the sea to drown.

Captain Chandler begged Rawlins for his life, reminding him that if it wasn't for him the pilot would still be working in Algiers as Villa Raïs's slave. Rawlins lectured him as he knelt on deck, berating him with 'the fearfulness of his apostasy from Christianity, the unjustifiable course of piracy, the extreme cruelty of the Turks in general, the fearful proceedings of Algiers against us in particular, the horrible abuses of the Moors to Christians, and the execrable blasphemies they use both against God and men.'[25]

But he did spare Chandler's life, along with those of his master John Goodale, the renegades who had helped the mutineers, and four Turks 'who were willing to be reconciled to their true Saviour'.[26] When the killing was done and the ship had been cleared of corpses, Rawlins assembled his men and led them in a prayer of thanksgiving. The *Exchange* arrived to a hero's welcome at Plymouth four days later, on 13 February 1622.

That summer Rawlins published his own account of his adventures (with a little literary help, no doubt). He dedicated it,

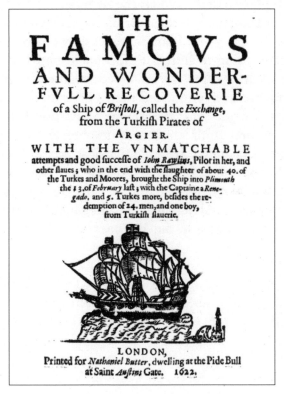

Rawlins's account of his escape, The Famous and Wonderfull Recoverie of a Ship of Bristoll

'an unpolished work of a poor sailor', to the Lord High Admiral, the Marquess of Buckingham, and, like the authors of the narratives about the *Dolphin* and the *Jacob*, he used the story to remind his readers of the courage with which ordinary English seamen faced the most appalling hardships. But in his preface he went further, asking Buckingham himself to show greater compassion:

> For though you have greater persons, and more braving spirits to lie over our heads, and hold inferiors in subjection; yet are we the men that must pull the ropes, weigh up the anchors, toil in the night, endure the storms, sweat at the helm, watch the biticle [binnacle], attend the compass, guard the ordnance, keep the night hours, and be ready for all impositions.[27]

Elsewhere, Rawlins's narrative suggests a hardening of attitudes, not so much in the brutal treatment he and his men meted out to their erstwhile masters (which the seventeenth century considered perfectly acceptable in the aftermath of any violent confrontation), as in the rage and contempt he showed towards Barbary and Islam. According to him, a European turned Turk for one of two reasons. Either captives convinced themselves that any religion would serve, and renounced their Christian faith in the hope of obtaining wealth and liberty; or they were tortured into submission, beaten until 'their tongues betray their hearts to a most fearful wickedness'. He railed against 'Mahometan tyranny', seethed at 'their filthiness and impieties' and ridiculed as superstition and witchcraft the religious rites he witnessed aboard ship.[28] The pirates of Algiers weren't just pirates; they were devils.

The Other had become the Enemy.

7

Treacherous Intents: The English Send a Fleet Against Algiers

*J*ames I's resolution in 1617 to 'draw our sword against the enemies of God and man' produced no immediate results, but it did at least lead to the creation of a commission of courtiers and merchants, who were charged with the task of putting the King's rhetoric into practice. They focused from the outset on Algiers, 'the nest and receptacle of the pirates', and the advice they received was that a frontal assault would fail.[1]

Sir William Monson, a one-time admiral of the Narrow Seas, suggested an international force of up to thirty-six English, Spanish and Dutch ships 'as most able to perform the service in respect of their strength and swift sailing'.[2] They should be prepared for a war of attrition lasting years rather than months, and since all the maritime nations of Europe would benefit, those who couldn't send ships and men should be asked to contribute to the finances. Spanish cooperation would be especially important: the fleets would need to be revictualled, careened and perhaps refitted every four or five months, and access to naval stations at Majorca, Alicante, Cartagena and Malaga was essential.

So was timing. It would be best to blockade the harbour at Algiers while the pirates were out on the cruise. None of the other friendly ports they might run for – Tunis, Safi, Agadir – could offer the same shelter as Algiers. But this meant stealth was important. 'If they understand of a greater force than their own to be made out against them', warned Monson, 'they will not adventure to put to sea.'[3]

Some members of the commission quailed at the diplomatic hurdles involved in organising an international force. Wouldn't it be simpler to stick with an exclusively English fleet and to ask the Spanish for the use of their ports? There were two objections to that. For one, Spain would benefit more than other nations from the destruction of the pirates, and popular opinion would not be happy at the idea of English ships and English sailors being sent to fight the Spaniards' battles at English expense. For another, an international operation meant the costs of mounting the expedition could be shared.

Everyone recognised that among the King's subjects, merchants and shipowners had the most to gain, so it was only fair that they should contribute the lion's share of the finances. London was the country's largest port, and the London companies were asked to stump up £40,000. Beyond the capital the provincial ports had to find another £9000 between them. But from each according to his trading links with the Mediterranean: the Levant Company was required to give £8000 and the Spanish Company £9000, while the Muscovy Company was assessed at only £1000.

The pattern of variation was repeated with the ports outside London. Bristol was asked for £2500, Plymouth, Exeter and Dartmouth for £1000 each. King's Lynn and Chester, which depended much less on the Mediterranean trade, had to give only £100 apiece, and Carlisle and Berwick weren't asked for anything at all.

Exactly how each body raised the levy was left up to them. Trinity House taxed ships using the port of London. The companies put a levy on imports and exports, as did most of the outports. And, predictably, the complaints and petitions and explanations of mitigating circumstances poured in to the government. The Muscovy Company said their £1000 was unfair, because they didn't trade with Barbary. The Spanish Company suggested the tax might be unconstitutional, and that, in any case, the Levant Company ought to pay more than them because their Mediterranean trade was much more extensive. Outports objected they were too poor to pay, or that their trade wasn't really affected by pirates. They claimed merchants would take their business elsewhere rather than pay levies, or that duties would harm local manufacturers, or that their neighbours deserved to contribute more than them.

The valiant but venal Sir Robert Mansell, leader of the 1620 expedition to Algiers

Politely, inexorably, the Privy Council considered – and usually overruled – each objection, and the money for the expedition started to trickle in. Meanwhile English diplomats were attempting to engage the Dutch and the Spanish in a joint venture, a process that proved harder than herding cats. After forty-one years of fighting for their independence against Spain, the United Provinces had concluded a twelve years' truce in 1609. It was an uneasy ceasefire rather than a peace treaty, and neither side trusted the other. The Spanish weren't happy with a Dutch naval presence in the Mediterranean, while the Dutch suspected that the Spanish were using the expedition against Algiers as a pretext for an unwelcome naval build-up. Both sides suspected James I of colluding with the enemy.

The English did their best to allay Dutch and Spanish fears. But as negotiations dragged on into 1618, then 1619, it became obvious to James and his advisers that the prospect of mounting a tripartisan expedition against Algiers was disappearing with the approach of the end of the Twelve Years' Truce in 1621. By the summer of 1620, England had come to an arrangement of sorts with Spain, who would put their Mediterranean ports at the disposal of the English and were in addition preparing to send a couple of squadrons into the Straits. The Dutch were sending a fleet of their own to patrol the western Mediterranean.

So, when, after three years of negotiation and preparation, an English expedition finally set sail on the first stage of its 2000-mile journey to Algiers, it was to all intents and purposes alone.

The Algiers expedition of 1620 was remarkable for many things, not least its leaders. The expedition's admiral and general-at-sea was Sir Robert Mansell, a naval administrator of long standing and, as Lieutenant of the Admiralty, second in rank only to the Lord High Admiral himself. (Sir William Monson, who had fallen from grace after being suspected of treasonable dealings with Spain, had hoped to stage a comeback by being given command of the expedition, but he was passed over.) Mansell chose as his rear admiral his own nephew Sir Thomas Button, the celebrated leader of an expedition to Hudson Bay who had spent the past seven years trying without much success to keep the coast of Ireland free from pirates. The vice admiral was Sir Richard Hawkins, an Armada veteran and the son of the great Sir John Hawkins, who had fought the Spanish Armada with Sir Francis Drake in 1588. Now about sixty years old, Sir Richard was still famous for his privateering exploits against the Spanish in the 1590s, which had ended in a desperate three-day fight against two heavily armed Spanish galleons off the Pacific coast at San Mateo, followed by an eight-year spell as a prisoner of war in Spain.

Neither the vice admiral nor the rear admiral had an unblemished record in public office. On his release from a Spanish jail in 1602, Hawkins had been compensated with the vice admiralty of Devon, a position he abused with gusto, letting pirates go free in return for a share of their loot. After a particularly awkward incident in which some personal valuables stolen from the Venetian ambassador turned up in his Devon home, Hawkins was fined, imprisoned and relieved of his post. Sir Thomas Button narrowly escaped punishment in 1605 for taking a bribe (two chests of sugar worth £42) to let a pirate go free. He came under investigation again in 1618 when a commission of enquiry discovered he had been receiving two royal pensions for the past ten years when he was entitled to only one.

But both men were models of probity in comparison to their leader. In an age in which public office and corruption went hand in hand, Sir Robert Mansell stood head and shoulders above his colleagues in his relentless, shameless pursuit of public funds which were not his to spend. After a spell as a privateer, and then as Elizabeth's Admiral of the Narrow Seas, in 1604 he obtained the post of treasurer to the navy, and clung to it for all it was worth for the next fourteen years. And it was worth a lot. He fitted out his own ship at the crown's expense, then hired it to the crown at an inflated rate, while simultaneously using it to carry private cargo. He routinely demanded bribes from naval suppliers as a condition of paying their bills. He ran a lucrative business buying timber and other materials from merchants, selling them to the navy at a handsome profit and, as treasurer, authorising the purchases himself. And when, in spite of his best efforts to stop it, the 1618 commission of enquiry into abuses in the navy began to examine his dealings, he resigned his post, mislaid his accounts and handed the commissioners a £10,000 bill for his travelling expenses, which they were unable to pay. Instead, they quietly dropped their investigation.

Mansell, Button and Hawkins were all venal men. But they were venal men in an age that routinely blurred the boundaries between service to the state and service to self, an age that regarded bribery, embezzlement and nepotism as legitimate business practices. No one raised an eyebrow, for example, when Mansell appointed his brother-in-law John Roper as one of his captains, his nephew Sir Thomas Button as his rear admiral, and yet another kinsman, John Button, as one of his officers. The only voice raised in complaint was Sir Thomas's, who was annoyed that he had been passed over for the vice admiral's job, which would have paid him £1 6s. 8d. (£1.33) a day instead of the 13s. 4d. (67p) he received as rear admiral.

And it is worth bearing in mind that courage and corruption aren't mutually exclusive qualities. Button and Hawkins had both distinguished themselves under fire, and if Mansell hadn't had the same opportunities to prove himself, his personal bravery was beyond question. He had a disabled right arm to remind him of a duel he had fought back in 1600, and during an embassy to Spain in 1605 he not only chased a pickpocket through the streets of Valladolid and into the house of a local judge, where he 'by force recovered a jewel stolen from his person',[4] but he also caused a stir at a diplomatic banquet when he noticed a Spanish guest secreting about his person a piece of plate that was meant as a gift for the English: he dragged the man into the middle of the hall and shook him till the silver fell out on the floor with a clatter. Sir Robert Mansell was a bold man, especially where his honour or his purse were concerned.

The fleet slipped out of Plymouth Sound early on 12 October 1620, heading towards the Lizard and then striking south across the Bay of Biscay to the coast of Spain and the Straits.

There were eighteen vessels in all. Mansell's flagship was the 600-ton *Lion*, Hawkins was in the 660-ton *Vanguard* and Button was in the *Rainbow*, also 660 tons. All three ships were relatively new, and each carried a complement of 250 men and 40 brass cannon. They were accompanied by three more of the King's ships, the *Constant Reformation*, the *Antelope* and the *Convertine*; ten armed merchantmen, hired for the purpose; a pinnace for inshore pursuit; and a supply vessel. Two more pinnaces were being built especially for the expedition, but they weren't ready and Mansell didn't want to delay any longer. Altogether the expedition consisted of 2250 men. Almost a third had been pressed into service.

Mansell had with him at least two men who had been on intimate terms with the enemy. Thomas Squibb, captain of a support ship, had been a captive at Algiers and was able to give valuable information on the state of the place. Robert Walsingham, the fearsome one-armed corsair captain who had so nearly taken the *Dolphin* off Sardinia, was also on the expedition: after being captured in Ireland in 1618 and condemned to death he had saved his neck by putting his considerable knowledge of Barbary pirates at the King's disposal.

James I's instructions, signed at Windsor on 10 September, were precise and prescriptive. Mansell was to cruise the western Mediterranean in pursuit of 'any pirates of what nation soever they be', but not to sail further east than Sardinia, because 'the islands of Archipelago' offered so many hiding places that 'it were a wild chase and to little purpose' to follow pirates who took refuge there. He was to go to Algiers and demand that the *pasha* hand over all of the King's subjects, whether they were slaves, renegades or free men. He was to demand restitution for all the English vessels taken by Algerian corsairs over the past five years and punishment for the pirates. And if he received no satisfaction he was to destroy the Algerian fleet.[5]

He was not to attempt 'any hostile act against the town', both for fear of offending the Ottoman Sultan, Uthmân II, and prompting reprisals against English merchants and diplomats in Istanbul, and also because Algiers was far too well defended for an open assault. Nor was he to put his ships at risk 'without some likelihood of success' — a catch-all phrase which meant that if the operation went wrong he was for it when he got home. If all else failed he was allowed to attack any pirates he found at anchor inside Algiers harbour; and he had explicit permission from James I to send in two or three of his smaller vessels as fireships — just so long as he used the hired merchant ships rather than any of the King's own.

The fleet was to rendezvous at Gibraltar, and Mansell put in there at the end of October, disembarking some sick crewmen and asking the Spaniards for news of pirates. John Button, who was aboard the *Constant Reformation* and who kept a journal of the expedition, recorded that the captain of a Spanish warship rowed over to the *Lion* and told Mansell that Turks were out and raiding further along the coast.

The fleet's next port of call was Malaga, sixty miles to the east, where Mansell split his forces into three squadrons and began the hunt in earnest. Sir Thomas Button's squadron spread out in a line, keeping about nine miles off the Spanish coast; Mansell's sailed on his bow, another nine miles out; and Sir Richard Hawkins's ships sailed on Mansell's bow, another nine miles out. The fleet could thus sweep a huge area as they moved eastward, further into the Mediterranean. To make the strategy more effective, the pinnace and 'two ships of least draught of water' were deputed to search the bays and coves for pirates as they passed. In case anyone tried to slip through their net during the night, the fleet agreed a password, 'Greenwich Tower'.

In the two weeks it took them to cruise the 250 miles from Malaga to Alicante, they didn't come across a single pirate.

After putting more sick crewmen ashore and victualling with wine, fresh water and other necessaries, Mansell struck out under full sail south-east for Barbary. He reached the Bay of Algiers on Monday 27 November 1620. The weather was so bad that the fleet was tossed around in the bay, and some of the smaller vessels were blown back out to sea before their anchors could take hold.

Keeping out of range of the Algerian guns, Mansell and Sir Thomas Button raised the white ensign, then a simple white flag with a red cross of St George in the canton, and the whole fleet saluted Algiers with their ordnance. The reply to the booming roar which rolled across the bay – at once a greeting, a gesture of respect and a show of force – was total silence.

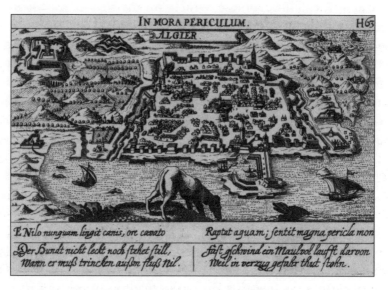

Algiers, 'the nest and receptacle of the pirates'

Mansell had sailed up to the walls of Algiers before. He had even attacked them before. 'The thundering artillery roared, the musketeers in numberless volleys discharged on all sides, the smoke (as it were) eclipsing *Titan's* refulgent Beams, filling all the air with a confused cloudy mist.'[6] But that was a pasteboard Algiers, and the battle took place in the safety of Whitehall one Saturday afternoon

in 1613, part of an elaborate water pageant which was staged to celebrate the marriage of James I's daughter Elizabeth to Frederick V,
count palatine of the Rhine and elector of the Holy Roman Empire.
Real life was more complicated (as Elizabeth was also discovering
– just as Mansell dropped anchor in the Bay of Algiers, Spanish
troops were overrunning the Palatinate and the Winter Queen and
her husband were fleeing into exile); and real-life Algiers was a great
deal more formidable than a pasteboard castle on the Thames.

The admiral waited impatiently for the storm to subside. The
next day, Tuesday 28 November, he sent Captain Squibb ashore to
present to the *pasha* the letter he carried from James I, setting out
England's demands. The delay was unlucky. Turbaned and jewelled
and seated on Turkish carpets and damask pillows, Kassan Kussa
received Squibb politely, welcoming him to his palace of marble
and porphyry, 'the most goodly house in Algier'.[7] He was prepared
to accept the letter, he said – but not until the next meeting of
the council of state, the *dīwān*. Since the *dīwān* only met on Saturday,
Sunday, Monday and Tuesday mornings, the fleet was going to have
to bob around in the bay in foul weather for another four days
before Mansell received any kind of official answer.

He wasn't happy when Squibb came back with this unwelcome
piece of news, and on the Wednesday he convened a council of
war aboard the *Lion* with Button, Hawkins and the other senior
officers to discuss whether the fleet should stay, or break off negotiations and adopt a more aggressive strategy. But what would that
strategy be? After some debate Mansell decided it would be better
to wait rather than 'to depart leaving his Majesty that sent me thither
unsatisfied and myself doubtful how to proceed'.[8] In any case, the
fleet's appearance had raised the hopes of the Christian captives; he
didn't want to disappoint the thousands of men and women 'who
had received great comfort by the sight of our approach'.[9]

The comfort was short-lived. That afternoon the English sailors
watched, appalled, as captives were herded down to the harbour and
forced into ships being made ready to sail. Meanwhile, pirate vessels
came and went, apparently unconcerned by the presence of an enormous battle fleet anchored in the bay; they even brought in two
English prizes, one from Great Yarmouth and another from Plymouth.

An infuriated Mansell sent his brother-in-law, Captain Roper,
to present the *pasha* with King James's demands, *dīwān* or no

dīwān. He explained that the English fleet was there to require restitution of, or compensation for, 150 ships taken by the Algerians over the past five years; the punishment or delivering up of all pirates and their *armadors* (shipowners); and the return of all English ships and goods currently at Algiers. In addition the admiral demanded that 'all his majesty's subjects, either slaves, renegades, boys or freemen, might be presently sent aboard me'.[10] The *pasha* listened politely again, and again said there was nothing he could do until the *dīwān* met on Saturday.

Although Kassan Kussa was the Sultan's viceroy and hence theoretically the man in charge of Algiers, real power lay with the *ocak*, the Turkish-speaking janissary elite, whose officers controlled the *dīwān*. Those officers were often major investors in pirate ventures, as well as providing them with fighting men. There were also the corsairs themselves to consider: the *pasha* couldn't afford to ignore the voice of the *tā'ifat al-ra'īs*, the powerful guild of corsairs which looked after their interests. And he had his own reasons for not wishing to interfere in their trade, since a percentage of the prizes and the cargo, human or otherwise, belonged to him by right as the Sultan's representative.

Ocak, *tā'ifat al-ra'īs* and *pasha* all profited in other, less obvious ways from the trade in captives. Contemporaries estimated the total number of European slaves in Algiers at the time at between 8000, which was plausible, and 50,000, which was not. They not only built houses and laid roads and acted as servants; some ran successful businesses for their masters, and kept their country estates, and repaired and sailed their ships. As a whole, they were absolutely essential to the Algerian economy. Backed by such a complex network of interests, the *pasha* was hardly going to smile sweetly and hand over captives, corsairs and compensation without a struggle.

When Saturday came round, he decided he wasn't going to allow the English into the *dīwān*. It was the main council meeting of the week, taking place in the great court of the *qasba* with a regular audience of a thousand or more people. Perhaps he thought it would give the English too public a forum; or perhaps there was just too much other business to attend to. But on Sunday morning Roper was brought before a much smaller, more select gathering of the *dīwān* which met in the courtyard of the *pasha*'s house. The officer carried the King's letter and had with him James Frizzell, an English agent who lived in Algiers. Since at least 1613 Frizzell had been looking after the Algerian interests of a powerful Levant Company merchant, Nicholas Leate. He 'well understood the course of their proceedings',[11] and may well have acted as Roper's interpreter, since all business was conducted in Turkish.

Roper began by formally presenting James I's letter to the *pasha*. The *pasha* said he couldn't read it.

Roper gave him copies in Turkish, Italian and Latin.

The *pasha* asked for letters of authority from Istanbul. When Roper said he had none, the *pasha* announced that he couldn't take notice of the King's letter without them.

Not a good start. Fortunately for the English, Frizzell had primed friendly members of the *dīwān* beforehand, and several now demanded to know exactly what was in this letter. Roper said the *pasha* was the proper person to explain it to them. The *pasha* said he couldn't understand it.

At this an exasperated Roper told the council he believed the contents 'were for the restitution of 150 sail of ships taken from his majesty's subjects . . . and the punishment of the offenders'; at which the *pasha* rose from his damask cushions and moved effortlessly to Plan B. It was so long since most of those ships were taken, he declared, that many of them had sunk. Others had been sold, along with their cargos. Most of the captured sailors were dead. That being understood, 'those that remained should be presently delivered'.[12]

Roper replied that this wasn't good enough, and Kassan Kussa countered with a list of English attacks on Algerian shipping, going back sixteen years to Richard Gifford's raid of 1604. He was told James I would certainly give satisfaction for any of his subjects' transgressions.

After listening to a noisy debate between the twenty-five senior officers of the janissary corps who made up the inner cabinet of the *dīwān*, the *pasha* rose from his cushions once again and proposed that losses sustained on both sides should be set against each other; that the city should return 'such ships and goods as were forthcoming';[13] and that all English captives, including those who had turned Turk but now wished to change their minds and their religion, should be released and handed over to the English. 'To all this the whole douana [i.e., the *dīwān*] assented.'[14]

Either Roper misunderstood the audience and its outcome (which isn't likely, considering he was accompanied by the experienced Frizzell), or the Algerians decided the quickest way to make him go away was to agree to his demands. They certainly made hardly any attempt to honour their pledges. No ships were forthcoming. No goods were forthcoming. And although the *dīwān* handed over to Roper a derisory eighteen captives, they promptly took them back (and placed Roper under house arrest) the moment Sir Robert Mansell suggested that for the future Frizzell's agent should keep a register of all English ships, men and goods brought in by pirates. The *dīwān* demanded a properly appointed consul, and it was only after Mansell dressed a hapless common sailor in fine clothes and put him ashore as the official representative of James I that Roper and the captives were released.

On Thursday 7 December, ten days after the fleet's arrival and four days after the *pasha*'s promise, one of the English captains brought word that men were unrigging the two new English prizes in the harbour and unloading all their goods. Admitting to himself at last that the Algerians had no intention of honouring their bargain, Mansell sent the *pasha* a cross letter 'to let him know how ill we took his perfidious dealing'.[15] The next morning the fleet weighed anchor and sailed out of the bay, with the admiral feeling foolish and complaining bitterly about 'the fair promises, faithless dealings and treacherous intents of the viceroy'.[16]

It was easy for contemporaries to criticise Mansell for his gullibility and his reluctance to fight. And they did. But having once opted for negotiation rather than intimidation, it is hard to think what else he could have done. The two new pinnaces still hadn't arrived, and without them to stop the pirates from slipping in and out along the shore he didn't have the resources to mount an effective blockade. There was now no question of surprising the Algerians. And the pointlessness of a blustering show of force was brought home to him while Captain Roper and the *pasha* were engaged in their diplomatic dialogue at the Sunday *dīwān*, when a Spanish squadron of six warships sailed into the bay in hot pursuit of pirates who had just burned a 700-ton ship off Cartagena and carried off 270 men. The Spanish admiral exchanged cannon fire with the shore batteries, but he knew better than to come within range of their guns and he left soon afterwards. 'The distance between them was so far', said John Button in his journal, 'that the shot falling short, no harm was done on either side.'[17] And no prisoners were recovered, he might have added.

For the next three months the English fleet cruised the western Mediterranean between Alicante, Malaga and Gibraltar, waiting for supply ships and pinnaces to arrive from England and searching without success for pirates. The succinct but disconsolate entries in John Button's journal tell their own story:

> The 27 [December] at night the rear-admiral's squadron went out to sea in pursuit of two Turks, pirates.
>
> The 29 the rear-admiral returned but saw no Turk.
>
> The fourth [of January] the *Constant Reformation* and the *Golden Phoenix* had order to go to sea to seek two pirates' ships which we heard were on the Christian shore.
>
> The fifth at night the *Reformation* and the *Phoenix* returned into the road [at Alicante] again, but met not with any.
>
> The 13 the *Reformation*, the *Samuel* and the *Restore* put to sea, to see if they could meet with any pirates.
>
> The 18 the *Reformation* with the other ships returned into the road, where we found the rear-admiral with his squadron like-wise returned, but met no pirates.[18]

On the single occasion when the fleet *did* encounter pirates – eight or nine accidentally sailed in among the English ships one night – a squadron chased them and fired at them but still couldn't catch them, 'by reason it was a dark night, and that they sailed better than our ships'.[19] The expedition's only trophy was a French merchantman captured on her way from northern Morocco to Algiers with a cargo of oil and some Moorish and Jewish passengers. Ironically, this was itself an act of piracy – although the vessel was crewed by Turks (who took to the boats and escaped) there is no suggestion that she was anything other than legitimate.

Mansell's men had seen virtually no action, yet casualty rates were high. The fleet had sickness aboard when it left England, and by the time it reached Gibraltar nineteen days later the situation was bad enough for the admiral to put an unspecified number of ailing crewmen ashore and arrange lodgings for them. One of his captains, a Virginia trader named John Fenner, died there. More sick men were put ashore at Alicante less than three weeks later, including thirty-seven from Mansell's own company. By the time the fleet regrouped at Alicante in the spring of 1621, sickness had claimed two more senior officers: Captain Eusabey Cave of the *Hercules*, one of the armed merchantmen, and Captain Arthur Manwaring of the King's ship *Constant Reformation*, 'a gentleman of an excellent temper . . . [whose] death bred a general lament in the whole fleet'.[20] Manwaring's chaplain, who had earned the crew's respect by selflessly ministering to them 'in the extreme of their sicknesses', was also dead. One of the pinnaces was unable to sail because its captain and master were too ill, and Mansell was now paying to lodge a substantial number of sick men in Malaga, including forty-two from the *Reformation* alone. Button's *Rainbow* was 'so grievously infested [probably with dysentery] that he had not able men in her to manage her safely'.[21]

Altogether more than 400 men were seriously ill. Mansell asked that a physician and two surgeons be sent out from England, complaining at the same time that 'the great sickness and mortality wherewith it hath pleased Almighty God to visit this fleet' was due to squalid living conditions, a lack of clean clothing and inadequate supplies.[22]

The ships were in no better shape. Hawkins, the oldest and most experienced of the three commanders, wrote to the Lord High Admiral in England that all three flagships — Mansell's *Lion*, Button's *Rainbow* and his own *Vanguard* — were 'very unfit for these seas' and needed to be replaced. Mansell followed this up with a detailed report from his master carpenter, who confirmed that the *Lion*'s hull was so leaky at the bows that in a head sea (when waves were running directly against the course of the ship) the crew had to man the pumps constantly to keep her afloat.

And all the English had to show for their efforts were a small French merchant ship and a handful of rescued captives.

There were two reasons the hunt had been so disappointing. In addition to the English fleet, twenty-two Dutch warships and two Spanish squadrons were patrolling the western Mediterranean over the winter of 1620–21. It didn't take long for the news to spread along the entire Barbary coast from Tangier to Tunis. As Sir William Monson had predicted, the corsairs were on their guard.

Even if the navies of three nations hadn't been cruising the high seas in search of them, it was the wrong time of year for them to be out. There would always be corsair captains who were bored enough, broke enough or reckless enough to venture out during the stormy winter months, but the season for Mediterranean piracy traditionally lasted from March or April until October, and over the winter most pirate ships were safely in harbour, being careened and repaired and refitted in preparation for the spring.

Mansell was feeling isolated and frustrated. His instructions from the Lord High Admiral were to remain in the Mediterranean for at least another six months, and James I was talking of maintaining a presence there for three years. The fleet was in desperate need of supplies, which proved inadequate when they eventually arrived, along with the two new pinnaces, in mid-February 1621. (And the word 'arrived' needs qualification: the supply ships had sailed from England with orders to go to Malaga, and their masters refused point-blank to obey Mansell's command to sail on to Alicante, forcing the fleet to weigh anchor and sail 300 miles to meet them and making him very cross indeed.) He didn't know how he was to receive fresh orders or supplies from now on, either, 'for being resolved in my intention to spend most of this summer on the Turkish shore, I know not whither the pirates may lead me'.[23]

At home, rumours were spreading that the expedition had turned into a fiasco. Government officials and diplomats started to distance themselves; the City merchants who had put up the money for it were muttering; and there were stories put about by Mansell's enemies that he had 'made an agreement with the pirates to [his] shame'.[24] Count Gondomar, the Spanish ambassador in England, complained that 'the English and those robbers are now all one',[25] and the Venetian ambassador sent a coded message home to the Doge reporting that the fleet was 'very short of provisions and money, upon which account the men complain and are half mutinous, some having deserted to join the pirates, while many have died of sickness'.[26] (There were in fact no desertions.)

To make matters worse, Admiral Mansell was fretting over his business interests in England. He had acquired a monopoly on glass-making in 1615, and had 'melted vast sums of money in the glass-business', according to James Howell, whom he sent abroad to look for foreign expertise. Though it was, again according to Howell, 'a business, indeed, more proper for a merchant than a courtier', Mansell clung tenaciously to his patent, investing some £25,000 in glass-works in London, South Wales, Dorset and Newcastle-on-Tyne, and news that elements in the government were trying to have the patent revoked added considerably to his woes.[27]

Mansell could have ignored his orders and gone home, arguing that crew shortages and an unseaworthy fleet made his mission impossible, and trusting to ride out the humiliation and the awkward questions. Or he could have continued patrolling the seas between the Straits and Majorca in the vague hope that his quarry would venture out before his demoralised men died of dysentery and his ships fell apart.

What he decided to do was to attack the corsair fleet as it lay in harbour. That April he hired a 120-ton polacre and three two-masted brigantines. All were fast and manoeuvrable in comparison to the lumbering warships, and the brigantines were equipped with nine pairs of oars each. Then he rented a house in Alicante and turned it into a bomb factory.

The harbour at Algiers was still protected from the elements by Khair ad-Din's great mole, the causeway of stone and earth that was six or seven yards wide and 300 yards long. The mole connected the city to a small fortified island in the bay, forming a giant capital J which, as one English observer noted, 'giveth shape to the port, where there are usually above an hundred vessels for piracy, and others'.[28]

Even if the fleet could manoeuvre through the shallow inshore waters until it was close enough to the mole to cause serious damage to the ships moored there, by doing so it would come within devastating range of the heavy ordnance mounted along the city walls. The other obvious course, a lengthy blockade, required the kind of reliable supply network that was conspicuously lacking. Mansell's best hope was to trust he would find a good number of pirate vessels moored within the mole when he returned, and to send in fireships to destroy them under cover of darkness.

Making grenades, from Nathaniel Nye's Fire-Works for Warre and Recreation *(1647)*

In the house at Alicante, his gunners went to work. They cooked up buckets of lethal wildfire from brimstone, gunpowder and petroleum oil; made a quantity of incendiary grenades; and prepared fire pikes which they would use to pin bags of explosive to the timbers of a pirate vessel. Mansell eschewed the traditional way of deploying fireships – setting fire to a couple of smaller ships and setting them adrift among the enemy – and opted instead for a more tactical approach. He had his men prepare two fireships, one of 100 tons and the other of 60. (John Button describes both as having been 'taken from the Turks' – presumably one was the Frenchman captured in February, but it isn't clear how they laid their hands on the other.) The one-armed reformado Captain Walsingham, whose previous career had provided him with first-hand experience of the harbour at Algiers, was given the command of one; a Captain Stokes had the other. Both were filled with incendiaries, piled high with dry timber, oakum, pitch, tar and brimstone, and equipped with chains and grapnels for fixing them fast to their victims. Their crews were to sail them into the mole, fasten them to a couple of suitable pirate ships, fire the incendiaries and at the last moment make their escape in longboats which they towed behind them for the purpose.

A third fireship, a much smaller single-masted barge, was also fitted out with incendiaries and iron grapnels: she was to be sailed right into the middle of the pirate fleet and set alight; and her crew were also to make their escape in a longboat.

The fireships were supported by the three brigantines Mansell had hired in Alicante. They carried fireballs, buckets of wildfire and fire pikes, all of which could be hurled on to the decks or jabbed into the timbers of the pirate ships.

Finally, there were seven longboats 'which we called boats of rescue', recalled John Button. They were to wait outside the mole. Armed with incendiaries to throw at any pirates they found within range, they were 'well-filled with armed men, who were to rescue and relieve the boats of execution if they should chance to be pursued by other boats or galleys at their coming off'.[29]

It was a desperately dangerous venture. The fireships and the brigantines would have to pass under the walls of Algiers, exposing their crews to fire from heavy ordnance and small arms. The mole itself had a strong parapet running its full length, and if this was properly manned and defended by the Turks, the English boats would be caught in a lethal crossfire. The element of surprise was crucial.

At the end of April the fleet moved to Majorca, where for weeks Mansell rehearsed the coming operation over and over again until the crews – more than 230 men in thirteen vessels – knew exactly what they were to do.

There was a full moon on the night of 24 May, and the tumbling clusters of low white houses gleamed through the darkness. Silhouetted against the hillside, the minaret of the Djemaa el-Kebir loomed over the harbour, a landmark for the little flotilla as it made its way across the bay. The stench of brimstone and sweat and fear was wafted away in the light south-westerly that carried the boats closer and closer to their quarry.

This was Mansell's fourth attempt to burn the corsair fleet. His own fleet had reached Algiers three days before, and the battered men-of-war had anchored within sight of the town while six of the merchantmen were deployed to patrol the coast 'to prevent the coming in of any pirates between the fleet and the shore'.[30] As soon as everyone was in place, the admiral had summoned Walsingham, Stokes and the captains of the brigantines and the 'boats of rescue' aboard the *Lion* to go over the plan one more time and give them their orders.

The crews were already aboard their vessels and ready to set off for the mole when Mansell decided to abort the operation. There was not enough wind to fill the sails of the two fireships, and Button, Hawkins and the other senior commanders advised against going in with just the boats and the brigantines.

The next night the men prepared again, and again the assault was called off, for the same reason. The night after that was stormy, but the flotilla braved gales, thunder and lightning to set out – only for the skies to clear and the wind to shift against them before they came near the mole, pushing them out into the bay and forcing them to abandon the attack for a third time.

The Algerians didn't show the slightest sign of being concerned at the reappearance of the English battle fleet. They didn't place an extra watch on the city walls. They didn't attempt to open negotiations. According to a Christian captive who escaped and swam out to the fleet, they hadn't even put guards on their ships, 'saving one or two in a ship'.[31] They simply didn't believe that Mansell would attack.

That night, the admiral watched from the deck of the *Lion* as his assault force approached the entrance to the harbour, in what was to prove their final attempt to destroy the pirate fleet. They were almost there. The open boats of rescue and the fireships were passing beneath the ramparts when once again the wind veered and began to push them slowly, inexorably, back out into the bay. 'The two ships with the fireworks having almost recovered the mouth of the mole', Mansell told the Marquess of Buckingham a few weeks later, 'the wind, to our great grief, turned to the opposite side of the compass'.[32]

As they milled around in the darkness calling to each other, a Captain Hughes cried out from the deck of one of the brigantines, 'Go *on*! Give the attempt with the boats!' The others took their cue from him, and pulling hard on their oars, the crews of boats and brigantines crossed into the harbour, chanting 'King James! King James! God bless King James!' Sentries on the walls raised the alarm, and the watchers out in the bay heard shouts and then the popping of muskets coming from across the water. The flotilla pressed on, returning fire as best they could in the darkness, and trying to keep the moored ships and galleys between themselves and the gunners and militiamen on the city walls. They lit their buckets of wildfire and grenades and hurled them on to the decks of one vessel after another, until seven of the pirate ships were burning. 'Striving in the end who should have the honour to come off last', said Mansell, 'the which at length, as a due to his former resolution and courage, they left to Captain Hughes, and so returned, all the ships continuing still their cheerful cry, "King James!"'.[33] As they rowed out from the cover of the moored ships, they came under sustained fire from the Algerians. Six men were shot dead and seventeen or eighteen wounded; four or five later died of their injuries.

It was all for nothing. The English boats made their way back to the fleet and the bab al Gazira, the great gate that connected the harbour to the town, burst open. Citizens, slaves, corsairs and soldiers streamed out along the mole and began to extinguish the flames. Almost immediately, clouds covered the moon and a sudden shower of rain made its own contribution towards undoing the work of Hughes and his fellow incendiaries. When dawn came Mansell reckoned only two pirate ships had been rendered unserviceable.

That day eleven pirates slipped into harbour past the English patrols, and although the admiral bided his time and waited for a favourable wind so he could send in the fireships again, he had missed his chance. Two Genoese captives who swam for their freedom a week after the attack told him 'the pirates had boomed up the mole with masts and rafts, set a double guard upon their ships, planted more ordnance upon the mole and the walls, and manned out twenty boats to guard the boom'.[34] They had also dispatched galleys east and west along the coast to warn off other pirates.

So Mansell retired to Alicante to refit his ships, to plan another assault and to await orders, supplies and reinforcements. The Spanish repeated their accusations of his being in league with the pirates. The supplies didn't come. Nor did the reinforcements. The orders did, but they were not what Mansell wanted: Lord Admiral Buckingham, anxious about rising tensions in the Narrow Seas following the end of the Twelve Years' Truce between Spain and the United Provinces, told him to send home Hawkins and Button with the *Vanguard*, the *Rainbow*, the *Constant Reformation* and the *Antelope*, and to carry on the fight against the pirates with what he had left.

He did as he was told, although the *Lion* was in such a poor state that she could not be kept at sea 'without eminent peril of perishing', so he swapped with Hawkins and kept the *Vanguard* for himself.[35] He also dismissed four of the merchantmen after their captains convinced him they were no longer fit for service. The Venetian ambassador, with his customary grasp of events, reported to the Doge that 'the twenty ships under Mansfilt [*sic*] have fought, defeated and captured some pirate ships and inflicted much damage upon the port of Algiers'.[36]

Mansell could be forgiven for feeling a little dispirited. But for all his many faults, he wasn't one to give up easily. He sailed round to Cadiz to refit and spent the month of July planning another attack on the harbour at Algiers, this time using galleys which he hoped to borrow from Spain. He intended to use the galleys – eleven would be good, but he reckoned he could make do with six – to blockade the harbour and to tow his remaining ships in close to shore, where their heavy guns could provide cover for his boats as they dismantled the boom. In spite of some misgivings, the Spanish agreed to provide him with 'a great supply of fireworks, galleys, and other vessels',[37] and the galleys had actually been dispatched to Majorca to await his arrival when he received fresh orders from home. He was being recalled to England, to patrol the Narrow Seas.

In October 1621, a year after they left England with such high expectations, the remains of Mansell's battered expeditionary force sailed into the shelter of the Downs, the anchorage off the coast of Kent which was the traditional gathering point for the fleet. In a final twist to the long comedy of errors, the government had changed its mind and decided to keep him in the Mediterranean, but he left for home before the orders countermanding his recall arrived. The adventure proved too much for his vice admiral, the elderly Sir Richard Hawkins, who collapsed and died in front of the Privy Council – of vexation at not having his expenses for the Algiers voyage paid, according to one contemporary.[38] Sir Thomas Button went back to chasing pirates round the Irish Sea. Mansell was left to bear the brunt of the criticism in Westminster alone.

No one could claim the mission had been a success – not even the Venetian ambassador, who reverted to saying that the English crews were so ill paid and ill disciplined that they deserted en masse to the Turks. Mansell's enemies seized the opportunity to condemn his failure of leadership. Sir John Coke, who had lost his place as deputy treasurer to the navy when Mansell took over back in 1604, and who as one of the Commissioners for the Navy had been involved in the 1618 attempt to bring him to book for corruption, described the fleet's early efforts as 'nothing but shooting and ostentation' and criticised the admiral for not spending more time at sea. Sir William Monson, still smarting from being passed over as commander of the expedition, agreed:

> Such was the misgovernment of those ships, and the negligence and vain-glorious humours of some to feast and banquet in harbour when their duty was to clear and scour the seas, that they rather carried themselves like amorous courtiers than resolute soldiers, by which means they lost the opportunity which offered itself to do hurt upon those hellish pirates.[39]

Monson also blamed Mansell for stirring up the pirates and thus actually making matters worse, a charge repeated by later historians. Josiah Burchett, author of the first general naval history of England, commented in 1720 that 'in return for the civility of [Mansell's] visit, his back was scarce turned, but those corsairs picked up near forty good ships belonging to the subjects of his master, and infested the Spanish coasts with greater fury than ever'.[40]

There was something in this. By the winter of 1621 MPs were complaining that the decay in trade was much greater than it had been in the summer 'by reason of pirates'.[41] In November two Portuguese carracks, big three-masted ships of the kind which dominated long-distance trade in the early seventeenth century, had almost reached home on their way from Goa on the west coast of India when they were attacked by seventeen Turks; one managed to get into harbour at Lisbon, but the other was sunk with the loss of all hands and cargo valued at nearly three million ducats. The following spring, merchants in the Exchange at London estimated recent English losses at £40,000. There were reports of savage behaviour, too. An English merchantman which resisted three Turks in the Straits was blown out of the water; its master and seventeen crew clung to the wreckage for hours, but the pirates refused to pull them out of the water and they all drowned. A group of women whose husbands were held captive in Algiers went down on their knees and wept in front of the Prince of Wales; they apparently obtained 'fair words' – a remarkable enough achievement for the shy and stammering Prince Charles.

It took an unusually virulent outbreak of plague along the Barbary Coast in the summer of 1622 to rein back the activities of the pirates. John Ward was among the casualties in Tunis; while merchantmen calling at Algiers reported that pirate ships lay abandoned for want of crew, and said that bodies were being thrown into the sea because there were so many dead. 'God grant it be true!', exclaimed the Venetian governor of Corfu.[42]

Sir Robert Mansell was robust in his response to his critics, blaming the failure of his mission on poor communications, inadequate supplies and bad weather – a fair assessment. He survived the whispering campaign against him, clinging to his Vice Admiralty of England and his glass-making patent; and even entered Parliament, so that he could secure an exemption for his precious patent from the Act of Monopolies.

One of his last appearances at Westminster – and in history – came in May 1641, when part of a ceiling in the Commons chamber gave way with a sudden crack, causing nervous MPs to assume they were under attack. There was an undignified stampede out of the chamber and into the adjoining Westminster Hall, where terrified members ran straight into Mansell, who drew his sword and commanded them to 'stand and fight like true Englishmen'. They didn't. If they had turned to glance backwards as they scrambled out into Palace Yard, they would have seen the old sailor, irascible and magnificent, advancing alone into the Commons chamber with his sword in his hand.

8

Fishers of Men:
The Sack of Baltimore

*T*he men didn't like passing through the Straits. It made them nervous.

Murad watched as one of the janissaries tossed the little bundle of candles over the side, an offering to the long-dead holy man who still promised them protection from the safety of his shoreline tomb.

Once he would have laughed. Now, without thinking, he murmured to himself the ancient form of words, at once a profession of faith and a prayer. There is no other God than God, and Mohammad is his messenger.

The candles vanished in the rolling sea.

Fifteen hundred miles away, on the coast of Co. Cork, the people of Baltimore were preparing for the first sighting of the glittering, rippling, silver-bright shoals of fish which meant security for the entire community for another year.

It was June 1631, and Baltimore had come a long way since

Captain John Jennings and his friends played hide-and-seek with the King's ships around the inlets and islands of Roaringwater Bay. Pirates still appeared from time to time, but the presence at Kinsale of the *Fifth Whelp*, a fast, well-armed new pinnace under the command of Captain Francis Hooke, made this particular corner of Ireland less attractive to them than it had been in the past.

As a result, Baltimore's black economy – the trading in stolen goods, the whores, the cattle and casks of ale left in isolated coves – had declined dramatically. The Protestant colony planted here at the beginning of the century had put down roots and all but ousted the native Catholic population; and a 'town of English people, larger and more civilly and religiously ordered than any town in this province', as the Lord Bishop of Cork had called it, was knuckling down to earning a more or less honest living.[1]

It prospered. That summer about 200 people were living in neat rows of houses beside the O'Driscolls' ancient Fort of Jewels which overlooked the harbour. A second group of more than 100 lived a few hundred yards below, close to a little cove. There were stalls, alehouses, workshops, brewers and bakers, a Friday market, a pretty stone-built church. The mayor, elected each year by twelve burgesses, presided over a weekly court; farmers and village people from all over West Cork came to the big three-day fairs which were held in June and October.

Baltimore wasn't entirely reformed. Its merchants still bought the occasional chest of sugar without enquiring too closely into its provenance. But these days the place owed its wealth not to pirates, but to a cousin of the herring, the humble pilchard.

Every summer, boys stood watch along the cliffs for the telltale shimmer on the waves which meant the arrival of the first shoals. As soon as one was sighted, the cry went up and men scrambled to put out to sea. They worked in teams: perhaps a dozen or more in the main vessel, the seine boat, and half a dozen in a smaller follower. The fishers were guided by huers who could track the shoal's movement from their vantage points on high ground; and at a given signal a seine net up to 400 yards long was dropped to form a vertical curtain. The crews of the seine boat and the follower rowed as hard as they could, one going clockwise and the other anti-clockwise, to draw the net round the shoal. When they met, they heaved up weighted draw ropes on the bottom of the net to trap the writhing mass of pilchards in a kind of purse. Then, using oval baskets, they emptied the fish into their boats and either set off in search of another shoal or turned for home.

It was a hard, frantic business, and the catch was just the start. The pilchards were unloaded in the cove and taken to storehouses called 'palaces' (from the old Anglo-Norman *palis*, meaning an enclosure), where they were arranged in layers, with salt between each layer. There they stayed for up to three weeks. Then the salt was shaken off and the fish were rinsed in fresh water before being taken to pressing houses, where they were tightly packed into casks and pressed with heavy weights. 'The pilchards are squeezed down', explained an eighteenth-century commentator on the Co. Cork pilchard industry, '[and] the barrels are again filled up and so again till they can hold no more. Under the casks are convenient receptacles to hold the oil, blood and water; the oil is got by scumming off the top. The fish being thus pressed, the barrels are headed and sent to market.'[2] A single catch might bring in 600 barrels of pilchards.

Baltimore revolved around the pilchard industry. It sustained not only the fishermen, but coopers and carpenters and rope-makers, shipwrights and merchants and factors. Most of the women worked in the palaces and pressing houses. Pilchard oil filled the lamps which lit their homes, and was used in preparing the leather they wore. Their great fear was that one day the notoriously unpredictable shoals wouldn't come.

Murad still marvelled at the way the janissaries would sit so still and silent, for hours on end. The motion of the ship meant little to them. The commands he gave his crew, as he sat cross-legged on his mat, they ignored. They had not come on this voyage to climb rigging or haul in the sails.

Sometimes they talked to each other, or smoked, or gambled. Sometimes they cleaned their muskets and oiled their scimitars. Mostly they just sat, in their tall red caps and long sashed robes and iron-heeled slippers, and looked out at the sea passing by.

In Dublin, a rumour reached the Earl of Cork that Algerian pirates were planning to attack Munster. His informant believed their target would be one of two recently built forts: Haulbowline, which commanded the mouth of Cork harbour; or Castlepark, put up in 1604 on a peninsula overlooking Kinsale. Unlikely though this seemed, the Earl took the intelligence seriously enough to pass it on to London. Cork and Kinsale were both ripe 'for Turks to lay eggs in', he told Viscount Dorchester, the King's Secretary of State, not setting much store by Captain Hooke and his *Whelp*.

There had been several security scares in these waters recently. In July 1630 Lord Esmonde, governor of the fort at Waterford, complained to London that 'the pirates on the coast are very bad';[3] and the same month Captain Hooke reported he was unable to engage with Spanish ships which had taken two prizes because 'the Irish fishermen warn them of our presence'.[4] That November, the mayor of Waterford warned the authorities that 'Cornelius O'Driscoll, an Irish pirate with his rendezvous in Barbary, is in the neighbourhood with a ship of 200 tons and 14 guns'.[5] Cornelius was one of the O'Driscolls who had ruled Baltimore before the coming of the English planters, and his appearance, together with the report that Turks were planning a visit to that part of Ireland, prompted the Earl of Cork to revive an idea proposed by Lord Deputy Chichester back in 1608, that Baltimore must be fortified to prevent its use as a safe haven by pirates.

The Earl ordered a map to be drawn up and sent to Viscount Dorchester, so that 'your lordship may observe how the town and harbour lyeth and how narrow the entry of the harbour mouth is, and how easily and fit it is to be fortified and secured'.[6] This map shows 1631 Baltimore in remarkable detail. Thirty-six houses, plumes of smoke rising gently from their chimneys, are grouped around the Fort of Jewels, with a further ten houses standing in two rows within the walls of the fort. The settlement down at the cove is represented by another twenty-six buildings. Most are obviously houses, but three pairs set apart on the shore could be the fish palaces and pressing houses.

In the bay, two seine boats and their followers are fishing, and a small fleet of six fishing boats lies in the cove. Two armed ships are anchored in deep water below the cliffs of Sherkin Island, which acts as a breakwater for the harbour, protecting it from the

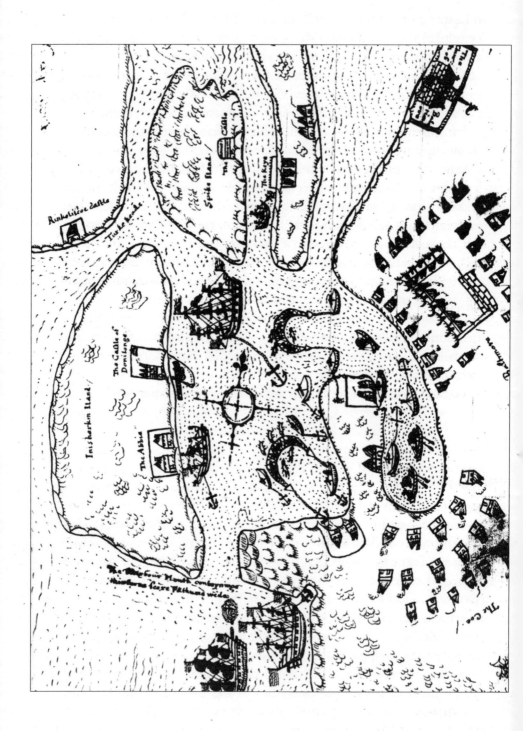

ravages of the Atlantic. A third ship is at anchor behind a little headland at the harbour mouth, just out of sight of the town, and a fourth puts out to sea in full sail, cannon blazing in salute. It isn't clear what these ships signify, although given that the anonymous cartographer has chosen to portray a snapshot of everyday life at Baltimore, most likely they are patrolling naval vessels and visiting merchantmen. The only sign of defence is a gun emplacement projecting out into the bay from the sixteenth-century Castle of Dunalong on Sherkin Island.[7] Heavy ordnance placed here would be capable of playing over the western side of the 500-yard-wide entrance to Baltimore harbour; but since Dunalong was still an O'Driscoll stronghold, the Earl of Cork presumably felt something a little more reliable was called for.

Viscount Dorchester's response to the Earl's proposal hasn't survived. The map – or a copy of it – found its way into the hands of Thomas Wentworth, who took up his appointment as the King's representative in Ireland, the Lord Deputy, in July 1633. Perhaps that implies the idea of fortifying Baltimore was passed back and forth from one government office to another. Wentworth did nothing about it, either.

In any case, by 1633 it was too late for Baltimore.

The two French ships were easy. Murad's men stripped them of ropes, rigging, canvas and everything else of value. They stripped their crews, too – seventeen Frenchmen, nine Portuguese and three Spaniards – and shackled them in the hold of the pirate vessel. But the ships themselves were worth nothing. Where Murad was going, they would be a liability. The men stove in their planking with iron bars and watched from the deck as they disappeared beneath the waves.

Murad was a veteran. As Jan Janszoon of Haarlem, he had worked with Suleiman Raïs, another Dutch renegade and a one-time member of Simon Danseker's crew. Around the time of Suleiman's death in 1620 Janszoon converted to Islam, took the name Murad and became a *raïs* himself, operating first out of Algiers, then from Salé on the Atlantic coast of Morocco, where he rose to become head of the *tā'ifat al-ra'īs*. He was back in Algiers by the spring of 1627, when

a Danish captive approached him with an offer to pilot an expedition
to the Northern Seas if Murad would buy him his freedom.

The result was an epic 5000-mile voyage to Iceland and back.
Murad's men, a motley mixture of Christians and Moslems, Franks
and Turks, free men and slaves, arrived off the Icelandic coast in
June 1627 and immediately began raiding small settlements, and
spreading terror and confusion. They took three Danish merchant
ships they found. They killed. They raped – the Icelanders were
shocked to see it was the European renegades rather than the
more disciplined janissaries 'that killed people, cursed and beat
them, and did all that is evil'[8]. Eventually in one final raid they
stormed ashore on 16 July 1627 at Heimaey, an island off the coast
which was inhabited by a little community of fishermen and
traders. Terrified at rumours of 'Turks with claws instead of nails,
spitting fire and sulphur, with knives growing out of their breasts,
elbows and knees',[9] the islanders mounted a half-hearted defence
and then surrendered. Murad was back in Barbary a month later.
He had with him 400 Icelanders, whom he sold in the slave market
of Algiers. The Icelandic liturgy still includes a prayer beseeching
God for protection against 'the terror of the Turk'.[10]

Now Murad was out on the cruise again. On Friday 17 June
1631, somewhere off Land's End, he caught up with a 60-ton
English ships out of Dartmouth and treated her as he had the two
French vessels. His men 'took therewith forth masts, cordage, and
other necessaries with all the men, and sunk the hull'.[11] Her crew
of ten were shackled and put down in the hold with the other
captives.

At least, nine of them were. The master, Edward Fawlett, traded
regularly with Ireland. He knew the lie of the Waterford coast,
the harbours and coves of Co. Cork. When he was questioned,
he made no secret of the fact. Realising he might prove useful,
Murad offered Fawlett his freedom in return for that knowledge.

And the raiding party sailed on.

'O Lord our heavenly father, high and mighty king of kings, lord
of lords, the only ruler of princes, which dost from Thy throne
behold all the dwellers upon earth, most heartily we beseech Thee

with Thy favour to behold our most gracious Sovereign Lord King Charles.'

It was the morning of Sunday 19 June and Baltimore was at prayer. The modern Protestant church stood on the shore of a small bay opposite the island of Ringarogy, a little way out of the town; and a long straggling line of men, women and children had walked along the cliff and down to the strand to that church, just as they did every Sunday. The talk as they picked their way over the coastal path would have been of ordinary things: the summer fair which was to take place the following weekend; the imminent arrival of the year's first pilchard shoals. Like its church, the Protestant community was young: there were plenty of small children to fidget through the long, long sermon.

And like its church, the community was set apart. Protestant settlers were not universally admired in Ireland. A resentment at English inroads, already common enough, had been fuelled in recent years by clumsy attempts to repress Catholic institutions and Anglicise Irish society. On St Stephen's Day 1629 there was a riot in Dublin when a 3000-strong crowd stoned the archbishop, the mayor and their officers for interrupting a Catholic service and attempting 'to lay hand upon the friars, and seize upon the house'.[12] Anyone who wore the traditional Irish cloak and woollen trousers was barred from bearing arms or keeping gunpowder. The time-honoured practice of carrying a skene (a short dagger) was outlawed. In fact, anyone who persisted in 'the barbarous custom of wearing mantles, trousers, skenes and such uncivil apparel . . . to the disgrace of this kingdom amongst civil nations' risked the humiliation of being brought before a sheriff and having their skene broken in two, and their cloak and trousers taken from them by force and cut up in pieces.

There is no evidence that the Baltimore planters ever tried to debag their neighbours or take a pair of scissors to an O'Driscoll *leine-chroich*. They were hard-working, decent people who kept to themselves, rather than arrogant colonialists determined to impose their culture and values on a native people. They were strangers in a strange land who wanted nothing more than peace and an opportunity to worship in their own way.

'In all time of our tribulation', intoned the minister in the little church on the strand that Sunday, 'in all time of our wealth, in the hour of death, and in the day of judgement' – he paused for the congregation's response.

'Good Lord deliver us.'

James Hackett was a Catholic and afraid. While the people of Baltimore knelt in prayer that Sunday morning, his 12-ton fishing boat was being boarded by pirates, and he and his crew of five were being quizzed by the pirate captain, 'Matthew Rice, a Dutch runogado'.[13]

Murad Raïs came upon Hackett's little mackerel boat as it put out its nets off the Old Head of Kinsale, about sixty miles west of Hackett's home at Dungarvan and forty miles east of Baltimore. By luck or by judgement the Earl of Cork's informant had been right – Murad's target was Kinsale, and although Edward Fawlett, the master of the vessel captured off Land's End, knew the coast, the renegade corsair was looking for someone with more detailed local knowledge of the harbour – a pilot who would be able to guide him safely up the River Bandon to where the town lies. During the Iceland raid in 1627 one of his ships had sailed into harbour while the tide was low and run aground. He'd learned his lesson then.

Murad also needed boats to take his men ashore. A prize crew piled into Hackett's vessel and went after a second fisherman from the Dungarvan fleet, while the captain interrogated Hackett about Kinsale and its harbour.

The man was scared and eager to please. He told Murad straight out that Kinsale was too hot for them. To get anywhere near the town they would have to pass under the guns of the King's fort at Castlepark, which stood on a small promontory on the west bank of the Bandon and covered the approach. And if they managed to negotiate *that* obstacle, they would sail straight into Captain Francis Hooke and the guns of the *Fifth Whelp*.

Murad was well armed. His own ship carried 200 men and twenty-four pieces of brass ordnance, and he was accompanied by another with eighty men and twelve iron guns. But that wasn't the point. He wasn't looking for a fight. So he listened carefully as Hackett offered to guide him to a far easier target less than a day's sail away. It didn't take him long to make up his mind: he ordered his ships to alter course for the west, and at ten o'clock that Sunday night the raiding party reached Baltimore.

They anchored just outside the harbour in the calm summer twilight, out of sight of the town at the mouth of a little inlet called the Eastern Hole. Fired up and keen for action, Murad himself led a small reconnaissance party, ordering his men to wrap sacking round their oars to deaden the sound of their rowing and taking as his guide not James Hackett, but Edward Fawlett, who clearly also knew Baltimore well. According to the official report of the incident, Fawlett 'piloted them all along the shore, and showed them how the town did stand, relating unto them where the most able men had their abode'.[14]

They were gone for more than two hours. Aboard the two ships, janissaries and corsairs waited in silence, listening for the shouts or the barking of dogs or the popping of muskets which would tell them their captain had been discovered. It was after midnight before Murad returned.

'We are in a good place', he told them with a smile. 'We shall make a bon voyago.'[15]

The water lapped against the shore in the darkness, and Baltimore slept.

At two o'clock on the morning of Monday 20 June, the pirates came ashore at the cove. There were 230 of them in all: eccentrically dressed European renegades, ragged Christian slaves and fearsome janissaries with drooping moustaches. Most carried muskets and scimitars. Some brought firebrands to set light to the thatched roofs of the little houses; others had iron bars to break down their doors.

The raiders ran up the pebbly beach in the darkness as quickly and quietly as they could and stationed themselves in groups of nine or ten outside the first houses. Then they waited.

But only for a matter of seconds. At a word from Murad, hell came to Baltimore, as the pirates smashed their way simultaneously

A Barbary Coast raïs, a corsair captain

into every home in the cove, screaming at the tops of their voices. Bleary-eyed, bewildered and half-asleep, families were punched and kicked and dragged out into the street, where the flames from the torches and the flickering light thrown by burning buildings showed them a scene beyond their nightmares. English renegades in Murad's crew were ordering them down to the boats in their own language, but others used *lingua franca*, Turkish, Arabic, perhaps even Gaelic. All used the unmistakeable language of violence and intimidation. People were milling around in the dark, crying, begging on their knees, calling for their children. One of the townspeople, a heavily pregnant woman named Joan Broadbrook, was separated from her husband in the confusion. He managed to escape inland; Joan was taken along with their two small children. John Davys put up a fight; he was killed. Timothy Curlew tried to defend his wife; he was killed, too, and his wife was taken. William Gunter was away from home that night: when he returned he found his home in ruins and no sign of his wife or their seven sons.

We know nothing about these people except for some names recorded in a tally of the lost after the raiders had gone: Bessie

Flood and her son; Bess Peeters' daughter; Richard Lorye, his wife, his sister and four children; John Harris, his wife, his mother, three children and a maid. There were ninety-nine in all.

Murad wasn't done with Baltimore yet. A dozen or so men were detached to herd his victims down to the boats, while James Hackett – who had come ashore with the corsairs and was playing his part as local guide with rather too much enthusiasm – led the pirates up towards the main part of the town, which lay about 500 yards away along a narrow coastal track. Like a good general, the pirate captain secured his line of retreat by deploying sixty musketeers to guard the track, while he and the remaining force of about 130 advanced into the town and began smashing their way into house after house.

Fugitives from the cove had got there before them. Although they broke into forty homes they only found another ten settlers; the rest had fled into the darkness or taken shelter behind the walls of the Fort of Jewels. Further up the hillside someone took a potshot at them; someone else began pounding a drum to warn the neighbourhood.

That was enough for Murad, who wasn't interested in becoming involved in a siege or a gunfight. He ordered his men back down to the cove. As quickly as they could, they pushed off the crowded little boats and rowed into the bay. Before daybreak they were aboard their ships and preparing to hoist their sails, while their bruised and frightened new captives – 22 men, 33 women and 54 children, 109 in all – were put below decks with the rest.

By sunrise the whole countryside was alive with fear and rumour. The mayor of Baltimore, Joseph Carter, scribbled a note to Sir William Hull, the deputy vice admiral at Leamcon:

> This last night, a little before day, came two Turk men of war of about 300 tons, and another of about 150, with a loose boat to set their men ashore, and they have carried away of our townspeople, men, women and children, one hundred and eleven, and two more are slain. The ships are at present going westward.[16]

The pirates were heading towards Leamcon and Crookhaven. Carter begged Hull to warn people.

At the same time the shocked burgesses of Baltimore dispatched a messenger cross-country to Castlehaven, ten miles to the east. A merchant ship was lying at anchor in Castlehaven harbour, and they pleaded with its master to set out in pursuit of the pirates. He could not be persuaded. The news of the raid was taken on to the Lord President of Munster, Sir William St Leger, at Mallow; and to Captain Hooke at Kinsale. On the Tuesday Sir William Hull reported (wrongly, as it happened) that the Turks were still in sight, plying off the south-west tip of Cork and waiting for more of their number to arrive for an attack on the returning Newfoundland fishing fleet later in the summer. St Leger urged Hooke to give chase. The burgesses of Baltimore urged Hooke to give chase. Everyone urged Hooke to give chase.

The *Fifth Whelp* was one of two naval pinnaces charged with scouring the seas around Ireland for pirates. The other, the *Ninth Whelp*, was commanded by Sir Thomas Button. The valiant but venal veteran of the 1620 Algiers expedition was still admiral to the Irish coast, and was supposed to patrol the Irish Sea while Hooke looked after St George's Channel and the western seas. However, Button spent most of his time ashore, leaving command of the *Ninth Whelp* to his lieutenant (and nephew) Will Thomas, while he concentrated on extracting money from the Admiralty. His current stratagem involved contracting to supply both *Whelp*s himself, but keeping Hooke on short, poor-quality rations and pocketing the difference. The previous October he had rather splendidly informed the Secretary to the Admiralty that he was too ill to travel and suggested that perhaps the pay and supplies due to both *Whelp*s might be sent directly to him at his house in Cardiff.

As a result of all this, Francis Hooke was engaged in an acrimonious dispute with Button, firing off letters of complaint to anyone in government who might listen. On 10 June 1631, only ten days before the Baltimore raid, he had written to Lord Dorchester: 'Victual goes through so many hands before it reaches us that we are made poor to make others rich. If only I could get the right to victual my own ship, I will engage my own life that the King's service will not be impeded in the future as it has been in the past.'[17] He was supposed to be in Limerick to escort a fleet of corn ships, he said. But as things stood, he felt unable to leave Kinsale unless he got some decent victuals on board.

Those victuals still hadn't arrived by the time of the raid. And so, unfortunately for Captain Hooke's subsequent career – and even more unfortunately for the Baltimore captives – he chose this moment to make a stand. For four days he refused point-blank to sail. When he finally did set out from Kinsale, there was no sign of Murad. Button remarked piously to the Admiralty on 'how dishonourable and how unchristianlike a thing it is, that these Turks should dare to do these outrages and unheard-of villainies upon his Majesty's coasts, by reason of the weakness of the guards'.[18]

Murad had little use for old people – they had no value. Before he hoisted sail for Algiers he sent ashore an elderly man and woman, Old Osbourne and Alice Heard. Edward Fawlett, James Hackett and another, unidentified, Dungarvan fisherman went with them.

Murad kept his promises.

They hanged James Hackett at the next assize. He and Fawlett were picked up and interrogated soon after being put ashore; and while the Englishman convinced the authorities that whatever he did to aid the pirates he did under duress, Hackett was not so lucky. The Lord Justices of Ireland, the Earl of Cork and Viscount Loftus, who shared the post of chief governor at the time, were of the opinion that he had 'expressed much disloyalty and dis-affection in bringing them [to Baltimore], when it appeared plainly that he might have put them into other harbours where they might have been taken, and so the mischief which happened might have been prevented'.[19] They made it clear to the judges of the Cork assize that the unfortunate man was to be arraigned and tried, that due process was to be observed, and that he should be found guilty. The judges did not disappoint: he was condemned and executed 'as an enemy to the state and country'.[20]

The raid caused outrage and alarm. The Justices of the Peace

for Pembroke begged the government to fortify Milford Haven
in south-west Wales, because they feared 'the accession of another
imminent peril by the Moors who have carried captives out of
Baltimore'.[21] The same month the Lord Justices of Ireland wrote
to the Privy Council with a list of the victims, describing the raid
as a disaster without precedent, even in wartime. It was an insult
to the King's honour, they said.

Charles I agreed. After two months of bickering, in which the
Lord Justices put the blame on Captain Hooke for refusing to stir
out of Kinsale at the crucial moment and on Button for staying
at home, and the Admiralty blamed the Justices for failing to
control the two sailors, and the two sailors blamed each other, on
23 August the King sent an impatient letter to Cork and Loftus,
urging them to discover exactly what had gone so wrong with
the defence of the realm that two Algerian pirate ships could sail
into an Irish harbour, abduct more than a hundred of his subjects
and sail away again without anyone doing anything to stop them.
'You shall inform us where the responsibility for this negligence
lies,' he told them. 'You blame the two captains appointed to guard
the coast, and they blame each other, but we are not satisfied with
these recriminations. You shall inform us about what was left
undone to guard against such a thing.'[22]

No one paid much attention to the captives. There was a rumour
that Murad was still hovering off the Irish coast; another that both
his ships had been taken by Spaniards off the Spanish coast. In fact
he made for the Straits and Algiers as soon as he left Munster. An
entry in a register of captives kept by the English consul at Algiers
records that on 28 July 'Morrato Fleming and his consort brought
from Baltimore in Ireland 89 women and children with 20 men'.[23]
(The figures were two out – there were 87 women and children.)
Two weeks later the consul informed London of the captives' arrival
and asked for money to pay their ransom. None came.

Autumn turned to winter, and in Dublin the two Lord Justices
were still pondering their response to the King's demand for
someone to blame. In January 1632 Lord Dorchester wrote from
Whitehall to say that Charles I was surprised not to have received
word from them regarding 'the Turkish piratical raid at Baltimore',
and this galvanised them into action. Their report went out of its
way to exonerate themselves. 'The attempt was so sudden as no

man did or with reason could expect it.'[24] The pirates were only in Baltimore for a few hours. Dublin was so far away. There were so many harbours in that part of West Cork that it was impossible to predict where a raid might take place or 'to guard every one of the places with competent strength to resist invasion'.

All of which was perfectly fair. But when it came to the *Whelps*, the Justices stretched the bounds of credibility. They did their best to put the blame for the raid squarely on Francis Hooke — 'we observed the *Fifth Whelp* oftentimes to lie idly and unprofitably in harbour while [your] subjects lay open to spoil at sea' — and announced disingenuously that only three weeks before the raid they had given Sir Thomas Button £200 to victual both ships, so how could Hooke pretend that want of victuals prevented him from leaving Kinsale in pursuit of Murad? Deliberately or not, that missed the point rather.

The year 1632 saw a flood of fear. The Algerians were bound to come back. Whitehall ordered more ships to be sent to Munster, in the expectation that 'the Turkish pirates who surprised some of his Majesty's subjects at Baltimore last summer will attempt the like again this next summer with greater forces and in divers places'.[25] A Captain Robert Innes urged the Irish authorities to ask the King for three or four Mediterranean-style galleys 'for preventing all piracies by sea and sudden depredations and landings of Turks and renegadoes'. Fast, manoeuvrable and versatile, they could be crewed by shaven-headed criminals who might be grateful to act as galley slaves for a fixed term in return for their liberty. Beacons were set up along the coast that year, and the President of Munster was authorised to arm the locals. 'But please take every care that arms are not put into the hands of disloyal people.'[26]

In Baltimore, the survivors put the pieces of their lives back together. A company of soldiers was stationed in the Fort of Jewels, and the mayor and burgesses offered to pay for the building of a blockhouse if the King would provide the ordnance for it. The burned-out houses in the cove were rebuilt — some of them, at least — but people drifted away, and the town never recovered. 'It is now a poor decayed fishing town', wrote one nineteenth-century historian, 'with not one tolerable house in it. Here are the ruins of an ancient castle of the O'Driscolls, [and] a few poor cabins.'[27] A Dutch renegade's accidental encounters with a Devon sailor and a Dungarvan fisherman had changed this corner of Ireland for ever.

In the winter of 1631–2 William Gunter, who had lost his wife and seven sons in the Baltimore raid, travelled to Dublin and then to London to plead for help from the government. The Lord Justices agreed he was a special object of pity and compassion. But no one acted, and Gunter never saw his family again. Like the rest of the captives, they simply vanished into Barbary.

A year later – and Murad Raïs answered the muezzin's call from the Djemaa el-Kebir as he always did, making his intention to pray and adopting the *qiyam*, both hands raised. How many of the Baltimore captives, strangers in a strange land, knelt as he did on their mats in a dusty North African city? How many of the Gunter boys chose to forget how they had once sat in the little church on the strand 1200 miles away and asked God to deliver them in the time of their tribulation, and now testified with Murad that there is no God but God and Mohammad is his messenger?

And who dares to blame them if they did?

9

Woeful Slavery:
William Rainborow's 1637
Expedition to Morocco

*S*ometimes, a slave escaped.

Francis Knight was an English merchant who was captured by Algerian corsairs in December 1631, six months after Murad's raid on Baltimore. He was twenty-three years old, and destined to spend the next five and a half years with a succession of masters in Algiers, 'that city fatal to all Christians'.[1]

In the summer of 1637 he was sold – for the fourth time in less than six years – to an Italian renegade, 'Ali Bitshnin, as a galley slave. 'Ali was a powerful figure in Algiers: 'one of the greatest slave-merchants that Barbary ever produced', said John Morgan in his eighteenth-century *Complete History of Algiers*.[2] He was also an ambitious corsair admiral, and in May 1638 Knight found himself embarked as an oarsman in a combined expedition of sixteen Algerian and Tunisian galleys which set out for Italy, with his master as commander.

With flags, standards and streamers blowing in the breeze, the fleet grouped at La Goulette and sailed up into the Tyrrhenian Sea, past volcanic Stromboli (where several of the inhabitants were so frightened at the sight of the Turks that they ran straight into the 'affrighting fires perpetually burning'[3]) and along the Calabrian coast, before doubling back through the Strait of Messina and into the Adriatic. They wrought havoc as they went, kidnapping hundreds of terrified citizens – including a bishop and fifteen nuns 'whom they prostituted to their lust'[4] – and destroying isolated farmsteads, small villages and big towns. Encountering no resistance at all, they burned fishing boats, slaughtered horses and cattle and laid waste to fields of corn. 'Thus was Italy the eye of Christendom infested by these rovers,' said Knight ruefully.[5]

In October a Venetian fleet caught up with 'Ali Bitshnin's galleys off the coast of Albania, and the corsairs were forced to seek refuge in the heavily fortified Ottoman garrison of Valona (modern-day Vlora), 'Ali persuading the governor of the castle to defend his men from the pursuing infidels, even though the raid was very definitely not sanctioned by the Sublime Porte. Fearing at one stage that the Venetians might storm ashore and capture their slaves, 'Ali and his captains placed them in one of the castle's towers, 1500 men, women and children 'all lying 10 and 10 in chains, [in] a place as dark as pitch, and a foot thick in dust'.[6] 'Ali eventually escaped inland, taking the Algerians, the Tunisians and all the slaves who could still walk with him. Among those left behind because they were too sick to travel was Francis Knight.

'God that had preserved us in so many inevitable dangers', recalled Knight in the account he wrote of his captivity, 'did also restore some of us to more than an ordinary strength of body . . . No sooner were we able to stand upon our legs, but we are studious how to bring to pass our liberty.'[7] On Saturday 22 October 1638, their Turk jailer went to a neighbouring town for the day, and while he was away the prisoners managed to unchain themselves, 'and the locks again so put in as to be taken out with our fingers'. Soon after midnight Knight and twelve others – a cosmopolitan bunch which consisted of three more Englishmen, a Welshman, a Jersey man, two Frenchmen, a Spaniard, a Majorcan, a Neapolitan, a Greek and a Maltese boy – slipped out of their chains while the jailer was sleeping. 'What became of our keeper I cannot tell,' Knight said a little uneasily. 'My consorts told me they had not done him any violence.'[8]

The fugitives took bread and water, and a rope that they used to scale the walls of the castle. Then they walked along the shore for a couple of miles in the darkness until they came on two little boats pulled up on the beach. They stove in the planks of one, and took the other out to sea, rowing for two nights and a day until they finally reached Venetian-held Corfu, about eighty miles south of Valona. Greek Orthodox monks sheltered them, and eventually they were brought before the governor of the island, who gave them passes to board a galley bound for Venice. From there Knight took passage on a Bristol merchant ship, the *Charles*, arriving in England in 1639, and the following year he published the story of his seven years' captivity, in the hope that it would rally support for 'my poor country-men, groaning under the merciless yoke of Turkish thraldom'.[9]

An opportunist escape from captivity like Knight's was unusual, but not unique. The master–slave relationship on the Barbary Coast was not at all clear, and those victims of piracy who were determined to find their way home sometimes exploited this ambiguity. In 1634 or 1635, for example, an English sailor named John Dunton was captured off Land's End in the *Little David*, which was bound for Virginia with fifty-seven men, women and children aboard. They were all taken to Salé and sold, including Dunton and his young son. Soon afterwards Dunton's Algerian master invested in a slaving expedition setting out from Salé for the south coast of England, and he sent Dunton as pilot, keeping the little boy behind in Algiers. The captain of the vessel was a Frieslander, John Rickles, who was also a slave; so was the gunner, Jacob Cornelius, and two other Dutch crewmen. The rest of the crew were Moors.

As they approached England, Dunton and the Dutchmen agreed they would try to bring the ship into port. They captured an English fishing boat with nine crew 'with intention to make a party against the Moors' and when they reached the Isle of Wight, Rickles called on the Europeans 'to stand up for their lives and liberties, whereupon they drove the Moors into the hold'.[10] They hoisted a white flag, hung the Salé colours over the stern into the water and sailed into port to give themselves up.

The ambiguities didn't end there. There was some question as to their real motives in taking the fishing boat, one of whose crewmen leaped overboard and drowned; and at their trial in

Winchester at the end of October 1636, the Dutchmen were
consistently referred to as renegados rather than slaves, and admon-
ished by the judge to repent their apostasy. At one point Captain
Rickles collapsed in a faint at the bar, 'which was occasioned, as
he himself stated, and as was conceived by the standers-by, seeing
the sweat run down his face ere he fell, by the consideration of
the foulness of his sin being laid open to him'.[11] Pirates who were
apprehended by the authorities, or who had simply had enough
of the life and came home, often claimed they had been enslaved
and forced into a live of piracy by their owners; and unless anyone
was found to bear witness against them, it was hard to prove they
were lying.

Rickles, Dunton and the other Europeans were all acquitted of
piracy, while the Moors were convicted and sentenced to death.
Two of them offered to convert to Christianity if it would save
their lives; others hinted that their comrades back home in Salé
would willingly exchange them for Christian slaves. The Europeans asked that none of the Moors should be allowed to go free,
in case word of what had happened got back to Barbary and their
countrymen suffered as a result. Dunton, though, pleaded with
the court to be given one of the Moors so that he could exchange
him for his ten-year-old son in Algiers. He also produced petitions from local fishermen who had had their own children and
friends taken, to the same purpose. They were all refused.

Exchange was the accepted way of liberating victims of piracy,
as it was any captive or prisoner of war. In the same year that
Dunton and the others seized their chance to escape, Charles I
received an anonymous letter proposing that idle and lascivious
women should be exchanged with the Turks for their male captives,
'so that one harlot might redeem half a dozen captives that are
made slaves to fulfil the lustful desires of the heathen Turks'.[12] (The
notion that Turks used men to gratify their sexual desires merely
because they couldn't find a suitable woman suggests the writer
was woefully ignorant of human sexuality. Or that he was a sailor.)
Tit-for-tat expeditions to capture sailors, fishermen or coastal
villagers who could in turn be exchanged for sailors, fishermen
and coastal villagers captured by the other side played a big part
in perpetuating the cycle of Christian–Moslem violence all round
the Mediterranean basin throughout the seventeenth century.

In general, citizens of Catholic Europe who had the misfortune to be taken by pirates had more chance of getting home than their Protestant counterparts, partly because there was more traffic between the nations which bordered the Mediterranean, and partly because ever since the Crusades, when the need arose to rescue Christians taken prisoner by the Saracens, the Catholic Church had operated two religious orders whose *raison d'être* was the redemption of captives held in the Islamic world. The clerical Order of Trinitarians, founded in France about 1193, and the lay Order of Mercedarians, which was founded in Barcelona twenty-five years later, worked extensively along the Barbary Coast, the former tending to send its monks to Tunis and Algiers, and the latter concentrating on Salé, Tetouan and the other Moroccan strongholds.

Redemptist friars negotiate to ransom European slaves

Mercedarian friars gathered goods, livestock, Moslem prisoners and, most importantly, money to ransom Christian slaves. They collected door-to-door, delivering sermons in churches and marketplaces, always emphasising the cruel treatment meted out to Christians by Moors and Turks, and the terrible possibility that captives might lose their souls by converting to Islam. When enough money had been collected to mount an expedition and all the necessary safe-conduct permissions had been obtained, those friars who had been chosen as redeemers set out, carrying a banner painted with an image of Christ's descent into limbo. If the expedition was successful, redeemers and redeemed made a triumphal entry into their city accompanied by all the local clergy, with the redemption banner at the head of a grand procession, followed by the redeemed all wearing the white Mercedarian scapular, and with the redeemers bringing up the rear.

The monks and friars who worked with the redemptist orders were dedicated men who cheerfully put their own lives at risk to save others. Unless it was absolutely impossible, they always travelled to Barbary themselves, rather than sending proxies; and if they found captives who were in danger of converting to Islam and there was not enough money to redeem them, they sometimes stayed behind as hostages in their place. But they weren't all that concerned about the saving of Protestant souls, and British victims of piracy had, by and large, to look to less formalised methods for their redemption.

Ransom was one; and licensed collections were regularly taken in British churches to buy the freedom of slaves. In 1643, for example, relatives successfully petitioned Parliament for collections to be held over a two-month period in churches in London, Westminster and the surrounding suburbs to raise money to ransom men who had been 'taken by Turkish pirates, carried to Algier, and there now remain in miserable captivity, having great fines imposed upon them'.[13] But poor private citizens were at the mercy of a government bureaucracy which moved very slowly and took its cut at every conceivable opportunity. Collectors took a percentage; officials at the Admiralty, which was supposed to organise the payment of the ransoms, took a percentage; consuls and merchants and the middlemen who brokered the handover took a percentage. And what money was left was often diverted towards securing the freedom of the more influential captives, leaving common sailors nothing but dreams of ever seeing their wives and families again.

Estimates of the numbers of European slaves in Barbary varied wildly from one observer to another. In 1634 the Trinitarian Pierre Dan reckoned that 32,000 were being held in Tunis and Algiers. Francis Knight, on the other hand, put the number of Christians 'groaning under the yoke of Turkish tyranny' in Algiers alone at nearly twice that number.[14] Inevitably, such rough estimates are less than reliable. But the threat was real enough, with corsair raiding parties making their presence felt right along the south coast of England. In September 1635 the governor of Pendennis Castle, Sir Nicholas Slanning, reported that six Turkish warships were off Land's End lying in wait for the return of the Newfoundland fishing fleet. 'This news terrifies the country,' he said. And well it might – a few days later the mayor of Dartmouth reported that two ships on the way home from Newfoundland had been taken by Turkish pirates less than ten miles off the Lizard. Sixty seamen were carried off 'to increase the number of the western captives'.[15] A thousand poor women petitioned Charles I to send an ambassador to Salé to plead for the release of their husbands, who were in 'woeful slavery, enduring extreme labour, want of sustenance, and grievous torments'.[16]

By 1636 there was a definite air of panic among the merchants and fishing fleets who operated out of the south coast ports. Shipowners from Exeter, Dartmouth, Plymouth, Barnstaple, Southampton, Poole, Weymouth and Lyme Regis got together and complained to the King that over the past few years they had lost an alarming eighty-seven vessels to piracy, which along with their cargos were worth £96,700. In addition, 1160 English seamen were kept 'in miserable captivity'; and the burden of caring for the wives and children of those captives was becoming intolerable. The petitioners begged that the Admiralty would issue letters of marque for taking the pirates, as well as mounting regular patrols 'of some nimble ships' to protect coastal waters.[17]

The raiders were back that summer. Another forty-two seamen were captured off the Lizard, and two fishing boats were taken by a Turkish man-of-war in full view of the fort at Plymouth. In September 1636, with the Newfoundland fleet due home at any time, the same group of merchants petitioned the King again, complaining there were now so many pirates about that 'seamen refuse to go [to sea], and fishermen refrain to take fish, whereby customs and imposts are lessened, merchandising is at a stand, petitioners are much impoverished, and many of them utterly undone'.[18] Plymouth organised monthly collections to ransom captives, and in October the Puritan Charles Fitzgeffry preached three sermons before the mayor of Plymouth urging compassion towards 'our brethren and country-men who are in miserable bondage in Barbary'. Taking as his text Hebrews 13:3, 'Remember them that are in bonds, as bound with them', Fitzgeffry's impressive rhetoric railed with an alliterative flourish against 'miscreant Mahometans' and urged his congregation to ponder the recent 'tragical transportation of our brethren from Baltimore into that Babylon, Barbary'.[19] Praising the men who had died trying to defend their families, he was in no doubt that they had the happier fate: 'Better it is to fall by the hands, than into the hands of those tyrannous Turks, whose saving is worse than slaying.'[20]

The miscreant Mahometans currently causing such havoc for West Country merchants and shipowners were the Salé rovers of Morocco. In 1613, during the last Spanish expulsion of the Moriscos, a group of Moriscos from Estremadura in western Spain found their way to Salé on the Atlantic coast of Morocco, where Mawlay Zidan allowed them to settle in a decrepit old fortress at the mouth of the Bou Regreg river. Taking their name from their home town of Hornacha in Estremadura, the Hornacheros repaired the fort and came to an informal arrangement with Mawlay Zidan, whereby they took care of his defences along that particular stretch of the North Atlantic coast in return for being allowed to make their living as privateers. Within a decade the Morisco settlement at 'New Sallee' had attracted several thousand Moslem exiles (and several hundred European renegades and outlaws), and when Mawlay Zidan died in 1627 the Hornacheros decided they were powerful enough to dispense with the patronage of his ineffectual successor, Abu Marwan Abd al-Malik. Encouraged by a charismatic religious leader named Mohammad al-Ayyashi, who was simultaneously waging a holy war against the Spanish and making a play for control of the north-western corner of Morocco, they broke away and set up their own small republic, presided over by a Grand Admiral and his council.

The Hornacheros signed a treaty with England in 1627, each side agreeing not to engage in acts of piracy against the other.

But the treaty broke down four years later, when the *William and John* of London got into a fight with a Salé man-of-war off Cape St Vincent. Each side blamed the other for the incident, but the end result was that the Salé rovers no longer felt any compunction about preying on English shipping.

In 1626 Trinity House had reckoned there were 1200 or 1400 English captives at Salé, all or mostly taken in the English Channel. 'When the ships are full of the King's subjects, the pirates return to Sallee, sell the captives in the common market, and then return for more.'[21] Ten years later, and five years after the breakdown of the treaty with the Hornacheros, a ransomed English sailor reported that ten Salé men-of-war were preparing to set out for the English coast, and the authorities at Plymouth were told that 200 Christian captives were landed at Salé on one single day. 'In times past,' complained West Country merchants, 'only the pirates of Algiers sometimes came into the English and Irish channels; now the pirates of Sallee are become so numerous, strong, and nimble in their ships, and are so well piloted into these channels by English and Irish captives' that no one dared put to sea.[22]

Something had to be done. The Salé corsairs of the Bou Regreg estuary were disrupting English trade, selling English citizens in markets from Tetouan to Tunis and putting the fear of Mohammad's God into coastal communities throughout the West Country. In the summer of 1636, pirates were seen lurking in the Severn estuary, and reports of losses started to pour in from ports along the coasts of Dorset, Devon and Cornwall. John Crewkerne, a representative sent from Weymouth to petition Charles I for help, told the King to his face that coastal patrols weren't enough, a view that (fortunately for Crewkerne) was seconded at the meeting by Archbishop Laud, who assured the merchant that 'whilst he had breath in his body he would do his utmost endeavour to advance so necessary and consequential a business'.[23]

The merchants of Exeter argued that as well as providing regular patrols, the King should issue letters of marque to allow suspicious vessels to be stopped and searched for 'supplies of munition and provisions for war'; that Exeter and the other western ports should be allowed to commission a ship or ships of their own to attack pirates in the Channel; and, most importantly, that the King should send a punitive expedition to mount a blockade of

Salé and to intercept those pirates who were out on the cruise as they returned home. Four ships of 300 tons each and two pinnaces could mount a blockade that would ruin the corsairs within a year.

Weymouth and Exeter weren't the only ports to propose direct action against the pirates of Salé. In June Captain Giles Penn, a Bristol merchant who traded regularly with Morocco, approached the Chancellor of the Exchequer, Sir Francis Cottington, and suggested the King should mount an expedition against 'the heathen moors of Sallee'.[24] Penn was well acquainted with the complex political scene in Morocco – he may have been acting at the behest of the sultan in Marrakesh, who saw an English naval blockade of Salé as an inexpensive way of bringing down the Hornachero rebels – and Cottington gave Penn enough encouragement for him to take his proposal further. In October 1636 he wrote to the Secretary of State, Sir Francis Windebank, and in December to the Lords of the Admiralty, each time setting out the requirements for a successful venture. The expeditionary force should consist of 800 men in four ships and two pinnaces, with 'able surgeons, doctors of physic, and good divines'.[25] Shirts and jackets should be provided for the poorer seamen, and the force should take some captured Moors along as exchange prisoners. Penn sketched out the political situation on the Bou Regreg: there was growing tension between the rovers in their fortress at New Salé and their erstwhile ally, the holy man Mohammad al-Ayyashi, who was based across the river in Old Salé. He ended by urging the fleet to set sail before the end of January. Otherwise the corsairs would leave on their spring cruise before it arrived.

And because it had all been his idea, and because private gain and public office were inseparable in seventeenth-century culture, Captain Penn asked the Admiralty to make him commander of the expedition – and 'surveyor of all goods taken in reprisal during the voyage'.[26]

The political will to suppress the activities of the Salé pirates and to secure the release of their English captives was there. And so, for a change, was the cash to fund an expedition. The writ for the first ship-money levy of 1634, which was directed solely towards the maritime counties, stated that one reason for its imposition was the need to finance action against 'thieves, pirates, and robbers of the sea'.[27] When writs, now extended to the inland counties, were issued in 1636 to fund the ship-money fleets for the following year, nearly £190,000 was collected. As resistance to the ship money began to grow, it would do the King no harm to produce a very public demonstration of how well that money was being spent.

At four o'clock on the afternoon of Friday 24 March 1637 three English ships anchored off New Salé and began a blockade of the harbour. There was a 400-ton merchantman, the *Mary*, which had been chartered for the voyage; and two 600-ton men-of-war, the *Antelope* and the *Leopard*. John Dunton, the English captive who had helped to steer his captors to the Isle of Wight and justice the previous year, had got a place as master aboard the *Leopard*, the expedition's flagship, still hoping for news of his little boy in Algiers.

Giles Penn was nowhere to be seen. Having accepted his advice and his proposal, the Lords of the Admiralty decided he wasn't the man to command the fleet, in spite of his plaintive assertions that he had no equal when it came to a knowledge of the Moroccan people. Their choice as 'general of the south squadron of the Salé fleet',[28] and Dunton's captain aboard the *Leopard*, was William Rainborow, a 49-year-old professional mariner and shipowner. One of the most respected figures in the English maritime world, Rainborow was a past Master of Trinity House, an adviser to the government on naval matters and the flag captain to the Lord High Admiral, the Earl of Northumberland, when the latter commanded the King's fleet in the Channel in the summer of 1636.

It was probably Northumberland who put his flag captain's name forward for Salé. Rainborow was known as a man who understood maritime warfare, and he had direct experience of dealing with corsairs: back in 1618 he had earned a commendation from the Levant Company for his service against pirates in the Mediterranean. And in 1628 he achieved considerable renown when, as the master (and co-owner) of the *Sampson*, a heavily armed merchantman that sailed back and forth between London and Istanbul for the Levant Company, he fought off an attack by four galleys manned by the Knights of Malta. The battle, which was 'as sharp as hath been upon these seas in many years', lasted for seven hours, during which time the pirates scored 120 hits on the vessel's hull, masts and rigging.[29] The English ambassador Sir Thomas Roe, returning home aboard the *Sampson* after more than six years at the Sultan's court, narrowly missed death when he was knocked flat by a flying piece of timber. (His wife's parrot was not so lucky – it was killed by a shot that smashed into the cabin.) But Rainborow, 'who behaved himself with brave courage and temper', gave as good as he got, and the galleys eventually retreated with the loss of 300 men. The *Sampson* lost the parrot, two sheep and one unnamed passenger.

Rainborow was a good leader, a good sailor and a good choice to command this expedition. But a series of events beyond his control meant that things were going badly. His fleet arrived off Salé seriously under strength. The *Hercules*, another merchant ship that had been chartered for the expedition, had lost its mainmast in a storm off the coast of Portugal and been forced to put in at Lisbon for repairs. And the *Leopard*, the *Antelope* and the *Mary* should have been supported by two 300-ton pinnaces, the *Providence* and the *Expedition*, specially designed for fast inshore work, intercepting any pirate galleys that might try to slip in and out of harbour by keeping to the shallow coastal waters where the big men-of-war couldn't follow. But neither vessel had been launched by the time Rainborow was ready to sail, and he made the decision to leave without them, fearful that, as Penn had pointed out, the corsairs might be gone when he reached Salé. And he was right not to wait: French and Spanish slaves who swam for the *Leopard* and their freedom when they saw the English fleet arrive told Rainborow that the renegade captains of Salé were on the point of setting off for the English coast on a slaving raid.

The harbour at New Salé was behind a small headland at the mouth of the river, out of sight and out of range of the English guns; and, for the moment at least, the corsairs had little to fear from their enemy. When the governor of New Salé, 'Abd Allah ben 'Ali el-Kasri, heard that the three ships which had appeared off the coast were English, his response was defiant: 'What care I

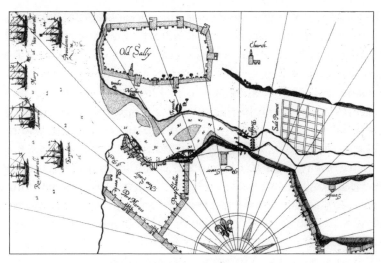

Rainborow's fleet stationed at the mouth of the Bou Regreg

for the King of England's ships, or all the Christian kings in the world? Am I not King of Salé?' And his reaction to the letter that Rainborow sent in to the citadel, demanding the release of all Christian slaves and 'satisfaction for ships and goods, and for all those Christians that they sold away both to Algier and other countries before we came here' was simple and, for the English, frustrating. He did absolutely nothing.[30]

Rainborow deployed the *Antelope* and the *Mary* to the north and south of the estuary, while he took the central position in the *Leopard*. The loss of the *Hercules* was inconvenient, but the absence of the two pinnaces was much more serious, as the English found out three days into their blockade, when a corsair arrived from Algiers. By staying close in to the shore, he sailed straight into harbour in the middle of the afternoon, notwithstanding that the *Antelope*, which had to stand off in deep water, 'did shoot above 100 pieces of ordnance at that ship'.[31]

There was no way of knowing when the other half of the fleet would turn up. (The *Hercules* sailed into Salé Road in mid-April, nearly four weeks after Rainborow and the others; the two pinnaces didn't arrive until the middle of June.) But as Rainborow pondered the unpleasant prospect of sitting helplessly at anchor while all the thirty or so vessels in the Salé pirate fleet slipped away in ones and twos, the watch on the *Leopard* reported that fighting had broken out along the shores of the Bou Regreg between the inhabitants of Old Salé, the walled port that lay on the northern bank of the river, and the corsair community on the south bank. It was more than just a skirmish, too: the battle lasted all day, 'and a great many men and horses were killed and hurt'.[32]

That evening a white flag of truce appeared on the ramparts of Old Salé. Rainborow dispatched a party of men in longboats, heavily armed and wary. They returned with two hostages, a request for a surgeon to treat the wounded and a letter from Mohammad al-Ayyashi, the rebel leader and holy man who had encouraged the corsairs to set up their own republic in the first place, and who was now using the old town as his headquarters. His hopes of enlisting the pirates of New Salé in his holy war to drive the Spanish out of their Moroccan enclaves had gone sour – their political and religious aspirations didn't match up to their passion for profit and privateering – and from taking the occasional potshot at each other across the Bou Regreg, the two communities had graduated to skirmishes and now to pitched battle.

Rainborow realised that this situation could work to his advantage. He agreed to al-Ayyashi's request for medical help and, while his surgeon's mate was tending the wounded, he opened peace negotiations with 'the Saint', as the English called the Moslem holy man.

This infuriated and scared the New Salé pirates. They accused al-Ayyashi and his men of 'turning Christian' – an ironic twist to the familiar English insult – and on 20 April they launched another assault on Old Salé. 'The two towns . . . were in fight very hard one against another,' wrote John Dunton, 'and did kill a great many men on both sides. We did stand and look upon them in our ships as they were at fight.'[33] The next day the Saint, convinced now that his enemy's enemy must be his friend, invited Rainborow's senior gunner ashore to inspect his fortifications, telling him 'he should have all the old town at his command, as castles, forts, and guns, and men, and all to lay siege and battery against the new town'.[34]

The *Leopard*'s gunner, Richard Simpson, had combat experience stretching back at least to the Duke of Buckingham's ill-fated 1627 expedition to La Rochelle, where by his own account he 'made many a shot . . . before any other'.[35] Now he was sent ashore with a couple of others to find suitable emplacements on the northern bank from which the fleet's heaviest guns could be brought to bear on New Salé – and on the corsair fleet, still at anchor in the shallow waters of the Bou Regreg. The English gunners mounted four of al-Ayyashi's guns on the ramparts of Old Salé and provided their new allies with shot, barrels of powder and expertise. Sending for the best gunners on each ship, Rainborow 'appointed every gunner and his company his day, and to take power and shot with them, and so to go to work with their ships to sink and burn them all'.[36]

Three of the corsair men-of-war were sunk the first day, and ten more in the coming weeks. The walls of Old Salé and New Salé were about 750 yards apart and, to achieve greater accuracy with their shot, English sailors excavated a huge defensive earthwork on the sandy northern river bank, half the distance from the enemy's city, where they set up a platform and mounted their heaviest guns.

Day in, day out the guns boomed, and the heavy shot rained down on ships and storehouses and homes. Timbers splintered and cracked. Plumes of dirt and dust filled the air. Dense clouds of smoke drifted across the river as raiding parties sent by al-Ayyashi set fire to the corsairs' corn in the fields. Ships that tried to slip in or out of harbour were intercepted or sunk or driven on to the shore, where the Old Salétians captured or killed survivors. Slaves ran for their freedom whenever the opportunity presented itself. Food began to run short. Pirates slipped away and deserted to the other side. And at the beginning of June those who were left in the city mounted a coup. The governor 'Abd Allah ben 'Ali el-Kasri was deposed, and the rebels sent him in chains to the new sultan at Marrakesh, the eighteen-year-old Mohammad ech-Cheikh el-Ashgar, in the hope that now they were at war with his enemy al-Ayyashi he would come to their aid, or at least intercede with the English. Dunton noted ruefully that although the English fleet had intelligence that this was about to happen, 'it was such a night, and so dark, and such a fog, that our boats could not meet with him'.[37]

A week later, on 13 June, the arrival of the two pinnaces and the sight of their crews using their oars to chase after a ship that was trying to get into harbour, as though they were swift Mediterranean galleys, alarmed the beleaguered pirates so much that they sent a delegation out to the *Leopard* to sue for peace. But Rainborow maintained his demand that the pirates not only surrender all their Christians, but also provide adequate compensation 'for all that ever had been taken by them', and the negotiations broke down.[38]

Unlike the blockade, which was maintained with awesome efficiency. On 3 July the *Leopard* forced a Salé man-of-war ashore, with the death of fifty-five Moors and Turks; on 12 July the *Providence* chased another into the arms of al-Ayyashi's men, who captured and killed its crew of eighty-five. Ships that came to trade at New Salé were all turned back. They included the *Neptune* of Amsterdam, which arrived with a cargo of gunpowder that, her captain claimed rather unconvincingly, was really intended for rebels further down the coast and not for the corsairs at all. Rainborow confiscated forty of the fifty-one barrels and sent the *Neptune* on its way.

On Thursday 27 July 1637, four months after the English fleet began its blockade, a Moroccan ship arrived off the coast of Salé. It brought a delegation from the young sultan. There was an English merchant named Robert Blake, who lived in Marrakesh and who had volunteered to act as interpreter; Mohammad el-Ashgar's personal representative; and, much to everyone's surprise, el-Kasri, the deposed ex-governor of New Salé. Instead of beheading el-Kasri, as the English had expected, the sultan had offered to restore him to office – but only if the corsairs would disband their republic and recognise Mohammad's authority, pay him a huge sum in customs duties which they had originally promised to collect on his behalf, and accede to all the English demands.

Rainborow's initial response was to bring el-Kasri aboard the *Leopard* and threaten to hang him, 'at which he trembled very much'.[39] On the Saturday, after talking with Blake, the besieged corsairs sent out thirteen Christian captives as a token of goodwill, and Rainborow finally agreed that el-Kasri and the sultan's official, or *qaid*, could enter New Salé to present terms to the besieged Moriscos. 'They desire to see whether you have any Moors amongst the renegadoes', Rainborow informed George Carteret, his vice admiral aboard the *Antelope*. 'If they say they be Moors, I pray let them have them. If they say they be Christians, I pray keep them.'[40]

The deal was done by Monday, and over the next three days another 293 slaves were handed over. 'They did make as much haste to bring our Christians aboard as they could,' wrote Dunton, 'because they would have us gone'.[41]

After four months the blockade was over. The English force suffered its share of casualties. One sailor had a leg blown off by the Moors while he was working on the gun platform on the exposed northern bank of the river. He survived, but others weren't so lucky. A member of the *Leopard*'s crew was shot in the head as the blockaders tried to set fire to two men-of-war that were leaving harbour. Two men from the *Hercules* were killed in the same action, both hit in the back by arrows; and thirty more were wounded in the arms and legs by small shot.

Against this, Rainborow had delivered a catastrophic blow to the Salé rovers, destroying more than a dozen ships and killing hundreds of men. By making alliances with both the Saint and the sultan (who remained implacable enemies to each other), he had completely destabilised the pirate republic. And if he hadn't managed to extract much in the way of compensation from New Salé, he *had* liberated its Christian captives. The final count was an impressive 348, comprising 302 English, Scottish and Irish, including 11 women; 27 Frenchmen, 8 Dutchmen and 11 Spaniards. The expedition was a tremendous success, by any standards. And there was more to come.

By 8 August 1637 all the freed slaves had been handed over. Rainborow sent off the *Antelope*, the *Hercules* and the two pinnaces, telling them to 'rove and range the coast of Spain, and to look for Turks' men-of-war'.[42] They were all back in England six weeks later, having cheerfully disregarded their instructions.

Meanwhile the *Leopard* and the *Mary*, reinforced by two supply ships which arrived from England days after the main fleet left for home, sailed down the coast to Safi, where Blake and the sultan's representative disembarked and set out for Mohammad's court at Marrakesh. They took with them Rainborow's son, one of his lieutenants, a couple of chastened representatives from the erstwhile corsair republic, and a mixture of ambitions and aspirations. Rainborow hoped that the delegation would secure the freedom of more British slaves, and that the sultan would undertake to suppress corsair bases on the Atlantic coast. Blake, who had commercial interests in Morocco, was trying to broker a trade agreement with England. The Moroccan *qaid* hoped for English aid against el-Ayyashi and other rebel leaders who were threatening the sultan's authority. At the very least, he looked to Charles I to put a stop to the activities of English merchants who happily traded guns to rebel strongholds further down the Atlantic coast at Essaouira, Agadir and Massa.

It was a month before the English party returned to Safi, and, when they did, they brought with them four Barbary horses, four hawks and sixteen English captives, all gifts from Sultan Mohammad to Charles I. They brought a draft treaty which confirmed the peace between England and Morocco. And they brought Mohammad's ambassador to the English court, a Portuguese renegade and his retinue of twenty-eight officials and servants. The sultan's letter to Charles I which accompanied them announced grandiloquently:

> We send to you the slave of our lofty abode and our emissary to you for sultanic purposes the favoured and most approved and noble and fortunate *qaid* Jawdar ben 'Abd Allah in the company of our servant the merchant Robert Blake . . . Our aforementioned slave has received from us that which he will deliver to you, so accept graciously what he will give to you and God (who is exalted) will fulfil the aims in going out and coming in.[43]

The sultan went on to urge King Charles to look kindly on Robert Blake, who had worked hard to broker the agreement. He ended on a particularly optimistic note. 'Your desires in this lofty territory will be fulfilled and your petitions all accepted and observed. We shall find none of them too difficult.'

At four in the afternoon of Wednesday 21 September, with a light wind and a calm sea, the *Leopard* hoisted its anchor and set sail for home.

As the shadows lengthened on a cold Sunday afternoon in November 1637, crowds of Londoners filled the narrow streets to watch a spectacular procession wend its way from Wood Street in the heart of the capital to the sprawling labyrinth that was the Palace of Whitehall. One of the City marshals led the way on horseback, accompanied by half a dozen servants who shouted and pushed people back, clearing a way through. Then came seven trumpeters, followed by four Moroccans in red livery. Each Moor led a fine Barbary horse covered with cloths of damask; two were equipped with saddles, bridles and stirrups 'plated over with massif gold of rare workmanship, esteemed each worth 1000 £.'[44] Next walked the sixteen freed slaves – the hawks that should have preceded them had been handed over to the King four days previously, because he feared 'their misusage from unskilful keepers'.[45] There were City captains with great plumes in their hats, ten Gentlemen of the Privy Chamber in black velvet (there should have been twelve, but two didn't turn up), and Charles I's master

The Moroccan ambassador to England, Jawdar ben 'Abd Allah

of ceremonies, Sir John Finet, who choreographed the entire procession.

But all eyes were on the figure who followed Finet. Flanked on his left by the Earl of Shrewsbury and on his right by Robert Blake rode Jawdar ben 'Abd Allah. His page walked beside him. One servant carried his scimitar, another had his slippers and part of his horse's golden harness. He was escorted by four footmen in blue livery and followed by eight more members of his household, 'Moors in their country habits on horseback'.[46]

The pageant marched slowly past the soaring Gothic walls of St Paul's Cathedral (covered in scaffolding to receive a classical facelift from Inigo Jones), and along Fleet Street, until it reached Temple Bar, where the Moroccan ambassador was met by a 400-strong contingent of Westminster's local militia, who formed up either side of the way as a guard of honour to escort him into Whitehall. There he was introduced to Charles I, and then to Henrietta Maria, whom he addressed in Arabic, interpreted by Blake. The four Barbary horses were presented to the King, along with the sixteen captives, and after a short private conference Jawdar ben 'Abd Allah returned through the darkness to his Wood Street lodging – this time in a royal coach, because it was so dark that he couldn't find his horse.

This spectacle was intended not only to honour the representative of a new and important ally, but also to provide a public display of English might, a loud proclamation of the Salé expedition's success against the pirates. From the moment Rainborow arrived in the Downs, his mission was hailed as a triumph. He was feted as a conquering hero. The King offered him a knighthood, which he turned down, accepting instead a gold chain and medal worth £300.

The procession through the streets of London by a symbolic group of freed slaves (most had been dropped off at Torbay in Devon as soon as the fleet reached England) was a first, and a vindication of the ship-money levy – as the King's ministers were quick to appreciate. 'This action of Salé is so full of honour', Thomas Wentworth told Archbishop Laud, 'that it should, me thinks, help much towards the ready and cheerful payment of shipping monies.'[47] Even Giles Penn was finally rewarded for having the idea in the first place: in December the King authorised him 'to be his Majesty's consul at Salé, and to execute that office by himself and his deputies in Morocco and Fez'.[48] John Dunton published an account of the expedition, mentioning sadly that his little boy in Algiers was now 'like to be lost for ever'.[49] Then he, too, disappeared for ever from the history books.

The ambassador stayed in London for six months, with the English treasury meeting his expenses to the tune of £25 per day while he and Blake ironed out the terms of the treaty with government ministers and City merchants. And he remained both spectator and actor in the King's self-congratulatory pageant. The great Twelfth Night revels hadn't taken place for three years: now they were reinstated. This year's masque, *Britannia Triumphans* by William Davenant and Inigo Jones, was a carefully orchestrated paean to 'Britanocles, the glory of the western world, [who] hath by his wisdom, valour, and piety, not only vindicated his own, but far distant seas, infested with pirates'.[50] While the French and Spanish ambassadors sulked because they hadn't received VIP invitations and squabbled over who had the better seats, the Master of Ceremonies made sure that Jawdar ben 'Abd Allah and his retinue were given prominent places in the new Masking House at Whitehall. They were, after all, part of the show.

Viscount Conway, a seasoned observer of court affairs, summed up the lavish reception given to the ambassador succinctly – and accurately. 'The reason of all', he wrote, 'is the shipping money.'[51]

10

The Yoke of Bondage:
A Slave's Story

'By break of day in the morning, we discovered three ships about three or four leagues to leeward.'[1]

The victims of Barbary Coast piracy produced dozens of captivity narratives. Most are harrowing. Some are heroic. The odd few are rather hateful. But everyone's story contains a sentence like this. The memory of fear is palpable, unstated, and common to all. The moment remains the same.

This particular moment, which came as the sun rose over the Atlantic Ocean on Saturday 10 August 1639, belongs to William Okeley, author of the most remarkable captivity narrative of them all. Okeley's ship, the *Mary* of London, was taking cloth and colonists to Providence Island, a settlement off the coast of present-day Nicaragua. The Providence Island Company was founded in 1629 by a group of English Puritan noblemen, who dreamed of creating a God-fearing sanctuary where Protestants could worship in their own way, free from interference by Church or state. They did, however, manage some interference of their own. In its short life Providence had already become notorious for its buccaneers, anti-Catholic crusaders who preyed on the Spanish silver fleet. As a hopeful Providence Island settler, Okeley was imbued with a fair amount of righteous Puritan xenophobia, ranting against Catholics, Turks, Jews, 'lying miracles', priests, friars, atheism, pride and impudence.[2]

When the pirates came into view that summer morning, the *Mary* was six days out from the Isle of Wight and travelling in convoy with two other vessels that were also making the crossing to the New World. Well out into the Atlantic by now and away from the corsairs' more obvious hunting grounds, she should have been safe.

The ship had suffered a run of bad luck ever since leaving Gravesend in June. For five frustrating weeks she lay becalmed in the Downs off the coast of Kent. Then, when the wind finally picked up and she was able to make her way around the south coast of England towards the Isle of Wight, the beer went sour. The crew had to throw it overboard and take in vinegar to mix with water for the rest of the voyage.

The *Mary* set off from the Isle of Wight on Sunday 4 August 1639 – and promptly ran aground on a sandbank, where she had to wait for the tide to lift her off. Rattled by their misfortunes, crew and passengers prayed for a fair wind – and reaped a whirl-wind six days later, in the shape of the three Algerian corsairs. 'God appoints it the moment when it should come about to blow us into the mouths of our enemies,' said Okeley.[3]

As soon as the as yet unidentified strangers were sighted, the masters of the English ships passed worried messages between them. They agreed that the best plan was to stay together, heave to and wait for the strangers to come up to them. The day wore on, the ships came closer and, even when it was obvious that they were pirates and steering a course towards them, the English resolved to stay and fight.

At dusk the corsairs were still a little way off, and the master of the *Mary* lost his nerve and gave the order to hoist sail. In the darkness the vessel almost managed to escape, but dawn saw the pirates closing fast. After a short fight in which six of the English were killed and others wounded, the pirates took control of the *Mary*. The survivors joined the crews and passengers from the other two vessels, both of which had been taken in the night. They were kept below deck in one of the corsairs' ships for five or six weeks, 'condoling of each other's miseries' in the stinking darkness and learning *lingua franca*.[4]

William Okeley's description of arriving in Algiers in chains reads disconcertingly like a page from a guidebook:

> Algiers is a city very pleasantly situated on the side of the hills overlooking the Mediterranean, which lies north of it, and it lifts up its proud head so imperiously, as if it challenged a sovereignty over those seas and expected tribute from all that shall look within the straits. It lies in the thirtieth degree of longitude and hath somewhat less than thirty-five degrees of north latitude. The city is considerably large, the walls being about three miles in compass, beautified and strengthened with five gates . . .[5]

The houses are fine, he says. The temples are magnificent. The castles are strong and the baths are stately.

But there is no such thing as a fair prison. And he at last admits that beautiful though Algiers is, 'in our eyes it was most ugly and deformed'.[6]

The prisoners spent their first night ashore in a 'deep, nasty cellar', one of the holding pens by the quay. The following morning they were herded en masse to the Hall of Audience at the palace and paraded in front of the *pasha*, Yûsuf II, who sat cross-legged on blue tapestry cushions in a gown of red silk and a great turban. The *pasha* had the right to one in every ten captives as his dividend (some accounts say one in eight, or even one in five) and, with ransom in mind, he usually chose those who seemed to be or claimed to be well born. Okeley was not, and he accompanied the remaining prisoners back to the bagnio, where they waited for market day.

It was a frightening time. On top of the disorientation and discomfort there was a dreadful apprehension as the prisoners remembered lurid tales of cruelty, male rape and forced conversion, of being beaten and tortured and made 'either to turn Turk or to attend their filthiness'.[7] Such things did happen. Slave-owners would deliberately mistreat new slaves before allowing them to write home for their ransom, just to give an added urgency to the pleas for money. Sodomy, both consensual and non-consensual, was more common in North Africa than in Britain, although not as ubiquitous as Europeans liked to maintain. And while most descriptions of Christian captives being tortured into converting to Islam rely on hearsay or are coloured by a strong element of anti-Islamic propaganda, there is no doubt that the more pious owners did bring pressure to bear on their slaves to become Moslems.

Okeley's induction into Algerian society was less dramatic than he expected, but still deeply humiliating. A few days after his encounter with the *pasha* he and the other prisoners were led out into the open market, or *bedestan*, where slaves and plundered goods were offered for sale. It was here, eight years earlier, that curious onlookers had watched as Murad Raïs's bewildered Baltimore captives were paraded up and down, had seen them clinging to each other and weeping as wives were taken from husbands and children separated from their parents.

A slave being flogged in Algiers

Now an old dealer with a staff marched each man up and down, while prospective purchasers poked and prodded. They examined Okeley's teeth – 'a good, strong set of grinders will advance the price considerably'.[8] They felt his arms and legs, and paid special attention to the state of his hands. Calluses were evidence that a man was used to labour, which was good; although, paradoxically, those with delicate or tender hands might command more money, since buyers 'will suspect some gentleman or merchant, and then the hopes of a good price of redemption makes him saleable'.[9]

When everyone had had a good look, the prisoners were made to sit in a row on the ground, and the old man took each in turn and led him round the market again, crying out 'Who offers most?' Prices varied wildly, depending on the profession of the captive, his or her physical state, and the perceived potential for ransom. Gunners and skilled artisans were in great demand. A professional soldier could sell for 200 Spanish dollars, nearly 50 English pounds. Once the bargain was struck, the slaves were taken once more to the *pasha*'s palace, their selling prices written on placards hung round their necks or on pieces of paper tucked into their hats. Yûsuf not only took his tithe of new prisoners, he also had the right to any of the remaining slaves if he was prepared to match the price offered in the *bedestan*.

Okeley was sold to a Morisco – he doesn't say for how much – and immediately received a sharp lesson in deference. His new master brought him home from the palace and left him in the care of his old father, who amused himself by sneering at Okeley's Christian faith. 'My neck was not yet bowed nor my heart yet broken to the yoke of bondage', the Puritan recalled.[10] He responded by miming a cobbler stitching, intending to suggest that Islam was nothing more than a patchwork of nonsense cobbled together by the Prophet, the Nestorian monk Sergius and a Jewish doctor named Abdallah. He referred to an anti-Islamic and anti-Semitic legend that was common in seventeenth-century Europe, which claimed that Mohammad had almost been converted to Christianity by Sergius, and that the Qur'an had been tampered with by Abdallah after the Prophet's death.[11]

You might think this was quite a hard mime to get. But get it the old man did. He flew into a frenzy, punching and kicking Okeley savagely. When his son came in and heard what had happened, he drew a knife on Okeley and was only prevented from stabbing him by his wife.

The new slave learned two lessons from the episode. One, that it was not a good idea to criticise another's religion; and two, that 'where the whole outward man is in bondage, the tongue must not plead exemption'.[12]

For the six months of his captivity Okeley worked as a domestic servant in his master's home until, in the late spring of 1640, he was suddenly sent to sea.

Like most wealthy Algerian citizens, his master invested in piracy, contributing a share of the finance for a voyage in return for a share of the prizes. When the ship in which he had an interest took an English merchantman with a cargo of plate and other rich commodities, he and his fellow investors were so encouraged by their success that they decided to fit the prize out as a corsair, increase her armament and send her on the cruise. Okeley was sent down to the shipyards to help with fitting her out for the voyage. Then he was told to join the crew.

He wrestled long and hard with his conscience over the morality of engaging in an action against fellow Christians. First he told himself that his job was only to manage the tackle, and that wouldn't kill anybody. But, he argued, the management of the tackle enabled the ship's guns to be brought to bear on a victim; so he could still be indirectly responsible for the deaths of Christians.

Next, he reasoned it might still be all right, because the pirates weren't actually going looking for Christians as such, just for anyone who was rich enough to be worth the risk and weak enough to keep that risk to a minimum.

He still felt uneasy. But his master came up with a solution to his troubles. 'He told me peremptorily, I must and should go.'[13]

The expedition wasn't a success. After nine weeks cruising inside and outside the Straits of Gibraltar all the corsairs had to show for their efforts was 'one poor Hungarian French man of war'.[14] The enterprise left Okeley's disappointed master in so much debt that, when the reluctant corsair got back to Algiers, he was thrown out on the street and told to get a job. He had to find his own lodgings, and he had to earn enough to pay his master two Spanish dollars every month.

The idea of the slave as an unfettered outworker was not as odd as it might sound. Security was tight in the case of galley slaves, whose lot was so harsh that they would go to any lengths to escape: their heads were shaved to mark them out and they were often kept in close confinement while ashore. Other Christians had a relatively free time of it, as Okeley found when he went looking for work. He first approached an English tailor, also a slave, who offered to teach him his trade and then changed his mind. Then he fell in with another English slave, who had set himself up as a general trader selling lead, iron, shot, alcohol and tobacco. Okeley had managed to save a little money, his master lent him some more, and he went into partnership with the man. 'That very night I went and bought a parcel of tobacco,' he said. 'The next morning we dressed it, cut it, and fitted it for sale, and the world seemed to smile on us wonderfully.'[15]

For the next three or four years Okeley worked hard and prospered. His partner turned out to be a drunk, and he faded into the background, to be replaced by an English glover, John Randal, who, along with his wife and child, had been with Okeley aboard the *Mary* when she was taken. Randal made and sold canvas clothes in the little shop they ran together, while Okeley dealt in wine and tobacco. He locked his goods away each night in a cellar he had rented for the purpose, and regularly buried his money for safe keeping.

His abiding concern was the welfare of his soul. The Algerians allowed their slaves freedom of worship (they were much more tolerant in this respect than most European nations), but there was no Protestant minister in the city. A Spanish Dominican, Father Joseph, celebrated Mass, but Okeley's hatred of popery was as venomous as his contempt for Islam. 'We were very much at a loss for the preaching of the Word,' he later recalled.[16]

God moved in a mysterious way to answer his prayers. In 1642 an Algerian corsair was on the cruise off the south coast of Co. Cork when he intercepted and captured a merchant ship bound for England. She was carrying 120 Protestant refugees who were escaping from the Great Rebellion, a wave of vicious sectarian fighting that was currently sweeping through Ireland.

For one of those refugees, a 22-year-old minister named Devereux Spratt, capture by pirates seemed the last straw. He had lost his mother and his eight-year-old brother during the recent siege of Tralee. He had nearly died himself of a fever in Limerick, and had survived two attacks by rebels on the road down to Cork. And now this – a thing 'so grievous that I began to question

Providence', he wrote in his journal, 'and accused Him of injustice in His dealings with me'.[17]

It was only when the despairing Spratt arrived in Algiers and realised that the Protestant slaves had no one to minister to them that he revised his opinion and found a divine plan in his capture and enslavement. So did Okeley, although he had the grace to wonder 'that the wise God should supply our necessities at the cost and charges of others of His dear servants'.[18] The Protestant community agreed to pay a levy to Spratt's master for his services, and before long he was conducting services three times a week in Okeley's storage cellar, to a congregation of anything up to eighty slaves. He was so successful in his preaching that, although his ransom was soon paid by English merchants based at Livorno, he elected to stay on as a free man, 'considering that I might be more serviceable to my country by my continuing in enduring afflictions with the people of God than to enjoy liberty at home'.[19]

Okeley's master never recovered from the financial disaster of his last venture into piracy, and his debts mounted until they reached a point where he was forced to sell off all his slaves. Okeley was passed to an old gentleman with a country estate twelve miles out of Algiers, who treated him exceptionally well. 'I found not only pity and compassion but love and friendship from my new patron,' he wrote.[20] The man took him into the country, showed him how markets operated, gave him produce to bring back to the city to share with his fellow Christians, and groomed him to take over the management of the estate. 'Had I been his son, I could not have met with more respect nor been treated with more tenderness.'[21]

Okeley's attitude towards the Algerians was complicated, ambiguous and very human. He naturally resented his enslavement and he kicked against Algerian culture, regarding it as brutish and cruel, and dwelling at length on the appalling punishments he saw being meted out to transgressors. A Dutch slave who threatened his patron with a knife had his arms and legs broken with a sledgehammer; a Turk was crucified for an unspecified offence, while another was thrown off a high wall on to a big meat hook and left there to die. Two Moors who struck Turks (presumably members of the janissary corps) had their right hands amputated and hung round their necks on strings. A third was dragged through the streets, his heels tied to a horse's tail: 'it was a lamentable spectacle to see his body all torn with the rugged way and stone, the skin torn off his back and elbows, his head broken, and all covered with blood and dirt'.[22]

This was a favourite topic with Christians in Barbary, who took possession of the moral high ground while conveniently forgetting how their own societies dealt with miscreants – the public and horribly inefficient hangings, the brandings and ear-croppings and nose-slittings. Okeley also loathed Islam with all the strength in his Puritan soul, and this deep contempt led him to view its rituals harshly. Ramadan, for instance, he saw as a perversion of Lent, 'an observation which they [i.e. Moslems] may be presumed to owe to that Nestorian monk who clubbed with Mahomet in the cursed invention of the Alcoran' (another reference to the Sergius myth). He ignored or was ignorant of the study of the Qur'an, which was an integral part of Ramadan, and regarded the dawn till dusk fasting as meretricious and insincere. 'When they have drunk and whored themselves into sin [each night], they fancy they merit a pardon by abstinence, a piece of hypocrisy so gross that whether it be to be sampled anywhere in the world, unless perhaps by the popish carnivals, I cannot tell.'[23]

Religious toleration was a rarity in Europe; and Okeley was amazed to discover that in Islam 'every man may be saved in that religion he professes' whether he was a Jew, a Christian or a Moslem; and that at the last, all will 'march over a fair bridge, into I know not what Paradise'.[24] Not that he condoned such a liberal attitude to salvation – he subscribed, after all, to a Puritan theology which believed most Christians were going to hell, never mind the unbelievers. He was impressed, however, by the respect which ordinary Algerians showed towards authority. 'It's worth admiration', he wrote, 'to see in what great awe they stand of the meanest officer, who is known to be such by his turban and habit.' These officers patrolled the streets and arrested violent offenders without weapons or helpers, because resistance was unthinkable.

And Okeley was prepared to notice and condemn the vices of Christians – particularly drunkenness, which he regarded as a European introduction. He hinted darkly at worse in the book he wrote about his experiences, claiming he could 'relate a passage during our captivity in Algiers that had more of bitterness in it than in all our slavery, and yet they were Christians, not Algerines; Protestants, not Papists; Englishmen, not strangers, that were the cause of it'.[25] But he refused to elaborate.

Almost imperceptibly, Okeley was becoming assimilated into Algerian society. He held fast to his own religion and his own kind, socialising primarily with other English captives, but step by step he became acclimatised to slavery and Barbary. 'The freedom that I found in servitude', he recalled, 'the liberty I enjoyed in my bonds was so great, that it took off much of the edge of my desire to obtain and almost blunted it from any vigorous attempt after liberty.'[26] Perhaps this was bound to happen when the repatriation rate for victims of piracy was as low as it was. Only one of the victims of the Sack of Baltimore had been ransomed, for instance. All the others, 106 of them, were dead, enslaved or turned Turk.

The man whose job it was to procure the release of captives in Algiers was James Frizzell, the Levant Company agent who helped Sir Robert Mansell during his unproductive negotiations in 1620. Three years later, England concluded a treaty with the Ottoman Empire which was supposed to signal the end of piratical attacks on both sides, the official recognition of English consuls in Algiers and Tunis and the repatriation of 800 English slaves. Frizzell was appointed to Algiers – by the Levant Company rather than the English government, which tended to leave such diplomatic initiatives to merchants along with the task of paying for them – and for the next two decades this influential but strangely elusive character did his heroic best to serve English interests in the city.

He began his long term in office with a success, by negotiating the release of 240 captives; but things went downhill from there. The *pasha* placed him under house arrest if *avanias*, the taxes levied on European merchants, weren't paid; and confiscated his goods if English pirates interfered with Algerian shipping. The Levant Company stopped employing him when it judged that trade with Algeria was just too dangerous and unprofitable. The English government ignored him. Frustrated relatives of captives spread nasty rumours that he was slow at handing over ransom money sent from England because he hoped captives would die in the interim so that he could pocket the cash.

And through it all it was Frizzell who kept the register of prisoners brought in by corsairs; Frizzell who badgered the English government with tallies of the lost, and tried to arrange the credit which would enable their friends at home to repatriate them; Frizzell who promised the *pasha* anything and everything that might lead to liberty for slaves, even – to quote a 1627 agreement he made with the *dīwān* – 'that he will restore to the city of Algiers all the ships and slaves of the Moslems taken by the English from the time of his appointment'.[27] In 1643, long after the Levant Company and the English government had dispensed with his official services, he was still being described in Parliament as 'Mr James Freesell, residing as consul at Argiers [*sic*]'.[28]

Scenes from the frontispiece to Okeley's account of his captivity, Eben-ezer

Frizzell was an English captive's best hope of repatriation. But it was a slim hope at best. Of 708 prisoners taken by pirates between 1629 and 1632, only twenty-four had been freed by the latter date. In 1637 Frizzell reported that 1524 English subjects had been taken by Algerian corsairs, and not 100 of them had been ransomed. And in any case, by 1644, when Okeley was losing his desire for liberty, Frizzell was old. He may even have been dead: after 1643 nothing more is heard of him in England.

After five years of slavery, William Okeley was jarred out of his complacency by the kindness of his master, who proposed that he give up the business in Algiers and take over the running of his country estate. 'If I once quitted my shop', Okeley reasoned, 'I should lose with it all means, all helps, and therefore all hopes to rid myself out of this slavery.' He might have a comfortable life as an estate manager for a benevolent patron; but 'fetters of gold do not lose their nature; they are fetters still'.[29] If he wanted to see England again, he had to act.

He had to escape.

Running away posed a new set of problems. Escape from Algiers was rare, and the few Christian slaves who succeeded did so either by seizing an opportunity while crewing a pirate ship near friendly coasts, or by taking a chance and swimming out to a European merchant vessel which might happen to anchor in the Bay of Algiers. The punishment for recaptured runaways was at the whim of their owners, and could be brutal: John Randal, the glover who went into partnership with Okeley for a time, was bastinadoed, receiving 300 strokes on the soles of his feet because he was suspected (wrongly, as it happened) of trying to escape. He was so badly injured that he had to give up work.

Okeley hit on an amazingly audacious plan. He meant to build a small boat in secret, in sections, in his cellar; then to dismantle it and carry it in pieces, so as not to arouse suspicion, to a secluded spot outside the city walls. Under cover of darkness he would put it back together and row or sail due north across 190 miles of open sea until he reached Majorca, where he would throw himself on the mercy of the Spanish governor.

He obviously couldn't do any of this on his own, and his first step was to sound out Rev. Spratt and other members of the English community. They all told him it was a brilliant idea, while at the same time discovering pressing reasons why they couldn't join him. After making discreet enquiries over the spring of 1644 he eventually recruited six fellow slaves, all Englishmen. John Anthony and another John, whose surname Okeley doesn't give, were carpenters. A third John, John Jephs, was a sailor. William

Adams was a bricklayer – not an obviously useful skill when it came to boatbuilding, but Adams regularly worked outside the city walls, carrying substantial pieces of timber which he used to level his work. These men had thirty-six years of slavery between them.

The other two conspirators aren't named at all. They were employed in washing and drying clothes down by the seashore, which meant they could both travel out of the city without being challenged, taking small pieces of the boat with them hidden in their laundry baskets. All seven men could come and go fairly freely during daylight hours, but, besides the sentries who manned the city gates around the clock, Algiers had an *ad hoc* system of watchmen and concerned citizens who would apprehend any slave they saw acting suspiciously beyond the walls.

The prospect of going home was exciting, and rather frightening. No one knew quite what to expect when and if they reached England again: the civil war had been raging for nearly two years, and unsettling scraps of news of the battle between King and Parliament had reached the Barbary Coast, brought by passing ships. Being the earnest Puritan that he was, Okeley also tussled with the propriety of deserting his kind patron – but only briefly. 'One thought of England and of its liberty and Gospel, confuted a thousand such objections and routed whole legions of these little scruples.'[30] His co-conspirators, on the other hand, became markedly less enthusiastic about the project when they stopped to consider the logistics of building a boat, smuggling it out of the city and then surviving the voyage. Again, Okeley's response was brisk. He told them that 'if we never attempted anything till we had answered all objections, we must sit with our fingers in our mouths all our days and pine and languish out our tedious lives in bondage. Let us be up and doing, and God would be with us.'[31]

That June, the cellar where Okeley stored his goods and where Spratt ministered to the Protestant congregation on Sundays was turned into a clandestine boatbuilding yard each night. The slaves got hold of a 12-foot-long piece of timber for the keel, which they cut in half and prepared for jointing: Adams the bricklayer might get away with carrying a 6-foot piece of wood out of the city, but one that was twice that length (and keel-shaped) would be a bit of a giveaway. The same held for the ribs of the boat. The carpenters hit on the ingenious idea of making each rib in three sections and boring two holes at each joint. They could quickly reassemble them simply by fitting nails into the holes, and each joint was designed to make 'an obtuse angle and so incline so near towards a semicircular figure as our occasion required'.[32]

They agreed it would be folly to use wooden boards for the hull: the hammering and sawing would attract too much attention. Instead, they bought enough stout canvas to cover the frame twice over, and one night Okeley and the two carpenters set about waterproofing it with hot pitch, tar and tallow.

That nearly brought the plan to an abrupt and tragic end. They worked in the close confines of the cellar, melting their materials in earthen pots, with the door closed and rags stuffed into every gap to prevent telltale steam escaping into the street. Before long the room was filled with noxious fumes. Okeley was overcome and staggered out into the night, gulping for breath before he collapsed. His comrades brought him to and dragged him back inside, but within a short time they were also complaining of nausea and dizziness.

Eventually the three men agreed to put their faith in God and work with the cellar door wide open, Okeley keeping lookout while the others applied the molten pitch. It took them two nights; when it was done, they crept 200 yards through the narrow, dark streets to Okeley's shop, where they stowed the canvas safely until it was needed.

Step by step the group got everything ready. They practised putting the boat together and taking it apart, and putting it back together again. They fashioned wooden seats, and made oars from pipe staves, and bought more canvas to use as a makeshift sail. They got hold of two tanned goatskins to use as water bottles, and decided to take fresh water, a small quantity of bread and nothing else, 'presuming our stay at sea must be but short, for either we should speedily recover land or speedily be drowned or speedily be brought back again'.[33] Okeley sold off the goods from his shop and entrusted the money to Devereux Spratt in a false-bottomed trunk made specially for him by John Anthony, one of the two carpenters.

By the end of June everything was ready. The keel, the ribs, the waterproof canvas and all the other bits and pieces had been smuggled out of the city and hidden in fields around a little hill which stood a safe distance beyond the walls and about half a mile from the coast. On the night of 30 June 1644, about an hour after dusk, the little party gathered by the hill, retrieved the parts of their boat and got to work in the darkness:

> The two parts of our keel we soon joined. Then opening the timbers, which had already one nail in every joint, we groped for the other hole and put its nail into it. Then we opened them at their full length and applied them to the top of the keel, fastening them with rope yarn and small cords, and so we served all the joints to keep them firm and stable. Then we bound small canes all along the ribs lengthways, both to keep the ribs from veering and also to bear out the canvas very stiff against the pressing water. Then we made notches in the ends of the ribs, or timbers, wherein the oars might ply, and having tied down the seats and strengthened our keel with the fig tree [to reinforce the keel they had cut down a small fig tree which stood on top of the hill], we lastly drew on our double canvas case, already fitted, and really the canvas seemed a winding sheet for our boat, and our boat a coffin for us all.[34]

Four of the group hoisted the boat on to their shoulders and carried it the half-mile to the sea. The other three followed in the pitch darkness, like mourners at a ghostly funeral.

When they reached the sea they all stripped naked and threw their clothes into the boat, tossed the goatskins and the bread in after them and dragged the craft as far out into the waves as they could manage. Then they jumped in.

It sank.

There were no leaks, and the frame held up to the waves. It was simply that the little dinghy couldn't bear the weight of seven men. This was enough for one of the washermen, who was already nervous at the prospect of going to sea in such a frail craft; he volunteered to stay behind. So they rescued the boat, bailed her out and refloated her; but she was still so low in the water that there was no question of taking her any further. They jettisoned most of their clothing, leaving themselves with just shirts or loose coats, but it was not enough. After an awkward pause, the second washerman waded ashore; and the remaining five slaves – Okeley, John Jephs the sailor, the bricklayer William Adams, and the two carpenters – said a prayer, bade their friends farewell, and set sail for Majorca.

They were still a long way from liberty. For the rest of the night they worked frantically to get clear of Algiers. Four men manned the oars while the fifth bailed out the seawater that was seeping through the canvas hull. But the wind was against them. When the sun rose at 5.30 the next morning they were still in sight of the ships in Algiers Road, making them redouble their efforts and row like men possessed. No one came after them, but they soon found another problem: their entire store of bread was soaked with seawater, 'like a drunken toast sopped in brine'; and the same seawater had seeped into the goatskins, bringing out the tanning liquor in the skins and turning the fresh water foul. In desperation they ate the bread anyway. There was none left on the third day. By then they were drinking their own urine.

They kept on, heading north all the time. One of the group – presumably John Jephs – had a small mariner's compass that he used to take their bearings by day. At night they followed the stars. By early on the fifth day they stopped rowing, too exhausted now to do anything but bail out the boat. They were ready to give up – blistered by the scorching sun, faint with hunger and dehydrated by the seawater they were now drinking. Their lives were saved by an unsuspecting turtle that was dozing in the sea. 'Had the great Drake discovered the Spanish plate fleet', said Okeley, 'he could not have more rejoiced'.[35] They hauled the unlucky creature aboard; chopped its head off; then drank its blood, ate its liver and sucked the warm flesh. 'Really it wonderfully refreshed our spirits, repaired our decayed strength, and recruited nature.'[36]

Around noon they sighted land. It was still a long way off but, overcome with relief, the whole crew leaped into the sea and swam for joy. They climbed back into the little boat and fell asleep and drifted. 'And here we saw more of divine goodness, that our leaky vessel did not bury us in the sea and we awaking find ourselves in the other world.'[37] But they rowed hard all night and all the next day, finally coming ashore on the coast of Majorca late on the night of 6 July, six days after escaping from Algiers and slavery.

Okeley and John Anthony went in search of fresh water, leaving the other three to keep an eye on the boat. The pair immediately got lost in a forest and fell out rather nastily over which way to go. 'Good Lord!' recalled Okeley, 'What a frail, impotent thing is man! That they whom common dangers by sea, common deliverances from sea, had united should now about our own wills fall out at land.'[38] After wandering around and arguing for a while, they came upon one of the watchtowers that lined the coast of Majorca, mostly built in the sixteenth and seventeenth centuries to provide advance warning of raids by corsairs. After they'd shouted up to the armed sentry and explained their circumstances – keeping a discreet distance in case they were fired on – the man threw them down a mouldy old cake. 'But so long as it was a cake, and not a stone, nor a bullet', said Okeley, 'hunger did not consider its mouldiness.'[39] The man also gave them directions to a nearby well. The pair returned to the boat, gathered up the others and went in search of the well. They were all in a bad way, wearing only their soaked shirts and limping on blistered feet, and they started bickering among themselves about what to do next.

The bickering stopped abruptly when William Adams suddenly collapsed at the side of the well, his throat so swollen that he couldn't drink. His comrades immediately rediscovered the sense of solidarity that had carried them across the Mediterranean. They lifted up their distressed comrade, who croaked 'I am a dead man', and forced him to take sips of water interspersed with little pieces of the cake. Slowly they managed to revive him.

The five of them slept beside the well that night, and went back to the sentry in the watchtower the next morning to ask for directions to the nearest town. It took them another two days to hobble the twelve miles to Palma.

The island was sparsely populated, and only as they entered the outskirts did they begin to attract serious attention. 'The strangeness of our attire, being barefoot, barelegged, having nothing on but loose coats over our shirts, drew a crowd of inquirers about us: who we were? whence we came? whither we went?'[40] Brought before the viceroy in the ancient Almudaina Palace, they answered questions on the strength of the Algerian fleet, the size of the

Algerian military. But what intrigued the viceroy most of all was the story of their escape. It so impressed him that he announced he would maintain them at his own expense until a passage to England could be arranged. The people of Palma held a public collection to buy clothes and shoes; and the prefabricated boat that had carried them across 190 miles of open sea was rescued from the beach where it lay and hung in Le Seu, Palma's great Gothic cathedral. It was still there, battered and now skeletal, nearly thirty years later, a monument to their miraculous deliverance.

William Okeley got back to a war-torn England in September 1644, just over five years after he had left for the Caribbean. The English merchant ship which was taking him home narrowly escaped capture by Turks off Gibraltar, a reminder that the threat of piracy had in no way diminished during his time in Algiers. The experience was so frightening that Okeley and the two carpenters went ashore and made the rest of the journey in stages, first to Cadiz, then overland to St Lucar before obtaining passage on another homeward-bound English vessel.

In London Okeley met up with Devereux Spratt, who had come home by more conventional means and who dutifully handed over his money, still in its false-bottomed trunk. Nothing more is heard of Okeley until 1675, when, with the help of an unidentified friend who tidied up his prose, he published *Eben-ezer, or, a Small Monument of Great Mercy appearing in miraculous deliverance of William Okeley, William Adams, John Anthony, John Jephs, John − , carpenter, from the miserable slavery of Algiers, with the wonderful means of their escape in a boat of canvas*. The book was sold by Nathaniel Ponder, a prominent Nonconformist bookseller who acquired the nickname of 'Bunyan' Ponder three years later through publishing John Bunyan's *The Pilgrim's Progress*.

Okeley reframed his Algerian experience as a Protestant parable, seeing his capture as evidence of the mysterious workings of Providence, and his escape as a testament to God's redemptive power. 'We called on Him in the day of our trouble,' he tells his readers in his lengthy and earnest preface; 'He delivered us, and we will glorify Him.' The book's title, *Eben-ezer* (Hebrew for 'stone of help'), is a reference to 1 Samuel 7:12, in which, after defeating the Philistines, Samuel took a stone 'and called the name of it Ebenezer, saying, Hitherto hath the Lord helped us'. The message is reinforced by the book's epigraph from Psalm 103: 'Bless the Lord, O my soul, and forget not all his benefits: Who redeemeth thy life from destruction; who crowneth thee with loving kind-ness and tender mercies.'

Okeley's readers were exhorted to take heart and take heed from the narrative. Servants who were unhappy with their lot should think themselves lucky that they were not slaves to Turks. Those whose thoughts turned towards sin should realise that, if provoked, God could punish them in terrible ways for their trans-gressions, just as He could reward them for their faith with the gift of eternal life. Everyone must learn to walk in the ways of righteousness, and remember that 'God can carry us to Rome or Algiers, or else send Rome and Algiers home to us'.[41] Even for those who would never see the bagnios of the Barbary Coast, slavery came in many guises.

11

Deliverance: The Liberation of Barbary Captives

*R*obert Blake and Jawdar ben 'Abd Allah left the English court and returned to Morocco in May 1638, taking with them fulsome expressions of friendship, a one-sided trade agreement which gave members of a newly founded English Barbary Company a monopoly to sell high and buy low, and some extravagant presents for the sultan, including a gilded coach painted with flowers and five Denmark horses to draw it, 100 lances, several pieces of fine linen and 'the king and queen's pictures drawn after the Van Dyck originals'.[1]

As they set sail from Portsmouth there were already rumours that Thomas Rainborow's triumph at Salé was unravelling, and by the early summer those rumours had been confirmed. The followers of Muhammad al-Ayyashi (the Saint) in Old Salé were ignoring the peace with the corsairs of New Salé; the corsairs were ignoring their promises of loyalty to the sultan, and English merchant vessels were ignoring the Anglo-Moroccan treaty and selling arms to the sultan's enemies. It was business as usual.

Or almost as usual. The threat from Salé rovers in the Narrow Seas did diminish in the wake of Rainborow's expedition, although this was as much to do with continuing civil unrest along the Moroccan coast. 'Abd Allah ben 'Ali el-Kasri, the leader of the Salé corsairs, was killed fighting the Saint's men across the Bou Regreg, and the citadel at New Salé was taken, besieged and retaken by different Morisco factions. When the sultan marched on the coast to restore order, his camp was overrun by hostile mountain tribesmen and he had to ride for his life; and in 1641 the Saint himself was killed in battle with the Moriscos he had ousted from New Salé, who had entered into an alliance with rival rebel groups.

The surviving Salé rovers eventually regrouped and resumed their activities against European shipping outside the Straits. In October 1641, for example, four English merchant vessels were on their way home from La Rochelle when they were intercepted by a heavily armed man-of-war, which rounded them up without a struggle, brought them back to New Salé and sold their crews to an Algerian merchant. In 1650 the Dutch blockaded Salé as Rainborow had done, in an unsuccessful attempt to put a stop to their activities. Seventy years later the Salé rovers were still a potent force: at the beginning of *Robinson Crusoe* Daniel Defoe has his eponymous hero surprised off the Canary Islands 'in the grey of the morning by a Turkish rover of Sallee' who captures the crew and carries them into Salé to be sold.

But for much of the mid-seventeenth century the dominant force along the Barbary Coast was Algiers, whose galleys and round-ships moved effortlessly and terrifyingly to fill the gap in the market; and their captain-general was 'Ali Bitshnin, the Italian renegade from whom Francis Knight had escaped at Valona in 1638.

Under a bewildering variety of names, 'Ali Bitshnin was a Barbary Coast legend. He was probably the Ali Pizilini who owned sixty-three Christian slaves in Algiers in 1619. He was certainly the Ally Pichellin who by the 1630s was 'for greatness renowned in all Africa';[2] the Ali Piccinino who terrorised and terrified Venetian merchantmen the length and breadth of the Adriatic; the Ali Pichinin who kept forty young pages 'for ostentation' but refused to let them out of doors for fear they might be sodomised; and, last but not least, the Alli Pegelin whose cheerfully impartial approach to spiritual matters enabled him to laugh at the Qur'an during Friday prayers while smiling benignly at a Carmelite priest who told him to his face that he was bound for hell because he had 'no other religion than an insatiable avarice'.[3]

Ironically, 'Ali Bitshnin is remembered today for building a mosque. The domed, almost Byzantine Djemaa 'Ali Bitchine still stands in the Bab al-Oued district at the heart of the Algerian *medina* – albeit in a rather mutilated state, having been turned into a Catholic church by the French. Put up in the early 1620s at 'Ali Bitshnin's command soon after he arrived on the Barbary Coast from the Adriatic, it was one of Algiers's first Ottoman mosques, and was built over a vast complex of basements and shops. His bagnio was nearby 'in a street of his house', according to the Spaniard Emanuel D'Aranda, who was captured off the coast of Brittany in 1640 and spent the next two years as 'Ali Bitshnin's slave. D'Aranda's description of the bagnio suggests that far from being the squalid slave pit of popular imagination, it was actually a thriving community resource:

> It had a very narrow entrance, which led into a spacious vault, and that received its light, such as it was, through a certain grate that was above, but so little, that at mid-day, in some taverns of the said bath, there was a necessity of setting up lamps. The taverners, or keepers of those taverns are Christian slaves of the same baths, and those who come thither to drink are pirates, and Turkish soldiers [i.e. janissaries], who spend their time there in drinking, and committing abominations. Above the bath there is a square place, about which there are galleries of two storeys, and between those galleries there were also taverns, and a church for the Christians, spacious enough to contain three hundred persons, who might there conveniently hear Mass. The roof is flat, with a terrace, after the Spanish mode.[4]

D'Aranda spent his first night as 'Ali Bitshnin's slave up on this roof terrace, under a coverlet provided for him by the *pasha*'s men. The next day he was ordered out (in *lingua franca*, 'the common language between the slaves and the Turks, as also among the slaves of several nations', he noted[5]) and set to work making rope in Bab al-Oued. He reckoned 'Ali Bitshnin kept about 550 Christian slaves of all nationalities in the bagnio; they spoke twenty-two languages between them – in addition to *lingua franca* – and included

Catholics, Lutherans, Calvinists, Puritans and a smattering of minor sectaries. For years a Dominican friar, 'a fat, corpulent person', celebrated Mass for everyone on Sundays and got drunk on week-days until, despairing of ever being ransomed, he converted to Islam, 'with extraordinary acclamations of the Moors and Turks'.[6]

The son-in-law of a legendary Albanian renegade named Murad Raïs the elder (not to be confused with the Dutch renegade Murad Raïs, who carried out the Sack of Baltimore in 1631), 'Ali Bitshnin was appointed Captain of the Sea in the early 1620s. As head of the *tā'ifat al-ra'īs*, the guild of corsairs, he managed to maintain an equi-librium of sorts between the interests of the corsairs, those of the merchant class which financed his raids and those of the janissary corps who were at once both eager for a slice of the pie and suspi-cious of anyone who threatened their supremacy. By the later 1630s he had become an immensely powerful figure in Algiers – so powerful, in fact, that European outsiders regarded him as the real head of state above the *pasha*, above even the *agha* who commanded the janissary corps. When he entertained on his country estate, the *pasha* was there, along with all the other naval commanders, the captains, 'the richest setters-out of galleys'.[7] When he went to sea, the admirals of Tunis and Tripoli were happy to serve under him.

Yet he remained an outsider, even in a community well used to making outsiders its own. He refused to provide his slaves with food, encouraging them instead to steal what they could, and allowing them out for two or three hours every evening to burgle, scavenge and pick pockets. On one occasion he had to stuff a cloth in his mouth to stifle his giggles during the call to prayers at the *pasha*'s palace. On another, his galleys were taking in water near Oran when a Moor came up to him and asked if he might be allowed to kill one of the Christian slaves, 'which is the most acceptable sacrifice that can be made to the Prophet'. The Captain of the Sea told him he'd be happy to oblige, and then gave a sword and a dagger to his biggest, roughest galley slave and sent him to chase the Moor away. When the man summoned up the courage to come back and complain, 'Ali Bitshnin laughed at him, saying there was no honour in killing a man who couldn't defend himself: 'Mahomet was a generous and valiant man; go and bid your *sherif* furnish you with a better explication of the Alcoran'.[8]

The problem in understanding 'Ali Bitshnin as a man and a leader is that most of our knowledge of him is both fragmentary and filtered through uncertain European eyes. And because the anecdotes are personal and partial, the picture is inconsistent. How is it that a convert to Islam who built one of Algiers's finest seventeenth-century mosques could mock the Qur'an? Or that to Francis Knight 'Ally Pichellin' was an arrogant, pompous tyrant – 'in truth we were all exquisitely miserable that were his slaves'[9] – while Emanuel D'Aranda, who knew him just as well if not better, saw him as that stock seventeenth-century figure, the jovial, amoral pirate who spurns convention and invites grudging admiration because of it?

The Captain of the Sea's reputation suffered some hard knocks in the late 1630s and early 1640s. The 1638 Battle of Valona, in which he commanded a combined Algerian and Tunisian force, ended disastrously with the loss of sixteen galleys and ten times that number of slaves. Violent recriminations flew so thick and fast in Algiers among janissaries, corsairs and merchants that the *pasha* declared it a capital offence for anyone to remove their thumbs from their girdles while they were arguing with another: 'the contending parties, blaming each other for the late miscarriage, could only vent their spleen by bitter invectives and reflections, scurrilous language, punches with their elbows, and, as occasion offered, now and then throwing their head in each others' jaws'.[10] 'Ali Bitshnin took a lot of the blame for the defeat – according to one source he was actually sentenced to death, but the sentence was rescinded. In 1643 he fell out with both the Ottoman court at Istanbul, for refusing to contribute to Sultan Ibrahim I's battle fleet against the Venetians without a hefty subsidy; and the Algerian janissary corps, for refusing to pay them money they claimed he owed them. Forced to flee Algiers for a time, he was reconciled with Ibrahim in 1645 and came back, only to sicken and die. It was popularly believed in Algiers that agents of the sultan had poisoned him.

But when 'Ali Bitshnin was at his peak, the galleys of the *tā'ifat al-ra'īs* took shipping from just about every European nation that ventured into the Mediterranean, and raided coastal villages from the Adriatic to the Atlantic. In the nine months to January 1640, English losses to pirates were estimated at nearly seventy ships and more than 1200 sailors, a figure which almost matched *nine years* of losses between 1629 and 1638. The casualties included the *Rebecca*, which was carrying a cargo of silver worth £260,000 to England: when the news of her capture broke at the beginning of 1640, it caused a slump in the pound and a crisis in European banking. (The corsairs who took her were so pleased with their prize that they gave the crew a boat and set them free.) Coastal raids on the British Isles, while not as common as they were in the western Mediterranean, where whole communities moved inland for fear of pirates and chains of watchtowers were built to give advance warning of their arrival, were still a reality. In the summer of 1640 the presence of Algerines off the Cornish coast caused first anxiety, and then downright panic when a raiding party landed by night at Penzance and captured sixty men, women and children. The following year, 1641, Algiers put no fewer than sixty-five pirate ships on the cruise, bearing out the opinion of the great Levant merchant Lewis Roberts when he listed Algerian commodities as 'Barbary horses, ostrich feathers, honey, wax, raisins, figs, dates, oils, almonds, castile soap, brass, copper, and some drugs; and lastly, excellent piratical rascals in great quantity, and poor miserable Christian captives of all nations'.[11]

Around one million Europeans were enslaved on the Barbary Coast during the seventeenth century

William Rainborow had proposed taking a fleet to Algiers in January 1638, as a follow-up to his Salé expedition of the previous year. But Algiers was a much more daunting prospect than Salé. Not for nothing was the city known in the Arab world as al-Mahroussa, 'the well-guarded'; the Algerians had developed, and were still developing, an elaborate defensive system of forts, batteries and ramparts. The walls were of brick and stone, with square towers and bastions and trenches, and there were seven fortresses, all built 'regularly according to the art of modern fortifications', well-manned and equipped with heavy guns – two of which, according to a guidebook of 1670, once belonged to the Devil Captain himself, 'Simon Dancer, a notorious Flemish pirate'.[12]

Rainborow suggested an expensive three-year-long blockade of the harbour by ten men-of-war and six pinnaces, reckoning that by the end of that period most of the Algerian vessels would be rotten and trade with the city would have been destroyed.[13] Around the same time Sir Thomas Roe reminded Parliament of an earlier proposal of his, in which he had argued for a trade embargo of the entire Ottoman Empire and the sending of a strong fleet to Alexandria, to attack Algerian and Tunisian vessels trading to the Levant. From there the fleet should 'range the coast of Barbary, land among the villages, and make prisoners of all men, women and children', exchanging the captives at Algiers and Tunis for English captives. If the corsairs refused to exchange, added Roe, the prisoners could be sold 'for money' in Majorca, Sardinia or Spain.[14]

Both schemes were ambitious. They would have been difficult to resource and manage at the best of times. And these were not the best of times. The Spanish assembled a fleet at Dunkirk in the spring of 1638, ostensibly to take on soldiers for an expedition to Brazil; English ships were needed to monitor its proceedings. The following January, deteriorating relations between Charles I and his Scottish subjects led the King to dispatch a fleet to blockade the Firth of Forth, rather than Algiers. And that autumn sixty-odd Spanish vessels faced a hundred Dutchmen off the coast of Kent, as a dozen English men-of-war looked on with optimistic instructions to 'take, sink, and destroy' any ship of either side which attempted anything which might be construed as disrespectful to England.[15]

In the spring of 1640 Charles I summoned a parliament, after eleven years of ruling without one. It was dissolved three weeks later when the King realised that the House of Commons was rather more anxious to discuss its long-held grievances than to vote him the financial resources he needed to resume his campaign against the Scots. But the Short Parliament was followed that November by the Long Parliament, so-called because it was to sit, in various incarnations, for the next twenty years; the members of the Long Parliament including a fair number of people whose involvement in overseas trade gave them a powerful interest in finding a solution to the problem of piracy. The Levant Company, the East India Company and the Massachusetts Bay Company were all represented by the four MPs for the City of London. Some London merchants held seats further afield, like John Rolle, a Turkey merchant who sat for Truro, and Edward Ashe of the Drapers' Company who sat for Heytesbury in Wiltshire. And local merchants predominated in the returns for the West Country, which had suffered more from the depredations of pirates than any other part of England.

Even outside the merchant class there were plenty of MPs who took a keen interest in the activities of pirates. William Rainborow, described as 'Captain Rainborow' in the Commons Journals, was returned for Aldburgh in Suffolk; Sir Thomas Roe was returned for Oxford University. And while one of the two members for Fowey in Cornwall was Jonathan Rashleigh, who came from a local merchant family; the other, Sir Richard Buller, was a lawyer and a commissioner for piracy. Richard King, who sat for Melcombe Regis in Dorset, was another lawyer and another commissioner for piracy. One of the provisions of the Offences at Sea Act of 1536, which aimed to make it easier to gain convictions against 'traitors, pirates, thieves, robbers, murderers and confederates upon the sea', was for the appointment of commissioners in the maritime counties who were empowered to try cases before a jury 'as if such offences had been committed upon the land within the same shire'.[16] While some commissioners regarded the job as more of a business opportunity than a judicial appointment, others pursued pirates with vigour and rectitude.

With a good many MPs having an interest in Algerian piracy

and its consequences, it isn't so surprising that in the midst of all its other pressing concerns, the Commons still found time to debate the problem. They also seemed to have received encouragement from the King himself: on 3 October 1640, exactly one month before the Long Parliament sat for the first time, Charles I had been presented with a petition from about 3000 of his subjects who were currently held captive in Algiers, where they were undergoing 'most unsufferable labours, as rowing in galleys, drawing in carts, grinding in mills, with divers such unchristianlike works most lamentable to express and most burdensome to undergo'.[17] (It isn't clear quite why rowing in galleys, drawing in carts and grinding in mills were 'unchristianlike' pursuits.) That December Parliament appointed a committee to look into the matter. It included Roe, Rainborow and Melcombe Regis's Richard King.

King was appointed chairman of the Committee for the Captives in Algiers, as it was called, and he reported back to the Commons in March 1641. Between them, he said, Algiers and Tunis were holding up to 5000 British subjects, and a fleet of thirty corsairs was expected off the English coast that summer. A further thirty pirate ships would be out on the cruise in the Mediterranean. There was no point in trying to ransom captives – that would only encourage the corsairs to take more, and it would persuade sailors to give in to their attackers without a fight, knowing their government would buy them out of trouble. Parliament should deploy six naval vessels 'to guard the western coasts against the Turkish pirates', and authorise private individuals to take reprisals against 'any Turkish, Moorish, or other pirates' – an idea which caused concern among other European states, whose ambassadors recalled the propensity of the English to abuse privateering licences.

The Commons agreed with the Committee's findings, but asked it to think of a way to finance the patrols and the liberating of captives. The response was devastatingly simple. A tax of 1 per cent levied on all goods coming into and going out of the kingdom would, in the words of the 'Act for the Relief of the Captives taken by Turkish Moorish and other Pirates', raise enough money for the 'setting forth to the seas a navy as well for the enlargement and deliverance of those poor captives in Argier [*sic*] and other places'.[18] The Act passed into law at the beginning of 1642.

This wasn't at all what the merchants of England had in mind.

It was 'more than trade can bear', complained the Levant Company. The Venetian ambassador maintained it was a clever ruse, so that Parliament could claim it was doing something about the pirate menace while diverting the revenue towards 'other emergencies, which certainly are plentiful'.[19] The Commons thought it necessary to convene another Parliamentary Committee to 'consider of the grievances pretended to be occasioned by the Bill for the Relief of the Captives of Algiers'.[20] Merchants avoided paying the tax by offering promissory bonds instead.

Optimists continued to press for a punitive expedition to blockade Algiers. Henry Robinson, a reformer, pamphleteer and fourth-generation City merchant, argued that even this wouldn't be enough. In *Libertas, or Relief to the English Captives in Algier* (1642), he wrote that an English fleet before Algiers wouldn't be able to prevent every single corsair from entering or leaving harbour; and that although the Ottoman sultan, Ibrahim I, had granted permission for England to attack Algerian pirates, it was in practice impossible to distinguish between pirate vessels and legitimate merchantmen. 'Scarce a ship of them, but is both merchant, and a pirate, many times in the self-same voyage';[21] and Istanbul would leap at the chance to retaliate against the English community there every time an Algerian 'merchant' was attacked. Even if Algiers were brought to its knees, other nations along the Barbary Coast would take its place 'and prove more pestiferous to us in matter of our commerce for the future'.[22] No, the only sensible course was for our Turkey merchants to sell up their businesses in the Levant (at a cost estimated by Robinson at £300,000) and come home. All trade with the Ottoman Empire must cease, and the government should then dispatch a fleet of forty ships into the Bosporus to blockade Istanbul itself. Cutting off the trade with the Mediterranean, within a year or two the blockade would 'raise the price of all provisions and merchandise, which used to come from thence, so much as will easily cause a tumultuous and rude multitude to rebel', thus forcing Ibrahim I to treat for peace.

This was, in fact, exactly the strategy which the Venetians adopted fourteen years later. In the continuing struggle between the Venetian Republic and the Ottoman Empire for control of Crete, Venetian troops in the eastern Aegean occupied the islands of Limnos, Samothraki and Bozca Ada at the entrance to the Dardanelles, and blockaded Ottoman trade routes to Egypt and the Mediterranean so effectively that, in Istanbul, famine 'scorched Moslems with the flame of misery and filled them with sorrow'.[23] But Venice was 700 miles closer to Istanbul than London was: the Republic had its own supply lines, its own bases in the eastern Mediterranean, and its own more pressing need to halt the Empire's westward march. Robinson was a little hazy as to exactly how an English blockade of Istanbul would force 'Ali Bitshnin and the *tā'ifat al-ra'īs* to free their captives and cease their piratical ways.

In any case, the question was academic. In August 1642 Charles I raised his standard at Nottingham, the plentiful 'other emergencies' to which the Venetian ambassador had referred coalesced and erupted into full-blown civil war and Parliament pushed to one side all the plans for a punitive expedition to Algiers or to the Ottoman capital. By the following year the prime movers on the Committee for the Captives in Algiers had all gone: Rainborow had died at the age of fifty-five; Roe and King had deserted Parliament to join their sovereign in Oxford.

But the victims of piracy – or, more accurately, their grieving relations at home – refused to go away. Desperate wives and mothers clustered every day in Westminster Hall, to petition individual MPs, to remind the great and the good of the human cost of piracy, to beg for alms. Wives were placed in an impossible position by the prolonged absence of their husbands, and the law was confused about their options. According to civil law, a woman could marry again if her husband had been gone for five years 'and nothing known whether he lived or no'. But common law dictated that a spouse couldn't remarry 'till the death of him or her that is missing be certainly known'.[24]

Uneasy at its failure to act, the Commons in the summer of 1642 ordered that the fines taken from members who came late into prayers should go to 'the poor women that daily attend the House, whose husbands are captives in Algiers'.[25] Still nothing happened, and the following spring seven of these poor women, unhappy that they had seen nothing of the promised 1 per cent tax on imports and exports, organised another petition on behalf of themselves and the thousands of others like them. Katherine Swanton, Elizabeth Chickley, Susan Robinson, Mary Savage, Mary

Taylor, Julian Morris and Lucie Michell – all we know of them
is their names. All they had in common was the fact that their
husbands had been taken by pirates, and that in spite of having
begged and borrowed money from friends and relatives, and selling
their possessions, they still couldn't raise the ransom that Algiers
demanded for the release of their men.

Parliament responded to the presence of the women with an
admission of failure. The plans 'for the setting forth of a fleet of
ships, for the suppressing of those pirates, and deliverance of those
poor captives . . . hath not taken that success which could be
wished'. In a half-hearted attempt to remedy the situation, the
Commons issued an ordinance which authorised collections to be
taken at churches in and around London, with proceeds going
towards the redemption of captives.[26] With a war on, ships, guns
and men were too precious to be wasted on a high-risk operation
to Barbary: ransom rather than liberation by force now seemed
the best course.

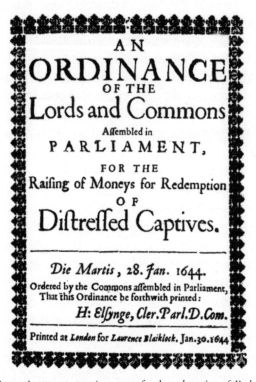

AN

ORDINANCE

OF THE

Lords and Commons

Aſſembled in

PARLIAMENT,

FOR THE

Raiſing of Moneys for Redemption

OF

Diſtreſſed Captives.

Die Martis, 28. *Jan.* 1644.

Ordered by the Commons aſſembled in Parliament,
That this Ordinance be forthwith printed:

H: Elſynge, *Cler.* Parl.D.Com.

Printed at *London* for *Laurence Blaiklock*. Jan.30.1644

One of Parliament's attempts to raise money for the redemption of Barbary slaves

Actually, that wasn't quite true. The very best course was to ask, politely but firmly. In July 1643 the Lords and Commons sent a London merchant who traded at Livorno with polite but firm letters for the *pasha* and the *dīwān*, desiring them 'to vouchsafe your justice and compassion unto those poor captives, and to grant them a speedy deliverance from their thraldom'.[27] A reply from the *pasha*, Yûsuf II, reached England about six months later, and, although it doesn't seem to have survived, Parliament understood its contents perfectly. Yûsuf and his council would be happy to negotiate a peace treaty with England, but slaves were commodities with a monetary value, and if the English wanted their captives released they would have to compensate the owners.

It is a measure of how seriously everyone viewed the piracy problem that even in the middle of a civil war – one which could still go either way – Parliament resurrected the 1 per cent levy on imports and exports with the aim of raising £10,000 for the captives' ransom. As an incentive, those merchants who came forward and answered for the bonds they had lodged in lieu of payment only needed to find a quarter of the amount they owed; and if more than £10,000 was raised, Parliament promised the surplus would go towards reimbursing them.

The levy, which gave the Lord Admiral and the Committee of the Navy responsibility for disposing of the money, was to continue for one year. It was still in operation at the Restoration seventeen years later. Cynics might say that Parliament had discovered a useful way of financing the navy. And they would be right: out of a total of nearly £70,000 raised by the levy, only £11,100 ever found its way to Barbary.[28]

Edmund Cason was the agent charged by Parliament with leading the negotiations with Yûsuf II and the *dīwān* of Algiers about the freeing of English captives. He is a shadowy figure. We know that in 1638 he owned a reasonable sized house near Old Fish Street at the northern entrance to London Bridge, and he is referred to in government records as a 'gentleman' rather than a merchant. He was never an MP, but he was a founder member of the powerful Committee for Taking Accounts of the Whole Kingdom, formed in February 1644, which meant he was also one of the City men empowered to supervise the collection of the levy for the redemption of distressed captives.

Cason's name first appeared in connection with the Algiers expedition on 15 August 1645, when the Lords and Commons agreed

> That Edmund Cason Esquire be sent as agent to Argier, with the ship and goods prepared, for the redemption of the captives in Argier and Tunis, and renewing the ancient peace with them. And it is further ordered, that the Committee of the Admiralty and Navy do draw up letters credential, commission, instructions, and all other documents fit for him: which the Speakers of both Houses are, upon presentation of the same unto them, to subscribe; that so the said agent may, with all speed, be sent away.[29]

In the late summer of 1645 (as it happened, just a few weeks after a raiding party of Turks landed on the Cornish coast and kidnapped 240 men, women and children[30]), Cason set sail for Barbary aboard the *Honour*, taking with him several thousands of pounds in cloth and ready money with which to ransom English captives.

The voyage was a disaster. The *Honour* sailed down the Portuguese coast and through the Straits, where she waited in the Bay of Gibraltar for favourable winds. While she lay at anchor, a fire broke out on board, and locals 'rescued' the cargo, which was never seen again. Cason managed to save some of the cash, and put it aboard an ancient Levant Company ship, the 140-ton *Diamond*; but a few days later the *Diamond* went down off Cadiz, and the money went down with it. 'Thus one affliction is added to another,' lamented the anonymous author of a contemporary pamphlet about the expedition, 'and misery, like waves, tread one on the other's heel. And now who could have otherwise thought, but that with this sad disaster, the work itself would have been laid aside?'[31]

But it wasn't laid aside. In July 1646 a determined Parliament issued a second order, identical in every way with their first, and an undaunted Edmund Cason set off once again for the Barbary Coast, now in the frigate *Charles*.

He had better luck this time. The *Charles* arrived safely off

Algiers on 21 September and Cason was granted an audience with the *pasha* the following day. Yûsuf entertained him well and agreed straight away to the idea of a peace treaty between the two countries. (Perhaps the £2500 which Cason offered him helped to make up his mind.) From now on, neither side would interfere with the other's shipping; any Englishman – and to all intents and purposes that meant any Briton – who was brought into Algiers as a captive would be released immediately. 'So this peace shall be continued,' declared the members of Yûsuf's *dīwān*, 'and that if it please God it shall not be broke, so long as the world endures and that God and the Great Turk's curse may fall upon him that breaks this peace'.[32]

As Cason must have anticipated, Yûsuf was less enthusiastic about giving up the English slaves. They had been bought in good faith, and their owners couldn't be expected to part with them for nothing. The agent tried initially to negotiate a single flat rate per head, but eventually he agreed to pay every owner the original purchase price of their slaves.

As those owners came to see him over the next five weeks, he and an Algerian scribe took down names, prices and places of origin. Judging from the partial list which survives, 50 per cent of the victims came from the West Country, as one might expect, and around 30 per cent from London. But there were also captives from every corner of the British Isles, from Swansea and Aberdeen and Newcastle and Youghal. 'Divers Turks and Moors caused us to set down much more than their slaves cost', complained Cason, but Yûsuf promised that no one would be allowed to cheat him.[33] Others thought they could get more money by holding out for a ransom: they made over their slaves to Tunisian friends who, because they weren't Algerian nationals, were exempt from the agreement. An unknown number of captives had converted to Islam, and they weren't part of the deal, because Cason didn't want them or because Yûsuf wouldn't release them or because they were happily settled in Barbary. In any case, Cason was told, 'the young men (after turned) they carry to Alexandria, and other parts to the eastwards'.[34] Even so, more than 650 men, women and children from England, Ireland, Scotland and Wales were entered on the register. Another 100 men at least were away on the galleys, sweating at their oars in a long and bloody Ottoman campaign to take the Venetian citadel at Heraklion on Crete.

The English were a tiny minority in a slave population which was estimated at between 30,000 and 40,000, and they were scattered all over Algiers. Most of the women and children worked in household service. The men worked as dockers and porters. They built ships and laboured on urban construction sites and outlying farms. They ran shops of their own in the *suks*, selling tobacco and wine, lead shot and iron goods. Wherever they were, on the quays and in the fields and in the bagnios, they heard the story that an Englishman had come to Barbary to take the lost ones home. Peter Swanton, whose wife Katherine led the 1643 Westminster petitioners, heard the news. So did Thomas Sweet, who had been captured off the Barbary Coast in 1639 and who, like so many slaves with special skills, was prized by his master, a French renegade: 'I do keep his books of accompts and merchandise, and that keeps me here in misery'.[35]

There were old men and boys. There were young mothers with babes-in-arms. There were whole families waiting patiently and impatiently for liberation. The Puritan Robert Lake waited, 'an ancient person . . . very wise and religious'. Joan Broadbrook, who had been taken in Murad Raïs's dawn raid on Baltimore fifteen years earlier, waited. John Randal, the glover who had worked making and selling canvas clothes in William Okeley's shop, waited with his wife Bridget and their little son for the moment when the three of them might see England again. There were slaves from Dartmouth and Dover and Liverpool and Lyme Regis and Southampton and Sandwich. There were masters of ships and carpenters, caulkers, coopers, sailmakers and surgeons. They all waited.

And they all wanted to go home.

The logistics of ransom were formidable. Cason had a limited amount of ready money and a consignment of cloth, which he could exchange for captives or sell. If he sold, he might get his price in doubles – the native Algerian currency – or in Spanish dollars, 'pieces of eight'. The exchange rates fluctuated, with a double worth around an English shilling and a dollar worth between 4s. 4d. and 4s.11d. (roughly 21.5–24.5p). The price per captive varied enormously. It depended on an individual's age, status and skills, and his or her master's greed. Cason paid a paltry £7 for one Edmond Francis of Dorset, and well over £80 for Elizabeth Alwin of London. The average price was just under £30 per captive, which was the usual rate for ransoming ordinary mariners and boys, but rather more than Cason had hoped to pay. 'The reason is, here be many women and children which cost £50 per head first penny, and [which their owners] might sell . . . for an 100 [pounds].'[36]

There were other charges to be paid over and above the purchase price. Normal expenses for redemption of slaves included port taxes and fees for taking a bill of exchange; payments to the *pasha* and the customs officer and the officials who inspected the outgoing ship carrying the slaves; gratuities to the interpreter and the janissaries who stood guard during negotiations. The final cost of liberating a slave whose ransom was set at 1000 doubles might end up being well over 1600 doubles. Cason managed to negotiate this down, but he still had to pay the *pasha* a charge of 6 per cent on all the money he brought into Algiers. He then had to pay twenty dollars in export duty for each slave, again to the *pasha*, and half duty to the *pasha*'s officers – a total of between six and seven pounds sterling. Food and drink for each freed slave on the homeward voyage came to between ten and fifteen shillings (50–75p) a person. It all mounted up.

Cason just didn't have enough money to redeem all the slaves. He wrote and explained to Parliament that he originally hoped 'to have taken away the better sort of people first, and the rest afterwards'; but that in the event he had opted for quantity rather than quality.[37] Swanton and Lake and the Randal family and Joan Broadbrook of Baltimore were all freed. Poor Thomas Sweet, whose French renegade owner was determined to hold out for a ransom of £250, was not. Sweet remained behind, still doing his master's accounts, 'when others that are illiterate go off upon easy terms for cloth, so that my breeding is my undoing'.[38] Altogether, Cason negotiated the release of 245 captives; they sailed for home aboard the *Charles* in the autumn of 1646.

That was quite an achievement, and both Houses of Parliament formally approved Cason's conduct. But more than 400 Britons were left behind. Cason urged Parliament to send more goods and money, and to make haste:

> I beseech your Honours not to think that this redemption may be part one year, and part another. And I desire your people may go home in summer, for I do assure you, their clothes be thin. I think two good ships and a pinnace will be fit to fetch away the rest of the slaves.[39]

The ships didn't come. And it isn't clear why. Perhaps it was just that government didn't move that quickly. In November 1651, four and a half years after Cason's letter reached England with the first group of redeemed slaves, the Parliamentary Committee of the Navy claimed to have got together 'ten or fifteen thousand pounds in pieces of eight' which they planned to send in the 44-gun *Worcester* 'for redemption of English captives in Argier, Tunis, and Tripoli'.[40] (The vagueness about the actual sum suggests that the operation had hardly reached an advanced stage.) The following March the *Worcester* actually set out for the Straits, but she had scarcely cleared the chain at Chatham when war broke out with Holland and she was recalled and ordered to the Downs.

Meanwhile, Cason was still in Algiers. His original orders had been to travel on to Tunis to negotiate the release of English captives there, but, because there were so many waiting for their freedom in Algiers, he had decided to wait with them. They were released in dribs and drabs as Cason found the money, and they went home whenever a suitable vessel could be found to take them. This didn't happen very often: in the summer of 1653 Cason informed Parliament that he had freed Mathew Aderam of Plymouth at the beginning of 1649, and that Aderam had acted as his servant without pay for the past four years, 'waiting in vain the arrival of a ship to take him to England'.[41] A few weeks later he announced that he wasn't going to lodge any more freed captives in his house, 'as some of them have been troublesome'.

From 1648 to 1653 Cason shared his duties and his house with Humphrey Oneby, a Barbary merchant dispatched by Parliament to be the English consul in Algiers. With Oneby's help, he continued to do a remarkable job. By trading on his own account or getting credit with other merchants, he managed to redeem the old captives and arrange for their passage home; and he ensured that any English man or woman who came into harbour aboard a foreign prize was freed and eventually repatriated. He placated the *pasha* and the *dīwān*, who, after ratifying the peace treaty, had become increasingly exasperated that every nation in Europe seemed to carry three or four English sailors and English colours to avoid being attacked by corsairs. (The *pasha* wasn't imagining things, either: the English factor at Livorno openly admitted that he was shipping a valuable consignment of Neapolitan wine in Italian merchantmen which had '2 or 3 Englishmen in each, with English colours, to save them from the Turks of Algiers'.[42])

And Cason sent back intelligence. No likeness of him survives, but we can still imagine him wandering down to the harbour through the narrow streets of brightly coloured houses to see the cosmopolitan prizes that the galleys of the *tā'ifat al-ra'īs* had brought home: a Frenchman carrying oil, figs and almonds; a Flemish hoy bound for Spain with a cargo of raw linen; a Portuguese intercepted on its way to Brazil; a little English fishing boat which had been taken by the Dutch and captured from them by the Algerians. And the occasional English sailor, brought in among the crew of another nation's vessel. 'Since my last', wrote Cason to the Navy Committee, 'we have eight men given us by the governors. We do not want to keep them if we could dispose of them with safety.'[43]

It is much harder to imagine how he felt as the months turned into years and he became just another Frank in a foreign land, as much an outcast from his own kind as the renegades who drank in the taverns and whored in the brothels and knelt at Friday prayers before setting out on the cruise. He had a widowed sister in England, and a merchant nephew whom he saw occasionally. Did he yearn to be back in London, doing deals and gathering gossip at the Royal Exchange? Did the *suks* and *fonduks* of Algiers come to feel more real than Cheapside and Cornhill, the Byzantine dome of the Djemaa 'Ali Bitchine more familiar than the soaring Gothic tower of St Paul's?

Unlike the hundreds of men, women and children he rescued, Cason never saw home again. He died in Algiers on 5 December 1654, eight years after he arrived there aboard the *Charles*, and the authorities carefully inventoried his goods and shut up his house until his nephew Richard could come out and take stock of his possessions. The fact that in 1652 Parliament could note that 'none of the vessels or mariners of this Commonwealth have been surprised by the men of Argier, since the confirmation of the peace in 1646' is some measure of his success.[44] The treaty he brokered may not have lasted so long as the world endures, but it demonstrated that cordial Anglo-Algerian relations were possible.

And that, in the volatile political climate of Barbary, was no mean achievement.

12

The Greatest Scourge
to the Algerines:
The Occupation of Tangier

Wenceslaus Hollar, Scenographer and Designer of Prospects to King Charles II, sat on the wall and watched the little procession trooping past along the breakwater that snaked out into the harbour. He sketched quickly: first the driver, flicking his whip at the flanks of his stocky Barbary horses, shouting, urging them on as the two-wheeled wagon, piled high with stones, bumped and shivered over the rutted ground. Then two workmen, deep in conversation, with picks on their shoulders and high crowned felt hats on their heads. Finally, a pair of wary soldiers in scarlet and green coats, keeping their eyes out for snipers who might lie hidden in the sandhills. A third soldier was on sentry duty on the shore, marching up and down outside a little guardhouse built against a massive outcrop of rock a few yards from the beach; ten more soldiers lolled around in the sun talking and smoking. They seemed relaxed, but their muskets were lined up ready against the guardhouse wall, and the ramparts and towers and gun emplacements which loomed over them were not for show.

Tangier was a dangerous place.

England acquired its first and only outpost on the Barbary Coast under the terms of Charles II's marriage treaty with the Portuguese infanta, Catherine of Braganza. The King announced the match at the opening of Parliament on 8 May 1661, telling the Lords and Commons that he would 'make all the haste I can to fetch you a Queen hither, who, I doubt not, will bring great blessings with her, to me and you'.[1] So she did. Catherine brought the English free trade with Brazil and the East Indies, the promise of a portion of £300,000 in ready money, and the trading centre the Portuguese had established on the west coast of India at Bombay.

A view of Tangier in 1669 by Wenceslaus Hollar

But the jewel in Catherine of Braganza's bridal crown was Tangier. The Portuguese, who had occupied the town since 1471, were in no position to hold it against the Spanish, with whom they were currently at war and against whom they needed the support offered by an alliance with England. The outpost's position on the Moroccan coast at the western entrance to the Straits of Gibraltar meant it possessed an obvious strategic value for any maritime power with trading interests in the Mediterranean. No vessel could pass through the Straits without being seen from Tangier during daylight hours, and regular night-time patrols by four or five men-of-war could easily intercept any which tried to slip through in darkness. If money were invested in building a proper harbour, ships could ride at anchor securely in all weathers and, as one of Charles II's admirals told him, a nation could 'keep the place against all the world, and give the law to all the trade of the Mediterranean'.[2]

The place could be developed into a commercial hub to rival Livorno or Genoa. Even Algiers, that 'den of sturdy thieves, form'd into a body',[3] would make use of the port when it wasn't actually at war with England, their ships anchoring in the bay while the Algerians sold their prizes in the market square and supplied themselves with fresh provisions.

Best of all, Tangier was perfect as a base for naval patrols engaged in convoy work and punitive raids against the corsairs. The Salé rovers, who still made a nuisance of themselves by preying on smaller merchantmen and fishing vessels off the Atlantic coast, were only 140 miles south; by careening and revictualling at Tangier, three or four small frigates could blockade Salé so that 'those inconsiderable rogues would by such care be soon reduc'd to nothing'.[4] Five hundred miles to the east, the pirates of Algiers were once again posing a serious problem, but a carrot-and-stick approach which made use of the base could yield results, as an ardent advocate of English occupation, Sir Henry Sheres, pointed out:

> Tangier well managed, may be rendered the greatest scourge to the Algerines in the world: and may afford them the best effects of friendship. For if in time of war we can force them from this so beloved station, and attack them or their prizes bound in or out; and in time of peace (which we cannot refuse them) they can be admitted to make use of Tangier, and the port, as their occasions require; they may perform their voyages in half the time, and with half the trouble of returning home, to refit and victual.[5]

Commercially, politically, militarily, the place was, as Charles II told his ministers, 'of that strength and importance, as would be of infinite benefit and security to the trade of England'.[6]

There were a few stumbling blocks. Tangier possessed no defensible harbour, only an open bay which offered no protection against the elements or an enemy. And potential enemies were gathering: Portugal was at war with Spain and the Netherlands, and both nations had designs on the place. Moreover, it was by no means certain that the Portuguese governor of the city would relinquish control to the English, royal wedding or no royal wedding. And last but not least, Tangier was surrounded on three sides by a hostile army of Moors. Their leader, 'Abd Allāh al-Ghailān, was trying to establish a breakaway state in northern Morocco, and his response to an infidel settlement in his territory was *jihad*.

On a foggy Wednesday in June 1661 an English war fleet of seventeen vessels commanded by the Earl of Sandwich in the *Royal James* weighed anchor in the Downs and headed out into the Channel. The Earl's official instructions were to sail to Algiers and to find the best means of persuading the Algerians to desist from searching English vessels and removing goods and persons from them. He could either negotiate a new treaty, or 'fight with, kill and slay, sink, burn or destroy the persons, fleets, ships and vessels belonging to the said town or government of the town of Algiers'.[7]

Sandwich arrived in the Bay of Algiers at the end of July and presented his demands to the governor, Ismail Pasha, who refused point-blank to agree to any treaty which didn't allow his men to search English shipping. This was the signal for an apparently inconclusive exchange of fire between the fleet and the town, after which the Earl moved out of range and waited for a favourable wind so that he could send his fireships into the harbour. It didn't come, and, after a week of watching helplessly as Algerian troops strengthened the boom across the harbour, reinforced their forts and mounted more guns, the fleet sailed away again.

But Sandwich had other business. Although there was no mention of it in his orders, one of his objectives was to visit Lisbon to arrange for the evacuation of Portuguese subjects from Tangier. Another was to monitor the movements of a Dutch fleet under Michiel de Ruyter which was also in the Mediterranean, also with the publicly declared purpose of suppressing the Algerian corsairs. (At one time or another every maritime power in western Europe used the corsairs as an excuse to justify its navy's presence in the Mediterranean.) With half an eye on that Dutch fleet, Sandwich was told to put in at Tangier and to ensure that nothing untoward

happened before the English governor could arrive to take possession. Henry Mordaunt, Earl of Peterborough, was appointed to
that post in September 1661, and Sandwich anchored in the Bay
of Tangier on Thursday 10 October to await his arrival.

By the beginning of January 1662 there was still no sign of
Peterborough. Sandwich, who had spent the winter in the bay
watching and occasionally pursuing Turks as they passed through
the Straits, was getting anxious. It wasn't the Dutch who worried
him but the threat from 'Abd Allāh al-Ghailān's Moors, and on
4 January he wrote to the Portuguese governor, Don Luis de
Almeida, with an offer of 400 men to help with the defence of
the town. The offer was refused.

Eight days later the mayor of Tangier took 140 mounted soldiers
– the town's entire contingent of horse – on a particularly ill-
judged raid deep into the hostile countryside beyond the network
of trenches and forts which divided the Portuguese from the
Moors. The raiders rounded up 400 cattle and a smaller number
of camels and horses, and captured thirty-five women and girls
before turning for home. Six miles from the gates of Tangier they
were ambushed by 100 angry Moors armed with muskets. The
mayor was shot in the head in the first volley, at which his men
forgot their booty and ran. Al-Ghailān's men killed another fifty-
one Portuguese in the chase that followed, which continued to
the gates of the town.

Beleaguered and in desperate need of reinforcements, Don Luis
had second thoughts about the Earl of Sandwich's offer, and within
days the 400 English seamen had been put ashore, armed with
muskets, pikes, swords and bandoliers. They stood sentry around
the town, and manned the walls day and night. Sometimes, when
they caught sight of Moors in the fields, they fired a volley or
two of small shot, 'to put them in fear and let them know that
the town was well manned'.[8] This went on for several weeks, with
the Earl torn between relief 'that now I have between 3 and 400
men in the town and castles, and the command of all the strengths
and magazines',[9] and anxiety that reinforcements might not arrive
until it was too late.

At noon on Wednesday 29 January 1662, Lord Peterborough's
fleet finally sailed into the Bay of Tangier, bringing with it 2000
horse and 500 foot. Peterborough took formal possession of the

town the next day, and Don Luis de Almeida presented him with the keys to the gates, a pair of silver spurs and a problem which would afflict the English for the next two decades.

Wenceslaus Hollar made his drawings of Tangier when he visited the town in the autumn of 1669 with Henry Howard, the newly appointed English ambassador to Morocco. By this time it had achieved a semblance of normality, but it had been a struggle. The Portuguese had carried away everything that wasn't nailed down when they left – and even some things that were, including doors, windows and floors. So large parts of the town were remodelled or rebuilt after the English moved in. The bulk of the population, which fluctuated between 1800 and 2600 men, women and children, consisted of soldiers and their families. There was also a fair number of quarrymen and engineers who were working on the building of the harbour; most were from Yorkshire and had also brought their families with them. And there was a community of around 600 English, Portuguese, Spanish, Dutch and Italian merchants, attracted by Charles II's decision in 1662 to make Tangier a free port. (Fairly free, at least: merchants plying the East Indies trade were barred, as were ships from English plantations in the Americas.)

Houses were generally low after the Spanish fashion, with walls of stone and mud, low-pitched roofs of tile, and walls and ceilings panelled with pine planks. The officers and senior officials had rather grander homes, but almost everyone had a little garden full of sweet herbs and shady orange trees. Vines were trained to run up pillars and along lattices of reeds, and they were heavy with grapes in the hot summers. Of the various Catholic churches which had served the town under the Portuguese, only two survived: the 'Cathedral', a plain aisled building without steeple or bells, about 30 yards square with ten side chapels, which belonged to the Dominicans; and St Jago's, which was turned into an Anglican church, rededicated to Charles the Martyr (the King's father, Charles I) and 'very well filled on Sundays'.[10] Some of the old Portuguese street names were retained – Terrero de Contrato, Escada Grande, Rua Nabo. Others were newly invented reminders of home: Butcher

Row, Cannon Street, Salisbury Court, even Pye Corner. A pavilion which stood between the town walls and the outer defences, 'where the ladies, the officers, and the better sort of people do refresh and divert themselves with wine, fruits, and a very pretty bowling-base', was called 'Whitehall'. The quarries just along the coast, where the North Yorkshire stonemasons had their base, was 'Whitby'.

The town was dominated by a vast Portuguese citadel which glowered down from a hill to the north-west of the residential district and occupied almost a third of the entire area within the walls. Reinforced and partly rebuilt by the English soon after they arrived, its lower ward ran down to the bay and was used as a parade ground for the garrison. The seaward perimeter was guarded by a little fortified blockhouse and magazine, renamed York Castle, which dated from before the Portuguese occupation and was once a refuge for pirates.

The Upper Castle was much grander. It contained the governor's house – a Portuguese dungeon which had been transformed into a 'noble, large and commodious' Restoration mansion, with formal gardens and spectacular views out over the Straits. Ranged against the ramparts of the Upper Castle were storehouses for munitions and provisions, and a neat row of officers' houses lay behind the governor's. To the west, a heavily fortified gatehouse and lookout post named Peterborough Tower after the town's first English governor opened on to a broken, hilly no-man's-land.

The governorship was not a passport to success in the world. The Earl of Peterborough was recalled to England after eleven months in office, amidst allegations of corruption and incompetence. (He foolishly took home with him the only plan of the wells and springs which supplied Tangier with water, which had been given to him by Don Luis – and, even more foolishly, he lost it.) Peterborough's successor as governor, the Earl of Teviot, managed a year in the post before he was killed in a Moorish ambush. During a bout of diarrhoea, the Earl of Middleton, who took up the governorship in 1668, got up in the middle of the night to hunt for a candle, fell over his sleeping manservant and broke his arm; he died two days later. The Earl of Inchiquin was recalled in disgrace after allowing the Moors to overrun the outer defences, although he managed to calm the King's anger by giving him a pair of ostriches. The Earl of Ossory fell into a fit of depression when he heard of his appointment as governor, and succumbed to a fever before he could even leave England. One lieutenant-governor was killed in action against the Moors; another died of dysentery, the 'bloody flux'.

In spite of his short tenure in office, the Earl of Teviot was the most successful of the nine governors who tried to rule Tangier during England's struggle to maintain its Barbary Coast outpost. A professional soldier and ex-governor of Dunkirk (which Charles II sold to Louis XIV in 1662), he arrived in the colony on May Day 1663, and immediately set about reviewing the garrison and opening peace talks with 'Abd Allāh al-Ghailān. These proved un-fruitful – al-Ghailān responded that 'the Mahometan law prohib-ited them to suffer the Christians to build any fortifications in Africa'[11] – and against a background of constant skirmishing Teviot began a network of redoubts, outworks and trenches which extended as a buffer for nearly half a mile beyond the walls.

There would eventually be thirteen forts – Anne, Belasyse, Bridges, Cambridge, Charles, Fountain, Giles, Henrietta, James, Kendal, Monmouth, Pole and Pond. Most were clustered to the south of the town, and only 200 or 300 yards beyond the walls; they were meant to do no more than slow down an enemy advance. But the two biggest, Henrietta and Charles, were more formid-able affairs, heavy bastioned blockhouses big enough to hold garrisons of 150 men. Charles Fort, which was built on a hill 600 yards from the town – a spot from which the Moors had liked to keep an eye on comings and goings in the town – carried enough victuals and ammunition to withstand a six-month siege, and was armed with thirteen heavy guns.

Henrietta Fort stood on a neighbouring hill about 300 yards away. Dogs guarded the outer perimeters, and snares and spiked balls were placed in the communicating trenches to slow down the Moors, who usually went barefoot. The Earl ordered that the long grass beyond the lines should be cut short so that snipers had no cover, and each night he went out himself to set ambushes 'to prevent surprisals, it being the Moors' custom to plant their ambuscade a little before day'.[12]

Stories of Teviot's courage began to circulate inside and outside the walls, and he did his best to live up to them. Within days of his arrival at Tangier he ordered his men to open the city gates, and then rode out – alone – to reconnoitre the ground, 'marking the best grass for hay, and the fittest places to essay a fortification'.[13] His sense of honour earned respect: when two of al-Ghailān's men were killed in a skirmish one Sunday morning, he ordered their bodies to be shrouded in white linen, placed on biers and covered with flowers. Then he rode out under a white flag with his troops in formation until he reached the Moors' lines, where he ceremoniously handed over their dead. By the spring of 1664 the Moors were saying that he was the Devil, that he had ships which could fly in the air and guns which fired without human intervention, that 'he never sleeps but leaning against some part of the works; and that having scaped so many dangers . . . it is in vain to resist and impossible to worst him'.[14]

Teviot's charmed life came to a sudden end on 3 May 1664, a year and two days after his arrival in Tangier and exactly two years after a force under Major William Fiennes had been massacred during a minor sortie against al-Ghailān's men. Warning his men to take special care on the anniversary of the day when 'so many brave Englishmen were knocked on the head by the Moors',[15] the Earl took a party of 400 horse to cut down a wood which the enemy used as cover about a mile and a half out of town; and although his scouts reported that there was no enemy activity in the area, his scouts were wrong. The party rode straight into an ambush and only thirty men made it back.

The Earl was not one of them. In London, they said it was little short of a miracle that he had survived so long: 'every day he did commit himself to more probable danger than this'.[16]

Aside from fortifying Tangier against al-Ghailān's attacks, the main priority for the colonists was the harbour. From the outset, the English plan was to build a breakwater in the bay: the Earl of Sandwich noted in his journal for 6 February 1662 that 'I went and sounded about the ledge of rocks, to see the most conven- ient place for making a mole'.[17] The following year Christopher Wren, then a young Oxford professor of astronomy with only a passing interest in architecture, was invited out to advise on its construction. He declined the offer, and his place was taken by

Jonas Moore, a professional surveyor who had worked on the Earl of Bedford's great fen drainage project in the 1650s, and who had just mapped the Thames for the Navy Board.

Moore was in Tangier in the summer of 1663, returning to London with 'a brave draught of the mole to be built there, and [the] report that it is likely to be the most considerable place the King of England hath in the world'.[18] The same year, in that cheery blurring of the boundaries between private interest and public good which characterised Restoration society, the Earl of Teviot contracted with the crown to build the mole at thirteen shillings per cubic yard. He had two partners: Sir John Lawson, vice admiral of Sandwich's fleet and the commander of a naval squadron in the Mediterranean; and the Yorkshireman Hugh Cholmley, who had recently established his reputation as an engineer with the construction of a new pier at Whitby. Teviot's death, followed by Lawson's recall to England on the outbreak of war with the Dutch in 1666, left Cholmley in charge. The contract was cancelled in 1669 and he was named as surveyor-general of the works, directly answerable to Charles II's Tangier Committee in London, of which he was a member, along with Samuel Pepys, the Duke of York, Prince Rupert and the Earl of Sandwich.

The great mole was one of the most ambitious pieces of engineering to be carried out by the English in the seventeenth century. By 1680, when it was still unfinished, it was 500 yards long, 90 feet wide and 18 feet high at low water. Several houses had been built on it, along with a battery armed with 'a vast number of great guns, which are almost continually kept warm, during fair weather, in giving and paying salutes to ships which come in and out'.[19] It was a symbol of English aspiration and English pride, 'the greatest and most noble undertaking in the world, (all other moles, as at Genoa, Malaga, Algier, etc. not deserving more than the name of a key in comparison of it)'.[20]

It was also a symbol of English extravagance, costing a mighty £340,000.

Cholmley brought over forty masons, miners and other workmen who had built his pier at Whitby – hence the name of their settlement, which consisted of stables, storehouses and quarters for the men and their wives at quarries a mile along the coast from the walls of the town. Cholmley and his wife and daughter moved into Tangier, living in a house by the church and leading the sociable and civilised life of a Restoration gentleman. Lady Anne Cholmley, the daughter of the Earl of Northampton, usually entertained the governor, the minister and a few other select guests after Sunday morning service. 'We had an extraordinary good dinner', wrote the governor's secretary after one such gathering; 'some wild boar baked in a pot the best of any I ever saw, good claret . . . rhenish, and a mighty strong beer called blue John.' On another occasion Lady Anne treated her guests to 'extraordinary good anchovies, potted wild boar, pickled oysters, and admirable claret'.[21] After dinner the Cholmleys would stroll along to Whitehall to watch a bowling match between the married officers and the bachelors; or enjoy entertainments put on by visiting Spanish actors at the governor's mansion; or sail out into the bay with their little girl, Moll, to see how work on the mole was progressing.

After a good start, it was progressing rather slowly. The Earl of Sandwich, who called in at Tangier in August 1668, reported that the mole was 380 yards long; but as it extended into deeper water the task of construction grew harder, while winter storms caused breaches in what was already there. Cholmley's original method was to drop loose stones on to the seabed, and then to build up on these foundations with massive masonry blocks cramped together with iron. The structure was protected from the weather by a row of projecting pillars on the seaward side, which helped to dissipate the force of the buffeting waves.

Sandwich brought with him a 'good ingenious man' named Henry Sheres to help with his survey of the work to date[22] and, the following May, Sheres returned to Tangier to act as clerk-examiner on the project. Later that year he travelled to Genoa to see the mole there, and when he returned he did his best to persuade Cholmley that the Genoese model, which instead of masonry blocks used massive wooden caissons or chests filled with stones, was a better and cheaper way of proceeding. Cholmley was reluctant to follow his advice – 'the work with chests seemed . . . superfluous', he said[23] – but as each winter brought another breach and another round of emergency repairs, and as it became obvious that the deep-water work had slowed to a snail's pace, criticism began to mount at home.

Tangier and its network of trenches and outlying forts

1 King's Batt.ⁿ 2 Governor's Reg.ᵗᵗ (2ⁿᵈ Queens). 3 1ˢᵗ Batt.ⁿ Dumbartons Reg.ᵗ 4 2ⁿᵈ do. do. 5 Adm.ˡ Herbert's Batt.ⁿ of Seamen.
6 2ⁿᵈ Batt.ⁿ Governors Reg.ᵗ (2ⁿᵈ Queens). 7. 8. 9. 10. 11 Forlorn Hope, 12 Detached parties at Anne Fort. 13 Do. do. Kendal Fort. 14 Reserve Cavalry.

In 1676, when a new contract for completing the mole was drawn up, Sheres was able, by using caissons, to undercut Cholmley's tender by £10,000, to the latter's distress. He left Sheres to it and took Lady Anne and little Moll back to England, where he entered Parliament and busied himself in court politics and self-justification.

The mole never was completed. 'Abd Allāh al-Ghailān's desultory assaults and ambushes came to an end in the late 1660s, when he was defeated by Mawlay al-Rashid, the Alawi sultan of Morocco. Tangier's troubles didn't end there. Neither al-Rashid nor his successor, the brutal Mawlay Isma'il, was particularly keen to see a fortified foreign enclave in their territory, and troops were frequently sent to chip away at the port's outlying defences.

They held off from making an all-out assault, and some recent British historians have suggested that the Moors deliberately waited in the hope that Sheres would finish the mole so that they could move in and take over a fully functioning ocean harbour. In fact the real bone of contention for successive Moroccan rulers was not the state of the mole but the growing system of outlying forts begun by Teviot. While they undoubtedly had designs on Tangier itself, they were determined that the English must not be allowed to expand their territory beyond the old limits set by the Portuguese. And with these forts the English were doing just that.

On Thursday 25 March 1680 the Irish governor of Tangier, the Earl of Inchiquin, dispatched seventy-five soldiers to relieve Charles Fort. The Moroccan *qaid*, 'Umar ben Haddu, was camped with an army of 7000 men less than a mile from the town; and his troops were digging a network of trenches and cross-trenches which was coming closer and closer to the forts which defended the English lines. This was something new. Sniper fire, ambushes and the occasional full-frontal cavalry charge were the tactics the Moors usually employed, not engineers and siegeworks. Now they were beginning a mine, an offensive tunnel, about 200 yards from Charles Fort, and cutting deep trenches between Kendal Fort and Pond Fort, and close to Henrietta Fort. Although they were only half a musket shot from Charles Fort, they made no attempt to fire on it; and 'our small firing did not much disturb them', wrote a soldier in the Charles Fort garrison, 'by reason of their being always under ground'.[24]

Four days later, on 29 March, the Moors cut through the lines of communication between the fort and the town, and that night the English soldiers could see hundreds of them working feverishly by moonlight to mark out new positions. In the morning the commanders of Charles Fort, Captain St John and Captain Trelawny, erected a 'cavalier', a raised gun platform, on the walls of one of their batteries, and from the vantage point it provided, 30 feet above the ground, eight or nine snipers overlooked and fired down into the Moorish trenches.

It made no difference. Day by day the siegeworks snaked around, through and beneath the English defences. 'Umar ben Haddu had brought in specialists from Algiers and the Levant, men who had learned their trade during the siege of the Venetian stronghold of Heraklion on Crete, which had fallen to the Ottomans in September 1669 after a campaign lasting twenty-eight months. With their help, the Moors were no longer the unmethodical neighbours they had been to the Portuguese, but were 'grown to a great degree of knowledge in the business of war'.[25]

At eight o'clock on the night of 11 April a force of between 500 and 600 Moors suddenly rushed at Henrietta Fort. They pitched long timbers up against a section of wall, covered the planks with boards and branches and brought in their pioneers to work on a mine under cover of the makeshift shelter. For more than seven hours the English commander, a lieutenant of foot named John Wilson, directed his men from the ramparts as they hurled hand grenades down on their attackers in the darkness and shot at them with small arms.

Just before dawn the Moors retreated without having managed to breach the wall, and Wilson, still not daring to open the gates of the fort, let down five men on ropes to clear away the timber siegeworks and burn them. They also decapitated two of the corpses left behind by 'Umar's army and raised the heads on poles 'in the sight of the Moorish camp, which all of that nation hold for the greatest indignity that can be put upon them, because, according to their Mahometan superstition, they hold that when they die, their bodies immediately are translated into paradise; but if they are dismembered they can in no wise enter'.[26] There were no more flower-strewn biers, no more expressions of mutual respect.

Torrential rains that week flooded 'Umar's trenches, but he maintained his grip on the siege. All of the outlying English forts were now cut off; day and night their troops were subjected to the sound of drums and pipes coming from the Moorish camp, and whenever they tried to communicate with the town by speaking trumpet, 'the Moors fell a-hallowing and shouting all along their lines'.[27]

At the end of April 1680 two renegades, a Frenchman and an Englishman, appeared before Charles Fort carrying a white flag. They brought the news that it had been undermined, and that 'Umar would give the order to light the gunpowder if Captains St John and Trelawny didn't surrender. The officers had one hour to decide.

To prove they weren't bluffing, the renegades brought a safe conduct for two English engineers to inspect the works. So they did, but the English remained defiant, telling 'Umar that they 'would stand it out to the last'.[28] Between three and four o'clock on the afternoon of Thursday 29 April the Moors sprang the mine; there was a low rumble deep in the ground, and then a huge plume of sand and dust erupted into the air – 40 yards short of the fort. Impatient to break the deadlock, 'Umar's pioneers had got their measurements wrong.

Nothing daunted, they set to work again, while 'Umar sent for more ordnance. On Saturday 8 May the defenders saw a group of Moors hauling 'carriages of great guns' up to a hill overlooking Henrietta. They were actually only fairly light cannon, a 2-pounder and a 6-pounder, but within twenty-four hours they had opened a breach in one of the fort's walls. Using their speaking trumpet, and shouting in Gaelic in the hope that no one in the Moorish camp would be able to understand them, the officers of Charles Fort got a message to Governor Inchiquin to say that Henrietta was about to fall to 'Umar and that the garrison of about 175 men was threatening mutiny. They couldn't hold out much longer – could they have permission to evacuate the fort?

Sir Palmes Fairborne, the deputy governor and commander-in-chief of the military at Tangier, was a professional soldier who had just returned from Europe. He and Inchiquin immediately

convened a council of war in the Upper Castle. They decided
that Henrietta Fort was lost (as indeed it was – Lieutenant Wilson
surrendered that very night), and that the men in the other
outlying forts must be brought into the town. A ship should stand
by the next morning to take on board the thirteen-man garrison
from Giles Fort, which lay on the coast close to the quarries at
Whitby, and at the same time the men from Charles Fort must
run for it across the 600 yards of open ground that lay between
them and the relative safety of the town walls. To cover their
retreat, 500 men would sally out from the town towards Moorish
lines in five groups: the main body, a right and left wing, a reserve
– and a 'forlorn-hope', which was the name given to the first
wave of soldiers in an assault, the men who bore the brunt of
the enemy's fire and enabled the main body to gain ground while
the enemy was reloading. (Apt though it sounds, the phrase is an
Anglicisation of the equally apt Dutch *verloren hoop*, which means
'lost troop'.)

The men in Charles Fort spent the night spiking and wedging
their heavy guns, so that 'Umar couldn't use them. At dawn the
Moors blew up Henrietta with a mine, and the attempt to rescue
the garrison of Giles turned into a farce when all but one of the
soldiers surrendered to the enemy because they were too scared
to swim out to the ship waiting to take them off.

Meanwhile, the men of Charles Fort broke all the small arms
they couldn't carry, and threw all their powder and hand grenades
into a counter-mine they had been digging to intercept 'Umar's
mine. They spoiled their provisions, and did their best to render
their surplus ammunition useless to the enemy. Then they waited.

The two captains had agreed between them that St John would
lead the retreat while Trelawny, who had his little son with him,
would bring up the rear. At seven o'clock they lit a fuse to the
train of powder which was to detonate the counter-mine. By the
time they opened the gates of the fort only one inch was left. As
they ran, two things happened in quick succession. The forlorn-
hope, which was led by a Scottish captain named George Hume,
emerged from the town and advanced relentlessly towards the
enemy trenches which criss-crossed the no-man's-land between
Tangier and Charles Fort, followed by the main body, then the
reserve and the two wings. And 'Umar's soldiers poured out of

their camp and into those trenches, determined to take both the fort and its garrison.

The counter-mine was sprung just as the retreating troops scrambled over the first trench, and the noise and confusion bought them a little time. Then they were over the second trench. The forlorn-hope was only a couple of hundred yards away. And still the Moors hadn't reached them.

Now there was only one trench left between them and the safety of the town. But it was the so-called Great Trench, the hardest obstacle of all, 14 feet deep and half-flooded with rainwater. Hundreds of armed sailors lined the ramparts of the town wall, firing volley after volley at the Moors, urging their comrades on. Hume's men were hurling grenades at the enemy as fast as they could.

The soldiers of Charles Fort were in the Great Trench, splashing through the mud and filth, when 'Umar's men caught up with them. St John was one of the first out. He took a musket ball in his side as he ran for the gate, but he managed to stagger inside. Trelawny wasn't so lucky. He was killed in the trench as he tried to pass his child over the parapet to safety. The boy was taken alive, along with fourteen others.

Thirty-nine soldiers made it back to safety. The rest died. The next day 'Umar invited the English to come out and retrieve their dead under a flag of truce. They had all been decapitated.

That afternoon he sent back their heads.

13

Breaches of Faith:
Making Peace with Barbary

*T*here had been a moment at the end of the 1640s when
England seemed to have achieved a peace of sorts with
the two most troublesome Barbary states. The treaty
which Edmund Cason had negotiated with Algiers in 1646 was
holding, due in part at least to his continued presence there; and
Thomas Browne, an agent appointed by Parliament, was dealing
with the authorities at Tunis for the release of English captives
and the confirmation of an agreement for England and Tunis not
to molest each other's shipping.

Tunis had gone through some major upheavals since the death
of Yûsuf Dey in 1637. His successor as *dey*, a capable Genoese renegade named Uṣṭâ Murad, encouraged and regulated piracy, played
off the interests of Tunisians against those of the Turkish janissary
corps and constructed a new and heavily fortified harbour for corsairs
on the north-east coast of Tunisia at Porto Farina (present-day Ghar
al Milh). But Uṣṭâ Murad Dey died in 1640; the next two *deys*,
Ahmad Khûja (1640–47) and Mohammad Lâz (1647–53), had to
contend with a particularly astute and powerful *bey*, Hammûda.

Under 'Uthmân Dey at the beginning of the century, the *bey* of Tunis had been a finance officer responsible for collecting taxes; since the nomadic tribesmen of the interior were reluctant to hand over their taxes, the process often involved an element of compulsion. Hammûda's father Murad Bey, a Corsican who had been captured by pirates as a child and converted to Islam, was thus able to gather together a private army separate and distinct from the janissary corps, which formed the basis of his political power as *bey*; and Hammûda, who inherited the beylicate in 1631 as a sixteen-year-old after Murad persuaded the Ottoman emperor to appoint him *pasha* of Tunis, continued the rise to power begun by his father. He built himself a palace at the Bardo a few miles outside the city, where he would be safe from the hostile janissaries, and consolidated his influential connections with both rural Tunisia and with Tunis itself. One of his wives, for example, was the daughter of a tribal chieftain, while another was the daughter of an important Provençal renegade. His good opinion was essential when it came to electing the *dey* and, in 1658, he followed his father's example by buying the office of *pasha* from the emperor.

Power in mid-seventeenth-century Tunis was delicately balanced between the *dey* and the *bey* and the *agha* of the janissary corps. All of them were happy to invoke the authority of the Sultan in Istanbul when it suited; all of them were equally happy to ignore him when it didn't. The Tunisian corsairs remained an important economic force in the community – the state still received 10 per cent of their prizes, the janissaries still accompanied them on raids, everyone who could afford to still invested in their ventures – but they were expected to conform to government policy and to prey only on those nations with whom Tunis had not concluded a treaty.

By and large they toed the line, even when it involved a loss of income all round. So when in April 1651 an English ship, the *Goodwill*, whose captain had contracted to carry thirty-two important Tunisian citizens from Tunis to Smyrna, was intercepted by Maltese galleys, and when that captain, a man named Stephen Mitchell, handed over those thirty-two Tunisian citizens without a struggle, the *dey*, the *bey* and the *agha* were understandably aggrieved. When word reached them that the captives had been put into the galleys of the Knights of Malta as slaves, their disappointment with their English friends was acute. And when they heard that Captain Mitchell had not only handed over their

comrades without a fight, but might actually have *sold* them to
the Knights, they were very cross indeed.

So were the townsfolk. There was a riot as a 500-strong mob
stormed through the streets looking for Englishmen and crying
'Stone the dogs who have sold our fathers, brothers, kindred and
friends!'[1] Members of the English community were taken into
custody for their own protection, and English property in Tunis
was confiscated until the captives were returned safely.

Subsequent events show how difficult it was to arbitrate when
complicated international episodes like this occurred. The Parlia-
mentarian naval commander William Penn, who happened to be
cruising with his squadron in the western Mediterranean in search
of the remains of the royalist fleet commanded by the late King's
nephew, Prince Rupert, remonstrated with the Grand Master of
the Knights of Malta. 'If by means of such necessity our merchants
should be subject to such deep inconveniences', Penn threatened,
'what resentment the State of England may thereupon make, I
cannot conclude.'[2] Meanwhile, Penn secured the release in Tunis of
the most senior of the English merchants, Samuel Boothouse, who
was allowed to travel to Sicily to obtain a letter from the Archbishop of Palermo in the name of the Viceroy of Sicily (who technically had feudal domain over the Knights) demanding the release
of the thirty-two Turks. Boothouse also tried to prosecute Captain
Mitchell in the English courts, and Mitchell was held on his return
to London, only to be released when no evidence was offered.

The Grand Master, who didn't take kindly to being squeezed
between Penn's squadron on the one hand and the Viceroy of
Sicily on the other, responded to English threats by pointing out
that the Knights of Malta were friends to England, but that since
the time of the Crusades their role had been to harry Turks, 'the
enemies of the name of Jesus Christ'.[3] Penn suggested the affair
might be solved if Tunis paid a ransom of 3200 dollars (£770) for
the lot. The Knights demanded a lot more than that. They wanted
40,000 dollars (£9600), and they refused to part with a single slave
until the entire sum was handed over.

The Tunisians decided reprisals were in order. Their corsairs
captured an English merchant ship, the *Princess*, and held her crew.

For the next couple of years, England had more pressing foreign affairs than Barbary to consider, in the shape of war with Holland. But when the First Anglo-Dutch War ended in 1654, the Commonwealth was in possession of a massive fleet, 160 strong; and that summer Cromwell and the Council of State sent twenty-four ships under the command of Admiral Robert Blake into the Mediterranean, where it was to remind other nations, principally the French and the Spanish, that England was a force to be reckoned with. While he was there, Blake's instructions included the liberation of English captives held by the Tunisians, the restitution of the *Princess* and the re-establishment of peaceful relationships with the *dey* of Tunis.

Admiral Robert Blake

Blake, an inveterately republican veteran of the English Civil Wars (and not to be confused with the Robert Blake who mediated between the English and the Moors in 1637–8), arrived off Tunis on 7 February 1655. The moment he anchored 'I did forthwith send ashore to the Dey of Tunis a paper of demands for restitution of the ship *Princess*, with satisfaction for losses, and enlargement of captives'.[4] There was a new *dey* in office: Mustafa Lâz Dey was Hammûda Bey's choice, and, since Hammûda had bribed the *agha* to support him, Tunis was experiencing a rare moment of co-operative government without the usual tri-lateral infighting.

The Tunisians received Blake politely, and expressed a desire to restore peaceful relations with England; but the thirty-two citizens taken from the *Goodwill* were still being held captive in Malta, and until they were freed the *dey* refused point-blank, in Blake's words, 'to make a restitution of satisfaction for what was past'.[5] It was stalemate; and the *dey* showed not the slightest sign of being intimidated by Blake's war fleet, even though it boasted around 900 guns and more than 4000 men. 'They entrust an English runnagardo with their causing', commented a suspicious John Weale, a junior officer with Blake's fleet who kept a journal of the voyage.[6]

The fleet needed to replenish its supplies of bread and fresh water, so Blake couldn't afford to stay in Tunis Road indefinitely. Moreover, he was a punctilious officer, and he was anxious that, although his instructions authorised him 'to seize, surprise, sink, and destroy all ships and vessels belonging to the kingdom of Tunis', they didn't specifically extend to actually entering Tunisian ports.[7] So he sent letters back to England asking for clarification and sailed for Cagliari Bay in Sicily to revictual his ships. On the way the fleet anchored for more than a week at Porto Farina, where they found nine corsairs (including the refitted *Princess*) drawn up close to the shore and unrigged. Blood-red colours were flying from the castle which guarded the harbour and from eight of the pirate ships; a silk flag of white and green flew from the corsair admiral's vessel. There were signs of frantic activity along the shoreline: batteries of guns were being erected, as was a sea of tents. And thousands of horsemen and infantry had gathered, flourishing their scimitars in the sunlight and firing at English boats which attempted a reconnaissance closer to the shore. The Tunisians were clearly preparing to repel an English invasion.

Blake was back at Tunis on 18 March, when he found Mustafa Lâz Dey less inclined to negotiate than before. Accusing the Tunisians of obstinacy, insolence and wilfulness – by which he presumably meant they still wanted their citizens back – he reported back to England that such 'barbarous provocations did so far work upon our spirits, that we judged it necessary for the honour of the fleet, our nation, and religion, seeing they would not deal with us as friends, to make them feel us as enemies'.[8] Having now resolved on commencing hostilities, he planned to fire the pirate fleet, which still lay in harbour at Porto Farina. After withdrawing his ships to Sicily – a deliberate ruse to lull his enemy into a false sense of security – he arrived back at Porto Farina on the afternoon of 3 April.

At sunrise the next morning the English fleet entered the harbour. The biggest men-of-war, including Blake's 60-gun flagship, the *George*, anchored within musket shot of the Tunisian fortifications and opened fire, taking advantage of a gentle breeze off the sea, which kept a pall of smoke between themselves and the enemy. Out of these rolling clouds emerged the English boats of execution filled with armed men and incendiaries, and at the sight of them the pirate crews, who had been returning fire with small arms, lost their nerve and swam for the shore. All nine vessels were boarded and set alight.

By mid-morning the operation was over and the English sailors were back aboard their ships. Twenty-five had been killed and about forty hurt, mostly by small-arms fire from the shore. The fleet continued to play its guns on the burning ships to deter any attempts to extinguish the flames. That night the English lay at anchor outside the harbour and watched them light up the sky like so many bonfires.

Leaving aside the question of who held the moral high ground, Blake's burning of the Tunisian fleet at Porto Farina was a remarkable action. 'Planned with care and executed with precision', said the twentieth-century naval historian J. R. Powell, it was the first time ever that 'the guns of a fleet had overpowered shore batteries'.[9] 'A piece of service as hath not been paralleled in these parts of the world', wrote young John Weale.[10] 'We have great cause to bless God for His mighty deliverance in the sight of the heathen' was the verdict of another officer.[11]

At home, the English hailed the burning of Porto Farina as a terrible demonstration of the nation's naval might. G.T.'s triumphalist and racist *Encomiastick* gives a flavour:

The poor Mahometans do trembling fly,
From their strong holds to mountains that were nigh
Whence like so many fiends of blackest hue,
(With scaring horrid faces) they might view,
In those sulphureous fiery streams below,
A new Gehenna, to their greater woe.[12]

England was also convinced that the friendly reception Blake received when he put in for supplies at Algiers six days after Porto Farina was entirely due to the shock and awe his action had caused throughout Barbary. This wasn't quite fair. The Algerians, increasingly adept at playing off one European power against another, had already decided that it was in their interests to maintain the peace with England – for the time being. When Blake's fleet first entered the Straits in November 1654, for example, four Algerines made a great play of handing over some English captives whom they had just rescued from a Salé pirate.

Blake himself was more circumspect about his victory, and with good reason. The action was a tactical triumph, but it didn't really achieve very much apart, of course, from preventing nine Tunisian ships causing any more mischief. Although he returned to Tunis and asked Mustafa Lâz Dey to reconsider his refusal to hand over English goods and captives from the *Princess* (he could no longer hand over the *Princess* itself, because Blake had just burned it), the *dey* stuck to his obstinacy, insolence and wilfulness. Moreover, he chose this moment to remind the admiral that Tunis was under the protection of the Ottoman emperor.

This was no hollow threat. Blake took it seriously enough to dispatch letters warning Sir Thomas Bendysh, the English ambassador at Istanbul, to expect reprisals against English merchants in the city. Bendysh went straight to the Grand Vizier as soon as he received the news, 'and very well pacified him concerning the burning of the ships at Tunis',[13] so the consequences Blake feared didn't materialise. But it wasn't until after April 1657, when the ransoms of the thirty-two captives held at Malta were finally settled (by the English), that a lasting peace between England and Tunis became a real possibility.

Even then the Tunisian government would only give up the

seventy-two English men and women it held when Admiral John Stoakes, who arrived off Tunis with six warships in 1658, agreed to pay out 11,250 dollars (about £2700) for their release. This cleared the way for formal articles of peace, which were agreed on 8 February 1658. They included a clause stipulating that 'if any English ships shall receive on board any goods or passengers belonging to the kingdom of Tunis, they shall be bound to defend both them and their goods ... and not deliver them to the enemy.'[14]

Maintaining good relations with the Ottoman Empire was important, as the *Lewis* affair demonstrates. In the summer of 1657 word reached London that Captain William Ell of the *Lewis* had turned up at Livorno with a cargo of rice, sugar and other provisions, which he was trying to sell. The problem was that these goods were the property of Sultan Mehmed IV, and Ell had contracted with the *pasha* of Egypt to take them from Alexandria to Istanbul.

This had the makings of a major diplomatic incident, as Sir Thomas Bendysh pointed out to Oliver Cromwell. All his carefully laid plans for furthering English interests in the Levant were in danger, he ranted, 'of being blasted by the unexpected and foul treachery and falseness of one (sorry I am, I must name an Englishman) William Ell, master of the *Lewis*'.[15] In London the Levant Company, which employed Ell, shared Bendysh's outrage. Trade was already poor because of the depredations of Turkish and Spanish pirates; and officials were in the middle of some delicate negotiations for the recovery of a Company ship, the *Resolution*, which had recently been taken by men-of-war from Tripoli. Ell's actions jeopardised everything, said the Company, 'to the great shame and scandal of the English, and disparagement of our ships, beside the evil consequences it may have on our trade'.[16]

Captain Ell's version of events was delivered to Secretary of State Thurloe at the beginning of September 1657, and it suggests the matter was more complicated than either Bendysh or the Levant Company appreciated. Ell claimed that, after he contracted to carry the Grand Seigneur's goods in January, he was kept hanging about at Alexandria for more than three months without any allowance for the delay. When he was finally given permission to set sail, armed Turks went with him and commanded him to put in at Rhodes, where he encountered a battle fleet of forty-four galleys and fifteen ships from Algiers, Tunis and Tripoli which was preparing to attack Venetian territory in the Aegean. The *Lewis* was held there for a further two months, during which time the Tripolitans amused themselves by threatening that the moment Ell had unloaded his cargo they were going to take over his ship and carry off two boys who were part of the crew 'to satisfy their inhuman, unnatural lust'.[17] Thoroughly rattled, Ell was ordered to accompany the fleet into the Aegean, unload at one of the Turkish-held islands and refit the *Lewis* for service against Venice. He was all too aware that the Venetians hanged any Christians they found supporting the Turks, and while the Tripolitans – the same pirates who had captured the *Resolution* of London – continued their threats against him, the captain-general of the fleet showed no inclination to protect them against 'this desperate destructive resolution of the Barbarian corsairs'.[18] So on 6 July, while the fleet anchored for the night off Samos, Ell seized his chance and made a run for it. The *Lewis* arrived at Livorno twenty days later.

It's impossible to know how much of this was true. But it cut no ice with the English government, or with Sir Thomas Bendysh, or with the English agent in Livorno. An aggrieved Ell complained that the Grand Duke of Tuscany was threatening to return him and his ship to the Turks because his behaviour was prejudicial to European interests in Turkey. He offered to hand over the balance due to the Grand Seignieur as soon as the goods were sold. In desperation he reminded Cromwell that he and most of his men had fought for their country against the Dutch in the last war. By way of reply Oliver Cromwell personally wrote to the Grand Duke, asking him to impound the *Lewis* and its cargo and to arrest the captain and crew. The disputed goods were sent to Istanbul – at Captain Ell's expense. The Turks refused to accept them, saying they were spoiled; and claimed further that they were only worth 16,000 dollars (£3840), while the original consignment was valued well over four times that amount.

While the English government went to some lengths to avoid upsetting Mehmed IV, its relations with the Barbary Coast states were complicated by the fact that Barbary was less inclined than ever to keep to Istanbul's rules. Almost the first thing the Earl of Winchilsea did when he presented his credentials to the Grand Vizier on his arrival in Istanbul in January 1661 was to draw his attention to renewed complaints about the behaviour of Algerian pirates, to which the Vizier airily promised redress. They both knew he didn't mean it.

Like France and Holland – the other two major European nations with trading interests in the Mediterranean – the English knew that as well as going through the motions with the Sultan and the Vizier, they would have to come to separate accommodations with the governments of Algiers, Tunis and Tripoli. The Dutch did their best to make themselves indispensable to the corsairs by supplying sails and munitions; the French relied on a shared hatred of Spain to endear themselves to Barbary; the English, after Blake's action at Porto Farina had boosted their confidence as a force to be reckoned with in the Mediterranean, developed a confrontational policy of cannon diplomacy.

The apparently inconclusive attack on Algiers which the Earl of Sandwich mounted in the summer of 1661, before he moved on to supervise the handover at Tangier, did more damage to the city than he realised. A month after he withdrew from Algiers he was surprised to hear from a Frenchman who'd just left the place that 'when we shot against Algiers we killed them many men and beat down many houses, and that they have made a great heap of our shot in the Palace yard'.[19] Back in England, where a restored monarchy wanted its own Porto Farina, the assault was hailed as a major victory: Turkish insolence had been answered by a terrifying display of naval power in which English guns battered down half the town, demolished the citadel, destroyed eighteen enemy ships and rescued 1100 Christian slaves.

This was a wild exaggeration. But it confirmed the obvious: that a powerful English presence in the Mediterranean at least had a chance of making Islamic pirates choose to prey on the merchant ships of *other* nations. Sandwich's vice admiral, the rough, tough career mariner Sir John Lawson, remained on the Barbary Coast

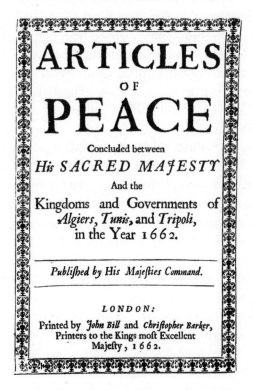

ARTICLES

OF

PEACE

Concluded between

His SACRED MAJESTY

And the

Kingdoms and Governments of
Algiers, Tunis, and *Tripoli,*
in the Year 1662.

Publiſhed by His Majeſties Command.

LONDON:

Printed by *John Bill* and *Chriſtopher Barker,*
Printers to the Kings moſt Excellent
Majeſty, 1662.

Sir John Lawson concluded peace treaties with Algiers, Tunis and Tripoli. They didn't last.

for the next four summers, harrying Algerian shipping and generally making his presence felt.

So effective was he that in the autumn of 1662 he managed to conclude three separate treaties within the space of thirty-six days. Hammûda was now *pasha* at Tunis, having appointed his son Murad as *bey*, and he confirmed articles of peace on 5 October. There were some very minor changes to the previous treaty, but the articles still included the clause about English ships defending their Tunisian passengers. Hammûda had not forgotten Captain Mitchell's lack of goodwill towards the Tunisians on the *Goodwill*. To be fair, nor had Charles II. In a proclamation issued at Whitehall he commanded the masters of all English ships carrying Turks or their goods 'to the utmost of their power, by fighting or otherwise, [to] preserve and defend them against any whatsoever'.[20]

The rest of the Tunis treaty was common-sensical, if a little biased towards the English. Neither side should seize the other's ships at sea or in port; both should treat the other's citizens with respect; any English merchant or passenger captured by Tunisian ships of war was to be released with their 'goods free and entire'.[21] And the ship of either party 'shall have free liberty to enter into any port or river belonging to the dominions of either party'.[22] (How often did Tunisian merchants sail up the Thames or enter the port of Bristol?) Encounters between the two nations on the high seas were formalised through a system of passes. Tunisian men-of-war were to be provided with certificates by the English consul at Tunis, and were required to produce them when they met a ship flying English colours. In return, the English vessel had to allow two men – and no more – to come aboard to verify that its crew was indeed predominantly English. It was common practice for Italian merchant ships to sail under English colours because they carried two or three English crew, 'to save them from the Turks'.[23]

On 10 November 1662, a month after concluding terms with Hammûda Pasha at Tunis, Lawson confirmed a treaty with Algiers. The details had been thrashed out the previous April, but the *pasha*, Ismail, had neglected to inform the *tā'ifat al-ra'īs* of the fact since, as a major investor in piracy, he was keen to prolong their activities against English shipping for as long as possible. All was now well. No Algerian was to give any English subject 'a bad word, or a bad deed, or a bad action'.[24] English slaves were to be set free on payment of their first market price. (Charles II asked the Church of England to stump up the cash, and more than 150 captives were redeemed the following January.) No more were to be bought or sold in Algiers or its territories.

More economically powerful and more of a threat, Algiers extracted 10 per cent custom duty on imports and exports, although this hardly operated in its favour – very soon the Algerian merchants were complaining that English traders didn't come to their city any more. All English ships sailing in the Mediterranean were required to carry a pass:

> The Algier ships of war meeting any merchant-ship belonging to the subjects of the King of Great Britain . . . have liberty to send one single boat, with but two sitters more than the common crew of rowers, and no more to enter on board

the said merchant-ship but the two sitters, without the express leave of the commander of the merchant-ship; that upon producing unto them a pass under the hand and seal of the Lord High Admiral of England, the said boat to presently depart, and the merchant-ship to proceed on his voyage.[25]

Examples of these passes were handed over to the authorities in the Barbary states for their men of war to carry to sea, so they could distinguish them from counterfeits. But even if the master of a vessel couldn't produce a pass, the Algerians were required to leave it alone as long as the majority of the company was English.

Lawson was a busy and determined man, with a strong and well-armed squadron. Between signing the Tunis treaty on 5 October 1662 and the Algiers treaty on 10 November, he also managed to agree 'a good and firm peace' with 'Uthmân, the *pasha* of Tripoli.

Until quite recently, the corsairs of Tripoli hadn't posed too much of a threat to European trade. For one thing, they weren't as adventurous as their comrades to the west, never venturing as far as the Straits, let alone into the Atlantic. For another, Tripoli was poorer than either Algiers or Tunis and the bloody battles for supremacy which frequently shook its hierarchy of *dey, bey, dīwān* and Istanbul-appointed *pasha* were more time-consuming. 'Uthmân was a Greek renegade who became *dey* in 1649 on the sudden but not unexpected death of the incumbent, another Greek renegade named Mohammad al-Saqisli. 'Uthmân moved quickly to secure the support of Mehmed IV, who appointed him *pasha*; and at the same time he secured popular approval by the excellent and simple expedient of lowering taxes.

This bought 'Uthmân time, but his hold on power depended on a juggling act involving a bewildering patchwork of different and often overlapping factions: Turkish janissaries; corsair captains; European renegades; native Tripolitans; *shaykhs*, who ruled the tribes in the deserts beyond the city walls; *kulughis*, the offspring of janissaries and local women who formed a separate, unempowered and resentful class in Tripoli as they did in Algiers and Tunis. Every one of these groups had to be placated, neutralised or actively suppressed.

'Uthmân's natural allies were the renegades; it was they who had propelled him to power in the first place, and he tried to ensure their continued support by rewarding them with positions of authority. For the same reason he built up the fleet – around half of the corsair captains in Tripoli were renegades – turning it into a strong force of some twenty-four ships.

It was the activities of this fleet which attracted the attention of Sir John Lawson's squadron. During the 1650s 'Uthmân's 'Tripoli men' preyed on Levant Company ships to such an extent that the Company petitioned Cromwell for help, while the port itself gained a reputation all the way along the Barbary Coast as a safe haven for pirates: an Englishman calling there in the spring of 1651 noted without surprise that one evening a Moroccan man-of-war from Salé, 1400 miles westward, sailed in with a prize. (The same Englishman also encountered renegades from Kent and Devon during his stay, and ransomed a captive so that he could return to his native Dorset.)

Lawson's articles of peace and commerce with 'Uthmân Pasha were basically the same as those he concluded with Tunis and Algiers. They announced a new start in relations between the two countries, the first clause of the agreement stating that 'after the signing and sealing of these articles, all injuries and damages sustained on either part shall be quite taken away and forgotten'.[26] Lawson installed a consul, Samuel Tooker, who, like most English consuls in seventeenth-century Barbary, was destined to have an unhappy time: promised a generous salary of £400 a year from the crown, he had only received £200 after eight years of service, while the 2 per cent consulage he was supposed to receive on goods imported and exported in English ships was withheld by 'Uthmân, who declared it was an unwarranted restraint on trade.

But Tooker's woes didn't count for much beside Lawson's considerable achievement – separate peace treaties with three of the four Barbary states. By the end of 1662 England had renewed the articles of capitulation with Sultan Mehmed IV, and had put in place signed and sealed agreements with Tripoli, Tunis and Algiers. If relations with Morocco were still a little rocky, at least Tangier was now a free port. English ships could move around the Mediterranean unmolested and were free to carry foreign goods and persons, 'a great advantage for the trade and reputation of England', commented Francesco Giavarina, the Venetian

Resident in London.[27] Joy in England was all the keener for the news that a Dutch fleet under Admiral de Ruyter was having less success in negotiating with Barbary. Tripoli refused terms; so did Algiers. Now the news from Livorno was that fourteen pirate ships were out on the cruise looking for Dutch merchantmen and saying that 'since they had a peace with the English, they should do well enough, and were resolved to make no further agreement' with the Netherlands.[28] The English government and the English people applauded Lawson's success in negotiating a good and firm peace with Barbary; and he returned home in January to a hero's welcome, 'with great renown among all men [and] mightily esteemed at court by all'.[29]

Tunis kept the articles of peace, although Hammûda Pasha allowed Algerian pirates to sell their prizes there; Tripoli could be difficult, especially in the years between 'Uthmân's overthrow and death in 1672 and the signing of a new treaty with England by 'the *pasha, dey, agha, dīwān*, and governors of the city and kingdom of Tripoli' in 1676: the troubled state had six *deys* in that four-year period.[30] But Tripoli posed less of a threat than Algiers because its corsair fleet was weaker – twelve ships in 1676 as opposed to at least fifty at Algiers. In any case, the treaty held after 1676, and the pirates of Tripoli focused their attention on capturing French shipping.

Algiers broke the treaty and broke it often. Algerian corsairs boarded English merchant ships on the high seas; they took foreign cargo, passengers and occasionally crew; and they treated English consuls in Algiers with contempt whenever they complained. (At least one consul was hacked to death.) And this, even though the articles of peace stated quite clearly that no one was to do the consul or any of the King's subjects 'any wrong or injury in word or deed whatsoever'; and that 'though there be strangers and their goods on board [an English vessel], they shall be free, both they and their goods'.[31]

The favourite explanation in Europe for the failure of the articles of peace was the one voiced by the veteran English naval officer Sir Thomas Allin: 'Never any one met with such artful, dissembling, hypocritical traitors in this world!'[32] His opinion was shared by Francesco Giavarina, who was standing in for the absent Venetian ambassador in London: 'Anyone who knows the Turks and especially those assassins of Barbary is aware that they rarely keep their word.'[33] It was shared, too, by Robert Browne, English consul at Algiers, who reported that it was 'impossible for any but those that have been eye-witnesses to believe the rash, unjust and inconsiderate proceedings of these people'.[34] Turks were treacherous – it was as simple as that.

Every nation constructs its own narrative of conflict. The English believed that, although in 1662 the 'perfidious pirates' of Barbary had made 'an entire submission to the English flag', they had proved to be 'faithless', going back on their word and committing 'new insolencies' on English shipping, for which the fleet would 'chastise' them. All these value-loaded words and phrases were used by the Earl of Clarendon, Charles II's Lord Chancellor, in an angry speech to the two Houses of Parliament in October 1665.[35] Consciously or not, Clarendon spoke of the Algerians as a conquered people.

The Algerian narrative was different. The English, declared the *dey*, were 'a people without faith, not observing their promise; they [have] made war with us without cause, and without declaring against us; they have taken vessels, and made slaves of our people'.[36] Algiers was convinced that nations with whom they had no treaty were packing their ships with English crew, or flying English colours illegally: 'English' ships with Spanish crews and Spanish goods were plying back and forth across the Straits to supply Tangier; Dutch vessels sailed under English colours, the Algerians claimed. This was perfectly true. When a Venetian merchant ship was intercepted by an English squadron off Sardinia while flying the flag of St George, its Dutch master freely admitted that for the past fourteen years he had 'got free of all Barbary corsairs with his Royal Highness's pass'.[37]

The Algerians couldn't accept that when they searched an English ship and found it carrying Turks and Moors as slaves for sale in another country they must let it go without saving their fellow Moslems. When they met a ship flying English colours and sent a boat to examine its credentials – something they were allowed to do under the terms of the treaty – they were often fired on 'and not suffered to come near enough to speak with and examine them, so that they cannot possibly tell who they are, and, for aught they know, foreigners'.[38]

England did make concessions. In the summer of 1669 as Sir Thomas Allin set off on a peacekeeping mission to Barbary, he was authorised by the Lord High Admiral, James Duke of York, Charles II's brother, to insert a new clause into the Algerian treaty declaring that no English ship could carry more foreigners than Englishmen, passengers or crew; and another that English ships would henceforth not carry any Moslems 'that are slaves or that are sent to be sold in any other country'.[39] On the same expedition Allin was told explicitly that he was to behave with 'all possible truth and fidelity' towards the Algerians. If they agreed to a new peace, he was to return to them all ships, goods and men he might have taken on his way through the Straits, without keeping anything back; and to give presents to the *pasha* (although James's suggestion that Allin might reward the Algerians with gunpowder seems rather rash in the circumstances).[40]

But it was a case of small carrot, big stick. The incident which had led the Admiralty to send Allin to Algiers on this occasion had involved the taking of an English ship carrying sixty-one Spaniards, whom the Algerians sold. If the *pasha* and the *dīwān* wouldn't agree to terms and promise to mend their ways, Allin was empowered to attack their ships wherever he found them, to go into harbour and fire their fleet, to sell any Turks and Moors he captured. In a separate and presumably secret order, the Lord High Admiral also told Allin that if conditions were favourable when he arrived at Algiers, he should attack the corsair fleet immediately without waiting to begin negotiations.

The weather was too calm for a surprise attack when Allin arrived at the end of August 1669, but when the *agha* and *pasha* responded to his demands by 'raving like so many mad dogs, calling us all their language would afford them', he deployed his considerable fleet of eighteen warships and three fireships to blockade Algiers, to patrol the coast for returning corsairs and their prizes and, as necessary, to convoy English merchant shipping through the Straits. Captives were sent to Spain or Minorca and sold, including non-combatants. Fifty-four men, women and children were dispatched to the slave market at Cadiz in September. Two months later Allin recorded that he left with the Spanish vice consul at Port Mahon on Minorca 'one blind, one lame, one old Moor and one about 30 years, to be sold for his Majesty's use'.

At Malaga in December 'we disposed of ten slaves I sold and one presented to the governor free for his civilities'.[41] The Turks didn't have a monopoly on slavery.

But they didn't have a permanent garrison on the moral high ground, either. The Algerian economy depended on piracy, to a much greater extent than its neighbour Tunis. In order to function as a state, Algiers needed to be free to prey on at least one of the major trading nations – England, France and the Netherlands. As all three engaged in an arms race during the third quarter of the century, building up powerful naval presences in the Mediterranean in response to the threat posed by the others, the *tā'ifat al-ra'īs* found it harder and harder to make a living. Like the English, the French and the Dutch periodically sought and enforced treaties that would safeguard their merchant shipping in the Mediterranean and which consequently curtailed the activities of the corsairs. With or without legitimate pretexts the Algerians had to break those treaties simply in order to survive.

In 1664 an English squadron had sailed into the bay of Algiers to demand that the Algerians kept to their side of the bargain. This show of force was followed by a renewal of the articles of peace, and a humiliating public confession from the Algerians that the breach was caused by their subjects, and theirs alone, 'for which', they promised in a certificate appended to the renewed articles, 'we have drowned one, banished another, some others fled to escape our justice, and divers have been imprisoned to give satisfaction in part to his most excellent majesty [Charles II]'.[42]

Five years later, in 1669, the *Mary Rose*, which was taking Wenceslaus Hollar and Henry Howard back to England from Tangier, was fired on by Algerian corsairs off the Spanish coast and chased into the Bay of Cadiz. They left off the attack, but only after eleven members of the *Mary Rose*'s crew had been killed, seventeen wounded, 'and the ship much damaged'.[43]

In 1671 Admiral Sir Edward Spragge, then in command of the Mediterranean fleet, came on seven new and heavily armed corsair vessels at anchor on the Algerian coast in the Bay of Béjaïa (known in Europe as Bugia or Bougie). The corsairs tried to defend themselves by throwing a boom across the bay made of their topmasts, yards and cables, all buoyed up with casks. But

Spragge's men cut the boom, and the fireship he sent in among the Algerians, the *Little Victory*, burned them all. 'Our lovely bonfires', the admiral wrote in his journal, 'was the most glorious sight that ever I saw, so great variety was in it, some of the ships' ports appearing in the flame, others their sterns, and some their timbers all naked. When the powder came to blow up, it was terrible.'[44]

By his own account, Spragge's squadron dealt a deadly blow to the Algerian fleet at the Battle of Bugia Bay, wounding the Algerian Captain-General and killing 300 janissaries and seven of his captains (including a renegade called Danseker – the Devil Captain's name had lived on, until then at least). The incident was followed by a palace coup in which the *agha* was murdered and power transferred to an old *raïs* named Mohammed Tariq, or 'Old Treky' as the English called him. With the new regime there was a renewal of the articles of peace.

Five years later Admiral Sir John Narbrough burned four ships of war in Tripoli harbour, destroyed Tripolitan merchant ships and bombarded the city itself, a prelude to a public apology by Tripoli for contravening their treaty with England and a payment of reparations to the value of £18,000 in money, goods and slaves. There was a renewal of the articles of peace.

By the later 1670s Algerians were taking English ships in the Channel, just as they had half a century earlier. Admiral Narbrough was blockading Algiers. English and Algerian ships were engaging in pitched battles in the western Mediterranean. And now there was no renewal of the articles of peace. England and Algiers were at war from 1677 until 1682, when the *dey* and his son-in-law Baba Hassan tired of the losses their fleet was suffering and concluded yet another treaty with Narbrough's successor in the Mediterranean, Sir Arthur Herbert. A list published in London in 1682 showed that between 1677 and 1680 153 British ships had been taken by the corsairs of Algiers. Some were small: the *Robert* of Dartmouth, for instance, captured on 29 October 1677 with its crew of six; or the *Speedwell* of Topsham, taken with five crew in September 1679. Some were not: the *Phoenix* of London, which was taken two days before the *Robert*, had forty-nine men on board. The *William and Samuel*, also of London, was blown up and twenty-five of its crew were killed in June 1679; the other twenty-

Mortars being used in an assault on a town. The introduction of ship-mounted heavy mortars gave European fleets a devastating advantage over the fortified cities of Barbary.

one were taken to Algiers to await ransom or slavery. Gregory Shugers, master of the *Danby*, escaped in his longboat with twenty-one of his crew when they were attacked; no one knew the whereabouts of the remaining twenty-five. The anonymous author of the list reckoned that altogether around 1850 seamen and passengers had been captured by Algerian pirates. When the ransoms of the sailors, at £100 a man, and the ransoms of the more important passengers, at anything up to £1000 each, were added to the value of the vessels and their cargos, he put the cost to England of Algerian piracy in those three years alone at anything up to half a million pounds.

It was 29 July 1683, and in the scorching heat of an Algerian summer janissaries and a few townspeople watched as a heavy Venetian cannon was dragged into position on the battery overlooking the bay. Out beyond the mole a French battle fleet lay at anchor.

Admiral Abraham Duquesne had visited Algiers before. In 1682, shortly after Herbert concluded England's most recent peace treaty with the *dey*, the French had arrived to demand terms and reparations from Mohammad Tariq. But Algiers had made peace with the Dutch, peace with the English. Old Treky could not afford peace with the French as well. So he refused Duquesne's demands, and the French admiral used a new and terrible weapon of war to punish him. Heavy mortars mounted on specially adapted ships known as bomb-ketches lobbed huge explosive shells into the city, causing terror among the population and destroying dozens of houses and shops. The great mosque was badly damaged, and thousands of people fled to the safety of the countryside, 'crying out with a general voice, that the world must needs be now at an end, that never such things as these were seen, that they certainly were not of man's invention, but sent by the Devil from Hell'.[45] Even the French consul, a saintly Vincentine priest named Jean Le Vacher, couldn't persuade the admiral to stop. It was only the prospect of the coming winter which made Duquesne withdraw with a promise to return.

Now Duquesne was back, and threatening once again to rain down on Algiers his 'allamode tennis balls', as the English consul at Tripoli called them.[46] At the first sight of the enemy ships there was a general panic, which was only exacerbated when the 64-year-old Père Vacher returned from an interview with the admiral and announced regretfully to the *dīwān* that the French weren't interested in negotiating. They wanted to hurt Algiers. They wanted to destroy the city.

Desperate to avoid a repetition of the previous year's bombardment, Baba Hassan, who was now the real power behind his father-in-law Mohammad Tariq Dey, panicked and handed over 560 French slaves without even asking Duquesne for ransom. The janissaries and the *tā'ifat al-ra'īs* were so incensed that they killed Baba Hassan. Old Treky fled to Tunis and the captain of the galleys, Hajj Hasan, was elected in his place.

Mezzo Morto, the 'half-dead', as everyone called the new *dey*, was of the opinion that begging for mercy did not become an Algerian.

Hence the cannon.

He sent word to Duquesne that if the bombardment of the previous year was repeated, the fleet could watch as he blew

Vacher and all the other French merchants and redemptionist priests living in Algiers from the mouth of that cannon. Still the heavy French bomb-ketches moved within range of the city, and Mezzo Morto's men dragged the old priest on to the gun platform and tied him across the barrel of the big Venetian artillery piece. More than a hundred years old, it was one of the most impressive guns the Algerians possessed. Handled by expert gunners it could fire a shot more than two miles with accuracy.

But on this summer day, accuracy wasn't needed. With a roar and a flash the first mortar shells sailed over the mole and landed with a thick crump in the city. And Jean Le Vacher said a prayer and exploded in a dreadful burst of blood and bone which splashed into the blue waters of the Bay of Algiers.

The mortar shells kept crashing down, and another twenty Frenchmen died in the same terrible way as Père Vacher. (The Dutch renegade who actually fired the cannon suffered from awful nightmares for the rest of his life.) Duquesne left without his articles of peace, but a French fleet was back in 1688. The population of Algiers fled, leaving the pounding mortars to wreck the city. For two weeks the ketches worked in shifts, dropping a total of 13,300 shells. When they left, the English consul went to survey the ruins. 'Three-quarters of the town is defaced,' he wrote, 'and I believe it will never be rebuilt in its former splendour.'[47] The following year Algiers signed articles of peace with France.

14

No Part of England: The Evacuation of Tangier

*T*he 1680 siege of Tangier was a triumph for Morocco and a disaster for English hopes of a permanent base on the Barbary Coast. The short-term consequences were dramatic enough: some of the explosives at Charles Fort failed to go off, and 'Umar ben Haddu managed to retrieve 3300 hand grenades and all of the guns, which his men unspiked and unwedged and turned on the town. They were helped by one of the captured English soldiers from Henrietta Fort, who turned Turk – or, rather, Moor – and was promptly promoted to master gunner in 'Umar's army. Four days after the fall of Charles Fort Inchiquin sued for peace. Of his thirteen outworks, ten were either demolished or in enemy hands, while the three remaining were 'not defensible, when it shall please the enemy to reduce them'.[1] Whitby and its stone quarries were lost, which meant that all work on the mole had to stop. 'We shall be brought to the condition the Portuguese were in', wrote an anxious member of the garrison, 'but we can't bring the Moors to the same they were in.' 'Umar and his Algerian and Levantine siege specialists had turned the Moors 'from a cowardly and inconsiderable enemy . . . to a puissant and formidable foe'.[2]

No one was surprised when the Earl of Inchiquin concluded a four-month peace with the *qaid* and set sail with his pair of ostriches for a difficult interview with Charles II and a quiet retirement at the O'Brien family home in Co. Cork. Nor when soldiers aboard ship in the Thames heard that they were destined for Tangier and 'leaped overboard to escape, where they were taken up half drowned and secured again'.[3] The English government responded to the news of 'Umar's victory by sending troops to reinforce Sir Palmes Fairborne and his survivors. A contingent of volunteers led by the young Earl of Plymouth, illegitimate son of Charles II, landed on 2 July 1680, along with 600 regular troops under the command of Colonel Edward Sackville of the King's Own Royal Regiment.[4] Over the summer their numbers were supplemented by twelve Scottish and four Irish companies led by Sir James Halkett, a major in Dunbarton's Regiment; by four troops of English horse and 200 Spaniards; and by 500 or so English seamen who were put ashore to help with the defence of Tangier by their admiral, Arthur Herbert. By the time Inchiquin's four-month truce with 'Umar ben Haddu expired on 19 September 1680, there were well over 3000 English, Irish and Scots soldiers crammed into the town. At five o'clock the next morning the gates of Tangier opened and this army marched out in battle array and took up positions on the site of Pole Fort, 300 yards south of the town.

The Moors were taken completely by surprise. They hurtled down from the mountains 'with violence, in twenties and hundreds in a rude, unexpert, promiscuous way to interrupt the work';[5] but the English were prepared for them, and by nightfall labourers under the direction of Henry Sheres and a Swedish military engineer, Major Martin Beckman, had erected a wooden stockade around the ruins of Pole Fort, strengthened it with earth and stone and garrisoned it with 500 men.

The sally was the start of a bout of vicious fighting which lasted for the next five weeks, as the two sides struggled for control of the no-man's-land of hills and ditches and ruined blockhouses surrounding Tangier. Dunbarton's Regiment lost 250 men and 24 officers killed or wounded in a single engagement. In retaliation, they made a pile of the enemy dead in plain view of the Moors and set about cutting off the corpses' genitals 'to make purses'.[6]

At the end of October, when another truce was called and

negotiations began between the sultan of Morocco, Mawlay Isma'il, and Charles II for a more lasting peace, England had managed to regain some of the territory it had lost in May. The victory, if victory it was, was bought at a heavy price. The Earl of Plymouth died early on in the fighting, not from wounds but from the dysentery he had contracted when he spent a night in Pole Fort and foolishly drank the water. Sir Palmes Fairborne was shot by a sniper on 24 October when he rode out with some officers to survey the defences; he died of his wound three days later as he sat on a balcony watching Colonel Sackville leading what turned out to be the final attack on the Moorish lines. Between six and seven hundred were killed altogether on the English side, and perhaps as many as 2000 Moors.

Back in England, questions were asked about Tangier. Parliament, obsessively and paranoically anti-Catholic in the wake of the Popish Plot, was anxious about the high proportion of Irish (and hence Catholic) troops in the garrison. About the fact that the Catholic Lord Belasyse, currently imprisoned in the Tower on charges of plotting to poison the King and muster a secret Catholic army, had once been a governor of Tangier, as had the Catholic Earl of Teviot. Even about the fact that the Dominican church in Tangier was prospering in a most sinister fashion.

The mole was unfinished, and, since the Moors retained control of the quarries at Whitby, there wasn't much prospect of it being finished in the near future. As things stood, after eighteen years of building work and £340,000 of expenditure the harbour was still virtually unusable by big ships, which crashed into each other in bad weather, fouled each other's lines and even broke from their moorings to be driven right out into the Straits in the westerly gales which lashed the coast from time to time. The flow of money assigned by the King out of his private revenue for the maintenance and service of the town, between £60,000 and £70,000 a year, was unsustainable, and when in November Charles asked Parliament to provide some financial support for Tangier, he was refused. Granted that the outpost was 'a place of consideration for trade, and a guard from pirates, where our ships may retreat',[7] the cost was just too great, as most of the MPs who spoke in the debate on the matter made clear. 'Tangier is no part of England, and for us to provide for it, as things stand now, is to weaken our own security,' said Sir William Jones. 'Tangier is not only a seminary for Popish priests, but for soldiers too', said William Harbord. 'I should be glad', said Sir William Temple, 'either that we never had it, or if it was by an earthquake blown up.'[8]

Samuel Pepys, 'sole counsellor' to Lord Dartmouth on his 1683 mission to Tangier

In the end the Commons linked a vote in favour of more money for Tangier to the King's acceptance of the Exclusion Bill, which would bar the Catholic Duke of York from succeeding to the throne. Charles wasn't prepared to put an ailing outpost on the Barbary Coast given to him at his marriage before the interests of his own brother. And for the time being, matters rested there in stalemate, with a beleaguered and undersupplied Tangier caught in the middle of a bigger battle between Parliament and crown.

Samuel Pepys was feeling a little bewildered. At only forty-eight hours' notice Charles II had ordered him to travel down to

Portsmouth. When he got there he was to board HMS *Grafton* and accompany Admiral Lord Dartmouth, a man he hardly knew and liked less, on a voyage to Tangier. He didn't know why they were going. He didn't know what his role in this mysterious expedition was to be. And he had been left to kick his heels in port for three days while Dartmouth rushed up to Windsor for a meeting with the King.

Now Dartmouth was back and Pepys was closeted with him in the admiral's cabin. It was raining heavily, and the *Grafton* rocked and swayed at anchor. Timbers creaked and groaned, the wind blew hard and sailors scrambled around uncertainly in the rigging. It was an August afternoon, but the interior of the cabin was dark, and the guttering tallow candles cast long shadows on Dartmouth's firm and faintly quizzical features as he quietly explained the King's orders. Their mission was to destroy Tangier.

The next morning, 14 August 1683, Dartmouth summoned Pepys to his cabin again and showed him the secret papers he had received from the King. The Earl of Sunderland, one of Charles II's two Secretaries of State, had urged the abandonment of Tangier back in 1680, but he lost office and the idea fell out of favour when he did, to be resurrected when he returned to power three years later. Now Charles was keen to push ahead. To ensure there were no leaks, Dartmouth's commission and instructions had been written personally by the King's other Secretary of State, Sir Leoline Jenkins, rather than being entrusted to a clerk. Those instructions appointed Dartmouth as admiral, captain-general, governor and commander-in-chief of Tangier, and ordered him 'to demolish and utterly to destroy the said city and the mole erected in the port belonging to it, so as they may be altogether useless, and no pirate or enemy of the Christian faith may at any time hereafter make their abode or retreat there'.[9]

Pepys's role was to act as 'sole counsellor' to Dartmouth and, in collaboration with an Admiralty lawyer, William Trumbull, to assess claims for compensation from the townspeople of Tangier. Other members of the party included Thomas Ken, who was aboard the *Grafton* as Dartmouth's chaplain (and who would later earn himself a place in history as one of the seven bishops sent to the Tower for objecting to James II's insistence on religious toleration for Catholics); Martin Beckman, the Swedish military engineer who had directed the fortifications during the 1680 counter-attack against the Moors; and Henry Sheres, who, ironically enough, was to be given the job of destroying the 'stupendious Mould' he had worked so hard to build.

None of these men knew the purpose of their voyage when they set sail that August. Dartmouth put a strict interpretation on his instructions, which urged him to take 'all imaginable care how to prevent strangers and our own subjects' from relaying the scheme to the Moors.[10] But by the time the *Grafton* anchored in Tangier Road four weeks later, word was spreading. Dr Trumbull was told after he went into a sulk at being excluded from Pepys's regular *tête-à-têtes* in Dartmouth's cabin. Two weeks out, Beckman was asked to produce a strategy for carrying out the demolition – a lengthy and complicated job involving engineers, fire masters, miners and drillers. (Most were to be supplied by the garrison, but a team of expert miners was taken aboard when the fleet called in at Plymouth.) He handed his plan to Dartmouth on 28 August, recommending that they begin preparatory work on mining the fortifications without waiting until the civilian population had been evacuated. 'I do not doubt,' he told the governor, 'but the news (though it be but guessing) of demolishing of the place will arrive before we shall arrive there.'[11]

When Pepys wasn't being seasick (which he was, rather a lot), he spent his nights watching the sailors dance on deck, and his days producing a paper for Dartmouth to justify the King's decision. 'Arguments for destroying of Tangier' was a model of clarity, and it reflected governmental thinking pretty accurately. England's high hopes for Tangier as a naval base and a major trading centre had not materialised; without the help of Parliament, which was conspicuously unforthcoming, the King could no longer afford to support it. Sooner or later it would fall either 'to some Christian enemy' or to the Moors, who would use the mole and the fortifications which had cost so much in blood and money, and would establish 'such a den of thieves and pirates, as would prove of worse consequence to the whole trade of the Levant . . . than all that can arise from the whole united force of corsairs infesting that sea at this day'.[12] It was better for the English to destroy Tangier than to let it fall into the hands of others.

George Legge, Lord Dartmouth, chosen to mastermind the dismantling of Tangier

The fleet arrived on 14 September 1683 to find a Moorish army camped outside the walls. This was going to make a clandestine demolition rather difficult, and Dartmouth hadn't bargained on it. It was no secret that Mawlay Isma'il had designs on Tangier; or that the Ottoman Emperor, Mehmed IV, was urging him to make holy war on all the Christian enclaves along the coast of Morocco – not only Tangier, but the Spanish and Portuguese outposts of Ceuta, Larache, Melilla and Mazagan. But the four-year truce that had been brokered in 1680 still had just over a year to run; and Dartmouth's latest intelligence had been that 'Umar ben Haddu's successor as *qaid*, 'Alī ben 'Abd Allāh al-Hammāmī, was eager to see it extended. What had gone wrong?

Before even stepping ashore, he invited the governor, Colonel Percy Kirke, aboard the *Grafton* and showed him the King's commission. Kirke was perfectly happy to hand over to Dartmouth. 'He do most seemingly collectedly bear it and very cheerfully,' Dartmouth told Pepys afterwards.[13] When the new governor read Kirke's intelligence report on recent events, he saw why. Relations between the garrison and al-Hammāmī had begun to deteriorate in May, when the *qaid* complained that some stained glass which Kirke had promised to get for him from England hadn't arrived. An escalating tit-for-tat exchange of sanctions followed. The Moors refused to sell the garrison straw for their horses until the glass arrived. The English refused (quite under-standably) to hand over a supply of gunpowder, even though this had been agreed as a condition of the truce. The Moors barred the English from walking outside the town walls. The English barred the Moors from entering the town. Now the *qaid* had gathered an army, with a view to intimidating the garrison; but there was still a chance to avoid war, reckoned Kirke, adding disarmingly that this was 'a work that seems to be reserved for your lordship's prudence and dexterity'.[14] Over to you, in other words.

Dartmouth thought briefly of simply telling al-Hammāmī his plans, but Pepys and Sheres managed to dissuade him. There was nothing for it but to press ahead in an increasingly uneasy and unreal climate of semi-secrecy. Pepys and Trumbull convened a court to hear claims of title to property, pretending that they were carrying out a general survey and valuation, although everyone in the town now suspected the real reason. Sheres went round declaring that the demolition work would take at least three months, which infuriated Dartmouth who insisted it could all be done in a fortnight. Colonel Kirke turned into a fawning yes-man, agreeing with every passing whim of Dartmouth's, and prefacing every utterance with the words 'God damn me!' His wife dropped heavy hints that she knew all about the imminent evacuation of the colony, while Dartmouth withheld everyone's letters from England in case they offered a clue as to his plans. Anxious to put on a show of force in front of the Moors, he brought 1000 seamen ashore and had them parade in full view of the enemy camp along with his soldiers, as though they were reinforcements for the garrison; but this only made matters worse, since al-Hammāmī now demanded to know why the English had sent such a powerful army to Tangier. Dr Trumbull grew so depressed at the thought of all the fees he could have been earning back in London that he asked to go home. Dr Ken kept up everyone's spirits by delivering sermons in which he denounced the vicious ways of the townspeople and the garrison.

If Pepys is to be believed, those ways were indeed rather vicious. 'Nothing but vice in the whole place of all sorts', he wrote in his private notes, 'for swearing, cursing, drinking and whoring'.[15] The hospital was full of syphilitics. Kirke had got his wife's sister pregnant and packed her off to Spain to have the baby. On one occasion he had sex with a woman in the middle of the market-place, and he kept a whore in a little bathing-house he had furnished for the purpose; while he was visiting her, his wife entertained the colonel's young officers in her bedchamber. Admiral Arthur Herbert, the admired commander of the Mediter-ranean squadron who managed to secure peace with Algiers, kept a house and a whore in Tangier. His officers proudly recounted stories of his exploits, such as the time when he got his surgeon dead drunk, had him stripped naked, 'and one of his legs tied up in his cabin by the toe, and brought in women to see him in that posture'.[16]

The garrison's soldiers were often drunk, both on and off duty, and they beat the townspeople and stole from them with impunity. Kirke himself was said to owe the local traders £1500, but when they asked him to settle his debts all they got was 'God damn me, why did you trust me?'[17]

On the afternoon of Thursday 4 October 1683, three weeks after arriving in Tangier, Lord Dartmouth went to the town hall and announced 'the great secret'. He had spent days working on his speech, discussing it with Pepys and Trumbull and making endless revisions. He took care to explain that everyone would be compen-sated for the loss of their property, all debts would be paid, trans-port home would be arranged at the King's expense. If he expected a hostile reception, he couldn't have been more wrong. Bells were rung in the steeples, bonfires were lit all over town in celebra-tion. The mayor and aldermen wrote a letter of thanks to Charles II for his compassion in 'rescuing us from our present fears and future calamities, in recalling us from scarcity to plenty, from danger to security, from imprisonment to liberty, and from banishment to our own native country'.[18] The officers of the garrison handed in an address for the King, expressing 'all the joy that our hearts are capable of' and telling him how much 'we applaud and admire the wisdom of your Majesty's counsels on this important affair'.[19] No one was going to miss Tangier.

Dismantling an entire community was a complicated business. Pepys compiled a list of 180 freeholders and leaseholders who needed to be compensated – civilians, army officers and absentee landlords. (Some were more absent than others: the list included the King of Portugal, legal owner of the Dominican church; and Sir Palmes Fairborne, who had been dead for three years.) There was some wrangling over values but things were settled within weeks, at a cost to the crown of about £11,300. Debts had to be proved and paid. Goods had to be inventoried – one careful soul catalogued the contents of the public library, which included Fuller's *Worthies of England*, the plays of Sir William Davenant and Pascal's *Mystery of Jesuitism*, but not Milton's *Paradise Lost*, which was marked 'lost'.

And the population, which had more than doubled since the 1660s, had to be shipped out. There were currently 4000 of the King's men – soldiers, sailors and engineers – in Tangier. Many had their wives and children with them (Lord Dartmouth reckoned there were 400 Christian children in the town). The civilian population had taken a dip after the siege of 1680, when a number of merchants and tradesmen moved to the safer shores of Spain, but it stood now at well over a thousand, and everyone must be moved to Christendom and safety.

The first vessel to go was a hospital ship called the *Unity*, which set sail towards the end of October carrying sick and crippled veterans and a sprinkling of women and children. A few days later the mayor boarded the *St David* and 'he and the best families of the citizens sailed away at break of day for England'.[20] Trumbull, whose grief at his loss of earnings was boring the garrison to death, was given permission to go home at the same time.

Even as the *Unity* was leaving the Bay of Tangier, Lord Dartmouth's engineers were excavating a series of experimental mines. On 19 October his master gunner, Captain Richard Leake, set off two explosive devices under the arches at the landward end of the mole, but the earth was so loosely packed that they did no damage. The next day Sheres, who seems to have taken charge of the demolition of the mole, drilled out a cavity, packed it with powder and detonated it to more effect. But there was a vast amount of earth and rubble to move. He computed it at 2,843,280 cubic feet, or 167,251 tons, and estimated that it would take a thousand men nearly eight months to clear the site.

The other teams were more efficient. By 5 November Dartmouth could report to London that the mines laid in the town and the citadel were all finished and ready to blow. In the meantime Sheres managed to break up the caissons at the seaward end of the mole, but he was still having huge problems with Sir Hugh Cholmley's earthworks. Dartmouth deployed 2000 men at a time to remove the rubble by hand and tip it into the bay: 'this good will follow', he said, 'that the harbour will be fully choked up by it'.[21] The sight of 2000 labourers swarming over the mole from dawn till dusk and hurling it stone by stone into the bay did give the watching Moors a bit of a clue that something was afoot; but by now Dartmouth had acquainted al-Hammāmī with his intentions. There was no point in secrecy.

On 21 January 1684 Dartmouth's officers reported that the mole was 'so entirely ruined and destroyed, and the harbour so filled with stones and rubbish' that it was 'in no capacity to give any kind of refuge or protection to the ships or vessels of any pirates, robbers, or any enemies of the Christian faith'.[22] The withdrawal of the English garrison had begun the previous week, when mines were sprung at Pole Fort and the other outlying defences, and the ground between them and the town walls was strewn with iron spikes to deter an opportunistic cavalry charge by the Moors. On 3 February Dartmouth gave the order to blow up one of the mines at York Castle, the old Moorish fortress on the shore, and another in the upper castle. The senior officers of the garrison gathered to hear Dr Ken read a prayer of thanks to God at the town hall, the church having been stripped of its furnishings, its seats, even its marble pavement, which Lord Dartmouth sent home to decorate the King's chapel at Portsmouth. For the next two days soldiers pulled down as much of the remaining buildings as they could, throwing the debris into the common sewer. At nine in the morning of 6 February the troops who were left ashore began to embark in small boats for the fleet at anchor in the bay, as one mine after another was blown. Rubble flew high into the air. Fires were started. Peterborough Tower in the Upper Castle collapsed with a roar 'on which many of the Moors appeared, giving a great shout'.[23]

Lord Dartmouth was the last to leave, springing the final mine himself before being rowed out in his barge to the *Grafton*, as thousands of Moors rode down from the hills towards the ruined town. He delayed sailing for home for several days, to negotiate the release of Lieutenant Wilson, the commander of Henrietta Fort who had been captured by 'Umar's soldiers four years earlier. 'I thought it not for your Majesty's honour to leave a commissioned officer behind that had behaved himself so very well in your service,' he told Charles II. 'And I believe [he] will do again upon a little encouragement, though at present his misfortunes and long captivity seem too much to have dejected him.'[24]

15
The King's Agent: Life in Late Seventeenth-Century Tripoli

'Is Majesty was this day pleased to honour me with his Commission under his Sign Manual and Privy Signet delivered me by the Right Honourable Henry Coventry Principal Secretary of State; thereby constituting me his agent and consul general in the city and kingdom of Tripoli in Barbary'.[1]

Thomas Baker's journal 'of whatsoever occurrences shall happen or be noteworthy' is a uniquely detailed English perspective on everyday life in a pirate city-state. But when he wrote these words on 2 May 1677, the career prospects of English consuls on the Barbary Coast were not happy. They were bullied, held hostage and even killed by their hosts; they were constantly pestered by desperate captives who expected them to stand surety for ransoms. Throughout the Ottoman Empire they were escorted by janissaries whenever they ventured out into the *medina*, since Moslems commonly responded to the sight of a European by punching him or spitting on him as he passed by. The district where a consul lived, often in closed collegiate communities, or *khans*, with other Europeans, was contemptuously referred to by Turks as the pig quarter.

And the reward for putting up with all this was to be ignored or forgotten by one's own government. 'I do verily believe,' complained James Frizzell in his last despairing dispatch from Algiers in 1637, 'that never any of his majesty's ministers hath been so neglected as I am.'[2]

Yet men like Thomas Baker were eager to serve, for all sorts of reasons: honour, the potential for advancement, the opportunity to make money on the side, the chance to make a life in an exotic and alien world. Baker's qualifications for the post were sound. He had close contacts with prominent Levant merchants and London financiers. As a young man he had worked as a factor in Algiers, and he had lived in Tunis in the late 1660s and early 1670s, where he made good friends, both Christian and Moslem. And his brother Francis was in Tunis now, acting as unpaid English consul.

Unlike his brother, Thomas was not prepared to work without pay. The Tripoli appointment came with a salary of £200 a year, and within days he had persuaded the government to increase it to £300 and to give him his first six months' pay in advance. He put his affairs in order, and arranged to take receipt of an expensive present of damask and brocade from the king to the *dey* of Tripoli. One evening in July he was brought by the Secretary of State, Sir Henry Coventry, into the Privy Garden at the Palace of Whitehall where he knelt and kissed the hands of Charles II and the Duke of York.

Ten days later he was aboard the *Plymouth* at Spithead and preparing to set sail for Barbary. He would not see the English coast again for another nine years.

Baker was not destined to see the shores of Tripoli anytime soon, either. The new consul travelled with Sir John Narbrough's Mediterranean fleet, and although Narbrough was charged with personally delivering him to the *dey*, he considered the task to be a low priority in comparison with the fleet's primary objective, which was to tackle a resurgence of Algerian attacks against English shipping. The voyage to Tripoli normally took no more than two or three months, but as summer turned to autumn, then winter, an impatient Thomas Baker sat helplessly aboard the *Plymouth* while Narbrough careered around the Mediterranean, chasing pirates, parleying with the authorities at Algiers, convoying Levant Company merchants to and fro from Zante and Cephalonia to the Straits, and calling in at Tangier and Cadiz and Malaga and Livorno and Alicante and Minorca – everywhere, it seemed, but Tripoli.

At least the consul wasn't bored. Narbrough's fleet, which at its greatest strength numbered a colossal thirty-five vessels, was engaged in frequent if often inconclusive naval warfare with the Algerians, who took more than sixty English ships in the year 1677 alone. In return, Narbrough captured five corsairs and destroyed seven more in the course of an expedition which lasted for nearly two years. Baker saw action several times, including a pitched battle off the coast of Spain, just outside the Straits of Gibraltar. The fight involved seven English ships and the 142-gun *Golden Rose of Algier*, commanded by a German renegade named Hassan Raïs: more than sixty English sailors were killed or wounded and 200 Turks died in the fight.

Baker's journal shows that casualties weren't confined to combat. The *Plymouth*, Narbrough's flagship, was only a few days out when, in saluting a homeward-bound frigate, one of her guns went off prematurely, 'and shot off Richard Robinson's hand at the wrist, whilst he was ramming the wad home'.[3] Drunken seamen suffered alcohol-induced fevers and fatal falls; an officer fell sick and died, from taking too much ice in his wine, according to Baker. One poor sailor was caught with his breeches down when the 7 a.m. watch gun was fired; contrary to normal practice it was loaded and the shot killed him 'as he was easing himself' over the side.[4]

By January 1679 Baker had been aboard one or other of Narbrough's warships for nineteen months with only brief spells ashore at Cadiz, Cartagena and a few other ports of call, and the admiral still showed not the slightest inclination to take him to Tripoli. In desperation he asked to be put on board the *Diamond*, which was convoying merchantmen to Alexandria and which could call in at Tripoli without too much difficulty. And finally, at eight in the evening of 5 April 1679, nearly two years after he received his commission from Charles II, the new consul arrived at his destination.

The minarets and towers of Tripoli

As the *Diamond* negotiated the narrow channel into the harbour the next morning, Baker stood on deck and looked out on the city which was to be his home for the next seven years. The ship moved slowly past shore batteries and gardens; past the forbidding walls of the vast Assaray Al-Hamra citadel and the shipyards that lay in their shadow; past the mosques with their slender minarets reaching for heaven – the Dragut Mosque, named for the sixteenth-century corsair who built it; the Mosque of Sid Salem, whose minaret was well known to European mariners as 'a mark to bear into the port';[5] the mosque of Al-Naqah, said to date back to the earliest days of Islam; and the mosque that 'Uthmân Pasha commissioned in the 1650s, part of a domed complex which included his mausoleum and a *madrasa*. At the opposite end of the shore to the citadel stood the Mandrake, a fortress which guarded the north-west approaches. Baker could glimpse, rising gently up the hill behind the high battlemented walls of the city, a sea of densely packed streets and alleys extending half a mile back towards the plains and the scrubby desert beyond.

Tripoli has a distinguished history. Founded in the seventh century BC by the Phoenicians, Oea, as it was known, was absorbed into the Roman province of Africa around the second century BC, along with the colonies of Leptis Magna to the east and Sabratha to the west. By the third century AD the coastal strip containing Tripoli, Leptis and Sabratha was known as the *regio tripolitana*, the region of the three cities.

Although Tripoli had its fair share of invasions and regime changes over the ensuing 1400 years or so – at different times it belonged to Egypt, to Sicily, to Tunis, to Spain and even to the Knights of St John, before becoming an Ottoman province in 1551 – there was still scattered evidence of its Roman past when Baker arrived to take up his post. The most substantial was (and still is) the magnificent Arch of Marcus Aurelius which marked the junction of the main north–south and east–west crossroads of the Roman city; but generations of Tripolitans recycled classical remains, and mosques, public buildings and private homes often boasted columns and capitals many centuries older than themselves.

Thomas Baker hadn't come to Tripoli to look at the vestiges of antiquity. He was there, as the King's commission put it, 'to aid and protect as well all our said merchants and other our subjects trading, or that shall trade or have any commerce, or that do or shall reside at Tripoli'.[6] And that meant ensuring that the Tripolitan corsairs kept to their side of the treaty agreed with Narbrough in 1676, and did not rob or otherwise molest English shipping. They could rob the Dutch; they could molest the French; they could do what they liked with Greek barks and Genoese pinks and Maltese galleys. But English ships must be allowed, in the words of the treaty, to 'freely pass the seas, and traffique where they please, without any search, hindrance or molestation'.[7]

Tripoli regarded itself as being at war with France and Holland; so technically, its fleet did not commit acts of piracy, but acted legally in attacking the merchant shipping of an enemy nation, just as Elizabethan privateers had operated against the Spanish, brandishing their exculpatory letters of marque.

Less concerned with definitions than with the threat to English shipping, over that first summer of 1679 Thomas Baker set down 'an exact list' of the fleet that lay in the little harbour beneath the city walls. Tripoli boasted thirteen vessels, with a fourteenth on the stocks. (This man-of-war had been under construction for five years, and the shipyard was so short of timber and other materials that it would be another five years before it was launched.) The vessels ranged upwards in size from a little galley carrying one gun and 150 men to the Captain of the Sea's flagship, its stern painted with a white half-moon, which was armed with forty-two guns and had a complement of 350. Six of the ships – the galley and the five biggest – were built in Tripoli; the rest were presumably converted prizes, since they originated in Provence (three), Genoa (two), Venice and Malta (one apiece).

Baker also noted the name and origin of each *raïs*. The corsairs of Tripoli were as cosmopolitan as their fleet. Seven were 'Turks', including the Captain of the Sea or admiral, 'Ali Minikshali, and his rear admiral, Karavilli; although this did not imply they were native Tripolitans. 'Ali was Greek and Karavilli came from Anatolia. Four others were Greek renegades, including 'Ali's vice admiral Mustafa; one was a Moor; and one, Ryswan Raïs, was a Frenchman. Ryswan commanded the memorably named Venetian prize *Souls in Purgatory*. Baker noted that its stern was painted with 'purgatory'; sadly there are no other details, although recycled Christian iconography clearly wasn't a problem for the Moslems of Tripoli, since the Genoese prize, which was commanded by a Greek renegade, regularly went out in search of Christians with a gilded figure of Mary Magdalene on its stern.

When every ship was carrying its full complement, more than 3000 janissaries and sailors might go out on the cruise. This seems impressive, but the fleet was considerably smaller than that of Tunis, which numbered twenty vessels, and it was dwarfed by Algiers's thirty-eight men-of-war, seven brigantines and three galleys.

It was also much less successful. Over that first summer of 1679 Baker watched 'Ali Raïs's ships go out 'a Christian-stealing' again and again, only to come back empty-handed.[8] Their range was limited: food was so expensive and they were so poor that they could only afford victuals for three or four weeks at a time. ('Corn is always dear, because their fields are sand' was Samuel Purchas's verdict on Tripoli back in 1614.[9]) At least six men-of-war were forced to turn to more respectable occupations. Three of them, 'having been long out in corso and meeting with no purchase', put in at Alexandria and took on legitimate cargos of rice and beans.[10] Two more went to the Dardanelles in search of timber to finish the warship in the yards; and the sixth was sent to Crete for supplies of corn.

In Baker's first six months in Tripoli the fleet took only two prizes, even though it was out for most of the spring and summer. One, the inappropriately named *Madonna of the Good Voyage*, was taken off Zante on its way to Istanbul with a cargo of Brazil-wood and sugar; the French crew escaped in a longboat. The other, also a Frenchman, was actually on her way into harbour at Tripoli when she was captured. It wasn't considered sporting to take a vessel in this way – the convention was that if a merchant managed to get within gunshot of the batteries, she should be allowed to come in unmolested. It shows how desperate the Tripolitans were for prizes that the *dey* ignored this, impounded the bark and made slaves of her fourteen crewmen.

Baker meticulously recorded the unimpressive comings and goings of the Tripoli fleet: he counted them out, and he counted them back – 'without any prize'.[11] In the middle of August 1679 half the fleet came back not only without prizes, but also without their admiral. 'Ali Minikshali had gone ashore with all his money and possessions at Heraklion on Crete, and announced he was staying there.

'Ali's decision to jump ship was related to his part in a failed attempt that summer to oust the *dey*, an Anatolian Turk named Aq Mohammad al-Haddad. The stability which 'Uthmân Pasha had imposed on Tripoli in the 1650s and 1660s was a distant memory in 1679, as was amply demonstrated by the fact that Aq Mohammad was the eighth *dey* to rule since 'Uthmân's death in 1672. Two *deys* had ruled for less than a fortnight, and one for a matter of hours.

Each change of government was accompanied by an inordinate amount of strangling, although the luckier outgoing officials were deposited alive on Djerba, the fabled island of the lotus-eaters described in Homer's *Odyssey*. (However attractive it might have been to Odysseus's men, it held little appeal for the Tripolitan exiles: according to John Ogilby's *Africa*, the land was barren and there were 'no cities, nor any thing else, but some huts, scattered here and there far from one another'.[12])

Aq Mohammad's hold on power was already shaky. A plot by *kulughis* to depose him while most of the janissary corps were out on the cruise with the fleet was forestalled in June, and the *dey* had eight of the ringleaders dismembered alive. 'The silly, but wicked animal,' declared Baker.[13] In July one of Aq Mohammad's exiled predecessors landed at Zuwarah, along the coast from Tripoli, joined forces with a group of disaffected Arabs and disappeared into the mountains of Gharyan, seventy miles south of Tripoli. The *dey* sent his *bey*, or commander of land forces, Hasan 'Abaza, to find out exactly what was going on, and to make certain that the powerful governor of Gharyan, Murad, was loyal to him.

He wasn't. Nor was Hasan, who came back to Tripoli with Murad as his deputy, called a full meeting of the *dīwān* and denounced Aq Mohammad. The *dey* was taken away in chains to face some rather rigorous questions as to the whereabouts of 394 pounds of gold which was missing from the treasury and, with a suitable show of modesty, Hasan reluctantly agreed to take his place as ruler. The next afternoon Aq Mohammad was shipped off to Djerba, 'a Christian and a negro being his whole retinue and dollars five hundred his subsistence'.[14] And the afternoon after *that*, a new admiral, vice admiral and rear admiral prepared to set out on the cruise. It was business as usual.

Baker's reaction to the coup was a very human irritation – he'd wasted Charles II's expensive present of damask and brocade on the wrong *dey*. But he loathed Aq Mohammad and liked Hasan 'Abaza; so he shrugged his shoulders, ensured that the new regime ratify the old articles of peace with England before the corsair fleet sailed (which it did); and settled into life in Tripoli.

Contacts with fellow countrymen were few. There was no sizeable English merchant community resident at Tripoli as there was further east, at Aleppo in Syria and Smyrna on the Aegean coast of Turkey; and Thomas Goodwyn, a friend who had accompanied Baker from Livorno in April, only stayed until September, preferring to try his luck in Tunis instead. Henry Caple, a ship's master liberated by Narbrough in 1676 who had acted as consul from then until Baker's arrival, left in a bad temper aboard the *Diamond*, having tried and failed to persuade the *dīwān* that Baker must pay him 1500 dollars (around £350) before being allowed to take up his post.

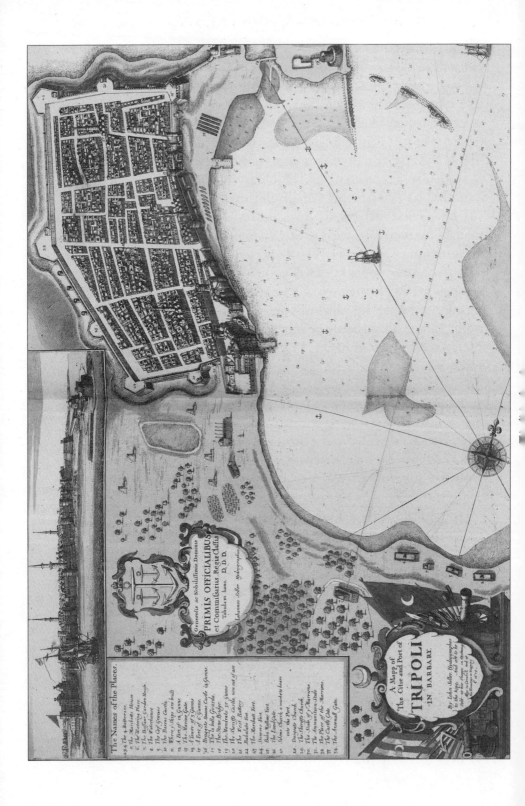

The Names of the Places.

1.2.3. The 3 Batteries.
4. The Marabotts House.
5. The Watering Place.
6. The Bassaw Garden House.
7. The Watch tower.
8. The Old Groyne.
9. Where 5 Ships are built.
10. The Bassaw Castle.
11. A Bridge in a Guine.
12. The Marina Gate.
13. A Tower of 5 Guines.
14. A Fort of 6 Guines.
15. Bragets bassaw Castle is Guines.
16. The la bella Guarda.
17. The Stone Bridge.
18. The Mandrake 30 Guines.
19. The Sheriffs Castle now out of use.
20. Slave Church a market houre.
21. The Fort Battery.
22. Balukhat Fort.
23. The Marabott Fort.
24. Summers Fort.
25. Baba Redwan Fort.
26. The Ramsfoote.
27. Sumers Fort.
28. Daragate Church.
29. The Sheriffs Church.
30. The Souk of 5 Marynes.
31. The Amomintum Shede.
32. The Place of the Marynes.
33. The Souk of Chio.
34. The Arsenal Gate.

Generosis ac Nobilissimis Dominis
PRIMIS OFFICIALIBUS
et Commissariis Regiæ Classis
Tabulam hanc. D.D.D.
Iohannes Seller Hydrographus

A Mapp of
The Citie and Port of
TRIPOLI
IN BARBARY.

By Iohn Seller Hydrographer
to the Kings

It wasn't until nearly a year later that the consul realised the full extent of Caple's duplicity, when it emerged that in the chaos of the handover, while the captains of the *Diamond* and the *Pearl* were taking their leave and the consulate was crowded with visitors come to pay their respects, the outgoing consul had bribed his secretary to slip a forged deed under Baker's nose in a sheaf of papers. Baker had signed it with the rest, not realising that it made over to Caple a sum of 4302 dollars (about £1000) which did not belong to him.

Baker doesn't say how he discovered the deception, but when he did, the secretary, a 59-year-old Venetian slave named Andrea Nassimbene, was hauled before the *dey* and formally accused. The man confessed straight away and was sentenced – rather to Baker's horror – to have his right arm chopped off. He had another trick up his sleeve, however (if that's not a hopelessly inappropriate expression in the circumstances). The moment sentence was pronounced he said to the *dey* that he wanted to convert to Islam.

This was a common ploy among Christian slaves trying to avoid harsh punishments. And sometimes it worked. But Hasan 'Abaza Dey wasn't having any of it. He told Nassimbene he couldn't. As he wrote to Charles II in a letter absolving Baker of any part in the deception, 'we had [Nassimbene] sent from our presence with insulting and threatening words as merits his falsity, to be taken to a public place where there should have been executed our sentence that his hand should be separated and chopped from his right arm'.[15] 'Should have been' because this was all too much for Baker, who leaped up from his seat in the court and, to quote Hasan 'Abaza Dey again, 'urged, prayed and beseeched us for a moderation of the penalty'. The sentence was commuted: Nassimbene had the right side of his head and the left side of his beard and moustache shaved, after which he was paraded through the streets in chains and then set to work in the quarries. He was also thrashed with a tarred rope by the Guardian of Slaves on the assumption that this would please the consul. It didn't.

The episode suggests Baker had a compassionate side, and this was borne out again and again during his stay. Two days after Nassimbene's trial, he was in the Assaray Al-Hamra citadel on business when he received word that a drunken janissary had burst into his house and stabbed one of his servants. He demanded satisfaction; and the soldier was duly sentenced to a thousand blows with a baton, which would almost certainly have killed him. Once again Baker pleaded with the *dey* to show mercy and the man was pardoned – thus earning the consul the gratitude not only of the culprit, but of the entire janissary corps.

He was an astute political operator, rigid in his determination to claim his rights as set out in the articles of peace (Article 16 clearly stated that the English consul should be allowed to live 'at all times with entire freedom and safety of his person and estate'[16]), but aware that there was power in magnanimity. When one of the port officers contravened the articles by preventing him from taking a boat out into the bay, Baker immediately demanded the man's dismissal. This was duly done, and the consul let him sweat for a few days before petitioning the *dey* for his reinstatement. He had made his point. And when Baker began to have problems with his interpreter, a Norfolk man named Edward Fountain, he opted for the gentler path again. Fountain, a convert who had taken the name of Hasan Agha, had a drink problem. Instead of firing the dragoman, Baker gave him a gold coin against a forfeit of ten that he couldn't stay away from alcohol for the next six months. He doesn't say whether or not he won the bet, but one suspects not, judging from the fact that a year later he noted in his journal that 'I cashiered my conceited, foolish, impertinent false, traitorous, base, drunken dragoman, who is called Hasan Agha'.[17]

Besides the impertinent, false Hasan Agha, Baker's household included at least one English servant, Thomas Landsford. He also employed a French secretary, and later a Venetian. There may have been an English chaplain – the articles of peace stipulated that the consul must be allowed a place to pray in – but, if so, Baker never mentions him or, indeed, makes any mention of his own religious observances. The majority of the 800 or so Christian slaves in the city were Italian and French Catholics, and their spiritual needs were catered for by a small community of missionary priests.

The consul's main sources of contact with home were the English merchant ships that called to trade or to take on supplies. And those contacts were few and far between. In his first year, Baker welcomed just five English ships to Tripoli.

In fact he only saw thirteen during his entire six-year stay. Some were regular visitors: the *Francis and Benjamin*, which regularly plied between Livorno and Barbary, put in at Tripoli four times between March 1680 and May 1681. Others came once and then vanished back into the Mediterranean. The *Content*, for instance, put in with forty-seven butts of Sicilian wine and some timber boards at the end of December 1679; she stayed in port for two months waiting for good weather before leaving for Malta and Messina with a cargo of dates and was never mentioned again. The following summer the *Resolution* arrived from Syracuse on its only visit during Baker's consulate, bringing 100 butts of wine. (An English butt was 105 gallons, or 477 litres.) Wine was a valued commodity in Tripoli, in spite of repeated attempts by Istanbul to outlaw the consumption of alcohol throughout the Ottoman Empire. At various times Baker recorded the arrival of consignments of wine from Sicily, Cephalonia, Zante, Livorno, Marseilles and Frontignan. The imperial edict banning alcohol from any town or village with a Friday mosque was clearly more honoured in the breach than in the observance on the Barbary Coast: one English visitor to Tunis in 1675 commented that 'they drink more freely wine [here] than in other parts of Turkey', while near the marine gate in Tripoli, slaves kept taverns 'where commonly all sorts of religion go to play from morning until evening'.[18] Baker's problems with his dragoman and the close encounter with the drunken janissary suggest the residents played hard.

At the end of his first year in Tripoli, Thomas Baker sat down and made out a list of all the prizes taken by the corsair fleet since his arrival.

It wasn't a long list. In fact, for a state whose economy depended on piracy, it was remarkably short. The corsairs had brought in five ships, and that included the little bark so unsportingly apprehended on her way into harbour. All five were French. Far and away the most valuable was the *St Louis*, a brigantine of fourteen guns homeward bound for Marseilles. Karavilli Raïs, the Tripolitan vice admiral, came upon her one night in October as she tried to slip through the channel between Sardinia and the coast of Tunis, and after a brief scuffle she surrendered.

The *St Louis* was on her way back from Sidon and Cyprus with a cargo of fine silk, cotton yarn, pistachio nuts and spices. She also carried fifty-two Christians. Baker initially valued the prize at 100,000 dollars without the slaves – more than £23,000. And although he later revised his estimate downwards slightly (to 98,000 dollars), the *St Louis* still represented 60 per cent of the entire year's haul which, including 152 Christian slaves valued at 300 dollars each, came to 165,200 dollars, nearly £39,000.

That seems a lot of money. But the Tripolitan captains had to set against it the expenses of successful and unsuccessful cruises. They still had to buy victuals, powder and shot, and maintain their vessels, whether they came home with a prize or not. When they did capture a prize, the treasury took a huge cut. (In 'Uthmân Pasha's time it rose as high as 50 per cent, which was one of the reasons for his overthrow.) Private individuals expected a return on their investment. And the corsairs themselves, sailors and janissaries, had to have their shares.

Corsairing was a precarious business: at least one *raïs* didn't manage to take a single prize in the whole time Baker was in Tripoli. 'I would to God Algier afforded no better sailors or soldiers!' noted Baker in his journal, as the *raïs*, whose name was Mustafa Qadi, set off on his thirteenth trip. (He was back a month later 'without a rag of purchase'.[19]) If it hadn't been for Karavilli Raïs's chance midnight encounter with the *St Louis*, the *tā'ifat al-ra'īs* would have had a very lean year indeed. And, as a result, so would the whole of Tripoli.

For the next five years Baker held to his habit of sitting down each April on the anniversary of his arrival in Tripoli, and making out a list of all the prizes and slaves brought in by the pirates over the past twelve months. Success rates varied dramatically. The year 1680–81 was a good one for them, if not for the eighteen French, Venetian, Ragusan, Genoese and Maltese vessels they captured: 'the damages which have accrued to the navigation of Christendom by the depredations of these corsairs' amounted to 428,100 dollars, or well over £100,000.[20] The following year was disastrous, with prizes and slaves valued at only 124,800 dollars (less than £30,000). The 1682–3 haul was better, at 204,500 dollars

(£48,000), but only because of the capture off Crete of 'the richest prize that was ever brought into this place by a single ship', the *Three Kings of Marseilles*, which was homeward bound from the Levant and was valued at 120,000 dollars (£28,200).[21]

Takings were down again in 1683–4 at 129,300 dollars (just over £30,000); and again, they would have been a great deal worse without the capture of a substantial French vessel, the *Golden Sun*, worth 50,000 dollars (£11,750). The year 1684–5, Baker's final one as consul, was the corsairs' worst. This time there was no big prize. They took sixteen ships, but all were small, and six were empty. Baker reckoned the lot, plus seventy-nine slaves, at a mere 105,500 dollars, or less than £25,000. Lean times.

Times were destined to become leaner yet. When Baker arrived in 1679, England was the only European nation to have a treaty with Tripoli, which meant that the Tripolitan corsairs felt no compunction in taking any vessel which wasn't flying English colours. The two other major trading nations in the Mediterranean, France and Holland, were keen to reach similar agreements. In April 1685 articles of peace with Holland were concluded, when a Dutch man-of-war arrived at Tripoli with masts, cables, 150 barrels of gunpowder and 3000 shot as presents for the *dey* and the other senior officers 'to confirm their peace with this government', said Baker.[22]

The French were also keen for peace. In 1680 a French squadron arrived at Tripoli with an offer to negotiate, but the overture was roundly rebuffed by the *dey*, who simply could not afford it. War with France was essential to the Tripolitan economy: during the six years of Baker's time as consul, French ships accounted for more than 75 per cent of all prizes taken by value.

The French persisted, and the presence in the Mediterranean of Admiral Duquesne and his fleet persuade the *dey* to change his mind. In December 1681 he accepted the presence of a French consul and an offer to begin peace negotiations – to the disgust of his captains who complained they could barely scrape a living by preying on little barks out of Genoa or Malta. At the end of 1682 they broke the peace by taking a Marseilles merchant ship on its way home from Syria with a valuable cargo, and faced with the prospect of having to give it back, the captains forced a full meeting of the *dīwān* at the citadel, where *raïs* after *raïs* argued for war.

The French were enemies to Islam and the Empire. They had not returned to confirm the treaty, as they had promised. And, most tellingly of all, 'as long as a peace were maintained with France t'would be time and money spent to no purpose to arm out these ships, whilst all the Italians would enjoy the same security to their navigation by abusing these Turks with French colours, French passes and French sham-captains'.[23]

The result was a declaration of war. The French consul was placed under house arrest; the *dīwān* agreed to keep the Marseilles merchant and make slaves of its crew and passengers. Six weeks later corsairs took the 120,000-dollar *Three Kings*. But Duquesne's robust response to the taking of French merchant ships in the Mediterranean, demonstrated by his ruthless bombardments of Algiers in 1682 and 1683, was a worry. It is significant that in the middle of all the clamours for war in the *dīwān*, one of the few voices raised in dissent was that of the Tripolitan admiral himself, leading the *dey* to tell him to his face that if he foresaw 'evil contingencies which might arise by the war', now was the time to say so. He was silent.[24]

The French would mortar-bomb the Tripolitans into submission three years later.

Faced with a difficult economic climate, Tripolitans began to cast around for alternatives to corsairing. Tunis had been quite successful in making the switch from piracy to agriculture and legitimate commerce, establishing control over the countryside beyond Tunis itself, extracting taxes from the inhabitants and exporting a range of commodities from staples like rice, dates and olive oil to sponges and coral. Visitors commented on the wealth of foodstuffs available: flatbread ('not unpleasant whilst it is new'[25]); sheep, goats and bullocks; fresh fish like mullet and bream; dates, oranges, lemons and limes.

The countryside beyond Tripoli, on the other hand, the Fezzan, just wasn't that fertile. It consisted mainly of mountains, steep ravines and inhospitable desert, and it was populated by equally inhospitable nomads. So Tripolitans' options were limited. They exported a certain amount of salt from the salt pans of Zuwarah along the coast; and they occasionally tried to supplement the income they derived from prizes by raiding coastal villages in Calabria and the Morea for slaves. They also began to look to the tribes of the interior, for tribute and for slaves. In 1682 Murad Bey, the governor who had helped to topple Aq Mohammad al-Haddad, and who was now general of land forces and the power behind the throne in Tripoli, returned from an expedition deep into the Fezzan, where his soldiers killed a tribal chieftain who refused to pay tribute, and brought away five hundredweight of gold and a thousand black slaves, who were later sold to Albania.

Peace meant poverty for Tripoli. And Baker knew it. He knew, too, that occasional forays into the Sahara for slaves wouldn't sustain the Tripolitan economy. The choice was war with England or war with France. In November 1682 he was relieved when Admiral Herbert's flagship, the *New Tiger*, arrived to confirm the articles of peace once again. The *dey* welcomed him with a spectacular display of arms on the shore. For three hours Murad Bey's soldiers drilled and exercised, while Herbert watched from a barge and the *dey* looked down from the battlements of the citadel, 'where he caused to be spread abroad a great flag of green silk most richly wrought with gold, a respect wherewith the Turks' most solemn festivals have not been known to be honoured'.[26] Herbert entertained Baker and most of the senior officers of the government to dinner aboard the *New Tiger*. Only Murad was absent, because he couldn't stand the rough sea. (That's why he was commander of land forces, presumably.) There were salutes and presents and expressions of mutual admiration, and the articles were once more confirmed, although that didn't stop Baker smuggling two fugitive slaves aboard in disguise. One was a Swede with a Newcastle wife; the other, a Muscovite named Gabriel, had been hiding in Baker's house for the past nine months.

Herbert's arrival was a relief to the consul. 'I do verily believe it will have turned the scale on our side,' he wrote in his journal as the *New Tiger* weighed anchor and sailed away. 'A poor barren country, an empty treasury, and a good peace continued with his majesty and the French king, destroys the very foundations of [Tripoli's] existence.'[27]

Baker was a familiar figure in Tripoli, in the *suks* and narrow streets, down by the harbour, around the courtyards and fountains of the Assaray Al-Hamra citadel. In the later seventeenth century, Europeans – those who weren't renegades, at least – tended to adopt the same dress all over Barbary and the Levant: a broad-brimmed beaver hat, a knee-length black silk suit, perhaps with high red stockings and a red waistcoat; and, for winter, a long grey woollen coat. Baker's journal gives fleeting glimpses of his day-to-day activities. One moment he is firing off an angry note to a *raïs* called Mustapha Four-Beards who is flying English colours from his bowsprit: 'I must have that flag immediately taken down and sent to my house without more ado.' (And it was.)[28] Another time he receives word that an English gunner from the *Francis and Benjamin* has decided to convert to Islam. He immediately sets off for the citadel, where he finds that the man, whose name is William, has already presented himself to the *dey*, announced his wish to turn Turk and made the *shahada*. Technically that means the consul is too late, but Baker pays no attention to such niceties. He drags William away from the *dey*, down to the harbour and aboard his ship, where he is locked up – for his own good, of course – until she sails three weeks later.

But Baker is tantalisingly reticent about life in Tripoli – with two exceptions. He takes a keen interest in court gossip about the power struggles and falls from grace and regime changes. *Deys* come and go: Hasan 'Abaza is packed off to the island of Djerba in June 1683; his replacement lasts for two days before being banished to Crete (Djerba is full, presumably) and himself being replaced by a Rumelian renegade, 'Ali al-Jazairi, who lasts for thirteen months before taking the boat to Djerba. The janissaries strike for their pay: the rear admiral, who is blamed for stirring them up, is abruptly taken off his ship as she's about to set sail for the Levant and put aboard a small boat for Djerba. The daughter of a high-ranking court official, 'the finest woman of the town', is murdered by one of the *dey*'s officers. The treasurer dies suddenly; Baker assumes he has been poisoned, but can't feel any regret since the man was no friend to the English and was in any case 'as malicious as ignorant'.[29]

The other facet of Tripolitan life which fascinates the consul is sex. Any kind of sexual relationship between a Christian man and a Moslem woman was in theory punishable by death (although the sentence was usually commuted to a heavy fine); and fraternising with the local women was frowned upon by both sides.

But six years was a long time to stay celibate. Whores plied their trade in the Greek and Jewish quarter by the Arch of Aurelius, and there were those taverns by the marine gate where 'all sorts of religion go to play from morning until evening'. Perhaps Baker was made of purer stuff. Perhaps that's why his thoughts lingered on stories of sexual transgression.

These stories are presented with little in the way of moralising, even though it is precisely because they are transgressions that Baker gets to hear about them. In the summer of 1683, for instance, the son of a Dutch renegade, 'a brisk young fellow of the town' is gang-raped in a tavern by thirty-six janissaries;[30] although the consul remarks that the rape was carried out without shame or fear of retribution, that's as far as his censure goes. He seems to maintain a bemused detachment, as he does when a Turk is given 500 strokes on his buttocks 'not for having committed the act of sodomy with a boy, but for that, after having so done, he threw him over the town wall, whereby he brake both his legs'.[31] That's it. It is as if Tripolitan homosexual mores can be marvelled at, but they are so impossibly alien that it is really none of his business to condemn them.

Baker is more comfortable with heterosexual misbehaviour. Sidi Usuph, the strikingly handsome brother of a revered holy man, is caught by the watch at two in the morning coming out of a woman's house. There is a scuffle and he is killed. 'Unlucky accident!' laments the consul. 'Thus to disoblige all the fine women of the town, who, besides the reverence they bore for ye holiness of his strain [i.e., his bloodline], were most of them at his devotion, so comely was his personage.'[32] And when three Christian slaves are caught outside the walls with three women, he takes a delight in describing how the women are paraded around the town riding backwards on asses with sheep's entrails draped around their necks. One of the men turns Turk to avoid punishment; the other two have to pay fines of 850 dollars (about £200) and receive a bad beating into the bargain.

'Upon my word', says Baker with a Pepysian flourish, ''Twas a dear bout!'[33]

Baker didn't concern himself exclusively with the welfare of His Majesty's subjects, although English strategic interests usually lay at the heart of everything he did. This sometimes led him down some unusual paths. On one occasion, at the request of Hasan 'Abaza Dey, he provided a Tripolitan *raïs* with a letter of introduction to Lord Inchiquin at Tangier, requesting the English garrison to offer the corsair protection as he headed out to hunt for shipping in the Atlantic. His justification, that this was 'no more than what he may reasonably claim by our capitulations with this government',[34] was technically correct, even though the *raïs*'s ship, a recently captured Genoese prize, was to be fitted out at Algiers, with whom England was currently at war. No doubt the prospect of the *raïs* harassing French shipping when he reached the Atlantic also played a part in the consul's thinking.

It was a difficult job, as the Giaume Ballester affair and its aftermath showed. Ballester was a Majorcan captain who was taken with his ship in the Gulf of Venice and brought back in chains to Tripoli. Initial efforts to arrange his release foundered on the fact that the *dey*, convinced Ballester had wealthy connections at home, set his ransom at an exorbitant 7000 dollars, or around £1650. His friends arranged to exchange him for a well-known Tripolitan being held at Naples, but this came to nothing when the Majorcan entrusted with the negotiations suddenly decided to convert to Islam and join the Tripolitan fleet. Baker was particularly appalled at the man's behaviour because he had been a guest in his house, and had actually gone from there to the citadel 'where he most infamously renounced his baptism and turned Turk'.[35]

In May 1684, two and a half years after his capture, Ballester was redeemed for just 2000 dollars (£470) – still a lot, but a lot less than 7000 dollars. The man who redeemed him was Thomas Baker, who received an order for 800 dollars from Ballester's friends and trusted the Majorcan's assurances that the rest would be repaid as soon as he was safe home. A redemption certificate was issued, and Ballester was released into Baker's custody while he waited for a ship to take him back to Majorca.

Four weeks later he was rearrested and thrown into one of the city's three bagnios.

Baker stormed up to the citadel to demand an explanation. He found the *dey*, 'Ali al-Jazairi, uncharacteristically calm and reasonable – but adamant. The captains had told him the Majorcan was worth twenty times more than 2000 dollars; and they were so powerful, claimed 'Ali al-Jazairi, that he couldn't contradict them.

The consul went back to his house fuming, and convinced that the *dey*'s days were numbered. He was right. Before the week was out 'Ali al-Jazairi was on his way to Djerba, and a new ruler, Hajj 'Abdallah al-Izmirli, had taken up residence in the Assaray Al-Hamra citadel. Baker gave him four days to settle in and then renewed his assault. At a meeting of the full *dīwān* he absolutely demanded that Ballester be given up. Not unless he stumped up another 3000 dollars, they said.

By his own account, this flagrant disregard for what was right goaded him into a bravura piece of brinkmanship. In front of the entire *dīwān* he declared that this affront was done not to him but to the King of England. That three English warships were at that very moment on their way to Tripoli from Livorno. And that the moment they arrived he was going to declare war.

He was bluffing, but it worked. The *dīwān* backed down and Ballester was immediately produced and taken to the consul's house. 'And so, with a present the *dey* made me of a pleasant young bear ended this troublesome business.'[36]

If only life were that simple. A couple of days later an English merchantman, the *Unity*, put in from Livorno with a cargo of French wine, and Baker asked its master, William Ferne, to take Ballester back to Livorno. The *Unity* left Tripoli with the redeemed captive aboard on 16 July 1684. Ten weeks later Captain Ferne was back, and he had two pieces of bad news. The first was that Ballester had died of a fever five days after arriving at Livorno. Including expenses, passage money and various gratuities, the consul had paid out 1320 dollars of his own money on the Majorcan's redemption; the prospect of getting his money back also died in Livorno. 'A good help to a poor Tripoli consul!' wailed Baker.[37]

However Ferne's second piece of news was potentially even more serious. The captain had picked up a handful of passengers for the return voyage to Tripoli, and among them was a prominent Tripolitan who had just been redeemed out of slavery at Livorno. Off the island of Pantelleria in the Strait of Sicily the *Unity* was overtaken by a Genoese pirate, Giovanni Maria Caratini. Ferne was carrying an English pass; the liberated Turk was carrying a

certificate of redemption. Neither of these facts cut any ice with
Caratini, who seems to have decided his international status – the
Genoese was sailing under Spanish colours in a Dutch man-of-
war and holding Sicilian letters of marque – entitled him to disregard legal niceties. He took the *Unity*'s cargo, which was worth
more than 10,000 dollars. He took four Jews who were travelling
to Tripoli. And he took the Turk.

This was a disaster. There were echoes of the business with the
Goodwill back in 1651, when Stephen Mitchell allowed the Knights
of Malta to board his vessel and take thirty-two Tunisians: that
incident had led to riots, reprisals and war. And the timing couldn't
have been worse. The Dutch were concluding their own articles
of peace with Tripoli and the French were pushing hard for the
dey to accept theirs. (That summer the *Unity* had brought news
of a massive French mortar attack on Genoa which pounded the
city into unqualified submission, and Tripoli was bracing itself for
a visit from Duquesne and his bomb-ketches.) Baker was convinced
the Tripolitans were looking for an excuse to break the peace
with England and, as he reported to the English government,
unless the navy moved swiftly to free the Turk and punish Caratini, 'they will be the more easily invited to take strangers' goods
and passengers out of our numerous unguarded shipping in these
seas'.[38]

Baker was tired. The climate at Tripoli had taken its toll on him,
and he suffered from gout, 'a most disingenuous unkind mistake!',
and other unspecified but chronic illnesses.[39] It was time to go home.
He had asked to be recalled in the spring of 1683, and now in a
coda to his report he repeated the request, 'which once more I
presume languishingly to remind you of'.[40] But before his letter
reached England a French bark came into harbour at Tripoli with
word that Caratini had panicked and destroyed the evidence, throwing
the Turk and the four Jews overboard. Shortly afterwards he was
himself captured by the Venetians, who put him and his crew to
work in their galleys. This gave some satisfaction to the Livornese
merchants who had lost their cargo, but not to the Tripolitans, who
believed Caratini was being punished for his piracy rather than for
killing the Turk; nor to the man's widow and children, 'whose
continual outcries and tears will neither be quicked nor dried up,
unless the person of the pirate be rendered here'.[41]

If the consul was hoping for swift and decisive action, he was destined to be disappointed. When a response finally arrived in May 1685 (from the pen of Samuel Pepys, reappointed as secretary to the Admiralty after his return from Tangier), it was noncommittal. The matter was in the hands of the King's Secretaries of State, and there it must rest, although Pepys did add that if it was up to him, something would certainly be done to give the Tripoli government satisfaction for the murder of her subjects.

It wasn't up to him, and as far as I can find out nothing ever was done. The peace with England held, however, even after the expected bombardment by French mortars – which took place over three days that June – persuaded the *dey* and the *dīwān* to conclude a treaty with Louis XIV.

Baker left no account of the French assault. That is because Pepys's letter ended with the welcome news that James II was recalling the consul to London; he could go home as soon as his replacement arrived. When that was we don't know – only that seventeen months later, on 23 October 1685, he 'returned into the King's presence and kissed his hand'.[42] But the letter from Pepys, carefully copied into his journal, is the very last entry, as though with his recall the urge to keep a record 'of whatsoever occurrences shall happen or be noteworthy' came to an abrupt end.

Thomas Baker was a good consul. He served his country more conscientiously than many public officials, and with less regard for his own pocket than most. If he was a man of his own time with all the prejudices that entailed – he called Islam, for instance, 'that accursed superstition', and the French, with rather more reason, the 'scum of the earth' – at least he was able to establish good relationships with individual Tripolitans, based on shared interest and mutual trust.[43] He was sorry when the treasurer of Tripoli was dismissed and banished to Crete, because he had been a 'constant friend' not only to English interests but also to Baker himself. (He put the blame for the treasurer's downfall on the man's interfering wife: 'Women hold an empire even amongst these barbarous nations, as well as in England.'[44]) He regarded the captain of the port, who was sacked a few months later, as 'my truly cordial friend'.[45]

One gets the impression that, for all his grumbling, Baker rather liked North Africa and North Africans, an impression confirmed perhaps by the fact that he went back. He was appointed consul to Algiers in 1691, and when he left the post in 1694 he went on to Tripoli to renew the articles before coming home for the last time – in a vessel provided by the *dey* of Algiers, who wrote that 'since his coming [he] has gained the love of all our people'.[46] The government reimbursed him £1389. 0s. 6¼d. for the redemption of captives in Algiers, Salé and elsewhere in Barbary during this second stint as consul, and he was able to end his time there with a remarkable declaration – that there were no longer any subjects of the crown taken under English colours in slavery anywhere in Algiers, Tunis or Tripoli.[47]

16

The Last Corsair:
Colonialism, Conquest and the
End of the Barbary Pirates

O n the morning of Saturday 17 June 1815, a lookout on
the USS *Constellation* spotted a frigate sailing alone
twenty miles off the Spanish coast at Cabo de Gata. She
was flying the Union Jack, but the captain of the *Constellation*,
Charles Gordon, suspected she was really an Algerian corsair sailing
under false colours. He ordered his crew to break out the flags
signalling 'Enemy to the South-east' to his commander in the USS
Guerriere, Commodore Stephen Decatur, and the entire American
squadron of eight ships turned in pursuit.

The strange frigate held her course. But she was poised for
flight, and when an overenthusiastic Captain Gordon raised the
Stars and Stripes, the ship took alarm and 'was immediately in
a cloud of canvas', in the words of a young midshipman who
was watching from the deck of the *Guerriere*.[1] As the Americans
gained on her she altered course and doubled back, amazing
them with her seamanship – and with the marksmanship of her
snipers, who picked off several sailors from vantage points in the
rigging. But she was outnumbered, outgunned and eventually
outmanoeuvred. The *Constellation* came within range and opened

fire; then the *Guerriere* did the same. In less than half an hour she surrendered.

The American prize crew that boarded the crippled frigate took 406 prisoners, many of them wounded. They were sitting quietly on the cabin floor below deck, 'smoking their long pipes with their accustomed gravity'.[2] About thirty had been killed, including the frigate's commander, and only now did the Americans realise what they had done. That commander was none other than the legendary Hamidou Raïs, the most distinguished fighter in the Algerian navy. For years Hamidou had been celebrated all over Barbary as the master of the seas, the champion of the holy war against the infidel. Now he was dead.

The Americans had killed the last of the great corsairs.

In the 130 years that had passed since the treaties of the 1680s, relations between the European powers and the Barbary states had achieved an uneasy equilibrium, in which piracy played an increasingly insignificant role. Britain, France and Holland, followed by the Danes, the Swedes and the Venetians, discovered that if the agreement and renewal of articles of peace were accompanied by the giving of presents and hefty cash payments, the corsairs would be more punctilious in their observance of those articles. The sums involved varied, but they were substantial. In the 1780s Great Britain was paying Algiers around £1000 a year to maintain the peace, roughly equivalent to £1.2 million today. The Dutch paid about £24,000 and the Spanish a colossal £120,000.

Algiers commanded the biggest bribes, since it still presented the biggest threat to European merchant shipping, but the other states also needed to be paid off. Spain, Austria, Venice, Holland, Sweden and Denmark all gave large sums to the Bey of Tunis. Venice handed over 3500 ducats a year to Tripoli; Sweden gave 20,000 dollars. An English colonel living in Morocco in the 1780s reported that the Sultan had announced his intention to declare war on the Dutch 'if their embassy (that is, their presents) does not soon appear . . . It is a tribute', admitted the Englishman; 'and we are all tributary to him.'[3]

There were good reasons why the European powers tolerated this rather distasteful system of paying for licences to trade. It was easier and cheaper than launching punitive expeditions, convoying merchantmen to and from the Levant and maintaining expensive squadrons on permanent station. And even less creditably, it ensured that the Barbary corsairs directed their attention towards poorer commercial competitors who couldn't afford to pay them off. Most tellingly of all, if one state were to break out from beneath what an American diplomat eloquently described as 'the dark cloud of shame which covers the great powers of Europe in their tame submission to the piracies of those unprincipled barbarians',[4] it would immediately place itself at a disadvantage in relation to its rivals.

An act of rebellion on the other side of the Atlantic led, indirectly, to the collapse of this tribute system. When the American colonies declared independence in 1776, Great Britain withdrew the safe-conduct passes which its merchant vessels carried throughout the Mediterranean. New passes were issued – but, understandably in the circumstances, the errant colonists were left off the mailing list.

This was a major blow for America. Between 80 and 100 ships from the thirteen colonies traded to the Mediterranean, exporting wheat, flour, dried fish, timber and other commodities and bringing back wine, salt, oil and Moroccan leather. In one year alone, 1770, the total value of American produce exported to southern Europe and North Africa was £707,000. And every one of the ships carrying this trade relied on being able to show British Admiralty passes if they were stopped by corsairs.

After the American War of Independence was over, the Continental Congress did its best to obtain protection in the Mediterranean from other friendly states – first France and then Holland. Both were polite; neither was prepared to help. In desperation, the Congress even asked Britain if she might help to negotiate with the Barbary states on its former colony's behalf. Britain declined.

The United States was left with no alternative but to embark on its own negotiations. In 1786 John Adams, then the US minister to the Court of St James's, held a series of meetings with Abdurrahman, the Tripolitan ambassador in London, who told him that a perpetual peace between their two nations was perfectly possible. It would cost a mere 30,000 guineas, and he let it be known he expected the Americans to pay him a commission of

£3000 for arranging it. (The conversation, said Adams, was carried on 'in a strange mixture of Italian, Lingua Franca, broken French, and worse English'.[5]) Abdurrahman went home without his commission, and John Adams went home without his treaty.

In 1794 the United States government set aside $800,000, partly as ransom for a hundred slaves who had been captured by Algerian corsairs since America lost the protection of Britain in the Mediterranean, and partly as tribute to the *dey* and his officials in return for agreeing a peace treaty. Joseph Donaldson, the Philadelphian sent to Algiers to negotiate with the *dey*, was not an obvious choice for a delicate diplomatic mission. A middle-aged, sour and rather surly man, his gout was so bad when he arrived in Algiers in September 1795 that he needed a crutch to walk and had to wear a huge velvet slipper on his afflicted foot. Nor was his temper improved by his being made to limp unaided all the way from the harbour to his lodgings, or by the curious crowd which followed him every step of the way, or by the fact that when he finally reached his house he had to climb a long flight of marble steps to reach his apartment. When he got there he collapsed on a couch, threw off his hat and swore so long and so loudly that one of the Algerians asked in amazement what was happening? What was the infidel saying? 'The ambassador is only saying his prayers and giving God thanks for his safe arrival,' he was told. 'His devotion is very fervent,' replied the Algerian.[6]

In spite of this inauspicious start, Donaldson's negotiations were a success, but it was a hard battle. The *dey* began by demanding $2,247,000 in cash, plus a pair of 36-gun frigates, an annual dona-tion of naval stores and 'presents' every two years. Donaldson coun-tered with an offer of $543,000; the *dey* said he would accept $982,000. They finally agreed on a price of $585,000, plus an annuity of naval stores and biennial gifts. It wasn't much, said the *dey*, but he agreed 'more to pique the British who are your inveterate enemies and are on very bad terms with me, than in considera-tion of the sum, which I esteem no more than a pinch of snuff'.[7]

It was a big pinch of snuff. The United States treasury estim-ated the eventual cost of the treaty, including all the expense involved in negotiating it, at nearly $1 million. When word of the United States' generosity got out, it made Europe anxious. The $585,000 that Donaldson had agreed with the *dey* was twice what the Dutch had just paid Algiers, and, as the European powers feared, the other Barbary states began to wonder if they had been selling their treaties too cheap.

By the end of the eighteenth century America had secured treaties with Morocco, Tripoli and Tunis as well as with Algiers, albeit at a much higher rate than the British. The *pasha* of Tripoli, Yûsuf Karamanli, extorted $56,484; and the *bey* of Tunis, Hammûda ibn Ali, charged $107,000. (The sultan of Morocco held out for an annual tribute and then had a change of heart and signed articles of peace for nothing.) In addition, Hammûda made it clear that he expected some very special presents on the occasion of his ratification of the peace between Tunis and the United States. The long list which the United States' minister in London, Rufus King, supplied to his Secretary of State for approval included a musket mounted with gold and set with diamonds, a gold repeating watch and chain set with diamonds, a diamond ring, a snuff box of gold set with diamonds and an enamelled dagger which was, inevitably, set with diamonds. The whole lot was bought in London at a cost to the American government of £7000.

John Adams, who became President of the United States in 1797, was philosophical about the idea of paying tribute to the Barbary states. His successor and political rival, Thomas Jefferson, was not. Even in the 1780s, when the United States had no navy at all and hence no independent means of defending its interests in the Mediterranean, Jefferson as vice president was unhappy at what he saw as a dishonourable course, telling Adams 'it would be best to effect a peace through the medium of war'.[8] By the time he beat Adams in the election of 1800, America had created a naval force large enough for a squadron to be dispatched to the Mediterranean in response to increasingly bellicose demands from Yûsuf Karamanli of Tripoli, who decided he wanted a revised treaty, another quarter of a million dollars and an annual payment of $20,000. The US squadron, which consisted of three frigates and a sloop, arrived off Gibraltar in July 1801 to find that Yûsuf had found himself a place in the history books. He had just become the first head of state to declare war on America.

The war between Tripoli and the United States was characterised on both sides by good luck, bad luck and expediency,
with flashes of discreditable behaviour and breathtaking heroism.
Yûsuf's corsairs hunted for American shipping, while unarmed
American merchant vessels went about their trade in the Mediterranean without regard for their own safety – or the interests of
their country, which would be jeopardised if the Tripolitans
managed to secure hostages. 'One single merchantman's crew in
chains at Tripoli would be of incalculable prejudice to the affairs
of the United States,' complained the US consul at Tunis.[9]

Yûsuf's men did capture one merchantman, the *Franklin*, in June
1802. She was sold along with her cargo at Algiers, and her nine-
man crew was taken back to Tripoli. They were eventually released
after the United States paid the *pasha* $6500.

Worse was to come for America. A brand new 44-gun frigate,
the *Philadelphia*, was blockading Tripoli when, at nine o'clock on
the morning of 31 October 1803, she caught sight of an enemy
vessel trying to slip into harbour. After an exchange of fire and a
pursuit which lasted for several hours the *Philadelphia*'s captain,
William Bainbridge, realised there was no hope of catching the
ship and gave orders to abandon the action – at which point his
frigate ran on to a submerged reef and stuck fast.

Bainbridge's crew did everything possible to float her off. They
cut the anchors, threw heavy lumber and even some of the guns
overboard, and eventually cut away the foremast and the main top-
gallant mast – all the while taking fire from Tripolitan gunboats
whose commanders had seen what was happening and set out to
capture her. At four that afternoon Bainbridge surrendered, and
the 307 officers and crew of the *Philadelphia* were taken ashore
and imprisoned. Bainbridge's distress was evident in the report he
sent to the US Navy Department the following day; the terms in
which it was couched speak volumes for the West's attitude to
Barbary. To strike one's colours to any foe was mortifying, he said;
'but to yield to an uncivilised, barbarous enemy, who were objects
of contempt, was humiliating'.[10]

Not every member of the *Philadelphia*'s crew shared his contempt.
At least five American sailors converted to Islam during their
imprisonment. Yûsuf reacted to his fighters' success by raising his
price for peace to $3 million and using his captives as a bargaining

counter in negotiations. (He threatened at one point to kill them all if the Americans attacked Tripoli.) The *Philadelphia* was salvaged and brought into harbour, and over the winter the Tripolitans went to work trying to repair and re-arm her.

Senior officers of the American navy in the Mediterranean considered attempting to rescue the *Philadelphia*, but decided it would be impossible to get her away from under the guns of the Tripolitan shore batteries. There was a chance, however, that a raiding party might fire her and this would at least prevent her from being used by Yûsuf against them.

The mission was given to a young naval lieutenant from Maryland, Stephen Decatur – the same Stephen Decatur who, as commodore in command of the American squadron in the Mediter-ranean, would kill Hamidou Raïs eleven years later. With a crew of volunteers and a Sicilian pilot, Decatur sailed a captured ketch renamed the *Intrepid* into Tripoli harbour on the night of 16 February 1804. He pretended to be a merchant and, claiming he had lost his anchors, requested permission to tie up alongside the *Philadelphia*.

Dr Jonathan Cowdery, the *Philadelphia*'s surgeon, was being held with the other officers in the American consul's former residence at Tripoli. He described what happened next:

> About 11 at night, we were alarmed by a most hideous yelling and screaming from one end of the town to the other, and a firing of cannon from the castle. On getting up and opening the window which faced the harbour, we saw the frigate *Philadelphia* in flames.[11]

Decatur's men had been found out as they approached the frigate. They stormed aboard, set fire to the ship and rowed out of the harbour and into American history books. Decatur became a national hero, 'the first ornament of the American Navy' whose 'gallant and romantic achievement' was memorialised in countless pamphlets, poems and paintings.[12]

The burning of the *Philadelphia* was an enormously courageous act, but it made little difference to the war. Yûsuf remained deter-mined to extract more money from the Americans, while they in turn were just as determined to break him – and to remove him from power.

The frigate Philadelphia *in flames*

A cornerstone of American strategy was a scheme to use Yûsuf's exiled brother, Ahmad Karamanli, as a focus for dissent; and, ultimately, to set him up in Tripoli as a puppet *pasha*. Unfortunately Ahmad was none too keen on the idea. William Eaton, the US consul in Tunis, tracked him down in Egypt and, after promising that American support would extend to the two men either triumphing within the walls of Tripoli or dying together before them, he persuaded Ahmad to join his motley expeditionary force of 10 American marines, 300 Arabs, 38 Greeks and about 50 other soldiers of various nationalities.

This ragtag army marched nearly 500 miles across the Libyan Desert from Egypt to Darna, a Tripolitan outpost to the east of Cyrene. They saw 'neither house nor tree, nor hardly anything green . . . not a trace of a human being'.[13] The Arabs and Christians argued with each other. They had no water for days on end. Their horses had no food. At one point Ahmad went back to Egypt, then changed his mind and rejoined the party. Nevertheless, they reached Darna on 27 April 1805. And when they got there, they took it.

This was a remarkable achievement. But if Eaton had hoped that Ahmad would inspire a rebel force to go on and capture

Tripoli, he was disappointed. No one joined the rebel army, while Eaton's men struggled for six weeks to fight off combined attacks by Arab tribesmen and forces sent by Yûsuf to relieve the town. Nevertheless, Eaton himself continued to believe on very slender evidence that it was only a matter of time before the country-side rose up and joined Ahmad's cause.

He never had the chance to test that conviction. On 11 June the USS *Constellation* arrived off Darna with the news that Yûsuf had suddenly caved in and made peace with America. There was no need to wait for a general rising. In one of the less creditable episodes of the war, Eaton, Ahmad, the marines and most of the Greeks sneaked aboard the *Constellation* and left their beleaguered Arab army behind to fend for itself.

The terms of the peace agreed between Yûsuf and the US consul-general, Tobias Lear, were that America should pay nothing for a new treaty, and that all prisoners would be exchanged man for man. The capture of the crew of the *Philadelphia* meant the Tripolitans currently held about 200 more prisoners than the Americans, so Lear agreed to acknowledge the imbalance by paying Yûsuf $60,000, $300 a prisoner.

The peace treaty was formally ratified in Tripoli on 10 June 1805. On finally meeting his former adversary, Lear commented with some surprise that Yûsuf was 'a man of very good presence, manly and dignified, and has not, in his appearance, so much of the tyrant as he had been represented to be'.[14] Abstract notions of the Other as barbarian are hard to sustain when you come face to face with the reality.

Considering the *pasha*'s opening offer had been a demand for $3 million, the treaty was a good outcome for America. But it was unpopular with Eaton, who was furious at being prevented from marching on Tripoli and still convinced that a show of force would have toppled Yûsuf; and it was unpopular with sections of the American press back home, which were uncomfortable with the cost, with the loss of honour, and with the way Ahmad Karamanli had been used and then discarded. A plaintive letter from Ahmad, now in exile, to the people of the United States of America pointed out that Eaton had agreed on their behalf to place him on the throne of Tripoli and that America had reneged on that agreement. (The reality was that Eaton had exceeded his authority in the promises he made to Ahmad.) The public didn't know that although Lear had begun negotiations by insisting that Yûsuf must immediately hand over members of Ahmad's family who were being held hostage in Tripoli, he toned down this demand and agreed to give Yûsuf *four years* to comply.

Amidst all the condemnations in the press, it was left to the Washington-based, pro-government newspaper the *National Intelligencer* to defend the new treaty. The *Intelligencer* poured scorn on the critics, and insisted that the payment of $60,000 to Yûsuf was entirely justifiable in the circumstances. Since the United States was dealing with 'barbarians . . . who made a practice of vending prisoners', it declared, 'the price demanded for our countrymen is very small. It amounts to about 233 dollars for each individual. This is not the value of a stout healthy negro.'[15]

Who says Americans don't do irony?

The US–Tripoli conflict came close to destabilising the entire Barbary Coast. Algiers threatened war with America because the annual tribute of naval stores was late in coming. Tunis threatened war because American vessels blockading Tripoli harbour persisted in stopping Tunisians and confiscating Tunisian goods. Morocco actually opened hostilities and detained two American merchantmen before the sultan thought better of it.

Of the European powers with interests in the Mediterranean, the Danes and the Swedes did their best to mediate between the two sides, and France promised that its consul in Tripoli would try to free the crew of the *Philadelphia*. The British consul, on the other hand, worked hard to maintain Yûsuf's hostility towards America – or so the Americans believed. But war between Britain and France broke out in May 1803; and Napoleon Bonaparte crowned himself Emperor of France the following year. Europe had more pressing matters to worry about than relations with North Africa. 'God preserve Bonaparte!' exclaimed one corsair. 'As long as other nations have him to contend with, they won't worry us.'[16]

That corsair was Hamidou Raïs. Hamidou belonged to a group of corsair captains whose careers flourished in a little renaissance of Algerian privateering around the turn of the century. It included Hamman, said by some sources to be his brother; Tchelbi, with whom he sailed in the late 1790s; Mustafa 'the Maltese' and Ali Tatar. Although the *tā'ifat al-ra'īs* was no longer the maker and breaker of *deys* that it had been in the seventeenth century, individual captains still commanded a great deal of respect in Algerian society. They lived in fine mansions with large households. Their exploits were celebrated in songs and poems.

Hamidou was a native Algerian, the son of a tailor. He went to sea as a boy in the 1780s, and by 1797 he had his own ship, a small, fast, three-masted xebec. That year he and Tchelbi Raïs sailed into Tunis with four valuable prizes: a Genoese, a Venetian and two Neapolitans; and when Algiers declared war on France in 1798 he captured the French factory at El Kala near the Tunisian border, and then sailed north to raid along the coast of Provence. Over the next two years his men took at least fourteen prizes worth half a million francs.

Algiers made peace with Napoleon at the end of 1801, by which time Hamidou had become one of his nation's most profitable corsairs. As a reward, he was moved to the brand new 44-gun *Mashouda*, one of two frigates which the *dey* commissioned specially from a Spanish naval architect, Maestro Antonio (the other was given to Ali Tatar). The *Mashouda* remained his flagship for the rest of his life. In 1805 he took several Neapolitans, an American schooner with a crew of fifty-eight and, after a fierce battle, a 44-gun Portuguese frigate, the *Swan*. The *Swan*'s 282 survivors were brought back to Algiers, and the poets sang of how Hamidou's heart was full of joy at overcoming the infidels, and how he arrived at the *dey*'s palace trailing behind him enslaved Christians and negroes.

Amid the stylised Algerian encomiums that celebrated Hamidou's successes, there is the occasional more prosaic glimpse into the character of this charismatic man. He was of medium height, with blond hair and blue eyes (not as unusual as one might think among native-born Algerians), and clean-shaven except for long drooping moustaches. Elizabeth Blanckley, the young daughter of the British consul-general in Algiers, was clearly smitten: years later she wrote that the *raïs*, who, when he wasn't hunting Christians, lived next door to the consulate, 'was one of the finest-looking men I ever saw, and was as bold as one of his native lions'.[17] She also recalled that Hamidou was 'not the most rigid observer of the Alcoran', since he used to drop round for a glass or two of Madeira with her father. 'His house and garden were kept up in the greatest order and beauty,' she said.[18]

Hamidou's domestic arrangements are unknown, although when Algiers was briefly at war with Tunis in 1810 and the *Mashouda* captured a Tunisian ship with four negro women aboard, one was reserved for his use. Presumably the young Elizabeth was unaware of what went on behind the walls of Dar Hamidou.

The Tuscan poet Filippo Pananti, who was taken when the *Mashouda* captured the Sicilian merchant ship in which he was a passenger, left a vignette of Hamidou at work. His description of the capture is vivid: one of the Sicilian sailors, who had already been enslaved once, had to be restrained from stabbing himself to death. Another seized a firebrand and tried to blow up the ship's powder magazine before the corsairs could board. When they did, passengers and crew were petrified:

[The pirates] appear on deck in swarms, with haggard looks, and naked scimitars, prepared for boarding; this is preceded by a gun, the sound of which was like the harbinger of death to the trembling captives, all of whom expected to be instantly sunk; it was the signal for a good prize: a second gun announced the capture, and immediately after they sprang on board, in great numbers. Their first movements were confined to a menacing display of their bright sabres and attaghans [long knives]; with an order for us to make no resistance, and surrender . . . and this ceremony being ended, our new visitors assumed a less austere tone, crying out in their lingua franca, *No pauro! No pauro!* Don't be afraid.[19]

To Pananti's surprise, Hamidou's men were kind and deferential towards the women captives, and besotted by their children. 'It was only necessary to send Luigina [one of the little girls] round amongst the Turks, and she was sure to return with her little apron full of dried figs and other fruits.'[20] Hamidou himself comes across as ingenious, arrogant – and amiable. He would sit cross-legged on deck for three or four hours each day, giving orders to his men, smoking and smoothing his long moustache. But he also invited the Italians into his cabin, 'where an Arab tale was recited, and what was still better, a cup of good Yemen coffee was handed round, followed by a small glass of rum'.[21]

By 1815 Algiers was at war with Portugal, Spain, several Italian states, Holland, Prussia, Denmark and Russia. The *dey*'s prize registries for thirty months from July 1812 to January 1815 show that Hamidou and the *Mashouda* brought home twenty-two prizes with cargos worth nearly two million francs. There was brandy, cocoa, coffee and sugar, wine and cloth and timber. The corsairs were generally careful to avoid direct attacks on shipping belonging to France and Great Britain, both of whom had navies powerful enough to deter any acts of aggression. But the smaller, weaker nations were fair game, and Hamidou's victims included Danes, Swedes, Greeks – and Americans. The *dey* of Algiers used the War of 1812 to renege on his treaty obligations with the United States; and although corsairs had a hard time finding American ships that hadn't already been captured by the British navy, one US brig, the *Edwin*, was taken off the southern coast of Spain in the summer of 1812 while on her way home from Malta and brought into Algiers, where her ten-man crew was imprisoned. Her captor was a frigate armed with two rows of cannon on each side; she may well have been the *Mashouda*.

Britain and the United States signed a peace treaty on Christmas Eve 1814. The following spring, outrage at the continuing detention of the *Edwin* and her crew led the administration in Washington to decide it had had enough of the corsairs. President James Madison and Secretary of State James Monroe co-signed an uncompromising letter to the *dey*, Hadji Ali:

> Your Highness having declared war against the United States of America, and made captives of some of their citizens, and done them other injuries without cause, the Congress of the United States at its last session authorised by a deliberate and solemn act, hostilities against your government and people. A squadron of our ships of war is sent into the Mediterranean sea, to give effect to this declaration. It will carry with it the alternative of peace or war. It rests with your government to choose between them.[22]

Madison made good his threat, dispatching two squadrons of warships to deliver his letter. It was one of these squadrons, commanded by Stephen Decatur in the *Guerriere* and carrying the American consul-general for the Barbary states, William Shaler, which encountered Hamidou Raïs and the *Mashouda* at Cabo de Gata on Saturday 17 June 1815.

Hamidou had been cruising off the Spanish coast that week, in company with a 22-gun brig, the *Estedio*, which had been taken from the Portuguese some years before. He had just sent the *Estedio* to reconnoitre further along the coast (she was run aground near Valencia by the Americans and captured the next afternoon), leaving the *Mashouda* alone to watch the merchant shipping passing on its way to and from the Straits.

Hamidou initially thought the American warships were British (and hence friendly), even though they were obviously changing course to close the distance between the *Mashouda* and them. Only when Captain Gordon of the *Constellation* raised the Stars and Stripes prematurely did the corsair realise what was happening. Immediately he ordered his men to crowd on sail and take evasive action. If the *Mashouda* could once get clear of the American guns she could give them a run for their money. There was a westerly wind, and Algiers lay 300 miles due east. He could reach home in two days.

The Americans, though eager, were inexperienced. Even before Gordon's gaffe with the colours, the captain of the squadron's flagship, the *Guerriere*, who had never commanded a ship in battle before, broke out the wrong signal, ordering the other ships to 'tack and form into line of battle'. If they had obeyed the signal, the *Mashouda* would have got away while they slowly manoeuvred into line. They didn't. On the deck of the *Mashouda* Hamidou told his lieutenant that if he died, 'you will have me thrown into the sea. I don't want infidels to have my corpse.'[23]

Hamidou managed to leave the *Constellation* behind him, but the *Guerriere* gained fast, forcing him to change course and double back on himself. In doing so he brought the *Mashouda* within range of the *Constellation*'s guns and Gordon opened fire, hitting the Algerian's upper deck. One of the flying splinters of wood struck Hamidou, hurting him badly; but he refused requests to go below and instead ordered a chair to be placed for him on the upper deck. There he sat, in pain and in plain view, urging his men on.

The *Mashouda* changed course again and an American sloop, the USS *Ontario*, passed her on the port beam and fired a broadside before sailing straight past her, the captain having misjudged her momentum. Minutes later the *Guerriere* manoeuvred alongside and fired a broadside from a distance of barely 30 yards. It tore into the Algerian's upper deck and Hamidou, who was still shouting orders and encouragement to his men, was killed outright.

Even in the heat of battle, his men obeyed his wishes before surrendering. The last corsair's broken body was thrown into the sea to save it from being defiled by the infidels.

Commodore Decatur's warships arrived in the Bay of Algiers on 28 June 1815 to find that the *dey*, the devout and authoritarian Hadji Ali, had been murdered by his own janissaries. So had his successor, Mohammad Khaznadj. (He lasted just sixteen days.) The current *dey*, Omar, was understandably feeling insecure, and the presence of a very hostile American squadron didn't help. Nor did the news that his finest naval commander had just been killed in battle by a hostile foreign power. Decatur and Consul-General William Shaler managed to make Omar's life even more difficult. They delivered President Madison's letter – and then presented a series of unprecedented demands. There were to be no more payments to the *dey*. On the contrary, the Algerian government was expected to pay $10,000 to America as indemnification for the seizure of the *Edwin*. All American prisoners were to be released immediately. All American property in Algiers was to be restored to its owners. If America and Algiers ever went to war again, captives were to be treated as prisoners of war rather than slaves. In return, Decatur would hand over the *Mashouda* and the *Estedio* and their crews. But there was no time for prevarication or retrenchment or even diplomacy. America demanded an immediate response.

The fortifications at Algiers were in a state of disrepair, and the *dey*'s navy wasn't strong enough to take on the heavily armed American warships. So Omar had no choice but to cave in. The official Algerian report on the encounter was painfully brief. 'Eight American warships met and seized an Algerian frigate and a brig.

They then came to Algiers, and when the news of the event spread, peace was concluded.'[24]

On the surface this was a tremendous victory for the United States. Decatur and Shaler had succeeded where the greatest powers in Europe had failed; and Decatur seized the moment. Acting on his own responsibility he sailed straight to Tunis, where he demanded and received similar terms and an indemnity of $46,000 from the *bey*; and then to Tripoli, where Yûsuf Pasha agreed to release Christian slaves and to hand over $25,000, which was, he claimed, all the ready money he had. In England, the radical polemicist William Cobbett applauded the United States for its strong action and sneered at Europe's moral cowardice. 'The extirpation of the royal nest of African pirates,' he declared, 'is an act which will be recorded in the pages of history to the eternal honour of the American people, while the long endurance of this haughty and barbarous race will for ever reflect disgrace on the nations of Europe.'[25]

But America underestimated its adversaries. The *deys* of Algiers had always known how to pick their battles, how to yield when it suited them and how to fight when they could win. While the American warships sailed for home and a heroes' welcome, Omar began to have second thoughts. When another American squadron arrived off Algiers in March 1816 carrying the treaty, which had now been ratified by the Senate and proclaimed by President Madison, the crew found the Algerians extremely restive and looking for excuses to reopen negotiations on more favourable terms. They considered it 'disgraceful to the faithful to humble themselves before Christian dogs', wrote Oliver Perry, the captain of the USS *Java*, the frigate that actually brought the ratified treaty across the Atlantic.[26]

Omar found his excuse to suspend the new treaty in what he described as America's breach of faith in failing to return the *Estedio* as Decatur had promised. The battered *Mashouda* had been allowed home almost immediately, but the Spanish, who were holding the Algerian brig, showed a marked reluctance to give it up, arguing that it had been captured in Spanish waters. When a Spanish squadron eventually turned up at Algiers with the *Estedio* in March 1816, Omar promptly announced that it was too late; the United States had broken faith and there was nothing for it but to return to the treaty that the gout-ridden Joseph Donaldson had negotiated back in 1795, complete with its system of annual gifts and payments.

While the United States pondered this awkward turn of events, Algiers, Tunis and Tripoli were caught in a greater struggle. In 1807 the British government had abolished the trade in slaves (although not the institution of slavery) throughout the British Empire, and in the years that followed it brought pressure to bear on other slave-trading nations to follow suit. Abolitionists and anti-abolitionists alike were quick to point out the hypocrisy of Britain's position – how could it be so eager to put a stop to the traffic in black slaves while it turned a blind eye to the enslavement of white Christians on the Barbary Coast? Even slave-owning nations like the United States voiced their criticism, oblivious to the inconsistencies of their own position: as far as slave-owners like President Madison were concerned, there was simply no equivalence between the situation of their own black Africans and that of white Christians who were being held by heathens. In May 1816 John Quincy Adams, then the US minister in London, assured the First Lord of the Admiralty, Viscount Melville, that if America had but one third of Britain's naval power, 'the Christian world should never more hear of tribute, ransom, or slavery to the African barbarians'.[27]

As it happened, only a few moments after Adams made this remark he was called in to see Viscount Castlereagh, the British Foreign Secretary, who informed him that a naval force commanded by Admiral Lord Exmouth was at that very moment anchored off Algiers. Exmouth's instructions were to negotiate a peace on behalf of the Kingdom of the Two Sicilies and Sardinia (which now also controlled Genoa); to point out that the Ionian Islands now belonged to Britain, which put them off-limits to corsairs; and to advise Algiers, Tunis and Tripoli 'of the rising indignation of Europe against their mode of warfare, and to advise them to abandon it and to resort to more creditable resources for the support of their Government'.[28]

Exmouth's expedition was a partial success. Tunis and Tripoli were both persuaded to abolish Christian slavery completely and, in the event of a future war with Christian states, to treat captives as prisoners of war. Between them both cities agreed to free around a thousand Neapolitans and Sicilians, although the admiral had to pay for them. He was given a further 400 Sardinians and Genoese at no extra charge.

His experience at Algiers was less happy. Omar agreed to hand over forty Sardinian subjects at 500 Spanish dollars a head, and a thousand Neapolitans at 1000 dollars a head. He also agreed to pay ransom of 500 Spanish dollars a head for eight Algerian slaves being held at Genoa. (Let's not forget that the Barbary states were the victims of slaving raids, as well as the perpetrators.) But slavery was still vital to the Algerian economy and Omar refused point-blank to end the enslavement of Christians. Exmouth and his aides were jostled by an angry mob on their way back to the harbour; the British consul-general was arrested with his wife, daughter and sister-in-law, and the consulate was overrun and occupied by armed men.

After a stand-off in which both sides prepared to fight, Exmouth decided he couldn't commence hostilities against Algiers without authority from his government. Omar agreed to send ambassadors to London and to Istanbul to discuss the British demands, and Exmouth and his fleet went home.

They found the British public up in arms. While Exmouth was still in Algiers and the tension between him and the *dey* was at its height, Omar had sent orders to arrest two communities of Italian coral fishermen who lived on the coast at Bona near the Tunisian border, and Oran, 200 miles west of Algiers. Both groups were technically under British protection. Omar had second thoughts and countermanded the orders, but his new orders arrived too late for the group at Bona, who were celebrating an Ascension Day Mass on the shore when Omar's janissaries arrived. They tried to resist arrest and in the ensuing fight a hundred were hacked to death and as many more were wounded.

The Bona massacre outraged public opinion in Britain, galvanised the British government into action and sealed Algiers's fate. On 26 August 1816 Lord Exmouth was back in the Bay of Algiers at the head of a formidable fleet of battleships, frigates and bomb-ketches, reinforced by a Dutch squadron that had asked to take part in a joint operation. 'The whole western horizon,' wrote William Shaler, who was watching from the US consulate, 'is covered with vessels of war.'[29] The Algerians were ready for them:

Omar had 40,000 soldiers manning his shore batteries and waiting to board any ship that came close enough, and there was a fleet of thirty-seven gunboats just inside the mole waiting to attack.

The next morning at eleven o'clock one of Exmouth's officers handed an ultimatum to the Algerian captain of the port, demanding the release of all Christian slaves, the abolition of Christian slavery and the repayment of the ransom money that had been paid over in May. The Algerian was told that Omar had three hours to respond and no more. At two o'clock the officer returned to the fleet. No answer had been received.

This was the signal for Exmouth's flagship, the 108-gun *Queen Charlotte*, to move slowly towards the shore, closer and closer, until she was barely a hundred yards from the mole, which was crowded with Algerian troops. The other battleships followed her in. Exmouth's pilot steered the *Charlotte* into position with her starboard broadside facing the shore batteries. She anchored by the stern and the crew gave three loud cheers. It was three o'clock.

For a moment there was nothing but silence and the sound of timbers creaking and water lapping. Then a flash came from one of the shore batteries, followed by a loud crack and the whizz of a shot sailing past the *Charlotte*. 'Stand by!' called Exmouth. A second shot rang out. He gave the order to fire, and the walls of Algiers shook at the sound of hell breaking loose.

The Algerians fought back, and they fought hard. The British 104-gun ship of the line *Impregnable*, which was slightly out of position and exposed to fire from the heaviest batteries, was hit 233 times and fifty of its crew were killed. And soon after the bombardment began, the Algerian gunboats sped out from the smoke that lay over the mole and made straight for the *Queen Charlotte* and the frigate *Leander*, which was nearby. 'With a daring which deserved a better fate',[30] the boat crews intended to board them both. Before they could come close enough, the *Leander* depressed its guns and fired on them to terrible effect. Thirty out of the thirty-seven gunboats were sunk.

By nightfall the Anglo-Dutch fleet had poured 50,000 shots into Algiers, more than 500 tons of iron. The bomb vessels, stationed right out to sea, lobbed 960 shells over the ramparts and into the city. William Shaler, whose consulate was blown to pieces around him, described the scene:

The spectacle at this moment [it was now midnight] is pecu-
liarly grand and sublime. A black thunderstorm is rising,
probably an effect of the long cannonade; its vivid lightning
discovers the hostile fleets retiring with the land breeze, and
paints them in strong relief on the deep obscurity of the
horizon.[31]

Shells and rockets streamed across the horizon, and there was
the desultory thud of gunfire from those ships still within range,
answered by shots from what remained of the Algerian shore
batteries.

Taking stock that night, the British fleet's surgeons counted 141
men killed and 742 wounded. Lord Exmouth had the skirt of his
coat torn off by a passing cannonball and received cuts to his face,
hand and thigh. The Algerians initially reckoned their losses at
about 600 dead and wounded, a figure later revised to 2000.

As the bomb ships moved into position at dawn the next day
to resume their bombardment, it became obvious that Algiers
couldn't take much more. Her navy was destroyed: as well as the
thirty gunboats that the *Leander* had sunk, Exmouth noted that
his ships had sunk or burned four large frigates, five large corvettes
and several merchant brigs and schooners. On the quays and around
the city, walls had been breached or completely destroyed, houses
were smashed to pieces, batteries were out of commission. 'Every
part of the town appears to have suffered from shot and shells,'
wrote Shaler. 'Lord Exmouth holds the fate of Algiers in his
hands.'[32]

Before resuming operations Exmouth sent another letter to
Omar under a flag of truce. It was uncompromising:

Sir,
    For your atrocities at Bona, on defenceless Christians, and
your unbecoming disregard of the demands I made yesterday,
in the name of the Prince Regent of England, the fleet under
my orders has given you a signal chastisement, by the total
destruction of your navy, storehouses, and arsenal, with half your
batteries.
    As England does not war for the destruction of cities, I am
unwilling to visit your personal cruelties upon the inoffensive

inhabitants of the country, and therefore offer you the same terms of peace which I conveyed to you yesterday in my sovereign's name. Without the acceptance of these terms, you can have no peace with England.[33]

Omar surrendered later that day.

Exmouth's bombardment marked the beginning of the end for piracy on the Barbary Coast. Unable to defend itself, Algeria ratified the disputed treaty with the United States in December 1816, although Omar insisted that the Americans should provide him with a certificate stating he had signed under compulsion. He struggled to maintain his authority in Algiers for another eight months, but an outbreak of plague added to a general feeling that he was somehow cursed, and in the summer of 1817 his janissaries confirmed it by strangling him.

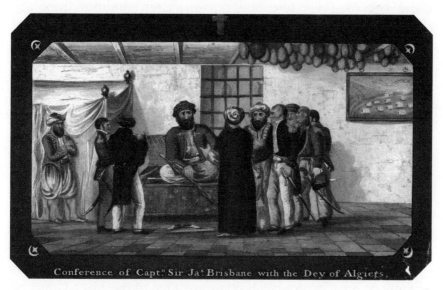

Conference of Capt.ⁿ Sir Ja.^s Brisbane with the Dey of Algiers,

Lord Exmouth's flag captain on the Charlotte, *James Brisbane, discusses peace terms with the* dey *of Algiers*

At the 1818 Congress of Aix-la-Chapelle the European powers debated ways of stamping out the corsairs completely; and although they couldn't agree on a resolution, Prince Metternich of Austria and the other heads of state did agree that Britain and France should send a joint squadron to warn the Barbary states 'that the unavoidable consequence of their perseverance in a system hostile to peaceful commerce, would be a general league among the powers of Europe . . . which might eventually affect their very existence'.[34]

As it turned out, their very existence was more profoundly affected by the greed and ambition of Europe.

George Davis and William Watts stood shivering on the gallows at Execution Dock. Crime and punishment had led them both to the other side of the world and back. Now they were about to leave that world for ever.

Watts had been transported to Tasmania in 1817 for stealing the bedding from a lodging house in Islington. Davis had followed him three years later, after being convicted at the Old Bailey of grand larceny. (He stole cutlery worth ten shillings from the kitchen of a house in Holborn.) The harsh conditions of the penal settlement at Hobart didn't persuade either man to the paths of righteousness; and in 1829, after re-offending several times, they were put aboard the brig *Cyprus* with sixteen other convicts and dispatched to the remote penal station of Macquarie Harbour on the west coast of Tasmania, where the worst of the worst ended up. En route to Macquarie the convicts had over-powered their guards and seized control of the ship, which they sailed, via Tahiti and Japan, to China. From there Davis and Watts had made their way back to England – only to be recognised, arrested and brought before the Admiralty Sessions in London on a charge of 'piratically and feloniously carrying away by force of arms' the *Cyprus*.

There was little doubt as to their guilt, and when the verdict was announced Sir Christopher Robinson, judge of the High Court of Admiralty, duly put on his black cap, informed the unfortunate pair that piracy was 'considered by the law of the land as a crime of the greatest magnitude'[35] and sentenced them to hang. On the morning of Thursday 16 December 1830 they were taken from their cells at Newgate Prison, put in a carriage and driven the three miles to Execution Dock where, as *The Times* reported succinctly the next day, they 'underwent the awful sentence of the law'.[36]

The deaths of George Davis and William Watts were less barbaric than those of the seventeen men who sought the fellowship of angels at Execution Dock back in 1609: the gallows was now equipped with a trap, making death by slow strangulation less likely; and the practice of leaving corpses until three tides had washed over them had been discontinued at the end of the eighteenth century. But an Admiralty official still led the procession on horseback, carrying his silver oar; the crowds still jeered; the prison chaplain still led prayers and the men still died. What made these particular executions noteworthy was that Davis and Watts were the last pirates to hang by British law at Wapping.

Piracy was on the decline in the nineteenth century, not only among British subjects but everywhere, as well-armed professional navies grew more effective at enforcing the rule of law on the high seas and the immensely powerful British navy pursued a vigorous anti-slavery policy. In 1856 the majority of maritime nations, including the Ottoman Empire, signed the Declaration of Paris, which outlawed privateering and the issuing of letters of marque and which brought to an end 350 years of quasi-legal Mediterranean piracy.

As the naval power of Algiers and the other Barbary states weakened and their ability to play off one European nation against another declined, the history of North Africa entered a new phase. On 14 June 1830, six months before Davis and Watts died at Execution Dock, a French force of 34,000 soldiers under the command of Marshal Louis-Auguste-Victor, Count de Ghaisnes de Bourmont, landed at Sidi Ferruch on the Algerian coast, fifteen miles west of Algiers. The pretext for the French invasion was the famous *affaire de l'éventail* of 1827, in which Hasan, the *dey* of Algiers, lost his temper with the arrogant French consul, Pierre Deval, and hit him across the face with his fly whisk in front of dozens of dignitaries and diplomats at a public feast to mark the end of Ramadan. The real reason for the invasion was to prop up the unpopular government of the French king, Charles X – an attempt that failed miserably, since news of the French victory had scarcely reached Paris when Charles was deposed in the July Revolution. But by then it was too late for Algiers. French withdrawal would have meant an embarrassing loss of face, and the invasion force stayed. Within twenty years the whole of Algeria was under French control.

In 1881, as a newly unified Italy cast a longing gaze at Tunis, the French used raids into Algiers by Tunisian tribesmen as an excuse to extend their influence eastward. An army of 30,000 crossed the border into Tunisia on 9 April 1881, entering the capital sixteen days later without meeting any real resistance, and Tunis was formally declared a French protectorate in June 1883. Morocco and Tripoli held on to their independence for a little longer; but by 1914 Morocco had been split between France and Spain, and Tripoli had been ceded to Italy by the Ottoman Empire, along with the rest of what is now Libya.

There's an obvious irony here. Fear of European conquest turned the Barbary states into pirate kingdoms in the first place, motivating Oruç and Khair ad-Din Barbarossa and their sixteenth-century corsairs to set out on their sea *jihad*. Without that fear of conquest, Barbary's socialised piracy would never have grown into the scourge of Christendom, its followers would not have become the shock troops on the front line of the defence of the Islamic world. And ultimately the only way Europe could find to deal with the scourge was to conquer Barbary, sweeping away the corsairs in a tidal wave of colonialism.

At the end of Byron's problematic poem *The Corsair*, Conrad, the eponymous hero, disappears into the night after he loses the love of his life. His pirate crew scours caves and grottos, searches shore and sea, calling his name 'till echo waxeth weak'; but they never find him. He has vanished into the air, leaving nothing behind but Byron's epigram:

> He left a Corsair's name to other times,
> Link'd with one virtue, and a thousand crimes.

The equally problematic pirates of Barbary left a thousand crimes behind them. Their one virtue, whether they were renegade Christian fugitives or devout Moslem warriors for God, was courage. Deplore the crimes, by all means.

But remember the courage.

Acknowledgements

Many people and institutions have helped me with this book. I would like to thank the staff of the various libraries and institutions I've haunted in the course of my research, including those at the British Library, Bristol University Library, the London Library and the National Archives at Kew. Thanks also to the Bodleian Library of the University of Oxford for permission to quote from the journal of Thomas Baker; and to the Duke of Devonshire and the Chatsworth Trust for permission to quote from the letterbook of the 1st Earl of Cork. I am particularly grateful to Andrew Peppitt, archivist to the Devonshire Collection, for his assistance and kindness.

I owe a personal debt of gratitude to Felicity Bryan, Jake Morrissey and Tricia Lankester for their comments, suggestions and sound advice; to Alex Bowler, whose considerable editorial skills are matched only by his endless patience and good humour; and to Fraser and Alfie Gill for their enthusiastic encouragement.

First and last my thanks, as always, to Helen.

Notes

Chapter 1

1 Anon., *The lives, apprehensions, arraignments, and executions, of the 19 late pirates* (1609). The executions of the eighteenth and nineteenth pirates were delayed until the following day amidst rumours of a pardon from the King, which in the event did not materialise.

2 *Ibid.*

3 *Ibid.*

4 *Ibid.*

5 Sir Arthur Chichester to Lord Salisbury, *Calendar of State Papers* (henceforth *CSP*) *Ireland*, 13 April 1608.

6 Sir Henry Mainwaring, *Discourse of the Beginnings, Practices, and Suppression of Pirates*, in G. E. Manwaring [sic] (ed.), *The Life and Works of Sir Henry Mainwaring*, Navy Records Society (1921), Vol. II, 15–16.

7 Lords of Council to President of Munster (Sir Henry Danvers), *CSP Ireland*, 27 September 1608.

8 Ferdinand Braudel, *The Mediterranean and the Mediterranean World in the Age of Philip II* (1975), I, 231. Braudel is quoting Paul Valéry.

9   Johannes Brenz, *Booklet on the Turk*, Wittenberg (1537); Veit Dietrich, *How Preachers Should Exhort the People to Repentance and Earnest Prayer against the Turk*, Nuremberg (1542); both quoted in John W. Bohnstedt, 'The Infidel Scourge of God: The Turkish Menace as Seen by German Pamphleteers of the Reformation Era', *Transactions of the American Philosophical Society*, NS, Vol. 58, No. 9 (1968), 50, 51.

10 Preface to Newton's translation of Agostino Curione's *A Notable Historie of the Saracens* (1575); quoted by Daniel J. Vitkus in his introduction to *Three Turk Plays from Early Modern England* (2000), 7.

11 Richard Knolles, *The Generall Historie of the Turkes* (1603), 1.

12 *Richard II*, IV, 1, 2076–8.

13 J. Morgan, *A Complete History of Algiers* (1731), 257.

14 D. Haëdo, *Topographia e historia general de Argel*, Valladolid (1612); quoted in Charles-André Julien, *History of North Africa* (1970), 280.

15 Morgan, *Complete History of Algiers*, 259.

16 *Ibid.*, 263.

17 In his lifetime and especially after the death of Oruç, Hızır was usually known in the West simply as 'Barbarossa'. Later writers added an attempt at his honorary name, calling him 'Hayreddin Barbarossa'.

18 Morgan, *Complete History of Algiers*, 293.

19 Lewis Roberts, *The Merchants Mappe of Commerce* (1638), 192.

20 *Ibid.*, 118.

21 Article 37, *The Capitulations and Articles of peace between the Majesty of the King of England, Scotland, France, and Ireland &c. And the Sultan of the Ottoman Empire*, Constantinople (1663), 11.

22 *Ibid.*, Article 19, 5.

Chapter 2

1   *CSP Venice*, 23 June 1608.

2   Anon., *The Seamans Song of Captain Ward the famous Pyrate of the world*.

3   Strictly speaking, letters of reprisal were something different. They allowed a merchant or shipowner who had been robbed by foreigners to recoup their losses by taking goods belonging

to the robbers' fellow countrymen. In practice, the terms were used interchangeably until well into the seventeenth century.

4 'A Proclamation ordained by the King's Highness ...', Harleian MSS 442, 170; reprinted in R. G. Marsden, *Law and Custom of the Sea*, Vol. I, Navy Records Society (1915), 156–7.

5 Piero Contarini, Venetian ambassador, 'Relation of England', December 1618; in *CSP Venice, 1617–19*.

6 *A Proclamation to represse all Piracies and Depredations upon the Sea* (1603).

7 Untitled proclamation, 8 July 1605.

8 'Report on England presented to the Government of Venice in the year 1607, by the illustrious Gentleman Nicolo Molin, Ambassador there', *CSP Venice*, 30 May 1607.

9 Anon., *The lives, apprehensions, arraignments, and executions, of the 19 late pirates* (1609).

10 Andrew Barker, *A True and Certaine Report of the Beginning, Proceedings, Overthrowes, and now present Estate of Captaine Ward* (1609), 5.

11 *Ibid.*, 5–6.

12 Quoted in Michael Oppenheim, 'The Royal Navy under James I', *English Historical Review*, Vol. 7, No. 27 (July 1892), 494.

13 *CSP Domestic Series*, 23 June 1597.

14 Nathaniel Boteler, *Six dialogues about sea-services between an high-admiral and a captain at sea* (1685), 26.

15 M. Oppenheim (ed.), *The Naval Tracts of Sir William Monson*, Navy Records Society (1902–13), Vol. II, 237.

16 Barker, *True and Certaine Report*, 7.

17 *Ibid.*, 8.

18 *Ibid.*, 9.

19 *Ibid.*, 10.

20 *Ibid.*, 10.

21 *Ibid.*, 11.

22 Anthony Nixon, *Newes from Sea of two notorious Pyrats* (1609), 2.

23 John Pory (trans.), Leo Africanus, *A geographical historie of Africa* (1600), 251.

24 Quoted in Godfrey Fisher, *Barbary Legend* (1957), 159.

25 Quoted in Charles-André Julien, *History of North Africa* (1970), 307.

26   Richard Hakluyt, *The principal navigations, voyages, traffiques and discoveries of the English nation* (1599), Vol. II, 1.128.

27   Myles Davies, *Athenæ Britannicæ* (1716), 97.

28   Pascual de Gayangos (trans.), *The History of the Mohammedan Dynasties in Spain,* Vol. II (1843), 394.

29   Quoted in David James, 'The "Manual de artillería" of al-Ra'is Ibrahim b. Ahmad al-Andalusi with Particular Reference to Its Illustrations and Their Sources', *Bulletin of the School of Oriental and African Studies, University of London,* Vol. 41, No. 2 (1978), 251.

30   *CSP Venice,* 17 May 1603.

31   John Ogilby, *Africa* (1670), 253.

32   Pory (trans.), Leo Africanus, *A geographical historie of Africa,* 247.

33   *Ibid.,* 249.

34   *Ibid.,* 248.

35   *Ibid.,* 249.

36   Ogilby, *Africa,* 251.

37   Nixon, *Newes from Sea,* 4.

38   Barker, *True and Certaine Report,* 12.

39   The pinnace never arrived. For reasons which aren't altogether clear, its crew kept sailing westward until they reached the Atlantic, stopping only when they were shipwrecked off the Balearic Islands. The survivors were picked up by a Dutchman and taken back to Tunis.

40   R. G. Marsden (ed.), *Law and Custom of the Sea,* Vol. 1, Navy Records Society (1915), 379.

41   By way of comparison, Henry VIII's great *Mary Rose* was rated at 700 tons, and the *Golden Hind*, in which Sir Francis Drake circumnavigated the world, was a vessel of just 120 tons.

42   Sean Jennett (trans.), *Journal of a Young Brother: The life of Thomas Platter* (1963), 117.

43   Marc' Antonio Correr to the Doge and Senate, 6 August 1609; *CSP Venice.*

44   Barker, *True and Certaine Report,* 13.

45   *Ibid.,* 14.

46   *Ibid.,* 13–14.

Chapter 3

1   Barker, *True and Certaine Report*, 16.

2   *CSP Venice*, 24 March 1608.

3   Barker, *True and Certaine Report*, 17.

4   *CSP Venice*, 5 November 1607.

5   *Ibid.*, 15 November 1607.

6   *Ibid.*, 2 October 1608.

7   *Ibid.*

8   *A proclamation against pirats* [*sic*], 8 January 1609.

9   Barker, *True and Certaine Report*, 18.

10 *Ibid.*, 18.

11 *Ibid.*, 24.

12 Nixon, *Newes from Sea*, 15–16.

13 Barker, *True and Certaine Report*, 15.

14 *Ibid.*, 1.

15 I owe this reference, and the wording, to Marc David Baer, *Honored by the Glory of Islam: Conversion and Conquest in Ottoman Europe* (2008), 197.

16 *CSP Venice*, 23 December 1610.

17 Samuel Rowlands, 'To a Reprobate Pirate that hath renounced Christ and is turn'd Turk', *More Knaves Yet* (1612).

18 Thomas Dekker, *If it be not good, the Divel is in it* (1612).

19 Robert Daborn, *A Christian Turn'd Turk*, in Vitkus (ed.), *Three Turk Plays from Early Modern England*, 198.

20 *Ibid.*, 230–31.

21 Rowland White to Sir Robert Sidney, quoted in Bernard Harris, 'A Portrait of a Moor', in Catherine M. S. Alexander and Stanley Wells (eds.), *Shakespeare and Race*, (2001), 29.

22 Stow, quoted in *ibid.*, 32.

23 Chamberlain, quoted in *ibid.*, 31.

24 Historical Manuscripts Commission (henceforth HMC), *Downshire*, 2 (1936), 160.

25 *Ibid.*, 186.

26 *CSP Venice*, 19 November 1609.

27 William Lithgow, *The Totall Discourse, of the Rare Adventures, and painefull Peregrinations of long nineteene Yeares Travayles* (1632 edn), 359.

28 *Ibid.*, 380.

Chapter 4

1   Anon., 'The sea-mans song of Dansekar the Dutch-man, his robberies done at sea' (n.d., 1609).

2   Nixon, *Newes from Sea*, 20–21.

3   *Ibid.*, 21.

4   *Ibid.*, 22.

5   *Ibid.*, 26.

6   *Ibid.*, 27.

7   *Ibid.*, 30.

8   *Ibid.*, 31.

9   *Ibid.*, 33.

10   Charles J. Sisson and Arthur Brown, '"The Great Dansker": Literary Significance of a Chancery Suit', *Modern Language Review*, Vol. 46 (1951), 341.

11   Nixon, *Newes from Sea*, 34.

12   *Ibid.*, 35.

13   *Ibid.*, 34.

14   William Okeley, *Eben-ezer: or, a Small Monument of Great Mercy* (1675), 5.

15   Dryden, *Limberham* (1678), I, i.

16   Katharine Prescott Wormeley (trans.), *The Plays of Molière*, Little, Brown and Company (1909), Vol. 1, 298.

17   Roberto Rossetti, 'An Introduction to Lingua Franca', see http://www.uwm.edu/~corre/franca/edition3/lingua5.html

18   Lithgow, *Totall Discourse*, 162.

19   Quoted as the epigraph to Henry and Renée Kahane and Andreas Tietze, *The Lingua Franca in the Levant: Turkish Nautical Terms of Italian and Greek Origin*, University of Illinois (1958).

20   Nixon, *Newes from Sea*, 10.

21   *CSP Venice*, 12 October 1609.

22   *Ibid.*, 31 October 1609.

23   *Ibid.*, December 1609.

24   *Ibid.*, 23 May 1610.

25   *Ibid.*, 21 September 1610.

26   *Ibid.*

27   *Ibid.*, 6 January 1611.

28   Lithgow, *Totall Discourse*, 381. Lithgow states that these events took place in 1616; but since he later buries Sir Francis

Verney (who died in September 1615), he must have his dates wrong. He also says that Danseker negotiates with the 'Bashaw', i.e. the *pasha* of Tunis, rather than the *dey*. At this point in Tunisian history the role of the temporary and Istanbul-appointed *pasha* is largely ceremonial, and it is much more likely that Lithgow means Yûsuf Dey, the *de facto* head of state.

29 Lithgow, *Totall Discourse*, 382.
30 *Ibid*.
31 Anon., 'The sea-mans song of Dansekar the Dutch-man'.

Chapter 5

1 *CSP Ireland*, 18 November 1612.
2 High Court of Admiralty, PRO 13/41/59 (24 July 1610).
3 *CSP Ireland*, 27 September 1612, Lords of the Council to Chichester.
4 *Ibid*., 25 July 1611, Skipwith to the Lord Deputy.
5 *Ibid*.
6 Whitbourne, *Westward Hoe for Avalon*, 42.
7 *CSP Venice*, 15 October 1612.
8 Whitbourne, *Westward Hoe for Avalon*, 42.
9 *CSP Venice*, 4 February 1612.
10 *Ibid*.
11 *Ibid*., 3 March 1613.
12 *Ibid*.
13 *Ibid*., 19 April 1612.
14 Mary Breese Fuller, 'Sir John Eliot and John Nutt, the Pirate', *Smith College Studies in History*, Vol. IV, No. 2 (January 1919), 76.
15 *Ibid*., 82.
16 SP Domestic, James I, 150/82; quoted in Fuller, 'Sir John Eliot and John Nutt, the Pirate', 88.
17 Quoted in Fuller, 'Sir John Eliot and John Nutt, the Pirate', 91.
18 Thomas Fuller, *The History of the Worthies of England* (1662), Herefordshire, 40.2.79.
19 Quoted in Manwaring (ed.), *Life and Works* (1920), Vol. I, 8.
20 Mainwaring, *Discourse of Pirates*, in Manwaring (ed.), *Life and Works* (1921), Vol. II, 11.

21 *CSP Domestic Series*, 5 July 1611.

22 Mainwaring, *Discourse of Pirates*, in Manwaring (ed.), *Life and Works* (1921), Vol. II, 10.

23 *CSP Colonial* (America and West Indies, 1, 16 March 1621); quoted in Manwaring (ed.), *Life and Works* (1920), Vol. I, 21.

24 *Ibid.*

25 Mainwaring, *Discourse of Pirates*, in Manwaring (ed.), *Life and Works* (1921), Vol. II, 22–3.

26 *Ibid.*, 26.

27 John Maclean (ed.), *Letters of George Lord Carew to Sir Thomas Roe*, Camden Society (1860), 35.

28 Mainwaring, *Discourse of Pirates*, in Manwaring (ed.), *Life and Works* (1921), II, 6.

29 *Ibid.*, 14.

30 *Ibid.*, 15.

31 *Ibid.*, 18.

32 *Ibid.*, 19.

33 *Ibid.*, 24.

34 *Ibid.*, 39–40.

35 *Ibid.*, 36, 37.

36 *Ibid.*, 36.

37 *Ibid.*, 26.

38 *Ibid.*, 31.

39 *Ibid.*, 32.

40 *Ibid.*, 33.

41 *Ibid.*, 25.

42 *Ibid.*, 27.

43 *Ibid.*, 25.

44 *Ibid.*, 42–3.

45 John Smith, *The True Travels, Adventures, and Observations of Captain John Smith, in Europe, Asia, Africa, and America* (1630), 59, 60

46 Daborn, *A Christian Turn'd Turk*, 16, 300–302.

47 Oppenheim (ed.), *Naval Tracts of Sir William Monson* (1912), Vol. III, 83.

48 This figure comes from J. F. Guilmartin Jr, *Gunpowder and Galleys: Changing Technology and Mediterranean Warfare at Sea in the Sixteenth Century* (1974), 198. My account of the advantages and disadvantages of the galley relies heavily on Professor Guilmartin's study.

49 *Ibid.*, 63.

50 John Fox, 'The Worthy Enterprise of John Fox, in Delivering 266 Christians out of the Captivity of the Turk' (1589), in Daniel Vitkus (ed.), *Piracy, Slavery and Redemption* (2001), 58.

51 Oppenheim, *Naval Tracts of Sir William Monson* (1912), Vol. III, 267.

52 *Ibid.*

53 Maclean (ed.), *Letters from George Lord Carew to Sir Thomas Roe*, 111.

54 *Cabala: sive Scrinia sacra. Mysteries of state & government in letters of illustrious persons in the reigns of Henry the eighth, queen Elizabeth, k: James, and the late king Charles* (1654), 206.

55 *CSP Venice*, 16 June 1616.

56 PRO SP 84/77, 182.

57 Quoted in M. Oppenheim, *A History of the Administration of the Royal Navy and of Merchant Shipping in Relation to the Navy from 1509 to 1660* (1896), 198–9.

58 *CSP Venice*, 5 October 1603.

59 PRO SP 14/90/f.136.

Chapter 6

1 Anon., *A Fight at Sea, Famously fought by the Dolphin of London* (1617), 2.

2 *Ibid.*, 3.

3 John Smith, *An accidence or The path-way to experience Necessary for all young sea-men, or those that are desirous to goe to sea* (1626), 19–24. (There are no pages 20–23. The edition is mispaginated.)

4 Anon., *A Fight at Sea*, 2.

5 William Bourne, *The Arte of shooting in great Ordnaunce* (1587), 54.

6 *Ibid.*, 56.

7 *Ibid.*, 55.

8 Anon., *A Fight at Sea*, 6.

9 *Ibid.*, 7.

10 *Ibid.*

11 J. Bullokar, *English Expositor*, 'Petroll' (1616).

12 Anon., *A Fight at Sea*, 9.

13   *Ibid.*, 8.
14   *Ibid.*, 3.
15   Anon., *A Relation, Strange and true, of a ship of Bristol named the Jacob* (1622), 2.
16   *Ibid.*, 4.
17   *Ibid.*, 5.
18   *Ibid.*, 7–8.
19   John Rawlins, *The Famous and Wonderful Recovery of a Ship of Bristol, called the Exchange* (1622), 9–10.
20   *Ibid.*, 13.
21   *Ibid.*, 14.
22   *Ibid.*, 19.
23   *Ibid.*, 33.
24   *Ibid.*, 31.
25   *Ibid.*, 31–2.
26   *Ibid.*, 32.
27   *Ibid.*, 2.
28   *Ibid.*, 9, 23, 8, 17.

Chapter 7

1   Oppenheim (ed.), *Naval Tracts of Sir William Monson* (1912), Vol. III, 107.
2   *Ibid.*, 80.
3   *Ibid.*, 83.
4   Clark, *Glamorgan Worthies* (1883), 12.
5   BL Add. MS 36445, 15–19.
6   John Taylor, *Epithaleamies, or Encomiastick Triumphall Verses …* (1613).
7   Ogilby, *Africa*, 221.
8   BL Add. MS 36445, f.22.
9   *Ibid.*
10   PRO SP 71/1/f.21v; quoted in David Delison Hebb, *Piracy and the English Government, 1616–1642*, Scolar Press (1994), 88. I am indebted to Dr Hebb's book, and to Michael Oppenheim's account in *The Naval Tracts of Sir William Monson*, Vol. III, 98–116, for my understanding of Mansell's operation in Algiers.
11   Quoted in Hebb, *Piracy and the English Government*, 88.
12   BL Add. MS 36445, f.23.

13   *Ibid.*
14   *Ibid.*
15   John Button, *Algiers Voyage* (1621) [no pagination].
16   BL Harl. MS 1581, ff.70–71.
17   Button, *Algiers Voyage.*
18   *Ibid.*
19   *Ibid.*
20   *Ibid.*
21   BL Harl. MS 1581, f.76.
22   PRO SP 94/24/f.124.
23   Kent Archive Office U 269 ON 6874, 22 January 1621.
24   Girolamo Lando, Venetian ambassador in England, to the Doge; *CSP Venice*, 7 May 1621.
25   Quoted in Hebb, *Piracy and the English Government*, 100.
26   Girolamo Lando, Venetian ambassador in England, to the Doge; *CSP Venice*, 11 June 1621.
27   The patent was declared void in 1623, but Mansell persuaded the Privy Council to grant him another immediately, on almost identical terms. He was still defending it twenty years later.
28   Ogilby, *Africa*, 222.
29   Button, *Algiers Voyage.*
30   *Ibid.*
31   *Ibid.*
32   Morgan, *Complete History of Algiers*, 649.
33   *Ibid.*, 650.
34   *Ibid.*, 651.
35   Button, *Algiers Voyage.*
36   *CSP Venice*, Girolamo Lando to the Doge and Senate, 30 July 1621.
37   Quoted in Hebb, *Piracy and the English Government, 1616–1642*, 104.
38   'Sir Robert and his crew are ill paid, and Sir Richard Hawkins, the Vice-Admiral, is dead of vexation', 27 April 1622; quoted without attribution in Clark, *Glamorgan Worthies*, 39.
39   Sir William Monson, 'The ill-managed enterprise upon Algiers in the reign of King James, and the errors committed in it', in M. Oppenheim (ed.), *The Naval Tracts of Sir William Monson*, Vol. III, 94–5.

40 Morgan, *Complete History of Algiers*, 648.
41 *Journal of the House of Commons*, 1, 5 December 1621
42 *CSP Venice*, 8 October 1622.

Chapter 8

1   *CSP Ireland*, 1606–8, 100.
2   Charles Smith, *The antient and present state of the county and city of Cork* (1750), 310–11.
3   *CSP Ireland*, 17 July 1630.
4   *Ibid.*, 19 July 1630.
5   *Ibid.*, 13 November 1630, enclosed with letter of 20 November from the Earl of Cork to Lord Dorchester.
6   Quoted in J. Coombs, 'The Sack of Baltimore: a Forewarning', *JCHAS*, 77 (1972), 60.
7   This part of the promontory is still known today as 'the platform', according to James N. Healy, *Castles of County Cork* (1988), 182.
8   Olafur Egilsson, quoted in Bernard Lewis, 'Corsairs in Iceland', *Islam in History* (1993), 242.
9   Quoted in Lewis, 'Corsairs in Iceland', 244.
10 *Ibid.*, 240.
11 PRO SP 63/252 81; quoted in Henry Barnby, 'The Sack of Baltimore', *JCHAS*, 74 (1969), 102.
12 Lord Wilmot to Lord Dorchester, *CSP Ireland*, 6 January 1630.
13 Barnby, 'The Sack of Baltimore', 102.
14 *Ibid.*
15 *Ibid.*
16 Richard Caulfield (ed.), *The Council Book of the Corporation of Kinsale* (1879), 20 June 1631.
17 *CSP Ireland*, 10 June 1631.
18 *CSP Domestic Series*, 5 July 1631; Button to Nicholas.
19 Chatsworth MSS, Earl of Cork's Letter-Book, 396.
20 *Ibid.*
21 *CSP Domestic Series*, 23 July 1631.
22 *Ibid.*, 23 August 1631.
23 Quoted in Des Ekin, *The Stolen Village: Baltimore and the Barbary Pirates* (2006), 240.
24 Chatsworth MSS, Earl of Cork's Letter-Book, 395.

25 *CSP Domestic Series*, 9 March 1632.

26 *CSP Ireland*, 6 April 1632.

27 Charles Smith, *The antient and present state of the county and city of Cork* (1779), I, 254.

Chapter 9

1   Francis Knight, *A Relation of Seaven Yeares Slaverie under the Turkes of Argeire* (1640), 1.

2   Morgan, *Complete History of Algiers*, 676.

3   Knight, *Relation*, 18.

4   Morgan, *Complete History of Algiers*, 666.

5   Knight, *Relation*, 19.

6   *Ibid.*, 24.

7   *Ibid.*, 27.

8   *Ibid.*

9   *Ibid.*, preface.

10 *CSP Domestic Series*, 26 September 1636.

11 *Ibid.*, 1 November 1636.

12 *Ibid.*, 1 January 1636.

13 'For the relief of captives', 25 April 1643; in C. H. Firth and R. S. Rait (eds.), *Acts and Ordinances of the Interregnum 1642–1660* (1911), Vol. III, 134.

14 Knight, *Relation*, preface.

15 *CSP Domestic Series*, 26 September 1635.

16 *CSP Domestic Series*, 1635 [undated].

17 *CSP Domestic Series*, 1636 [undated].

18 *Ibid.*, 1636.

19 Charles Fitzgeffry, *Compassion towards Captives* (1636), 17, 46.

20 *Ibid.*, 47.

21 'Trinity House of Deptford Transactions', 1609–35, *London Record Society*, 19 (1983), 72–8.

22 *CSP Domestic Series*, 2 September 1636.

23 Quoted in Hebb, *Piracy and the English Government*, 236.

24 *CSP Domestic Series*, 4 August 1636.

25 *Ibid.*, December 1636.

26 *Ibid.*

27 John Rushworth, *Historical Collections of Private Passages of State*, II, 257.

28 John Dunton, *A True Journey of the Salley Fleet* (1637), 25.

29 Michael Strachan, 'Sampson's Fight with Maltese Galleys, 1628', *The Mariner's Mirror*, Vol. 55 (1969), 287.

30 Dunton, *True Journey*, 5.

31 *Ibid.*, 5.

32 *Ibid.*, 5–6.

33 *Ibid.*, 7.

34 *Ibid.*, 8.

35 *CSP Domestic Series*, 31 March 1635. Simpson spent time in Plymouth jail in 1635, accused of saying 'that some of the chief commanders in the late action to the Isle of Rhé were either fools, cowards, or traitors' (*ibid.*). His defence, unusually robust for the time, was that they were indeed fools, cowards or traitors.

36 Dunton, *True Journey*, 9.

37 *Ibid*, 13.

38 *Ibid*, 15.

39 *Ibid*, 19–20.

40 *CSP Domestic Series*, 29 July 1637.

41 Dunton, *True Journey*, 20.

42 *Ibid*, 21.

43 Mohammed IV to Charles I, Marrakesh, September 1637; in J. F. P. Hopkins (trans.) *Letters from Barbary 1576–1774* (1982), 15.

44 Albert J. Loomie (ed.), *Ceremonies of Charles I: the note books of John Finet* (1987), 230.

45 *Ibid.*, 233.

46 *Ibid.*, 234.

47 William Knowler (ed.), *The Earl of Strafford's Letters and Despatches*, Vol. II (1739), 138.

48 *CSP Domestic Series*, 30 December 1637.

49 Dunton, *True Journey*, 'Epistle Dedicatorie'.

50 Inigo Jones and William Davenant, *Britannia Triumphans* (1638), 2.

51 Knowler (ed.), *Strafford's Letters*, Vol. II, 124. Jawdar ben 'Abn Allah and his retinue were placed in a box at the King's left hand, and just behind his seat. The next day Charles told Finet off for not giving them even better places.

Chapter 10

1 William Okeley, *Eben-ezer: or, a Small Monument of Great Mercy* (1675), 3.

2 *Ibid.*, 'Upon this book' (prefatory poem).

3 *Ibid.*, 3.

4 *Ibid.*, 5.

5 *Ibid.*, 6.

6 *Ibid.*, 8.

7 Rawlins, *The Famous and Wonderfull Recoverie of a Ship of Bristoll* (1622), 8.

8 Okeley, *Eben-ezer*, 9.

9 *Ibid.*, 11.

10 *Ibid.*, 12.

11 The story first surfaces in a medieval Christian text, the *Apology of al-Kindy*.

12 Okeley, *Eben-ezer*, 14.

13 *Ibid.*, 16.

14 *Ibid.*, 16.

15 *Ibid.*, 19.

16 *Ibid.*, 22.

17 Devereux Spratt, 'Journal', in T. A. B. Spratt, *Travels and Researches in Crete* (1865), Vol. I, 385.

18 Okeley, *Eben-ezer*, 23.

19 Spratt, 'Journal', in T. A. B. Spratt, *Travels and Researches in Crete*, 386. Spratt left Algiers in 1645 or 1646 and returned to Ireland, where he got a living at Mitchelstown, Co. Cork.

20 Okeley, *Eben-ezer*, 41.

21 *Ibid.*, 41.

22 *Ibid.*, 31.

23 *Ibid.*, 26–7.

24 *Ibid.*, 28.

25 *Ibid.*, preface.

26 *Ibid.*, 41.

27 SP 102/2 72; in Hopkins (trans.), *Letters from Barbary* (1982), 90.

28 *Journal of the House of Commons*, 5 July 1643.

29 Okeley, *Eben-ezer*, 42.

30 *Ibid.*, 47.

31   *Ibid.*, 50.
32   *Ibid.*, 52.
33   *Ibid.*, 57.
34   *Ibid.*, 63–4.
35   *Ibid.*, 73–4.
36   *Ibid.*, 74.
37   *Ibid.*, 76.
38   *Ibid.*, 80.
39   *Ibid.*
40   *Ibid.*, 84.
41   *Ibid.*, preface.

Chapter 11

1   Loomie (ed.), *Ceremonies of Charles I*, 250.
2   Knight, *A Relation of Seaven Yeares Slaverie under the Turkes of Argeire*, 16.
3   Emanuel D'Aranda, *The History of Algiers and its Slavery*, trans. John Davies (1666), 161. 'Ali Bitshnin makes an appearance in the eighteenth-century picaresque novel *The Adventures of Gil Blas,* as 'Hali Pegelin, a Greek renegado', who steals the heart of the passionate Donna Lucinda.
4   D'Aranda, *History*, 12.
5   *Ibid.*, 14.
6   Okeley, in Vitkus (ed.), *Piracy, Slavery and Redemption* 161. D'Aranda later heard that the friar was persuaded to convert back to Christianity, at which he was burned to death by his captors.
7   D'Aranda, *History*, 164.
8   *Ibid.*, 256–7.
9   Knight, *Relation*, 9.
10   Morgan, *Complete History of Algiers*, 669–70.
11   Roberts, *Merchants Mappe of Commerce*, 70.
12   Both quotes Ogilby, *Africa*, 223, 224.
13   Hebb, *Piracy and the English Government*, 263.
14   *CSP Domestic Series*, 26 January 1638.
15   *Ibid.*, 23 September 1639.
16   28 Henry 8, c. 15, subsequently named the Offences at Sea Act 1536.

17 *CSP Domestic Series*, 3 October 1640.

18 *Statutes of the Realm*, V, 1628–80 (1819), 134–5.

19 *CSP Venice*, 7 February 1642.

20 *Journal of the House of Commons*, 21 February 1642.

21 Henry Robinson, *Libertas, or Relief to the English Captives in Algier*, 3.

22 *Ibid.*

23 Quoted in Marc David Baer, *Honoured by the Glory of Islam*, 57.

24 Thomas Edgar, *The lawes resolutions of womens rights* (1632), 66. I owe this reference to Nabil Matar, *Britain and Barbary 1589–1689* (2006), 83.

25 *Journal of the House of Commons*, 1 June 1642.

26 *Acts and Ordinances of the Interregnum, 1642–1660*, 25 April 1643.

27 *Journal of the House of Lords*, 6: 5 July 1643 (1802), 120–23.

28 Hebb, *Piracy and the English Government*, 272.

29 *Journal of the House of Commons*, 15 August 1645.

30 A Venetian diplomat, in a commendable but uncharacteristic burst of pedantry, said that 'I fancy they call them Turks when they are really corsairs of Algiers' (*CSP Venice*, 8 September 1645).

31 Edmund Cason, *A Relation of the whole proceedings concerning the Redemption of the Captives in Argier and Tunis* (1646), 7.

32 *Ibid.*, 16.

33 *Ibid.*, 11.

34 *Ibid.*

35 Thomas Sweet, *Dear Friends* ['The long and lamentable bondage of Thomas Sweet, and Richard Robinson'] (1647), 1.

36 Cason, *Relation*, 12.

37 *Ibid.*, 13.

38 Sweet, *Dear Friends*, 1.

39 Cason, *Relation*, 14.

40 *Journal of the House of Commons*, 28 November 1651.

41 *CSP Domestic Series*, 26 July 1653.

42 Charles Longland to Robert Blackborne, *CSP Domestic Series*, 13 April 1657.

43 Cason to the Navy Committee, *CSP Domestic Series*, 2 April 1653.

44 *Journal of the House of Commons*, 14 January 1652.

Chapter 12

1   Richard Chandler, *The History and Proceedings of the House of Commons*, I, 1660–1680 (1742), 31.

2   Edward Hyde, Earl of Clarendon, *The Life of Edward, Earl of Clarendon* (1838), Vol. I, 494. The admiral was Sir John Lawson, who had visited the place.

3   Sir Henry Sheres, *A Discourse touching Tanger [sic]* (1680), 16.

4   *Ibid.*, 18.

5   *Ibid.*, 16.

6   Clarendon, *Life*, I, 334.

7   Carte MSS, Vol. 74, f.389; reprinted in R. C. Anderson (ed.), *The Journal of Edward Mountagu, First Earl of Sandwich*, Navy Records Society (1929), 289.

8   Basil Lubbock (ed.), *Barlow's Journal of His Life at Sea in King's Ships, East and West Indiamen and Other Merchantmen from 1659 to 1703*, I, 70.

9   Sandwich, *Journal*, 116.

10   George Philips, *The Present State of Tangier* (1676), 41.

11   Anon., *A Brief Relation of the Present State of Tangier* (1664), 3.

12   Lancelot Addison, *A Discourse of Tangier under the Government of the Earl of Teviot* (1685), 7.

13   *Ibid.*, 6.

14   Anon., *Brief Relation*, 8.

15   Latham and Matthews, *The Diary of Samuel Pepys*, 2 June 1664.

16   *Ibid.*, 15 June 1664.

17   Sandwich, *Journal*, 118.

18   Latham and Matthews, 28 September 1663.

19   Philips, *Present State of Tangier*, 32–3.

20   *Ibid.*, 31.

21   John Luke's Journal, quoted in E. M. G. Routh, 'The English at Tangier', *The English Historical Review*, Vol. 26, No. 103 (July, 1911), 477.

22   Latham and Matthews, 22 September 1667.

23   Sir Hugh Cholmley, *A Short Account of the Progress of the Mole at Tangier* (1679), 4.

24   *An Exact Journal of the Siege of Tangier* (1680), 1.

25   Samuel Pepys in Edwin Chappell (ed.), *The Tangier Papers of Samuel Pepys*, Navy Records Society (1935), 78.

26 Anon., *A Faithful Relation of the Most remarkable Transactions which have happened at Tangier* (1680), 3.

27 Anon., *An Exact Journal of the Siege of Tangier* (1680), 3.

28 *Ibid.*, 4.

Chapter 13

1 Samuel Boothouse, *A Brief Remonstrance of Several National Injuries and Indignities perpetrated on the Persons and Estates of publick Ministers and Subjects of this Common-Wealth, by the Dey of Tunis in Barbary* (1653), 2.

2 *Ibid.*, 22.

3 *Ibid.*, 25.

4 Blake to Secretary Thurloe; 14/24 March 1654/5; in J. R. Powell (ed.), *The Letters of Robert Blake*, Navy Records Society (1937), 291.

5 *Ibid.*

6 J. R. Powell (ed.), 'The Journal of John Weale 1654–1656', *The Naval Miscellany*, IV, Navy Records Society (1952), 106.

7 Blake to Secretary Thurloe; 14/24 March 1654/5; in Powell (ed.), *The Letters of Robert Blake*, 292.

8 Blake to Secretary Thurloe; 18/28 April 1655; in *ibid.*, 294.

9 Powell (ed.), *The Letters of Robert Blake*, 274.

10 Powell (ed.), 'The Journal of John Weale 1654–1656', 109.

11 'A Letter from the George'; in Powell (ed.), *The Letters of Robert Blake*, 320.

12 G. T., *An Encomiastick, or, Elegiack Enumeration of the Noble Atchievements [sic], and Unparallel'd Services, done at Land and Sea, by that truly honourable generall, Robert Blake* (1658), 21. 'Gehenna' appears in early Jewish, Christian and Muslim texts as hell, a place of torment for sinners.

13 Charles Longland, agent at Livorno, to Secretary Thurloe, 30 July 1655; in Thomas Birch (ed.), *A Collection of the State Papers of John Thurloe*, III (1742), 663.

14 *CSP Domestic Series*, 27 February 1658. Stoakes went on to conclude a similar treaty with Tripoli.

15 Sir Thomas Bendysh to the Lord Protector, Constantinople, 22 October 1657; Vol. XIII, 233.

16 Levant Company to Sir Thomas Bendysh, 10 September 1657; *CSP Diplomatic Series*, 1657–8.

17 Anon., *A brief Relation or Remonstrance of the Injurious proceedings and Inhumane cruelties of the Turks, perpetrated on the Commander and company of the Ship Lewis of London* (1657), 3.

18 *Ibid.*, 4.

19 Anderson (ed.), *The Journal of Edward Mountagu*, 98.

20 Charles II, *Proclamation touching the articles of peace with Argiers, Tunis, and Tripoli*, 29 January 1663.

21 Charles II, *Articles of peace concluded between his sacred majesty and the kingdoms and governments of Algiers, Tunis, and Tripoli in the year 1662* (1662), 14.

22 *Ibid.*, 11.

23 *CSP Domestic Series*, 13 April 1657.

24 Charles II, *Articles of peace* (1662), 4.

25 *Ibid.*, 7.

26 *Ibid.*, 20.

27 Francesco Giavarina, Venetian Resident in England, to the Doge and Senate; *CSP Venice*, 15 December 1662.

28 *Mercurius Publicus*, no. 40, 2–9 October 1662, 663.

29 Latham and Matthews, 5 January 1663.

30 Charles II, *Articles of peace & commerce between the most serene and mighty prince Charles II . . . [and] Tripoli* (1677), title page.

31 Charles II, *Articles of peace concluded between his sacred majesty and the kingdoms and governments of Algiers, Tunis, and Tripoli in the year 1662* (1662), 7.

32 Quoted in R. L. Playfair, *The Scourge of Christendom* (1884), 90.

33 Francesco Giavarina, Venetian Resident in England, to the Doge and Senate; *CSP Venice*, 14 July 1662.

34 Quoted in Playfair, *Scourge of Christendom* (1884), 86.

35 Charles II, *His Majesties Gracious Speech to Both Houses of Parliament, Together with the Lord Chancellors, Delivered . . . the 10th of October, 1665* (1665), 6–8.

36 *A Letter Written by the Governour of Algiers, to the States-General of the United Provinces* (1679), 1–2.

37 BS Sloane 2755, f.24. His Royal Highness was James, Duke of York, in whose name as Lord High Admiral passes were issued.

38 Playfair, *Scourge of Christendom*, 145.

39 Instructions from the Duke of York to Sir Thomas Allin, 29 June 1669; in R. C. Anderson (ed.), *The Journals of Sir Thomas Allin*, Vol. 2, Navy Records Society (1940), 231.

40 Instructions from the Duke of York to Sir Thomas Allin, 29 June 1669; *ibid.*, 232.

41 MS Tanner 296 f.131; reprinted in *ibid.*, 242.

42 *Articles of Peace Between His Sacred Majesty Charles the Second . . . and the City and Kingdom of Algiers* (1664), 8.

43 Wenceslaus Hollar, *A True Relation of Capt. Kempthorn's Engagement, in the Mary-Rose, with seven Algier Men of War* (1675).

44 Historical Manuscripts Commission, *Dartmouth* MSS III (1896), 6.

45 Anon., *The Present State of Algeir* [*sic*] (1682), 2.

46 C. R. Pennell (ed.), *Piracy and Diplomacy in Seventeenth-Century North Africa: The Journal of Thomas Baker, English Consul in Tripoli, 1677–85*, Associated University Presses (1989), 171.

47 Cole, quoted in Playfair, *Scourge of Christendom*, 158.

Chapter 14

1 Anon., *An Exact Journal of the Siege of Tangier* (1680), 13.

2 *Ibid.*

3 *CSP Domestic Series*, Charles II, 10 August 1680.

4 The King's Own, which was first raised for service in Tangier, was originally called the 2nd Tangier or the Earl of Plymouth's Regiment of Foot.

5 John Ross, *Tanger's* [*sic*] *Rescue; or a Relation of The late Memorable Passages at Tanger* (1681), 11.

6 *Ibid.*, 23.

7 Anchitell Grey, *Debates of the House of Commons*, VIII (1769), 11.

8 *Ibid.*, 5, 7, 19.

9 Edwin Chappell (ed.), *The Tangier Papers of Samuel Pepys*, Navy Records Society (1935), 58.

10 *Ibid.*, 65.

11 *Ibid.*, 71.

12 *Ibid.*, 83.

13   *Ibid.*, 16.

14   Historical Manuscripts Commission, *Dartmouth* MSS III, 92.

15   Chappell (ed.), *Tangier Papers*, 89.

16   *Ibid.*, 101.

17   *Ibid.*, 95.

18   Historical Manuscripts Commission, *Dartmouth* MSS III, 96.

19   *Ibid.*, 96–7.

20   Chappell (ed.), *Tangier Papers*, 50.

21   Historical Manuscripts Commission, *Dartmouth* MSS III, 34.

22   *Ibid.*, 44.

23   *Ibid.*, 53.

24   *Ibid.* I, 105.

Chapter 15

1   Thomas Baker, 'A Journall or Memoriall of whasoever Occur-rences shall happen or bee noteworthy Begunn at London . . . 1677', Bodleian MS Eng. Hist. c.236, 2 May 1677. My under-standing of Baker's journal and his time in Tripoli owes a great deal to C. R. Pennell's excellent *Piracy and Diplomacy in Seventeenth-Century North Africa: The Journal of Thomas Baker, English Consul in Tripoli, 1677–1685*, Farleigh Dickinson University Press (1989).

2   Quoted in Playfair, *Scourge of Christendom*, 50.

3   Baker, 'Journall', 7b (9 August 1677).

4   *Ibid.*, 8a (8 October 1677).

5   John Seller, 'Tripoli', *Atlas Maritimus* (1676).

6   Baker, 'Journall', 3a (2 May 1677).

7   Charles II, *Articles of Peace and Commerce Between . . . Charles II . . . [and] the Noble City and Kingdom of Tripoli in Barbary* (1676), 5.

8   Baker, 'Journall', 31b (5 May 1680).

9   Samuel Purchas, *Purchas his Pilgrimage, or Relations of the World and the Religions* (1614), 606.

10   Baker, 'Journall', 22a (11 June 1679).

11   Baker, 'Journall', 21a (20 April 1679).

12   Ogilby, *Africa*, 276.

13   Baker, 'Journall', 21b (9 June 1679).

14   *Ibid.*, 24a (26 September 1679).

15 *Ibid.*, 17 February 1680. The original text is in Italian: this translation and the following are from Pennell, *Piracy and Diplomacy*, 200.

16 Charles II, *Articles of Peace*, 12.

17 Baker, 'Journall', 39a (13 May 1681).

18 A. Holstein, 'Journal of a voyage to the Kingdom of Tripoli in Barbary, 1675–6', BL Sloane 2755.

19 Baker, 'Journall', 71a (16 July 1684); 71b (24 August 1684).

20 *Ibid.*, 38a (10 April 1681).

21 *Ibid.*, 59a (11 March 1683).

22 *Ibid.*, 84a (11 April 1685).

23 *Ibid.*, 57b–58a (29 December 1682).

24 *Ibid.*, 58a (29 December 1682).

25 'Dr. Covel's Diary (1670–1679)', in J. Theodore Bent (ed.), *Early Voyages and Travels in the Levant* (1893), 120.

26 Baker, 'Journall', 54a (7 November 1682).

27 *Ibid.*, 56b (18 November 1682).

28 *Ibid.*, 38b (14 April 1681).

29 *Ibid.*, 71a (24 July 1684).

30 *Ibid.*, 63a (30 June 1683).

31 *Ibid.*, 41b (15 October 1681).

32 *Ibid.*, 40a (30 June 1681).

33 *Ibid.*, 47b (23 May 1682).

34 *Ibid.*, 32a (1 June 1680).

35 *Ibid.*, 49a (4 August 1682).

36 *Ibid.*, 69b (13 June 1684).

37 *Ibid.*, 72b (23 September 1684). Baker needed deep pockets: when he returned to England he put in a claim for £651 11s. 6d. in expenses (*CSP Domestic Series*, 4 June 1687).

38 *Ibid.*, 73b (7 October 1684).

39 *Ibid.*, 79a (15 December 1684).

40 *Ibid.*, 73b (7 October 1684).

41 *Ibid.*, 80b (15 December 1684).

42 *CSP Domestic Series*, 8 November 1686.

43 Baker, 'Journall', 36b (5 January 1681); 75a (3 November 1684).

44 *Ibid.*, 62a (3 June 1683).

45 *Ibid.*, 64b (5 September 1683).

46 SP 102, National Archives, f.98; quoted in Fisher, *Barbary Legend*, 281.

47 When he was retired and living in London Thomas Baker was involved in distributing government grants to poor Turks in England, just as he had helped Christians when he lived in Tripoli and Algiers. The Treasury Books of the later 1690s contain several references to him signing money orders to provide food, clothing and relief for distressed Algerians stranded in England – a pleasing counterpoint to his role as consul.

Chapter 16

1 Quoted in Frederick C. Leiner, *The End of the Barbary Terror* (2007), 95.

2 Mordecai M. Noah, US consul at Tunis; quoted in J. de Courcy Ireland, 'Raïs Hamidou', *The Mariner's Mirror*, Vol. 60, No. 2 (1974), 196.

3 Alexander Jardine, *Letters from Barbary, France, Spain, Portugal, &c*, 2 vols (1788), 1, 68–9.

4 J. M. Forbes, US minister to Denmark, 6 September 1815, William Shaler Papers, Collection 1172, Historical Society of Pennsylvania; quoted in Leiner, *The End of the Barbary Terror*, 152.

5 Adams to Jefferson, 17 February 1786, Jefferson Papers XIX; quoted in Ray W. Irwin, *The Diplomatic Relations of the United States with the Barbary Powers 1776–1816*, (1931), 40.

6 James Leander Cathcart, *The Captives: Eleven Years a Prisoner in Algiers*, 170.

7 *Ibid.*, 184.

8 Jefferson to Adams, 11 July 1786, *Diplomatic Correspondence of the United States of America* (1837), Vol. I, 792.

9 William Eaton to Secretary of State, 3 February 1802; quoted in Irwin, *Diplomatic Relations*, 117.

10 Captain William Bainbridge to the US Navy Department, 1 November 1803; in Thomas Harris, *The Life and Services of Commodore William Bainbridge* (1837), 81.

11 Jonathan Cowdery, *American Captives in Tripoli*, Boston (1806); in Paul Baepler (ed.), *White Slaves, African Masters* (1999), 168.

12 Samuel Putnam Waldo, *The Life and Character of Stephen Decatur* (1822), 19; R. Thomas, *The Glory of America: comprising*

Memoirs of the Lives and Glorious Exploits of Some of the Most Distinguished Officers (1836), 196.

13   Paschal Paoli Peck, 4 July 1805; in *U.S. Gazette*, 11 October 1805.

14   Tobias Lear to the US Secretary of State, 5 July 1805, *American State Papers, Foreign Relations*, II, 717; quoted in Irwin, *Diplomatic Relations*, 153.

15   *National Intelligencer*, 6 November 1805.

16   Albert Devoulx, *Le Raïs Hamidou*, Algiers (1859), 72. My account of Hamidou's life relies heavily on Devoulx's biography, and also on J. de Courcy Ireland, 'Raïs Hamidou', *The Mariner's Mirror*, Vol. 60, No. 2 (1974), 187–96.

17   Elizabeth Broughton, *Six Years' Residence in Algiers* (1839), 200.

18   *Ibid.*

19   Filippo Pananti, *Narrative of a Residence in Algiers* (1818), 34.

20   *Ibid.*, 45.

21   *Ibid.*, 46.

22   Quoted in Leiner, *The End of the Barbary Terror*, 109.

23   Devoulx, *Le Raïs Hamidou*, 144.

24   *Ibid.*, 133–4.

25   Quoted in Leiner, *The End of the Barbary Terror*, 152.

26   Alexander Slidell Mackenzie, *The Life of Commodore Oliver Hazard Perry* (1840), II, 115. Perry believed that Omar was being egged on by the consuls of Europe, who were jealous of the United States' achievement. He was probably right.

27   Charles Francis Adams (ed.), *Memoirs of John Quincy Adams* (1874), III, 354.

28   *Ibid.*, 356.

29   William Shaler, *Sketches of Algiers, Political, Historical, and Civil* (1826), 279.

30   Edward Osler, *The Life of Admiral Viscount Exmouth* (1835), 219.

31   Shaler, *Sketches of Algiers*, 281.

32   Dispatch to James Monroe, dated 13 September 1816; quoted in Playfair, *Scourge of Christendom*, 271.

33   Exmouth to Omar Dey, 28 August 1816; in Shaler, *Sketches of Algiers*, 290–91.

34   Congress of Aix-la-Chapelle, Protocol No. 39, 20 November 1818; trans. and reprinted in Shaler, *Sketches of Algiers*, 302–3.

35   *The Times*, 5 November 1830.

36   *Ibid.*, 17 December 1830.

Bibliography

A Letter Written by the Governour of Algiers, to the States-General of the United Provinces (1679).

A Perfect Diurnall.

Abou-El-Haj, Rifaat, 'An Agenda for Research in History: The History of Libya between the Sixteenth and Nineteenth Centuries', *International Journal of Middle East Studies*, Vol. 15, No. 3 (August, 1983), 305–19.

Abun-Nasr, Jamil M., 'The Beylicate in Seventeenth-Century Tunisia', *International Journal of Middle East Studies*, Vol. 6, No. 1 (January, 1975), 70–93.

Abun-Nasr, Jamil M., *A History of the Maghrib in the Islamic Period*, Cambridge University Press (1987).

Adams, Charles Francis (ed.), *Memoirs of John Quincy Adams* (1874).

Adamson, John, *The Noble Revolt: The Overthrow of Charles I*, Weidenfeld & Nicolson (2007).

Addison, Lancelot, *A Discourse of Tangier under the Government of the Earl of Teviot* (1685).

Anderson, R. C. (ed.), *The Journal of Edward Mountagu, First Earl of Sandwich* (Navy Records Society, 1929).

Anderson, R. C. (ed.), *The Journals of Sir Thomas Allin*, Navy Records Society (1940).

Andrews, K. R., *Elizabethan Privateering*, Cambridge University Press (1964).

Andrews, K. R., 'Sir Robert Cecil and Mediterranean Plunder', *The English Historical Review*, Vol. 87, No. 344 (July, 1972), 513–32.

Anon., *A Brief Relation of the Present State of Tangier* (1664).

Anon., *A brief Relation or Remonstrance of the Injurious proceedings and Inhumane cruelties of the Turks, perpetrated on the Commander and company of the Ship Lewis of London* (1657).

Anon., *A Faithful Relation of the Most remarkable Transactions which have happened at Tangier* (1680).

Anon., *A Fight at Sea, Famously fought by the Dolphin of London* (1617).

Anon., *A Relation, Strange and true, of a ship of Bristol named the Jacob* (1622).

Anon., *An Exact Journal of the Siege of Tangier* (1680).

Anon., *The lives, apprehensions, arraignments, and executions, of the 19 late pirates* (1609).

Anon., *The Present State of Algeir* [*sic*] (1682).

Anon., *The Seamans Song of Captain Ward the famous Pyrate of the world* (n.d., 1609).

Anon., *The sea-mans song of Dansekar the Dutch-man, his robberies done at sea* (n.d., 1609).

Appleby, John C. (ed.), *A Calendar of Material Relating to Ireland from the High Court of Admiralty Examinations 1536–1641*, Irish Manuscripts Commission (1992).

Aylmer G. E., 'Place Bills and the Separation of Powers: Some Seventeenth-Century Origins of the "Non-Political" Civil Service', *Transactions of the Royal Historical Society*, 5th Series, Vol. 15 (1965), 45–69.

Baepler, Paul (ed.), *White Slaves, African Masters: An Anthology of American Barbary Captivity Narratives*, University of Chicago Press (1999).

Baer, Marc David, *Honored by the Glory of Islam: Conversion and Conquest in Ottoman Europe*, Oxford University Press (2008).

Bak, Greg, *Barbary Pirate: The Life and Crimes of John Ward*, Sutton (2006).

Barker, Andrew, *A True and Certaine Report of the Beginning, Proceedings, Overthrowes, and now present Estate of Captaine Ward* (1609).

Barnby, Henry, 'The Sack of Baltimore', *Cork Historical and Architectural Society Journal*, Vol. 74, No. 220 (1969), 100–29.

Bent, J. Theodore (ed.), *Early Voyages and Travels in the Levant*, Hakluyt Society (1893).

Birch, Thomas (ed.), *A Collection of the State Papers of John Thurloe* (1742).

Bohnstedt, John W., 'The Infidel Scourge of God: The Turkish Menace as Seen by German Pamphleteers of the Reformation Era', *Transactions of the American Philosophical Society*, New Series, Vol. 58, No. 9 (1968), 1–58.

Boothouse, Samuel, *A Brief Remonstrance of Several National Injuries and Indignities perpetrated on the Persons and Estates of publick Ministers and Subjects of this Common-Wealth, by the Dey of Tunis in Barbary* (1653).

Bosworth, C. E., *An Intrepid Scot: William Lithgow of Lanark's Travels in the Ottoman Lands, North Africa and Central Europe, 1609–21*, Ashgate (2006).

Boteler, Nathaniel, *Six dialogues about sea-services between an high-admiral and a captain at sea* (1685).

Bourne, William, *The Arte of shooting in great Ordnaunce* (1587).

Braudel, Ferdinand, *The Mediterranean and the Mediterranean World in the Age of Philip II*, Fontana (1975).

Broughton, Elizabeth, *Six Years' Residence in Algiers* (1839).

Bullokar, J., *English Expositor* (1616).

Button, John, *Algiers Voyage* (1621).

Cabala: sive Scrinia sacra. Mysteries of state & government in letters of illustrious persons in the reigns of Henry the eighth, queen Elizabeth, k: James, and the late king Charles (1654).

Calendar of State Papers Colonial, 1574–1738, Her Majesty's Stationery Office (1860–1970).

Calendar of State Papers Relating to English Affairs in the Archives of Venice, Her Majesty's Stationery Office (1864–1947).

Calendar of State Papers, Domestic Series, Her Majesty's Stationery Office (1856–1972).

Calendar of State Papers, Ireland, Her Majesty's Stationery Office (1860–1912).

Cason, Edmond, *A Relation of the whole proceedings concerning the Redemption of the Captives in Argier and Tunis* (1646).

Cathcart, James Leander, *The Captives: Eleven Years a Prisoner in Algiers*, Herald Print (1899).

Caulfied, Richard (ed.), *The Council Book of Youghal* (1878).

Cavaliero, Roderic E., 'The Decline of the Maltese Corso in the XVIIIth Century: A Study in Maritime History', *Melita historica: Journal of the Malta Historical Society*, Vol. 2, No. 4 (1959), 224–38.

Chandler, Richard, *The History and Proceedings of the House of Commons*, 14 vols (1742–4).

Chappell, Edwin (ed.), *The Tangier Papers of Samuel Pepys*, Navy Records Society (1935).

Charles II, *Articles of peace & commerce between the most serene and mighty prince Charles II . . . [and] Tripoli* (1677).

Charles II, *Articles of Peace and Commerce Between . . . Charles II . . . [and] the Noble City and Kingdom of Tripoli in Barbary* (1676).

Charles II, *Articles of Peace Between His Sacred Majesty Charles the Second . . . and the City and Kingdom of Algiers* (1664).

Charles II, *Articles of peace concluded between his sacred majesty and the kingdoms and governments of Algiers, Tunis, and Tripoli in the year 1662* (1662).

Charles II, *The Capitulations and Articles of peace between the Majesty of the King of England, Scotland, France, and Ireland &c. And the Sultan of the Ottoman Empire*, Constantinople (1663).

Charles II, *His Majesties Gracious Speech to Both Houses of Parliament, Together with the Lord Chancellors, Delivered . . . the 10th of October, 1665* (1665).

Charles II, *Proclamation touching the articles of peace with Argiers, Tunis, and Tripoli*, 29 January 1663.

Chatsworth MSS, Earl of Cork's Letter-Book.

Cholmley, Sir Hugh, *A Short Account of the Progress of the Mole at Tangier* (1679).

Claire Jowett, 'Piracy and politics in Heywood and Rowley's *Fortune by Land and Sea* (1607–9))', *Renaissance Studies*, Vol. 16, No. 2 (2002), 217–33.

Clarendon, Edward Hyde, Earl of, *The Life of Edward, Earl of Clarendon*, 2 vols (1857).

Clark, G. N., 'The Barbary Corsairs in the Seventeenth Century', *Cambridge Historical Journal*, Vol. 8, No. 1 (1944), 22–35.

Clark, George. T., *Glamorgan Worthies: Some Account of Sir Robert Mansel Kt . . . and of Admiral Sir Thomas Button Kt.* (1883).

Coate, Mary, 'The Duchy of Cornwall: Its History and Administration, 1640 to 1660', *Transactions of the Royal Historical Society*, 4th Series, Vol. 10 (1927), 135–69.

Cook, M. A. (ed.), *A History of the Ottoman Empire to 1730*, Cambridge University Press (1976).

Coombes, J., 'The Sack of Baltimore: a Forewarning', *Cork Historical and Architectural Society Journal*, Vol. 77 (1972), 60–61.

Corbett, Julian S., *England in the Mediterranean: A Study of the Rise and Influence of British Power within the Straits 1603–1713*, 2 vols, Longmans, Green and Co. (1904).

Cowdery, Jonathan, *American Captives in Tripoli*, Boston (1806).

Daborn, Robert, *A Christian Turn'd Turk: or, The Tragicall Lives and Deaths of the two Famous Pyrates, Ward and Dansiker* (1612).

D'Aranda, Emanuel, *The History of Algiers and its Slavery*, trans. John Davies (1666).

Davies, C. S. L., 'The Administration of the Royal Navy under Henry VIII: The Origins of the Navy Board', *The English Historical Review*, Vol. 80, No. 315 (April 1965), 268–88.

Davies, Myles, *Athenæ Britannicæ* (1716).

Davis, Robert C., 'Counting European Slaves on the Barbary Coast', *Past and Present*, No. 172 (August, 2001), 87–124.

De Cossé-Brissac, Philippe, 'Robert Blake and the Barbary Company 1636–1641', *African Affairs*, Vol. 48, No. 190 (January, 1949), 25–37.

De Slane, B. Mac Guckin, *Ibn Khallikan's Biographical Dictionary*, Paris (1843).

Dear, I. C. B. and Kemp, Peter, *The Oxford Companion to Ships and the Sea*, Oxford University Press (2006).

Deasy, George F., 'The Harbors of Africa', *Economic Geography*, Vol. 18, No. 4 (October, 1942), 325–42.

Dekker, Thomas, *If it be not good, the Divel is in it* (1612).

Devoulx, Albert, *Le Raïs Hamidou*, Algiers (1859).

Dryden, John, *Limberham* (1678).

Dunlop, R., 'The Plantation of Munster 1584–1589', *English Historical Review*, Vol. 3, No. 10 (April, 1888), 250–69.

Dunton, John, *A True Journal of the Salley Fleet* (1637).

Dury, Giles (ed.) *Mercurius Publicus: Comprising the Sum of Forraign Intelligence; with The Affairs now in Agitation in England, Scotland, and Ireland* (1659–63).

Earle, Peter, *Pirate Wars*, Methuen (2003).

Edgar, Thomas, *The lawes resolutions of womens rights* (1632).

Ekin, Des, *The Stolen Village: Baltimore and the Barbary Pirates*, O'Brien Press (2006).

Firth, C. H., and Rait, R. S. (eds), *Acts and Ordinances of the Interregnum 1642–1660* (1911).

Fisher, Godfrey, *Barbary Legend*, Oxford University Press (1957).

Fitzgeffry, Charles, *Compassion towards Captives, chiefly towards our Bretheren and Country-men who are in miserable bondage in Barbarie* (1637).

Fotheringham, J. K., 'Genoa and the Fourth Crusade', *The English Historical Review*, Vol. 25, No. 97 (January, 1910), 26–57.

Friedman, Ellen G., 'Christian Captives at "Hard Labor" in Algiers, 16th–18th Centuries', *The International Journal of African Historical Studies*, Vol. 13, No. 4 (1980), 616–32.

Fuchs, Barbara, 'Faithless Empires: Pirates, Renegadoes, and the English Nation', *ELH* (formerly *English Literary History*), Vol. 67, No. 1 (Spring 2000), 45–69.

Fuller, Mary Breese, 'Sir John Eliot and John Nutt, the Pirate', *Smith College Studies in History*, Vol. IV, No. 2 (January 1919).

G. T., *An Encomiastick, or, Elegiack Enumeration of the Noble Atchievements [sic], and Unparallel'd Services, done at Land and Sea, by that truly honourable generall, Robert Blake* (1658).

Glete, Jan, *Warfare at Sea, 1500–1650*, Routledge (2000).

Gordon, M. D., 'The Collection of Ship-Money in the Reign of Charles I', *Transactions of the Royal Historical Society*, 3rd Series, Vol. 4 (1910), 141–62.

Greene, Molly, 'Beyond the Northern Invasion: The Mediterranean in the Seventeenth Century', *Past and Present*, No. 174 (February, 2002), 42–71.

Grey, Anchitell, *Debates of the House of Commons*, 10 vols (1769).

Guilmartin Jr, J. F., *Gunpowder and Galleys: Changing Technology and Mediterranean Warfare at Sea in the Sixteenth Century*, Cambridge University Press (1974).

Hakluyt, Richard, *The principal navigations, voyages, traffiques and discoveries of the English nation* (1599).

Harris, Bernard, 'A Portrait of a Moor', in Catherine M. S. Alexander and Stanley Wells (eds.), *Shakespeare and Race*, Cambridge University Press (2001), 23–36.

Harris, G. G. (ed.), 'Trinity House of Deptford Transactions, 1609–35', *London Record Society*, 19 (1983).

Harris, Thomas, *The Life and Services of Commodore William Bainbridge*, Philadelphia (1837).

Healy, James N., *Castles of County Cork*, Mercier Press (1988).

Hebb, David Delison, *Piracy and the English Government, 1616–1642*, Scolar Press (1994).

Hirst, Warwick, *The Man Who Stole the Cyprus*, Rosenberg (2008).

Historical Manuscripts Commission, *Dartmouth* MSS 3 vols. (1887–96).

Historical Manuscripts Commission, *Downshire* MSS II (1936).

Hollar, Wenceslaus, *A True Relation of Capt. Kempthorn's Engagement, in the Mary-Rose, with seven Algier Men of War* (1675).

Holstein, A., 'Journal of a voyage to the Kingdom of Tripoli in Barbary, 1675–6', BL Sloane 2755.

Hopkins, J. F. P. (trans.), *Letters from Barbary 1576–1774*, Oxford University Press (1982).

Ireland, J. de Courcy, 'Raïs Hamidou', *The Mariner's Mirror*, Vol. 60, No. 2 (1974), 187–96.

Irwin, Ray W., *The Diplomatic Relations of the United States with the Barbary Powers 1776–1816*, University of North Carolina Press (1931).

James I, *A proclamation against pirats [sic]*, 8 January 1609.

James I, *A Proclamation to represse all Piracies and Depredations upon the Sea* (1603).

James, David, 'The "Manual de artillería" of al-Ra'is Ibrahim b. Ahmad al-Andalusi with Particular Reference to Its Illustrations and Their Sources', *Bulletin of the School of Oriental and African Studies, University of London*, Vol. 41, No. 2 (1978) 237–57.

Jardine, Alexander, *Letters from Barbary, France, Spain, Portugal, &c*, 2 vols (1788).

Jennett, Sean (trans.), *Journal of a Young Brother: The life of Thomas Platter*, Muller (1963).

Jones, Inigo, and Davenant, William, *Britannia Triumphans* (1638).

Jónsson, Már, 'The expulsion of the Moriscos from Spain in 1609–1614: the destruction of an Islamic periphery', *Journal of Global History*, Vol. 2 (2007), 195–212.

Journal of the House of Commons 1547–1699, 12 vols (1802–3).

Journal of the House of Lords, Vols 1–20 (1832–4)

Julien, Charles-André, *History of North Africa*, Routledge & Kegan Paul (1970).

Kahane, Henry and Renée, and Tietze, Andreas, *The Lingua Franca in the Levant: Turkish Nautical Terms of Italian and Greek Origin*, University of Illinois (1958).

Knight, Francis, *A Relation of Seaven Yeares Slaverie under the Turkes of Argeire* (1640).

Knolles, Richard, *The Generall Historie of the Turkes* (1603).

Knowler, William (ed.), *The Earl of Strafford's Letters and Despatches*, 2 vols (1739).

Kunt, Metin Ibrahim, 'Ethnic-Regional (Cins) Solidarity in the Seventeenth-Century Ottoman Establishment', *International Journal of Middle East Studies*, Vol. 5, No. 3 (June, 1974), 233–9.

Kyle, C. R., 'Parliament and the Palace of Westminster: An Exploration of Public Space in the Early Seventeenth Century', *Parliamentary History*, Vol. 21 (2002), 85–98.

Lane-Poole, Stanley, *The Barbary Corsairs* (1890).

Latham, Robert, and Matthews, William (eds.), *The Diary of Samuel Pepys*, 11 vols, HarperCollins (1995).

Leiner, Frederick C., *The End of the Barbary Terror*, Oxford University Press (2007).

Lewis, Bernard, 'Corsairs In Iceland', *Islam in History*, Open Court Publishing (1993), 239–46.

Lithgow, William, *The Totall Discourse, of the Rare Adventures, and painefull Peregrinations of long nineteene Yeares Travayles* (1632).

Loomie, Albert J. (ed.), *Ceremonies of Charles I: the note books of John Finet*, Fordham University Press (1987).

Lubbock, Basil (ed.), *Barlow's Journal of His Life at Sea in King's Ships, East and West Indiamen and Other Merchantmen from 1659 to 1703*, Hurst & Blackett, 1934.

Lybyer, A. H., 'The Ottoman Turks and the Routes of Oriental Trade', *The English Historical Review*, Vol. 30, No. 120 (October, 1915), 577–88.

Mackenzie, Alexander Slidell, *The Life of Commodore Oliver Hazard Perry*, New York (1840).

Maclean, John (ed.), *Letters of George Lord Carew to Sir Thomas Roe*, Camden Society (1860).

Manwaring, G. E. (ed.), *The Life and Works of Sir Henry Mainwaring*, 2 vols, Navy Records Society (1920–21).

Marsden, R. G., 'The High Court of Admiralty in Relation to National History, Commerce and the Colonisation of America. A.D. 1550–1650', *Transactions of the Royal Historical Society*, New Series, Vol. 16 (1902), 69–96.

Marsden, R. G., 'The Vice-Admirals of the Coast', *The English Historical Review*, Vol. 22, No. 87 (July 1907), 468–77; Vol. 23, No. 92 (October 1908), 736–57.

Marsden, R. G., 'Early Prize Jurisdiction and Prize Law in England', *The English Historical Review*, Vol. 25, No. 98 (April, 1910), 243–63.

Marsden, R. G. (ed.), *Documents Relating to Law and Custom of the Sea*, 2 vols, Navy Records Society, 49–50 (1915–16).

Matar, Nabil (ed. and trans.) *In the Lands of the Christians: Arabic Travel Writing in the Seventeenth Century*, Routledge (2003).

Matar, Nabil, 'The Renegade in English Seventeenth-Century Imagination', *Studies in English Literature, 1500–1900*, Vol. 33, No. 3 (Summer 1993), 489–505.

Matar, Nabil, 'Muslims in Seventeenth-Century England', *Journal of Islamic Studies*, Vol. 8, No. 1 (1997), 63–82.

Matar, Nabil, 'English Accounts of Captivity in North Africa and the Middle East: 1577–1625', *Renaissance Quarterly*, Vol. 54, No. 2 (Summer 2001), 553–72.

Matar, Nabil, *Britain and Barbary, 1589–1689*, University Press of Florida (2006).

Mathew, David, 'The Cornish and Welsh Pirates in the Reign of Elizabeth', *The English Historical Review*, Vol. 39, No. 155 (July, 1924), 337–48.

Maxwell, Baldwin, 'Notes of Robert Daborne's Extant Plays', *Philological Quarterly*, Vol. 50, No. 1 (January, 1971) 85–98.

Menage, V. L., 'The English Capitulation of 1580: A Review Article', *International Journal of Middle East Studies*, Vol. 12, No. 3 (November, 1980), 373–83.

Morgan, J., *A Complete History of Algiers* (1731).

Nixon, Anthony, *Newes from Sea of two notorious Pyrats* (1609).

Ober, Frederick A., 'A Look at Algeria and Tunis', *Journal of the American Geographical Society of New York*, Vol. 21 (1889), 287–324.

Ogilby, John, *Africa* (1670).

Okeley, William, *Eben-ezer: or, a Small Monument of Great Mercy* (1675).

Oppenheim, M., 'The Royal and Merchant Navy under Elizabeth', *English Historical Review*, Vol. 6, No. 23 (July, 1891), 465–94.

Oppenheim, Michael, 'The Royal Navy under James I', *English Historical Review*, Vol. 7, No. 27 (July 1892), 471–96.

Oppenheim, M., 'The Royal Navy under Charles I', *English Historical Review*, Vol. 8, No. 31 (July, 1893), 467–99; Vol. 9, No. 33 (January, 1894), 92–116; Vol. 9, No. 35 (July, 1894), 473–92.

Oppenheim, M., *A History of the Administration of the Royal Navy and of Merchant Shipping in Relation to the Navy from 1509 to 1660*, John Lane (1896).

Oppenheim, Michael (ed.), *The Naval Tracts of Sir William Monson*, 5 volumes, Navy Records Society (1902–13).

Origo, Iris, 'The Domestic Enemy: The Eastern Slaves in Tuscany in the Fourteenth and Fifteenth Centuries', *Speculum*, Vol. 30, No. 3 (July, 1955), 321–66.

Osler, Edward, *The Life of Admiral Viscount Exmouth* (1835).

Pananti, Filippo, *Narrative of a Residence in Algiers* (1818).

Parker, Kenneth, 'Reading Barbary in Early Modern England, 1550–1685', in Birchwood, M., and Dimmock, M. (eds.), *Cultural Encounters Between East and West, 1453–1699*, Cambridge Scholars Press (2005), 77–105.

Pennell, C. R. (ed.), *Piracy and Diplomacy in Seventeenth-Century North Africa: The Journal of Thomas Baker, English Consul in Tripoli, 1677–85*, Associated University Presses (1989).

Phelps, Wayne H., 'The Early Life of Robert Daborne', *Philological Quarterly*, Vol. 59, No. 1 (Winter 1980), 1–10.

Philips, George, *The Present State of Tangier* (1676).

Playfair, R. L., *The Scourge of Christendom* (1884).

Pory, John (trans.), Leo Africanus, *A geographical historie of Africa* (1600).

Powell, J. R. (ed.), *The Letters of Robert Blake*, Navy Records Society (1937).

Powell , J. R. (ed.), 'The Journal of John Weale 1654–1656', *The Naval Miscellany*, IV, Navy Records Society (1952).

Priestley, E. J., 'An Early 17th Century Map of Baltimore', *Cork Historical and Architectural Society Journal*, Vol. 89 (1984), 55–8.

Purchas, Samuel, *Purchas his Pilgrimage, or Relations of the World and the Religions* (1614).

Raithby, John (ed.), *Statutes of the Realm*, Vol. 5, 1628–80 (1819).

Rawlins, John, *The Famous and Wonderful Recovery of a Ship of Bristol, called the Exchange* (1622).

Raymond, Andre, 'Islamic City, Arab City: Orientalist Myths and Recent Views', *British Journal of Middle Eastern Studies*, Vol. 21, No. 1 (1994), 3–18.

Rghei, Amer S., and Nelson, J. G., 'The Conservation and Use of the Walled City of Tripoli', *Geographical Journal*, Vol. 160, No. 2 (July, 1994), 143–58.

Roberts, Lewis, *The Merchants Mappe of Commerce* (1638).

Robinson, Henry, *Libertas, or Relief to the English Captives in Algier* (1642).

Ross, John, *Tanger's [sic] Rescue; or a Relation of The late Memorable Passages at Tanger* (1681).

Routh, E. M. G., 'The English at Tangier', *The English Historical Review*, Vol. 26, No. 103 (July, 1911), 469–81.

Rowlands, Samuel, *More Knaves Yet* (1612).

Rushworth, John, *Historical Collections of Private Passages of State*, 8 vols (1721).

Russell, Michael, *History and Present Condition of the Barbary States* (1835).

Seller, John, *Atlas Maritimus* (1676).

Senior, Clive, *A Nation of Pirates: English Piracy in its Heyday*, David & Charles (1976).

Shaler, William, *Sketches of Algiers, Political, Historical, and Civil* (1826).

Sheehan, Anthony J., 'Official Reaction to Native Land Claims in the Plantation of Munster', *Irish Historical Studies*, Vol. 23, No. 92 (November, 1983), 297–318.

Sheres, Sir Henry, *A Discourse touching Tanger [sic]* (1680).

Shuval, Tal, 'The Ottoman Algerian Elite and Its Ideology', *International Journal of Middle East Studies*, Vol. 32, No. 3 (August, 2000), 323–44.

Sisson, Charles J., and Brown, Arthur, '"The Great Danseker": Literary Significance of a Chancery Suit', *The Modern Language Review*, Vol. 46, No. 3/4 (July–October, 1951), 339–48.

Smith, Charles, *The antient and present state of the county and city of Cork*, 2 vols (1774).

Smith, John, *An accidence or The path-way to experience Necessary for all young sea-men, or those that are desirous to goe to sea* (1626).

Smith, John, *The True Travels, Adventures, and Observations of Captain John Smith, in Europe, Asia, Africa, and America* (1630).

Spratt, Devereux, 'Journal', in T. A. B. Spratt, *Travels and Researches in Crete* (1865).

Stambouli, F., and Zghal, A., 'Urban Life in Pre-Colonial North Africa', *The British Journal of Sociology*, Vol. 27, No. 1 (March, 1976), 1–20.

Steckley, George F., 'Collisions, Prohibitions, and the Admiralty Court in Seventeenth-Century London', *Law and History Review*, Vol. 21, No. 1 (Spring 2003), 41–67.

Strachan, Michael, 'Sampson's Fight with Maltese Galleys, 1628', *The Mariner's Mirror*, Vol. 55 (1969), 281–9.

Sumner, Charles, *White Slavery in the Barbary States*, Boston (1847).

Sweet, Thomas, *Dear Friends* ['The long and lamentable bondage of Thomas Sweet, and Richard Robinson'] (1647).

Tenenti, Alberto, *Piracy and the Decline of Venice 1580–1615*, Longmans (1967).

Thomas, R., *The Glory of America: comprising Memoirs of the Lives and Glorious Exploits of Some of the Most Distinguished Officers*, Philadelphia (1836).

The Times, 5 November 1830, 17 December 1830.

Tinniswood, Adrian, *The Verneys: A True Story of Love, War and Madness in Seventeenth-Century England*, Jonathan Cape (2007).

Vitkus, Daniel J. (ed.), *Three Turk Plays from Early Modern England*, Columbia University Press (2000).

Vitkus, Daniel (ed.), *Piracy, Slavery and Redemption*, Columbia University Press (2001).

Waldo, Samuel Putnam, *The Life and Character of Stephen Decatur*, Connecticut (1822).

Weiss, Gillian, 'Barbary Captivity and the French Idea of Freedom', *French Historical Studies*, Vol. 28, No. 2 (Spring 2005), 231–64.

Whitburn, T. (ed.), *Westward Hoe for Avalon in the New-found-land* (1870).

Wolf, John B., *The Barbary Coast: Algeria Under the Turks, 1500 to 1800*, W.W. Norton (1979).

Index

and Ottoman Empire in sixteenth
century, 9, 10, 25
Ward in, 14, 25, 30, 31, 32–3, 37, 38,
39–40, 41, 45, 49–50
Ottoman Empire's objective in, 25,
27
janissaries in, 25, 27
'Uthmân comes to power in (1598),
27
'Uthmân's achievements in, 27
'Uthmân's enthusiasm for piracy,
27–8, 30
description of, 30–2
Ward dies from plague in, 50, 125
Danseker sent by the French to
negotiate with, 64
Danseker's reception and death in,
64–5
Mainwaring in, 76, 77, 78
singled out for mention in
Mainwaring's *Discourse*, 81–2
Dutch threat to, 86
Trinitarians work to redeem captives
in, 147
number of European slaves held in,
149
Browne negotiates with authorities
in, 220
changes in leadership (1637–53), 220
role of *bey* in, 220–1
relations with England between 1651
and 1658, 221–7
treaty with England (1662), 230–1,
232
success in moving away from piracy,
268
European powers make payments to,
278
and United States, 281, 286, 292
Exmouth's expedition to, and
agreement with, 293–4
France extends influence into, 300
brief references, 3, 7, 11, 19, 29, 34,
48, 52, 55, 56, 58, 63, 83, 85, 89,
173, 191, 200, 228, 229, 233, 234,
240, 255, 258, 259, 261, 265, 266,
276, 288
Tunisia, 27, 31, 82, 220, 221, 300 *see also*
Tunis

Turkey, 12, 13, 228 *see also* Istanbul;
Ottoman Empire
Turkish language, 58, 61
Tuscany, Grand Duke of, 228
Twelve Years Truce, 17–18, 106, 123
Tyrrhenian Sea, 143

Uluj Ali, 10
'Umar ben Haddu, 215, 216, 217, 218,
219, 242, 243, 248, 253
United Provinces *see*
Netherlands/Holland/Dutch
Republic/United Provinces
United States, 277–8, 279–86, 289–93, 297
Unity (hospital ship), 251
Unity (merchantman), 273–4
Upper Castle, Tangier, 209, 218, 252
Ustâ Murad Dey, 220
Uthmân II, Sultan, 109
Uthmân Dey of Tunis, 27–8, 30, 31, 32,
33, 35, 38, 40, 41, 43, 44, 45, 46,
49, 220–1
Uthmân, *pasha* of Tripoli, 232–3, 234,
257, 260, 266

Vachere, Père Jean Le, 240, 241
Valencia, 290
Valona, 144–5, 184
Battle of (1638), 187
Vanguard, 108, 116, 123
Venice, 5, 6, 12, 13, 16, 35, 48, 61, 75,
144, 145, 192–3, 228, 278
Gulf of, 272
and John Ward, 14–15, 30, 34, 36–7,
38–9, 40, 41
pirate attacks on ships of, 30, 34,
36–7, 52
Verney, Sir Francis, 43, 47–9, 50
Vienna, 6
Viliena, Viceroy, 52
Villa Raïs, 97
Villefranche, 71, 78
Virginia, 16
Vlissingen, 52, 61

Wales, 140
Walsingham, Robert, 92, 108, 119, 121
Wapping, 1–3, 15, 299 *see also* Execution
Dock